T0211324

Enterprise Drupal 8 Development

For Advanced Projects and
Large Development Teams

Todd Tomlinson

Apress®

Enterprise Drupal 8 Development: For Advanced Projects and Large Development Teams

Todd Tomlinson
Tigard, Oregon, USA

ISBN-13 (pbk): 978-1-4842-0254-8   ISBN-13 (electronic): 978-1-4842-0253-1
DOI 10.1007/978-1-4842-0253-1

Managing Director: Welmoed Spahr
Editorial Director: Todd Green
Acquisitions Editor: Louise Corrigan
Development Editor: James Markham
Technical Reviewer: Anshul Jain
Coordinating Editor: Nancy Chen
Copy Editor: Kezia Endsley
Artist: SPi Global
Cover image designed by Freepik

Distributed to the book trade worldwide by Springer Science+Business Media New York, 233 Spring Street, 6th Floor, New York, NY 10013. Phone 1-800-SPRINGER, fax (201) 348-4505, e-mail orders-ny@springer-sbm.com, or visit www.springeronline.com. Apress Media, LLC is a California LLC and the sole member (owner) is Springer Science + Business Media Finance Inc (SSBM Finance Inc). SSBM Finance Inc is a **Delaware** corporation.

For information on translations, please e-mail rights@apress.com, or visit http://www.apress.com/rights-permissions.

Apress titles may be purchased in bulk for academic, corporate, or promotional use. eBook versions and licenses are also available for most titles. For more information, reference our Print and eBook Bulk Sales web page at http://www.apress.com/bulk-sales.

Any source code or other supplementary material referenced by the author in this book is available to readers on GitHub via the book's product page, located at www.apress.com/9781484202548. For more detailed information, please visit http://www.apress.com/source-code.

Printed on acid-free paper

This book is dedicated to my wife Misty, for the sacrifices that she made by spending evening and weekends alone as I was locked away in my office researching and writing this book, and my daughters, Emma and Anna, for missing out on so many activities due to my focus on this book.

Contents at a Glance

About the Author xv

About the Technical Reviewer xvii

Introduction xix

■Chapter 1: Introduction to Drupal 1

■Chapter 2: Building a Practical Software Development Process and Team 9

■Chapter 3: Engineering Drupal 29

■Chapter 4: Creating Modules for Drupal 8 45

■Chapter 5: Drupal 8 Theming... 89

■Chapter 6: Leveraging Your Content 137

■Chapter 7: Optimizing Your Site Architecture... 173

■Chapter 8: Integrating Drupal 8 213

■Chapter 9: Building a Smart Administration User Interface 233

■Chapter 10: Scaling Drupal... 261

■Chapter 11: Drupal 8 DevOps.. 271

■Chapter 12: Migrating to Drupal 8 281

■Appendix A: Contributing to the Drupal Community 293

■Appendix B: Additional Resources 297

■Appendix C: Creating a Drupal 8 Profile 301

Index... 305

Contents

About the Author .... **xv**

About the Technical Reviewer .... **xvii**

Introduction .... **xix**

■**Chapter 1: Introduction to Drupal** 1

Content Management Systems 1

    Drupal 2

    Drupal Core 2

    Contributed Modules 2

    Drupal Themes 4

Creating Content 4

Taking Drupal 8 to the Enterprise 7

Summary 8

■**Chapter 2: Building a Practical Software Development Process and Team** 9

A Methodology for Building Your Site on Drupal 9

Building a Drupal Team in Your Organization 15

    Project Manager 15

    Senior Architect 17

    Business Systems Analyst 19

    Development Lead 20

    Developer 21

    Site Builder 22

    User Experience (UX) Designer 23

Visual Designer 24

Themer 25

Site Builder 25

Quality Assurance Specialist 26

Site Administrator 27

Summary 28

■Chapter 3: Engineering Drupal 29

Engineering the Foundation 29

Defining the Components of Enterprise Drupal 30

Network and Web Server 31

Database Servers 32

Drupal 8 Core 33

Drupal 8 Contributed Modules 35

Custom Modules 36

The Pillars of a Drupal 8 Solution 36

Taxonomy 38

Summary 44

■Chapter 4: Creating Modules for Drupal 8 45

The Purpose of Drupal Modules 45

The Foundation of Drupal 8 Is a Suite of Modules 46

Key Skills 47

Developing Your First Drupal 8 Module 47

Step 1: Create the Module's Directory 48

Step 2: Create the Module's Info File 48

Step 3: Create the Module File 49

Step 4: Create the Module's Routing File 50

Step 5: Create the Module's Controller 51

Step 6: Add a Menu Item 52

Step 7: Add a New Menu Item 54

Step 8: Add a New Function to the Module 54

Creating Blocks 57

Building Custom Forms 62

Interacting with Entities 71

    Finding Existing Entities 71

    Creating Entities 76

    Creating, Updating, and Deleting Entities Programmatically 81

Summary 87

Chapter 5: Drupal 8 Theming 89

The Role of a Drupal Theme 89

The Twig Templating Engine 89

The Structure of a Drupal Theme 90

Creating the Theme Files 91

    Adding Regions to the Theme 93

    Twig Syntax 96

    Twig Variables 96

    Conditionals, Looping, Filters, and Math Functions in Twig 98

    Twig Template Files 104

Standard Twig Templates 107

    Modifying the page.html.twig Template File 108

    Modifying the node.html.twig Template 114

    Modifying the block.html.twig Template 117

    Modifying the field.html.twig Template 118

Exposing Variables to Twig 121

Applying CSS to Your Theme 127

    Creating the Stylesheets 127

    Creating the libraries.yml File 128

    Loading the Libraries Through the .info.yml File 128

Adding JavaScript to Your Theme 129

Adding JavaScript and CSS Libraries to Template Files 131

Working with Breakpoints 131

Creating Advanced Theme Settings 133

Using Subthemes 134

Summary 136

■Chapter 6: Leveraging Your Content 137

Content Staging 137

Content Staging and Site Preview Use Cases 137

The Drupal 8 Solution for Content Staging and Synchronization 138

Installation, Configuration, and Use of the Content Staging Framework 140

Search 148

What Is Apache Solr? 149

To Install or Not To Install 150

Required Modules 150

Setting Up OpenSolr 150

Adding the Schema.xml File OpenSolr 152

Integrating Views and Solr 157

Advanced Features of Solr 161

Multilingual Support 163

Getting Started with Multilingual Support 164

Configuring Multilingual Capabilities 164

Configuring Entities 168

Translating Content 170

Summary 171

■Chapter 7: Optimizing Your Site Architecture 173

Content Types 173

Simplifying the Editorial Interface 175

Removing Options from the Node Edit Form 178

Content Types versus Entity Types 179

Leveraging Taxonomy 189

    Taxonomy as an Entity 189

    Building Multipurpose Pages Using Taxonomy 193

The Location of Content in an Enterprise Setting 207

    Using Apache SOLR 208

    What Does a Solr-Based Solution Require? 208

    Consuming Indexed Information Through Views 209

Off-the-Shelf versus Custom Development 209

Summary 211

■Chapter 8: Integrating Drupal 8 213

Using RESTful Web Services in Drupal 8 213

    RESTful Modules in Drupal 8 Core 214

    Retrieving Content Through REST 215

    Creating a Node Through REST 216

    Updating and Deleting a Node Through REST 220

Using REST for Other Entity Types 222

Generating Lists of Content Using Views and REST 222

    Generating Output in Other Formats 227

Using Views to Expose Content to External Sources 228

Creating Custom RESTful APIs 229

    Creating the Custom Module 229

Other Integration Options 232

Summary 232

■Chapter 9: Building a Smart Administration User Interface 233

Use an Administration Focused Theme 233

    Enabling Different Admin Themes 233

    The Seven Theme 234

    The Adminimal Theme 235

Update the Administration Menu 236

Simplify Content Types 236

    Organizing the Fields 236

    Using Hierarchical Select 240

    Using Field Collections 241

Use the Workbench Module 243

    The Workbench Module 244

    The Workbench Access Module 246

    Setting Up Workbench Access 246

    Setting Up Roles and Permissions 249

    Demonstrating Access Restrictions 252

Use Workbench Moderation 253

    Configuring Workbench Moderation 254

    Defining Workbench Moderation User Roles and Permissions 257

Summary 260

■Chapter 10: Scaling Drupal 261

Understanding Potential Performance Bottlenecks 261

Drupal Cache 262

    Enabling Drupal Cache 262

    Caching Views 263

    Caching Blocks 264

    External Caching Mechanisms: Varnish Cache 264

Using a Content Delivery Network (CDN) 265

    How CDNs Work 266

Considering Nginx Over Apache 266

Using Memcache or Redis 267

Optimizing MySQL 267

Scaling Hardware 269

Hosting Your Drupal 8 Site 270

Summary 270

■**Chapter 11: Drupal 8 DevOps** **271**

Traditional Versus DevOps 271

The Benefits of Embracing DevOps 272

Adopting DevOps 272

DevOps Best Practices 273

Drupal 8 Continuous Integration and Deployment 274

    The CI/CD Process Flow 274

    CI/CD Tools 275

Automated Testing 275

    Writing PHPUnit Tests for Classes 275

    Writing Functional Tests 276

    Write Functional JavaScript Tests (PHPUnit) 277

Executing Tests 277

Other Testing Tools 277

Summary 279

■**Chapter 12: Migrating to Drupal 8** **281**

The Migrate Modules in Drupal 8 Core 281

Migrating Themes 287

Migrating Modules from Drupal 7 to Drupal 8 288

Contributed Modules 290

Summary 291

■**Appendix A: Contributing to the Drupal Community** **293**

User Support 293

Documentation 293

Translations 294

Testing 294

Design and Usability 294

Donations 294

Development 294

    Ways to Contribute Code: Drupal Core, Contributed Projects, and Patches 295

    Improving Existing Projects and Core with Patches 295

    Contributing New Projects 295

    Collaboration Rather than Competition 296

■Appendix B: Additional Resources 297

Drupal Modules 297

Drupal Themes 297

Drupal Documentation 297

Where to Go When You Have Problems 299

Where to Host Your Drupal Site 299

Where to Go to Learn HTML and CSS 299

Video Tutorials 299

Drupal Podcasts 299

■Appendix C: Creating a Drupal 8 Profile 301

Picking a Machine Name 301

Creating the File Structure 302

The .info.yml File 302

The .install File 303

The .profile File 303

Configuration Files 304

Default Content 304

Index 305

About the Author

Todd Tomlinson is the Senior Enterprise Drupal Architect at a multibillion-dollar high-tech manufacturing company. Todd's focus over the past 22 years has been on designing, developing, deploying, and supporting complex web solutions for public- and private-sector clients all around the world. He has been using Drupal as the primary platform for creating beautiful and feature-rich sites since Drupal 4.

Prior to his current position, Todd was the Vice President of ServerLogic's national Drupal consulting practice, Senior Director of eBusiness Strategic Services for Oracle Corporation, where he helped Oracle's largest clients develop their strategic plans for leveraging the Web as a core component of their business. He is also the former Vice President of Internet Solutions for Claremont Technology Group, Vice President and CTO of Emerald Solutions, Managing Director for CNF Ventures, and a Senior Manager with Andersen Consulting/Accenture.

Todd has a BS in Computer Science, an MBA, and a PhD (ABD).

Todd is the author of six Drupal-related books, including *Enterprise Drupal 8 Development, Beginning Drupal 8, Pro Drupal 7 Development, Beginning Drupal 7, Beginning Backdrop,* and *Migrating from Drupal to Backdrop*. He is a contributing author to *Drupal Watchdog* magazine, and a frequent guest of various Drupal podcasts.

Todd's passion for Drupal is evident in his obsession with evangelizing the platform and his enthusiasm when speaking with people about the possibilities of what they can accomplish using Drupal. If you want to see someone literally "light up," stop him on the street and ask him, "What is Drupal, and what can it do for me?"

About the Technical Reviewer

Anshul Jain has been involved with Drupal since Drupal 5 came into the world. He is a full stack developer, proficient in a variety of technologies. He is currently working as a Senior Technical Specialist at a multinational company.

He has developed numerous web sites in Drupal for small to giant clients. He also takes sessions on Drupal to train his team and coworkers. He has contributed to Drupal 7 core and is also a maintainer of some contributed modules.

Apart from Drupal, he has worked on developing mobile apps using hybrid frameworks like PhoneGap, Ionic, Angular 2, jQuery mobile, and SAPUI5. He has also published an Android app in his drupal.org profile, https://www.drupal.org/u/anshuljain2k8.

Anshul can be contacted at anshuljain.php@gmail.com or anshuljain@mumbaicolors.com.

Introduction

In its relatively short life, Drupal has made a tremendous impact on the landscape of the Internet. As a web content management system (CMS), Drupal has enabled the creation of feature- and content-rich web sites for organizations large and small. As a web application framework, Drupal is changing the way that people think about web application development. When I experienced the power of the Drupal platform for the first time, I knew that it was something more than just another content management solution. When I saw how easily and quickly I could build feature-rich web sites, I shifted gears and focused my entire career around Drupal. While working with hundreds of organizations, I was often asked, "Where can I go to find information for someone who is new to Drupal?" Unfortunately there wasn't a comprehensive resource that I could point them to, and thus began my journey and passion of writing books and magazine articles about Drupal.

I'm also often asked, "What is Drupal?" The short answer is, "Drupal is an open source web content management system that allows you to quickly and easily create simple to complex sites that span everything from a simple blog, a corporate site, a social networking site, or virtually anything you can dream up." What you can build with Drupal is limited only by your imagination and the time you have to spend with the platform.

As an open source platform, Drupal's community is constantly improving the platform and extending the functionality of the core platform by creating new and exciting add-on modules. If there's a new concept created on the web, it's likely that there will be a new Drupal module that enables that concept in a matter of days. It's the community behind the platform that makes Drupal what it is today, and what it will become in the future. I'll show you how to leverage the features contributed by the community, making it easy for you to build incredible solutions with minimal effort.

The very act of picking up this book is the first step in your journey down the path of learning how to use Drupal. If you will walk with me through the entire book, you'll have the knowledge and experience to build complex and powerful Drupal-based web sites. You'll also have the foundation necessary to move beyond the basics, expanding on the concepts I cover in this book.

Learning Drupal is like learning any new technology. There will be bumps and hurdles that cause you to step back and scratch your head. I hope the book helps smooth the bumps and provides you with enough information to easily jump over those hurdles. I look forward to seeing your works on the web and hope to bump into you at an upcoming DrupalCon.

CHAPTER 1

■ ■ ■

Introduction to Drupal

This chapter provides a basic overview of what a content management system (CMS) is, how Drupal 8 fills the role as an enterprise class CMS, the major building blocks of Drupal 8, and how to create content on your new Drupal 8 web site.

Content Management Systems

In its simplest form, a *CMS* is a software package that provides tools for authoring, publishing, and managing content on a web site. "Content" includes anything from a news story, a blog post, a video, or a photograph, to a podcast, an article, or a description of a product that you are selling. In more general terms, content is any combination of text, graphics, photographs, audio, and video that represents something visitors to your site will read, watch, and hear.

A CMS typically provides a number of features that simplify the process of building, deploying, and managing web sites, including the following:

- An administrative interface
- A database repository for content
- A rich user interface to associate content that is stored in the database with a web page on the site
- A toolset for authoring, publishing, and managing content
- A component for creating and managing menus and navigational elements
- The tools required to define and apply themes
- User management
- A security framework
- Taxonomy and tagging to organize content by category
- Online forms
- E-commerce capabilities

There are hundreds of CMSs available (check out `www.cmsmatrix.org`). They range from simple blogging-centric platforms, such as WordPress, to complex enterprise-class content management solutions, such as Drupal.

© Todd Tomlinson 2017

T. Tomlinson, *Enterprise Drupal 8 Development*, DOI 10.1007/978-1-4842-0253-1_1

Drupal

Drupal is a free and open source CMS written in PHP and distributed under the GNU General Public License. Drupal stems from a project by a Dutch university student, Dries Buytaert. The goal of the project was to provide a mechanism for Buytaert and his friends to share news and events. Buytaert turned Drupal into an open source project in 2001, and the community readily embraced the concept and has expanded on its humble beginnings, creating what is now one of the most powerful and feature-rich CMS platforms on the Web. Individuals, teams, and communities leverage Drupal's features to easily publish, manage, and organize content on a variety of web sites, ranging from personal blogs to large corporate and government sites.

The standard release of Drupal, known as Drupal core, contains basic features that can be used to create a classic brochure web site, a single- or multi-user blog, an Internet forum, or a community web site with user-generated content. Features found in Drupal core include the ability to author and publish content; to create and manage users, menus, and forums; and to manage your site through a web browser–based administrative interface.

Drupal was designed to be enhanced with new features and custom behavior by downloading and enabling add-on modules. There are thousands of additional modules (known as contributed or "contrib" modules) that extend Drupal core's functionality, covering a broad spectrum of capabilities, including e-commerce, social networking, integration with third-party applications, multimedia, and other categories of capabilities.

Drupal can run on any computing platform that supports both a web server capable of running PHP version 5.5.9+ (including Apache, IIS, lighttpd, and nginx) and a database (such as MySQL, SQLite, or PostgreSQL) to store content and settings.

Drupal Core

When you download and install Drupal, you are installing what is commonly called Drupal core. Core represents the "engine" that powers a Drupal-based web site, along with a number of out-of-the-box features that enable the creation of a relatively full-featured web site. The primary components of Drupal core include capabilities to create and manage the following:

- Content
- File uploads/downloads
- Menus
- User accounts
- Roles and permissions
- Taxonomy
- Views to extract and display content in various forms such as lists and tables
- WYSIWYG-based content editor
- RESTful web services

Drupal core also includes a feature-rich search engine, multilingual capabilities, and logging and error reporting.

Contributed Modules

Although Drupal core can be used to build feature-rich web sites, there are likely situations where core lacks the functionality needed to address specific requirements. In such cases, the first step is to search through the thousands of custom modules, contributed by developers from all around the world to the

Drupal project, for a solution that meets your needs. It's very likely that someone else had the same functional requirement and has developed a solution to extend Drupal core to provide the functionality that you need.

To find a contributed module, visit the `drupal.org` web site at `drupal.org/project/project_module`. You will find a general list of categories and the current number of contributed modules (for all versions of Drupal) contained within each. Here is a short sampling of the types of categories and the number of modules you can find in each (modules are added to the list on a daily basis, and the number of modules in each category will have grown considerably since the time of this writing):

- Administration (1655)

- Commerce/Advertising (808)

- Community (733)

- Content (2679)

- Content Display (2169)

- Content Construction Kit (CCK) (710)

- Developer (1494)

- E-commerce (1245)

- Media (1083)

- Mobile (212)

- Third-party Integration (2616)

- Utility (2695)

To find modules that are supported on Drupal 8, select 8.x for the "Core Compatibility" search filter.

A few of the most popular contributed modules, and the ones that you will likely want to install, include the following (also check out the "Most Installed" list to the right of the search filters):

- *Drupal Commerce*: A full-featured web storefront module that provides all of the mechanisms required to sell products (physical as well as electronic downloads), collect credit card payments, and manage shipments. If you want to sell something on your web site, this is the module you will want to use.

- *Display Suite*: Allows you to take full control of how your content is displayed using a drag-and-drop interface.

- *Calendar*: Provides the ability to create and render a list of events on a calendar.

- *Backup and Migrate:* Handles scheduled backups of content in your Drupal database, with the ability to restore the database to a previous state based on one of the backup files created by this module. This is a must-have module for any production web site. You may also use this module to migrate content from one Drupal site to another.

- *Google Analytics*: Provides a simple-to-use form for setting up Google Analytics on your site. Google Analytics is a free service that tracks the number of visitors to your web site, where those visitors came from, what search terms they used to find your site, the pages they visited while on your site, how long they spent on your site, and many other useful metrics that will help you view and understand the usage of your web site. For more information on Google Analytics, visit `www.google.com/analytics`.

- *Pathauto*: Creates search engine–friendly URLs by automatically generating a "pretty" URL that is based on the page's title (such as www.example.com/examples instead of the default Drupal URL of www.example.com/node/1234).

- *Scheduler*: Provides the ability to specify the date that a node will become published on the site, and the date when a node will no longer be published. This allows a content author to create a node now and have it not appear on the site until some date in the future.

Drupal Themes

A *theme* is the Drupal component that defines how the pages on your web site are structured and the visual aspects of those pages. A Drupal theme defines attributes of your web site such as:

- How many columns of information will be presented on a page (a three-column layout with a left, center, and right column; a two-column layout with a narrow left column and a wide right column for content; a one-column layout, and the like)

- Whether a page has a banner at the top

- Whether a page has a footer

- Where navigational menus appear (at the top of the page, under the banner, in the right column, and so on)

- The colors used on the page

- The font and font size used for various elements on a page (such as headings, titles, and body text)

- Graphical elements, such as logos

Drupal core includes a number of off-the-shelf themes that you can use for your new web site. You may also download one or more of the hundreds of free themes that are available at drupal.org/project/project_theme, or you can create your own theme by following the directions found at drupal.org/documentation/theme.

Creating Content

A web site without content would be like a book without words, a newspaper without news, and a magazine without articles: hardly worth the effort of looking at. Drupal 8 makes it easy to create, publish, and manage content on your new web site. Let's look at how simple it is by creating your first piece of content. If you haven't installed Drupal 8 yet, visit www.drupal.org/docs/8/install and follow the step-by-step process for installing and configuring Drupal 8 core.

There are multiple paths for getting to the content-authoring screens in Drupal. I'll focus on the simplest, but there are several paths for creating content in Drupal 8.

On the front page of your new web site, you will see an Add Content link beneath the "No front page content has been created yet" message on your homepage. In the left column, you will also see an Add Content link in the Tools menu (see Figure 1-1). Click either of the links: they both take you to the content editing form, where you will create your first piece of content.

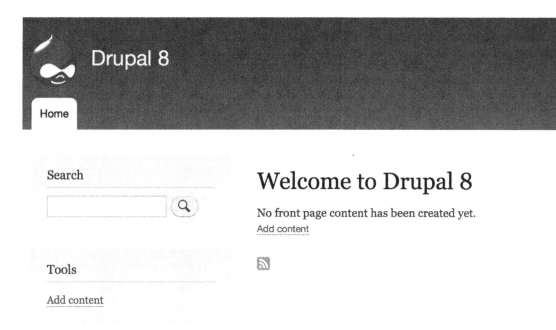

Figure 1-1. *Click either Add Content link to get started*

Next you'll see a list of the content types that you can use (see Figure 1-2). Drupal 8 comes with two basic content types: an article and a basic page. Both content types provide you, the author, with a text field for entering the title of the content item and a body text area where you can write. Different content types provide additional elements. In the case of an article, you have the ability to enter "tags" for categorizing your content and an image. I cover tagging and several other content types later in the book, as well as the capability for creating your own custom content types.

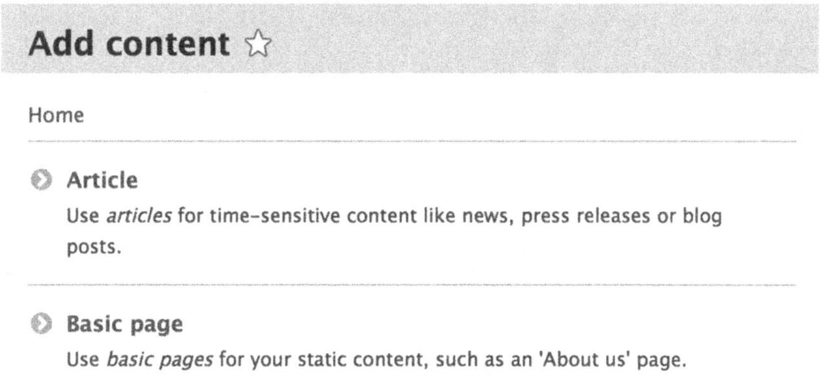

Add content ☆

Home

⊘ **Article**
Use *articles* for time–sensitive content like news, press releases or blog posts.

⊘ **Basic page**
Use *basic pages* for your static content, such as an 'About us' page.

Figure 1-2. *Selecting your content type*

5

Start with the simplest content type, a page, as the basis for your first content item on your new web site. Click the Basic Page link, which opens the content creation form for creating that content type (see Figure 1-3). On this form, enter the title of your first article and some text into the body area. After you have entered the title and body of your article, click the Promotion Options link in the right sidebar, and from the list of options presented, notice the Promoted to Front Page checkbox. When this option is checked, it tells Drupal to display this article on the front page of your site. If it is not checked by default, click on the checkbox to select it. Finally, scroll down to the bottom of the page and click the Save and Publish button.

Create Basic page ☆

Home » Add content

Title *

Body (Edit summary)

| **B** | *I* | ⊕ | ⊗ | ≔ | ≔ | 99 | 🖾 | Format | ▾ | ⊙ Source |

Text format   Basic HTML   ⬦   About text formats ⓘ

(**Save and publish** ▾)   (Preview)

Last saved: *Not saved yet*
Author: admin
○ Create new revision

▸ MENU SETTINGS

▸ URL PATH SETTINGS

▸ AUTHORING INFORMATION

▸ PROMOTION OPTIONS

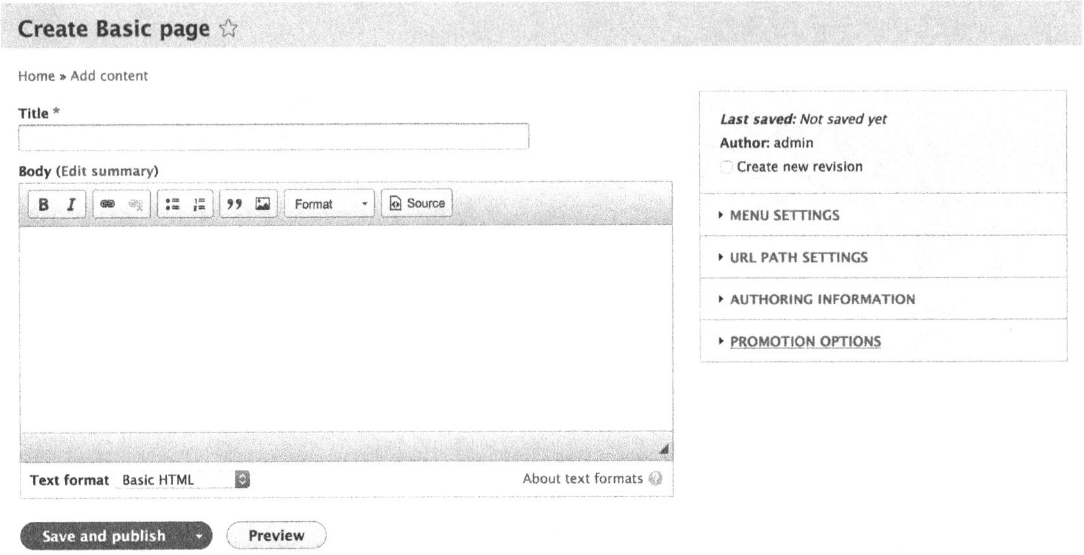

Figure 1-3. *Creating a basic page*

By clicking the Save and Publish button, the content you just authored will be immediately displayed on the front page of your web site (see Figure 1-4).

Figure 1-4. *Voila, you are published!*

Congratulations! You've authored and published content on your new Drupal web site. There are many other content authoring, publishing, and management features that I cover throughout the remainder of this book. You are well on your way to building incredible web sites on Drupal.

Taking Drupal 8 to the Enterprise

Creating a basic page on your new Drupal 8 web site is only the first step in the journey of creating an enterprise class web site on Drupal 8. There are many other features and capabilities that you should consider, such as:

- Categorizing content to make it easy for your site visitors to find the content they are looking for, while also making it easy for the editorial team to author content and have it appear exactly where they want it to show with minimal effort. Drupal 8's taxonomy system is a perfect solution to this issue.

- Delivering compelling content to a global visitor base by leveraging the multilingual capabilities of Drupal 8.

- Integrating the selling of your products or services into the content on your web site, creating a seamless experience between content and commerce. Drupal Commerce is a world-class platform for selling physical and virtual good such as ebooks, etickets, and memberships. And it's Drupal, so you have all of the content-creation, content-management, and site-building features of Drupal at your fingertips.

- Equipping your organization to successfully build, deliver, scale, and support Drupal.

- Looking at Drupal 8 as more than just a tool to build your web sites. Drupal 8 is a web application development framework that can be leveraged to build any web facing application, and you have access to the thousands of contributed modules that provide a wealth of functional capabilities that you can leverage in your applications.

- Scaling Drupal to effectively support the level of activity in your organization.

The remainder of this book focuses on these topics and other areas that are critical to the success of building and sustaining enterprise class applications and web sites on Drupal 8.

Summary

This chapter focused on the basics of what a CMS is, the base functionality available in Drupal core, how to extend the functional footprint of Drupal core by adding contributed modules, Drupal themes, and creating your first content item in Drupal. If you are new to Drupal 8, I suggest reading *Beginning Drupal 8* (published by Apress) to provide a strong foundation in the capabilities of Drupal 8.

Chapter 2 covers the process and organizational best practices associated with creating a high-performance Drupal team in your organization.

■ ■ ■

Building a Practical Software Development Process and Team

With the powerful capabilities that are available in Drupal 8 there is a tendency to jump in and immediately begin building before stepping back and defining the requirements and architecting an effective and efficient solution framework. It is an easy trap to step into, one that I have found myself victim to over the years, but in the end, taking time to define what you're trying to build before you begin the development process will save you countless hours of rework and frustration as you try to maintain, support, and sustain a solution that is held together with duct tape and bubble gum. Another common approach is to simply move your web site from one platform to another, replicating the potential inefficiencies from one solution framework to another. The "paving the cow path" approach often results in a solution that works, but it typically fails to provide breakthrough capabilities that will differentiate your organization in its respective markets, and it will likely take more time to try to force fit your old site's structure and components into Drupal, which in many cases is significantly different from an architectural perspective, resulting in a less than optimal solution.

There is a better way, and the process doesn't have to be long and arduous. Done correctly you'll end up with a solid foundation and a set of reusable components that will speed the development of future Drupal solutions. You will also step into the development process with a higher level of assurance that what you are building is what your customer, whether internal or external, wants. You'll also have the opportunity to enjoy your weekends, as you won't be fighting fires as your site "tips over" and slowly melts due to a poorly planned out solution.

A Methodology for Building Your Site on Drupal

While there isn't a formal "Drupal Methodology" for building sites on Drupal, there are several industry best practices and processes that you may want to follow as you embark on the journey of creating a new Drupal web site. The process described in Table 2-1 may seem overwhelming and more complex and involved than what you think you need to build your new site, but from 30,000 plus hours of Drupal experience under my belt I've found that it's good to at least think about these steps. Not every step is appropriate for every site; simple sites will typically require less up-front definition, whereas a complex enterprise-wide, multilingual site may take significant analysis and definition before installing Drupal and beginning the build process.

© Todd Tomlinson 2017
T. Tomlinson, *Enterprise Drupal 8 Development*, DOI 10.1007/978-1-4842-0253-1_2

Table 2-1. *A Methodology for Building Your Drupal Site*

Phase	Task	Activity
I		**Starting Your Project** The seven tasks in this phase are focused on helping you think about and define what your site is going to be. Drupal is a lot like a stack of lumber: you could build virtually any type and style of house with an appropriately sized stack of lumber. However, you wouldn't start picking up boards and nailing them together without first knowing the details of the house that you are going to build. Think of this phase of the project as defining the blueprint of your new site. In this phase, you're documenting key aspects of your site on paper, and not in Drupal. Once you have an understanding of what it is you're going to build, you can embark on the construction activities.
	A	**What is your new web site all about?** Write down, in narrative form, what the purpose of your new site is and, in general, describe the audience that you intend to target with your site. Think of this document as your "elevator pitch," meaning if you met someone in an elevator and they asked you what your web site was about, you could recite this document verbatim before the two of you left the elevator. This activity forces you to define in concise terms what it is you are building and who is going to view the site.
	B	**Identify who is going to visit and use your web site** List the various types of visitors who you intend to target with your new web site. Examples of visitor types for a library site might be children, teens, young adults, adults, jobseekers, and senior citizens. A favorite technique is to use a blank piece of paper and on this paper draw a "box" representing a browser window with your web site in that browser window. Draw a number of stick figures around the box and label each one with the type of visitor that "person" represents.
	C	**Identify the content that you are going to deliver to your visitors** A common mistake in the web site construction process is the "field of dreams" mentality: "if I build it they will come." Well if "they" come to your site, what content are you going to present to "them" so they stay on your site, look around, and bookmark your site for future visits? You may want to use a blank piece of paper for each visitor type, drawing a stick figure on the left and listing the content that this person would be interested in seeing on your site. There will likely be duplication between various visitor types, and that is okay, but it is important to step into the "shoes" of each visitor type to think about what content you are going to provide each visitor that will make them pay attention and return to your site in the future. Examples of content types might be, for a library web site, book reviews, movie reviews, music reviews, recommended reading lists, and a list of upcoming programs at the library.
	D	**Identify the functionality that you are going to deliver to your visitors** Content is typically only one aspect of what constitutes a web site; there may be interactive features that you want to deliver, such as blogs, surveys, videos, audio, discussion forums, online forms, e-commerce, RSS feeds, or other interactive features. In this task, list all of the interactive features that you want to provide to your visitors.

(continued)

10

Table 2-1. (*continued*)

Phase	Task	Activity
	E	**Define the site's structure** Examine the types of content and functionality documented in the previous steps; you will start to see logical groupings or categories. You may see logical groupings based on a topic or subject, or you may see groupings based on specific visitor types. Using a library site as an example, you might see that there is a logical grouping of content across all visitor types that are focused on book reviews. You might also see a logical grouping of content that is focused on senior citizens and their use of community resources. Each of these logical groupings may, and probably should, become a major page on your web site.
	F	**Define custom content types and taxonomy structureDrupal:methodology, building sites** There may be types of content that do not fit the off-the-shelf Drupal 8 content types. An example might be that you identified "Events" as a type of content. An Event has a title, a start date, a start time, an end date, an end time, and a location. It might be advantageous to create for events a custom content type that enforces the entry of those additional details, rather than relying on the author to remember to enter those values in the body of a generic page. In this step, you should create a list of custom content types and the attributes (such as start date and start time) associated with each content type. While defining content types, it's also time to think about taxonomy and how you are going to categorize content on your site.
	G	**Define the navigational structure of your web site** With an understanding of the visitor types, the content that they will want to see on your site, and the logical groupings or major pages that will make up your site, you can now define the navigation (menus) for your site. If you know that a specific visitor type is a primary visitor of your web site, you should make it easy for that visitor to find the information that they are seeking. The typical mechanism for doing that is to provide some form of menu or menus. In this task you would identify all of the links that you want to provide to your site visitors and how those links should be organized (as menus). Using the library example, you may decide that you want a primary menu at the top of the page that provides links to About the Library, Locations and Hours, and How to Contact the Library. You may decide that you want a secondary menu that links visitors to pages for Books, Movies, Music, and Events. You may decide that you want another menu that helps to direct specific visitor types to pages that are focused on their specific interest areas, such as links for youth, teens, adults, senior citizens, and business owners. You can take the concept to another level of detail by defining drop-down menu items for certain menu links; for example, under the Books menu you may want to provide a link to Recommended Books, What's New, and What's on Order.
	H	**Create wireframes** For every major page on your site, create a wireframe (`wikipedia.org/wiki/Website_wireframe`) that depicts the elements that will appear on each page. Use the wireframes to validate that you have identified all of the types of content that will be rendered on your page, as well as all of the non-content elements (e.g., call to action, advertisements, etc.) that will appear on your page. There are many free and commercially available tools in the market. Checkout Pencil at `pencil.evolus.vn`.

(*continued*)

Table 2-1. (*continued*)

Phase	Task	Activity
	I	**Document the inventory of site components**
		With an understanding of what the site needs to deliver to its end users, and the desired site structure, the team should develop a comprehensive inventory of the components required to support the requirements of the organization. Depending on the complexity of the site, the inventory may consist of annotated wireframes, where every element on a page is defined to a level of detail required to construct and test that component (e.g., this is a block that is editorially curated with a call to action). For more complex sites a spreadsheet may suffice as the means for documenting the inventory of what must be built to successfully build and deploy the required functionality. The benefits of a spreadsheet are that it is easier to identify common elements that are shared across pages on the site and the relative scope and the volume can determine size of the effort and complexity of elements required to assemble the site. The inventory should contain the pages that must be built, the content types that must be created, the taxonomy that is required, the menus, blocks, and views required to assemble each component of the site. To the extent possible, the architect should work with the business systems analyst and UX designer to identify the correct source of information for a given element (e.g., this is a list of articles tagged as news story, sorted by date published in descending order, showing the title and the first 300 characters of the body). This step will also provide the details required by the quality assurance team to build the test plans, scenarios, and conditions required to test the site.
II		**Setting Up Your Drupal Environment**
		Now that you have an understanding of what you're going to build, the next phase is to set up your Drupal environment to begin the construction process.
	A	**Decide where you are going to host your new web site**
		You can easily build your new web site on your desktop or laptop and then deploy that site on a hosted environment, or you can choose to build the site in the environment where you are going to host the production version of your web site. Either approach works well. However, at some point in the near future you are going to want to deploy your site with a commercially viable hosting provider or use your organization's own hosting platforms. To find a list of commercial hosting providers that support Drupal, visit `www.drupal.org/hosting`.
	B	**Install and configure Drupal**
		Following the step-by-step instructions found at `www.drupal.org/docs/8/install`, install Drupal on either your local desktop/laptop or on your hosting provider's environment.
III		**Choosing a Visual Design**
		Picking or designing your Drupal theme is one of those activities that you can choose to do early in the process, midway through the development process, or near the end of your efforts. For most people, having a sense of what the site is going to look like helps visualize the layout as it will look in its final state. There may be circumstances where you can't pick or design the theme up front, such as the case where the organization you are building the site for doesn't have their branding completed (including logo, colors, iconography, fonts, and so on). In that case it is still possible to continue with the construction activities using a generic theme.

(*continued*)

Table 2-1. (*continued*)

Phase	Task	Activity
	A	**Look for an existing theme that matches what you are trying to accomplish** Hundreds of themes are available on drupal.org, and there is likely one that comes close to the layout and design that you would like to use on your site. To see the list of themes, visit drupal.org/project/themes. If you can't find a theme that matches your requirements, you can use one of the various "starter" themes listed on the Drupal site (such as Bootstrap) as a place to start.
	B	**Implement your site's specific design elements** If you pick an off-the-shelf theme from drupal.org (versus creating one from scratch), you will likely want to change the theme's logo, colors, and so on. The topic of theme development is beyond the scope of this book; however, you can read up on the concepts behind Drupal themes and discover which files you want to look in to make changes to customize the theme at www.drupal.org/documentation/theme.
IV		**Downloading and Installing Contributed Modules** In Task D of Phase I, you documented the functionality that you want to deliver to your site visitors beyond just content (such as interfaces to legacy systems that provide content to your site, commerce capabilities, integration with your marketing automation tools, integration with your customer relationship management system, and other functionality). In this phase you will search for, install, and enable the modules that you need to address the desired functionality.
	A	**Identify the modules required to address the desired functionality** Some of the functionality may be addressed by Drupal 8 core modules (such as Views), while other functionality may require searching for an appropriate module. To look for modules, visit www.drupal.org/project/project_module. Using the filters available at the top of the page, narrow the search to those modules that are based on the functionality that you want to fulfill on your site. If you're struggling to find the right module, a good resource to use is the drupal.org forums. The community is extremely helpful, and posting a quick question asking for advice on which module to use for a specific feature or function may cut down on your research time as well as save you from picking the wrong module for the job.
	B	**Download and install required modules** Once you've identified the right modules to address the required functionality on your site, follow the instructions listed in Chapter 11 for installing, enabling, configuring, and setting permissions for each of the modules.
V		**Creating Custom Content Types** If you identified custom content types in Phase I, Task E, now is a good time to create those content types. Use the list of content types and the list of attributes for each type.
VI		**Creating Views** There may be pages on which you want to provide a list or table view of content. Now is a good time to construct those views to support creation of pages in the next step.
VII		**Creating the Physical Pages** Use the techniques described in this book to create the actual pages (for example, use the Panels module to create complex page layouts). Create the various pages that you defined in Phase I, Task E.

(*continued*)

13

Table 2-1. (*continued*)

Phase	Task	Activity
VIII		**Finishing Up the Menus on Your Site** With the pages in place, you're now ready to finalize the menus on your site. Revisit the navigational structure you defined in Phase I, Task F to ensure that you've addressed all of the navigational requirements for your new site.
IX		**Finalizing the Configuration** At this point, the site should be configured and ready to go. In this phase, make sure that you have created all of the user roles, have assigned the appropriate permissions to those roles, and have configured how users accounts will be created.
X		**Creating Content** Now that you have the site configured, content types created, views defined, panels created, and user roles and permissions defined, it's the time to create content on your site.
X		**Testing Your Site** With your site nearly ready for production, now is the time to test to make sure that everything works as you expect it to. Make sure you test the site as an anonymous user (not logged into the site). It is also a good idea to create test accounts for each of the user roles that you have defined and to visit the site while logged into each account to ensure that the roles and permissions are working as you had envisioned.
XI		**Deploying to Production** It's now time to deploy your site to your production-hosting environment.
	A	If you created your site on your desktop or laptop, you'll need to copy the entire Drupal directory to your production web server, and you'll need to back up your database and restore it on your hosting environment.
	B	If you created your site on a hosting provider's platform, you are already there and don't need to move your site.
XII		**Administering Your Site** Monitor and manage your new Drupal web site.

Several have asked if this methodology is a traditional waterfall approach, where the phases and tasks are executed sequentially, or whether the approach is adaptable to agile. My answer to that question is it depends on how your organization prefers to execute projects. If you are more comfortable in a traditional waterfall approach then follow the process sequentially. For those of us who have adopted the agile way of life, the approach may be to break the phase I and II tasks into sprints 1 and 2, and for the remaining phases and tasks into sprints that allow you to deliver incremental functionality until you have a minimal viable product (MVP) that can be launched, with additional sprints adding new functionality to your site. There isn't a right or wrong answer; the only answer is to use what works for your organization and those who make up your team.

While this may not be a comprehensive methodology that addresses every aspect of building large complex enterprise class web sites, it is the ninety-percent solution that addresses the majority of the needs for most organizations. The key is to "know before you go" or you'll likely end up in the ditch.

Building a Drupal Team in Your Organization

As with methodologies, there isn't a one-size-fits-all definition for the organizational structure that will ensure your team's success in delivering Drupal solutions to the enterprise. There are however a set of roles, responsibilities, and skills that form the foundation of an effective Drupal team and you will need to address coverage of these skill sets in your organization. The roles described in this section are recommendations based on the types of work that encompass a typical Drupal project, and in most organizations, team members assume the responsibilities of one or more of these roles, and in some instances, your Drupal team may consist of only one person.

Project Manager

Drupal projects are typical of all IT projects in that there are a number of tasks that need to be accomplished and resources that must be managed to ensure that those tasks are completed on-time, within budget, and meet the quality standards of the organization. On most Drupal projects the project manager role can be a part-time responsibility; however, large-enterprise scale site builds may require one or more project managers based on the size and scope of the effort.

Roles and Responsibilities

The role of the project manager encompasses the following key responsibilities.

Planning and Forecasting

1. Reviews project requests, prepares estimates, creates the project plan, develops the cost justification for the project.

2. Implements and manages project management tools that enable scheduling, budget tracking, resource allocation, resource balancing, time tracking, reporting, and communication of tasks, budgets, and schedules to those assigned to projects.

3. Responsible for the estimating template for all project-related work.

4. Creates and manages detailed project plans:

    a. Ensures that project schedules are accurately defined at the start of a project.

    b. Ensures that project budgets are accurately defined at the start of a project.

    c. Defines the staffing required to meet the project schedule with the skills required to meet the project budgets.

    d. Ensures that resources are loaded across projects in a manner that meets or exceeds utilization targets.

5. Maintains and publishes (weekly) accurate weekly, monthly, quarterly, and annual forecasts:

    a. Resource loading and requirements

    b. Utilization

    c. Project burn rate and earned value

6. Maintains a rolling 90-day forecast of utilization by individual team members and the availability of each team member during that 90-day period.

7. Coordinates with project stakeholders and product owners.

8. Works with accounting to set up jobs in tracking system.

Project Execution

1. Ensures that project schedules are met during the project (tasks are completed on time).

2. Ensures that project budgets are met during the project (tasks are completed within budget).

3. Manages work to ensure that resources meet utilization targets.

4. Ensures that all team members are assigned work, know what the scope of work is, know what their budgets are, and know what the schedule is.

5. Creates the tickets or other mechanisms used to communicate work tasks to staff.

6. Manages the project's scope and change request process. Secures change orders for out-of-scope items.

Reporting

1. Provides weekly status reports (written) to all stakeholders and product owners with active projects (tasks completed, tasks in progress, tasks to be started the next period, current budget, open issues, closed issues, and project schedule).

2. Reconciles time submissions with project schedules and budgets.

3. Reports weekly status to leadership.

Minimum Qualifications

1. Bachelor's degree with a focus on computer science

2. PMP certification preferred

3. Five years of project management experience

4. General understanding of Drupal, content management systems, web design, and web development

5. Expert level understanding of project management tools (MS Project, Project Server, or similar)

6. Expert level understanding of project accounting (managing project financials)

7. Expert level understanding of resource management/resource leveling

8. Outstanding communication skills (written and verbal)

9. Expert level understanding and experience in managing a diverse group of people

Metrics and Measurements

1. Project estimates and project plans are created and delivered to stakeholders and product owners in a timely fashion.

2. All resources are aware of assigned tasks, scope, budget, and schedule.

3. All projects delivered on schedule and on or under budget.

4. All resources meet utilization targets.

5. Reports are deemed accurate and are generated on a weekly basis:

    a. Resource utilization—current week and forecast for 90 days

    b. Project budget analysis and schedule

    c. Project status reports

6. Scope is controlled across all projects.

7. Change requests are identified, written up, and delivered to stakeholders and product owners. Secures signatures on change requests.

8. Provides details to accounting to support tracking project costs.

Senior Architect

The senior architect is responsible for defining the overall solution and ensuring that the right components are in place to ensure success of the project. The architect works closely with the business and the development staff to ensure that requirements are accurately translated into a viable Drupal-based solution, which includes contributed modules, custom modules, content types, and taxonomy. The architect also works closely with the development team to develop best practices for code management and deployment and works with the business team to ensure that requirements are accurately defined and translated into solutions that can be implemented in Drupal.

Roles and Responsibilities

1. Translates business requirements into viable Drupal solutions (information and technical architecture).

2. Sets and documents the team's architectural standards:

    a. Development tools and processes

    b. Standard Drupal core and contributed modules that are used to create Drupal solutions in the organization

    c. Custom development best practices, tools, and methods

    d. The server architecture used for development, test, and productions

    e. The deployment processes including tools, processes, roles, and responsibilities

    f. Estimating metrics used by the project manager to accurately define the level of effort and resources required to develop a Drupal solution in the organization

3. Sets and oversees the architectural standards on all projects.

4. Coaches and mentors team members on the use of the standards.

5. Remains current on Drupal core and contributed modules and updates standards based on emerging capabilities, tools, and trends.

6. Participates as the Drupal subject matter expert (SME) in key discussions with stakeholders and product owners.

7. Reviews project estimates for accuracy and completeness.

8. Is the senior technical resource on all projects.

9. Works with the project manager to ensure that project templates are up to date.

10. Participates in the Drupal community as the organization's senior Drupal visionary.

Minimum Qualifications

1. Five years of Drupal development

2. 10 years in information technology

3. Demonstrated expertise in Drupal architecture and Drupal application development

4. Demonstrated expertise in PHP development on MySQL

5. Demonstrated expertise in server architecture (Apache, MySQL, Linux, and PHP)

6. Demonstrated knowledge of software development best practices

7. Demonstrated expertise in project estimating

8. Demonstrated ability to mentor, coach, and lead teams of developers

9. Outstanding written and verbal communication skills

Metrics and Measurements

1. Architectural standards defined and communicated to the team

2. Projects adhere to architectural standards

3. Team members well versed in architectural standards and are applying them to projects

4. The team's methodology is defined, documented, and updated with lessons learned and best practices

5. The team's development tools are identified and deployed, and the team is trained on use of the tools

Business Systems Analyst

The business system analyst (BSA) is the primary liaison between the development team and the business stakeholders and product owner. The BSA is responsible for collecting and documenting business requirements and then communicating those requirements to the architect, development lead, site builders, and quality assurance team members. BSAs have a general understanding of Drupal and the platform's capabilities.

Roles and Responsibilities

1. Acts as the primary liaison between the business and the Drupal team.

2. Gathers requirements from the business, documenting them in a form that supports the process of defining the detailed architecture required to support the business needs of the organization.

3. Supports the architect, developers, site builders, and quality assurance team members, reviewing specifications to ensure that the solution delivered meets the business requirements.

4. Stays current with Drupal's functional capabilities so they can communicate the platform's ability to support the organization's business needs.

5. Performs assigned tasks within budget and on schedule.

Minimum Qualifications

1. One to five or more years of experience in gathering and documenting detailed business requirements

2. One or more years of experience working with Drupal development teams

3. Excellent verbal and written communication skills

Metrics and Measurements

1. Thoroughly and accurately gathers and documents the organization's business requirements.

2. Requirements are detailed enough for the architect and development team to translate into technical specifications that result in a Drupal solution that meets the business needs.

3. Ensures that the quality assurance team successfully translates business requirements into test scenarios and conditions.

4. Remains current on Drupal's functional capabilities.

5. Completes assigned tasks within budget and schedule.

Development Lead

The development lead is the primary developer on a project, taking overall responsibility for the site building and custom development activities on the project. The development lead works closely with the architect to ensure that the solution meets the defined business requirements and the developers understand the requirements. The development lead also works closely with the site administrator to ensure that the development, test, and live environments are set up properly to support the project and solution. This person coaches and mentors the other developers on the team and leads by example.

Roles and Responsibilities

1. Works with the architect to identify, implement, and train the team on the use of standard development tools, methods, and practices.

2. Reviews assigned tasks (tasks assigned to self as well as tasks assigned to team members). Ensures that scope, schedule, and budget are understood before beginning work on a given task.

3. Performs assigned tasks within budget and on schedule.

4. Works with the project manager and helps monitor the developers to ensure that they are performing tasks within scope, schedule, and budget.

5. Accurately logs time on each task.

6. Alerts team lead/project manager immediately upon identification of scope, schedule, or budget issues (tasks assigned to self as well as tasks assigned to team members).

7. Understands and adheres to architectural standards as defined by the team's architect.

8. Monitors team members' work for adherence to architectural standards defined by the team's architect.

9. Utilizes team's source code control process and commits changes daily (at minimum).

10. Works with the project manager to ensure that tickets are created and assigned to team members. Reviews ticket assignments to ensure the tickets are assigned to the proper team members based on skills. Reviews tickets to ensure that team members are fully utilized and will meet utilization targets.

Minimum Qualifications

1. Five or more years of development experience in a commercial environment

2. Previous team leadership experience

3. Five or more years of experience in application development in a Drupal environment (Drupal APIs and Drupal templates)

4. Five or more years of experience in developing applications using PHP, MySQL, and JavaScript

5. Five or more years of experience in site building on Drupal

6. Demonstrated people management and leadership skills

7. Strong communication skills

Metrics and Measurements

1. Completes assigned tasks within budget and schedule.

2. Ensures that team members complete tasks within budget and schedule.

3. Controls scope on assigned tasks—tasks assigned to self as well as team members.

4. Immediately alerts project manager of scope, budget, or schedule issues.

5. Actively mentors and coaches team members.

6. Actively identifies and contributes improvements to the team's tools, processes, and architecture.

7. Immediately alerts architect and development lead of design or architectural issues that will affect scope, budget, or schedule.

Developer

A developer is responsible for installing and configuring Drupal core and contributed modules as well as developing custom modules as required to support business requirements. The developer works closely with the lead developer to ensure that they understand the functionality that they are tasked with creating and to develop solutions that adhere to the organization's standards. While a majority of the tasks performed by developers are focused on PHP, they should also be well versed in JavaScript and the development tools used by the team.

Roles and Responsibilities

1. Works with the lead developer and architect to review assigned tasks.

2. Develops Drupal solutions that fulfill the stated requirements, using the organization's standards, tools, and processes.

3. Collaborates with other developers and site builders.

4. Completes tasks within the allocated time and budget.

5. Reports issues in a timely fashion.

6. Alerts team lead/project manager immediately upon identification of scope, schedule, or budget issues.

7. Remains current on Drupal development best practices.

Minimum Qualifications

1. One or more years of experience in application development in a Drupal environment (Drupal APIs and Drupal templates)

2. One or more years of experience in developing applications using PHP, MySQL, and JavaScript

3. One or more years of experience in site building on Drupal

Metrics and Measurements

1. Completes assigned tasks within budget and schedule.

2. Solutions developed meet the defined functional and technical requirements.

3. Solutions developed adhere to the organization's defined standards and best practices.

4. Defect rates are below the defined standards for the development team.

Site Builder

A site builder focuses on the tasks of creating Drupal sites as enabled through Drupal core and contributed modules. This person is an expert at selecting and installing contributed modules, configuring Drupal core and contributed modules, and using the administrative tools associated with menu creation, page creation, blocks, and views. Site builders may have some coding experience and expertise, but coding in PHP and JavaScript is not a significant portion of their tasks.

Roles and Responsibilities

1. Maintains expertise in Drupal site building best practices and modules (e.g., views and panels).

2. Reviews assigned tasks and ensures that scope, schedule, and budget are understood before beginning work on a given task.

3. Performs assigned tasks within budget and on schedule.

4. Alerts team lead/project manager immediately upon identification of scope, schedule, or budget issues.

5. Understands and adheres to architectural standards as defined by the team's architect.

6. Understands and utilizes the team's standard development and/or design tools.

Minimum Qualifications

1. One or more years of Drupal site building experience in a commercial environment

2. Demonstrated experience and expertise in site building on Drupal using standard site building approach (views, panels, panelizer, and taxonomy)

Metrics and Measurements

1. Completes tasks within budget and schedule.

2. Immediately alerts project manager of scope, budget, or schedule issues.

3. Actively identifies and contributes improvements to the team's tools, processes, and architecture.

4. Demonstrates growth in understanding and usage of Drupal site building tools, techniques, and best practices.

User Experience (UX) Designer

The UX designer is responsible for translating the business' requirements into sitemaps and wireframes that represent how users will interact with the new Drupal solution. They work closely with the business team, BSA, architect, and visual designer.

Roles and Responsibilities

1. Interviews business stakeholders, product owners, and the BSA to gather the information required to support the creation of assets used to convey the user experience for the new site.

2. Develops the sitemap that represents the overall structure of the new site.

3. Develops detailed wireframes for all the pages on the site and annotates the wireframes with enough detail to support the definition of the Drupal components required to support the functionality on each page.

4. Reviews the user experience designs with the business, solicits feedback, updates the designs, and gathers approval signatures on the design.

5. Works with the visual designer to define the elements that require styling.

6. Works with the architect, development team, and the quality assurance team to ensure that the user experience is accurately and completely translated into the final Drupal solution.

Minimum Qualifications

1. One or more years of user experience design in a commercial environment

2. Outstanding verbal and written communication skills

3. Keeps current on UX best practices and tools

Metrics and Measurements

1. UX designs accurately and thoroughly reflect the requirements of the business and its end users.

2. UX designs reflect the organization's and industry's best practices.

3. UX designs are achievable in a Drupal-based solution.

4. Wireframes are detailed enough to support the technical design and site building activities.

5. Sitemaps are detailed and complete.

6. Completes tasks within budget and schedule.

Visual Designer

This role is responsible for creating visual designs for Drupal sites to be developed by the team that encompass the organization's branding and design standards. The designs cover each of the elements on the wireframes developed by the UX designer and are detailed enough to support the development of Drupal themes.

Roles and Responsibilities

1. Creates visual designs using the team's standard design tools (Photoshop and Illustrator).

2. Creates visual designs that adhere to the organization's branding and visual standards and guidelines.

3. Understands the constraints on visual design that are present in a Drupal environment and develops visual designs that work with Drupal.

4. Works closely with the UX designer and themers to ensure that the visual designs are accurately represented in the Drupal theme and all elements of the UX are properly represented in the theme.

Minimum Qualifications

1. One or more years of web visual design commercial environment

2. Demonstrated expertise in using Photoshop and Illustrator

3. One or more years of developing visual designs for Drupal

Metrics and Measurements

1. Creates visual designs that are accepted by stakeholders and product owners with limited rework (less than 10% of the total effort to create the design attributed to rework).

2. Creates visual designs that are easy to use by themers.

3. Completes tasks within budget and schedule.

4. Immediately alerts project manager of scope, budget, or schedule issues.

Themer

The themer is responsible for translating the UX and visual designs into a Drupal theme. The themer uses the Photoshop (or equivalent) visual design as the foundation for creating the TWIG (Drupal's theming engine) template(s), style sheets, and JavaScript as required to create the theme. The themer works closely with the UX designer, the Visual Designer, and the development team.

Roles and Responsibilities

1. Creates Drupal themes from visual designs (HTML, CSS, Drupal TWIG template files, and JavaScript).

2. Understands and adheres to the organization's branding and visual standards and guidelines.

3. Understands and adheres to architectural standards as defined by the team's architect.

4. Understands and utilizes the team's standard development and/or design tools, including source code control.

Minimum Qualifications

1. One or more years of Drupal theme development experience

2. Demonstrated expertise in using Photoshop

3. Demonstrated expertise in HTML/CSS/JavaScript and Drupal TWIG templates

4. Demonstrated understanding of Drupal base themes

5. Demonstrated experience in developing responsive themes, including HTML5 and CSS3

Metrics and Measurements

1. Creates Drupal themes that adhere to ServerLogic standards and best practices.

2. Completes tasks within budget and schedule.

3. Immediately alerts project manager of scope, budget, or schedule issues.

Site Builder

A significant portion of building a Drupal site is focused on configuration and building elements such as menus, blocks, views, and if your site uses Panels, page building. All of these activities are performed through the Drupal administrative interface and do not require coding. This role may be performed by the BSA once the requirements have been gathered, or by junior developers.

Roles and Responsibilities

1. Creates menus, blocks, views, and pages using the organization's standard architecture and approach.

2. Tests components to ensure they meet the functional, technical, and design requirements.

3. Reviews assigned tasks and ensures that scope, schedule, and budget are understood before beginning work on a given task.

4. Performs assigned tasks within budget and on schedule.

5. Alerts team lead/project manager immediately upon identification of scope, schedule, or budget issues.

Minimum Qualifications

1. One or more years of Drupal site building experience (menus, blocks, views) in a commercial environment

Metrics and Measurements

1. Successfully completes tasks within budget and schedule.

2. Actively identifies and contributes improvements to the team's tools, processes, and architecture.

3. Immediately alerts project manager of scope, budget, or schedule issues.

4. Immediately alerts architect and development lead of design or architectural issues that will affect scope, budget, or schedule.

Quality Assurance Specialist

A Drupal site requires the same level of testing diligence as any application developed and deployed in the organization. The Quality Assurance (QA) specialist is responsible for developing the test plans, test scenarios, test cases, test data, expected results, and in the case where an organization uses automated testing, the test scripts required to execute the tests. The QA specialist works closely with the BSA during the creation of the test plans and cases. The QA specialist also works closely with the development team to support the investigation and remediation of failures in the system to successfully fulfill a test condition.

Roles and Responsibilities

1. Defines test plans, test scenarios, test conditions, test data, and expected results.

2. Identifies tools that will improve the team's ability to effectively test sites as they are developed and deployed.

3. Uses automated testing tools, if any, to facilitate execution of tests.

4. Executes tests, evaluates results, and reports bugs identified during the process.

Minimum Qualifications

1. One to five years of software testing experience in a commercial environment, preferably in a Drupal environment

2. Demonstrated experience and expertise testing strategies and tools

3. Excellent verbal and written communication skills

4. High level of attention to detail

Metrics and Measurements

1. The number of bugs that are found in the production environment continues to decrease over time as new features are implemented.

2. Completes tasks within budget and schedule.

3. Actively identifies and contributes improvements to the team's tools, processes, and architecture.

4. Immediately alerts project manager of scope, budget, or schedule issues.

5. Immediately alerts the team of trends in defects discovered during testing.

6. Trains the entire team on testing best practices and tools.

Site Administrator

The site administrator is responsible for the day-to-day operations of the organization's Drupal sites, ensuring that the site(s) are operational, performing as required, accessible to the users of the system, and are backed up to support disaster recovery. The site administrator is responsible for the full stack of technologies required to host the Drupal site(s), and the connections of that stack to external systems required to support the functional requirements. The site administrator is responsible for supporting the development team, ensuring that system level tools are available and operational for tasks such as source code control, continuous integration, testing, and deployment. Site administrators are also responsible for ensuring that security patches and updates to Drupal core and contributed modules are successfully applied and implemented in a timely fashion.

Roles and Responsibilities

1. Develops processes and procedures for effectively monitoring and managing the organization's Drupal instances.

2. Monitors and manages the organization's hosting environments and Drupal instances.

3. Ensures all Drupal instances are backed up and that the backups are successful.

4. Identifies performance bottlenecks and remediates the issue.

5. Identifies failures and communicates the failures to the development team for remediation.

6. Reviews and applies Drupal core and contributed module security patches.

7. Reviews and applies version updates to Drupal core and contributed modules.

8. Assists in the installation and configuration of new contributed modules.

Minimum Qualifications

1. One to five years of web site administration experience in a commercial environment

2. Demonstrated experience and expertise in managing environments running UNIX/Linux/Nginx, Apache, PHP, and MySQL

3. Demonstrated experience monitoring and managing Drupal sites

4. Demonstrated experience with installing Drupal security patches and installing new contributed modules

5. Demonstrated experience and expertise using git

Metrics and Measurements

1. Ensures that site uptime is within the service-level requirements set by the organization.

2. Actively identifies and contributes improvements to the site administration tools and processes.

3. Actively monitors `drupal.org` for security patches, core updates, and contributed module updates and applies patches and updates as appropriate.

Summary

There are many dimensions that will define the success of a Drupal project in your organization. Having a well-defined development methodology that is consistently used by the members of your team is key to building sustainable and repeatable processes. Realizing that it takes a team with a diverse set of skills and expertise is another dimension of the puzzle of assembling a Drupal solution. In this chapter I provided a general methodology that has worked well for me over the past 30,000 hours of building Drupal solutions for organizations, large and small, and the skills that are typically required to design, build, and support enterprise class Drupal solutions. But a methodology and a team is only the beginning of the process. In the next chapter, I describe how to engineer the Drupal architecture required to support the requirements of your organization.

CHAPTER 3

Engineering Drupal

Drupal is a powerful framework for building enterprise solutions that range from simple web sites to complex web-enabled applications. While Drupal 8 off-the-shelf could be used to build any of the broad spectra of solutions, there are best practices for engineering enterprise class Drupal. The chapter covers the key principles for determining the best approach, and the details involved in successfully engineering a solution that is scalable and adaptable.

Engineering the Foundation

Constructing anything requires an understanding of the requirements of what you are about to build, whether it is a bridge, an automobile, a house, a pizza, or a Drupal site. Building anything without a thorough understanding of the requirements will likely result in having to rebuild some or all of the foundation. If you begin building an automobile and later find out that the true requirements include the ability to tow a travel trailer and haul eight adults then you may have to radically shift the architecture of the two-seater convertible that you just about completed, a task that would likely require starting over. When building enterprise class Drupal, the best approach involves a thorough understanding of the needs of the various constituents that the solution must support. Having spent the past 12 years and 33,000+ hours working as the architect of enterprise class Drupal solutions, it's key that you understand high-level goals and objectives such as:

- What type of sites will the organization create? Are they primarily delivering marketing information? Is online commerce a key consideration? Is there an online community component (user generated content)? Will the sites be multilingual? Are the sites functionally similar or are there wide variations in the types of sites that will be built? Understanding this aspect will help you determine whether all sites can be constructed from a common distribution or whether the variance in functionality will require multiple base platforms on which to build and launch Drupal sites.

- How many different web sites (domains) will the organization construct over the next one to three years? Understanding the number of different sites will help determine whether to build each site independent of the others, whether to use a solution such as Drupal's multisite architecture, or whether a custom enterprise distribution from which each site inherits a majority of its structure and functionality is in order.

© Todd Tomlinson 2017

T. Tomlinson, *Enterprise Drupal 8 Development*, DOI 10.1007/978-1-4842-0253-1_3

- Is there an existing Drupal distribution that closely matches the functional and technical requirements for the organization's sites? For example, does Drupal Commerce, Open Scholar, Open Publish, Open Government, Open Atrium, or other distribution closely match your organization's requirements? Does the organization already have Drupal sites in place? If so, is one or more of those sites a candidate for building an enterprise class Drupal distribution for the organization?

- Will Drupal integrate with other non-Drupal systems in the enterprise? If so, what role does Drupal play? Is it a provider of information to external applications and web sites? Is it a consumer of content from other applications and sites? Is it both? If Drupal is primarily a provider of information to other enterprise application, having a robust user interface may be lower priority than having a well architectures services layer for providing REST APIs.

- What user interface best serves the consumers of information contained in the organization's sites? Does the Drupal interface suffice? Does AngularJS or another decoupled user interface provide a better interface? Headless or decoupled Drupal is becoming a more popular option for organizations that want to be more creative in the presentation of content to their users than what is typically accomplished through the traditional Drupal frontend. A prime example is `weather.com`, which uses a decoupled approach with AngularJS as the presentation layer and Drupal as the decoupled provider of content.

Answering these questions will not provide the detailed level of specifications required to fully define the approach required to build an Enterprise Drupal architecture; however, it will provide the overall guidance as to how the individual pillars of the architecture need to be engineered to address the organization's needs.

Defining the Components of Enterprise Drupal

With a general understanding of the fundamental requirements for your enterprise class Drupal 8 site, the next step is to begin the process of examining each component that will form the architecture and define how your organization's requirements will impact each of the components (see Figure 3-1).

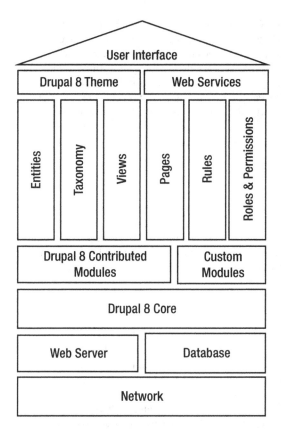

Figure 3-1. *Components of Enterprise Drupal 8*

Network and Web Server

The network and web server architecture required to support Enterprise Drupal 8 plays a significant role in the performance of your site, and there are several aspects that you should consider while engineering your solution. Most Drupal sites use Apache HTTP servers as their web server and Apache does well in that role. However, as your sites' traffic volumes grow, the load placed on the web servers often tax Apache's ability to serve pages quickly enough to ensure acceptable page load times.

Apache often faces what is called the *C10K problem*, which means that Apache has a difficult time supporting more than 10,000 concurrent connections, and in fact in most cases Apache falls far short of delivering adequate performance well before the 10,000 connections limit is reached. Apache's approach is to allocate memory to every additional connection, resulting in swapping to disk as concurrent connections increase. As the number of connections climb the performance quickly spirals downward, leading to unhappy site visitors and headaches for the operations team of your site. Nginx takes a slightly different approach, whereas Apache's approach is to fork a new process for each new inbound connection, where each new fork is allocated resources to process the connection, Nginx queues requests and processes them without allocating resources to each request. The result is lower overhead and faster responses to requests.

Drupal itself also consumes memory and CPU for each request that it receives, similar to Apache, but performance is often negatively impacted at significantly fewer than 10,000 connections. To resolve Drupal's own resource bottlenecks, the best practice is to employ reverse proxy servers. Reverse proxy servers receive request from browsers and then examine each request and determine what to do with it. They either carry out the request itself or send it on to the web server and Drupal for fulfillment of the request. Reverse proxy servers also provide the ability to cache static files (images, CSS files, and JavaScript files) separate from dynamic pages. A reverse proxy server may also cache PHP generated web pages, such as those pages generated by Drupal. By serving up pages from cache, Drupal never sees that request, as the request is fulfilled by the reverse proxy server. Using multiple reverse proxy servers also provides the ability to balance the load across several servers, further reducing the amount of time required to respond to requests.

Many of the biggest Drupal hosting providers, such as Pantheon, use Nginx and reverse proxy servers to ensure that the sites they host perform as desired. Your organization my choose to implement this same architecture in house, or you may rely on hosting providers to provide the infrastructure required to support your anticipated traffic volume.

Database Servers

The web and reverse proxy servers are the first line of defense in solving Enterprise Drupal 8 performance and scalability issues, while the database is a close second as the next area to focus on when engineering Drupal.

As an enterprise class platform, Drupal 8 requires the same level of capabilities and power as any other enterprise application, such as your enterprise resource planning (ERP), customer relationship management (CRM), human resources (HR), or other enterprise class applications.

Selecting the Database Platform

The de facto standard for most Drupal implementations has been MySQL. It was the first database supported by Drupal and continues to be the most popular option for most organizations. Drupal is optimized for MySQL, and while Drupal also supports PostgreSQL and SQLite, not all contributed modules support non-MySQL databases. There are also options for using Oracle and Microsoft's SQL Server databases, although using either of those databases is not considered the mainstream approach for Drupal.

While MySQL meets the performance requirements of most Drupal implementations, there are two MySQL "clones" that provide even higher performance and scalability options as they have replaced key component of the database engine focusing on performance. MariaDB is a fork of MySQL created and maintained by a team of MySQL engineers who left the organization when Oracle purchased the rights to MySQL. Percona is similar to MariaDB, but instead of a fork of MySQL, it is a branch of the main MySQL master branch. The primary difference between the two is that MariaDB diverged from MySQL at a point in time and continues down its own path, whereas Percona shadows MySQL and will continue to be tightly in alignment with the MySQL master branch. Many of the large-scale hosting providers use MariaDB as the database engine for their service offerings.

While MariaDB and Percona typically outperform MySQL, any of the three options are viable candidates to support an Enterprise Drupal implementation.

Clustering MySQL to Improve Performance

Traditionally Drupal sites often ran on a single instance of MySQL, and for many sites, that architecture supported them well until they hit a threshold of page views where the database became a bottleneck. After exhausting the options to tune MySQL to support the transaction volumes, the only alternative is to deploy more than instance of a MySQL server and employ clustering to distribute the workload across servers. This approach provides virtually unlimited database server resources and resolves the issue of the database as the bottleneck. While you may address some of the performance issues through reverse proxy servers and advanced caching mechanisms, it is wise to consider engineering your Enterprise Drupal architecture as a MySQL cluster to avoid having to retrofit your architecture at a later point.

For more information about MySQL clustering, visit `mysql.com/products/cluster`. As a point of reference, a standalone MySQL server may be tuned to deliver 250,000 to 500,000 queries per second, whereas a MySQL cluster, configured properly with the right number of servers and resources, can deliver 200 million queries per second.

Drupal 8 Core

There are several aspects of Drupal 8 core that you should carefully examine and consider while engineering your Enterprise Drupal 8 platform, and many of those options are discussed throughout this book. However, when launching your Enterprise Drupal 8 initiative, there is one aspect that will dictate how you engineer and build your Drupal sites. That aspect is how you want to build sites across your organization. There are three general alternatives:

- Single site
- Multisite
- Distribution

Single Site

A single-site architectural approach focuses on building each site or application by starting with Drupal core and adding the contributed and custom modules required to address the functional and technical requirements for that specific site or application. This approach works well and has been the de facto standard for many organizations. A single site solution framework works best for organizations in which every site and application is significantly different and there is little opportunity to leverage a common framework across all sites and applications. In this case, a common framework would likely be limited to Drupal core and a small number of contributed modules. While there may still be value in developing a common platform, the benefits are not as significant as the other architectural approaches. While it may seem as the easiest alternative to building sites in your organization, you will likely come to the realization that having to maintain dozens or even hundreds of independent sites is overwhelmingly complex and costly. Fortunately there are better ways, as described in the next two sections.

Multisite

Drupal multisite is an approach that has been around for nearly 10 years and is employed as the primary structure for hosting sites on Acquia. A multisite architecture consists of a single codebase with each site or application having its own database and configuration.

The benefit of this approach is that you only have to maintain a single instance of Drupal and contributed modules. An update to Drupal core, contributed, or custom module applies to all sites hosted in a multisite-based architecture. The benefits of a single codebase is often the primary benefit of a multisite architecture; however, there are potential pitfalls, such as:

- A single erroneous update to a module can take all of your sites down, as all sites share the same codebase.
- Scalability may be an issue, as all sites are running on a single instance. A distribution-based approach, on the other hand, provides the ability to spin up independent containers as increased demands warrant additional resources.
- Administrative access to a multisite architecture is difficult to restrict to single sites for tasks like updating a custom module.

Multisite is widely used in large organizations and is a viable approach, but there are tradeoffs that may be addressed by using a distribution-based model.

Distribution

Using a common distribution is the third approach and is based on the concept of assembling a "packaged" solution that addresses a majority of the functional and technical requirements for all sites and applications in an organization. This approach is nearly identical to using one of the community contributed distributions as the foundation for your site—for example, using Drupal Commerce Kickstart, Open Atrium, or Open Public as the upstream distribution on which you build all of your sites.

A distribution based approach starts with engineering a common Drupal footprint that addresses a majority of the functionality across the types of sites in your organization. You then create that site with the core building blocks to address that functionality, such as:

- Drupal 8 core

- Contributed modules

- Custom modules

- Entity types that address the common content requirements

- Taxonomy that addresses a consistent enterprise categorization of content using a common terminology

- Views that render content in ways that are consistent across the organization

- Page templates that address the common layouts used in the organization

- Common enterprise-wide navigational elements (menus)

- Common blocks

- An enterprise-wide search framework

- Integration with legacy enterprise applications and content

It is possible to assemble a common distribution that addresses a majority of the needs of the organization, fulfilling 80% of the common requirements. Creating a new site using a distribution is relatively straightforward—you clone the distribution from a centralized source code control system such as GitHub, install the distribution, and expand on the functionality provided by the distribution where necessary to address a site's specific requirements.

By setting the upstream master of the cloned site to the distribution's repository on, for example GitHub, you have the ability to pull updates and enhancements from the distribution into localized versions of the distribution, making the process of rolling out updates, patches, security updates, and expansion of functionality a relatively simple process. There are hosting providers, such as Pantheon, that provide this capability as part of their enterprise hosting packages, or you can build it yourself.

Profiles

If you select Drupal multisite or a distribution as the approach for building your Drupal 8 platform, you may consider creating one or more installation profiles. Installation profiles combine core Drupal, contributed modules, themes, and pre-defined configuration into one download. Installation profiles provide specific site features and functions for a specific purpose or type of site. They make it possible to quickly set up a complex, user-specific site in fewer steps than installing and configuring elements individually.

As an enterprise is it likely that there won't be a "one-size-fits-all" profile to address every type of site in your organization. For example, you may have a site that is primarily a marketing web site, while another site delivers technical product information to customers who purchase your products, and yet another site is primarily a commerce web site where you sell products and services. While it is possible to build three different distributions to address those three very divergent sites, it is more effective, efficient, and less complex to build a single distribution using installation profiles.

Don't underestimate the power of installation profiles, as they may save your development team countless hours of spinning up new Drupal 8 sites for the various constituents in your organization. See Appendix C for details on how to create a Drupal 8 installation profile.

Drupal 8 Contributed Modules

When engineering your Drupal 8 solution, it is likely that you will need to step outside the capabilities of Drupal 8 core to address the functional requirements of your organization. While Drupal 8 core is feature rich, it can't address every possible requirement from every conceivable use of Drupal 8 in organizations around the world. Combining Drupal 8 core with contributed and custom modules will provide the foundation for addressing your organization's specific needs.

Many organizations fall short when engineering their Drupal footprint by overlooking contributed modules that may solve their functional and technical requirements and, instead, developing custom modules that must then be maintained by their organization. The task of finding the right contributed module or combination of modules is often a tedious one, but the long-term payoff of using contributed modules instead of developing custom modules is significant, especially when considering the cost of upgrading your custom modules to the next major version of Drupal.

There are no easy shortcuts to finding the proper contributed modules to address your functional requirements, other than searching through drupal.org and finding other similar use cases and how people solved those issues. When evaluating contributed modules, there are a few things to keep in mind:

- How many sites report that they are using the module? If the number is small, for example less than 50, closely examine the functionality to determine why more people aren't using the module.

- Check the issue queue and read through the bugs that people are reporting. If they seem significant and there are a lot of them, you may want to consider a different path. The sheer number of issues may not always be a good indicator though, because many heavily used modules have issues that number in the hundreds. They key is to look for critical issues and determine how actively people are working on them.

- Check the date of the last update to the released (non-dev) version of the module. If the module hasn't had a release in several months and there are several outstanding bugs that have been reported and worked on, understand that you may have some additional work to do to apply the patches that developers have submitted to address critical functional and technical bugs.

- Look for known conflicts with other contributed modules in the issue queue. If you have the modules that are reported as conflicting you may want to look for an alternative solution, as implementing that module may break other functionality on your site.

- Look for hooks that provide you with the ability to augment the module. A *hook* is a function that allows you to directly interact with the module to modify some aspect of the module's functionality, such as adding or modifying content that is being processed by that module. A module that provides 80% of the required functionality but has hooks is better than a module that provides 90% of the functionality without the ability to modify the functionality through a hook.

- When presented with multiple options to solve a functional requirement, examine the two modules carefully. Not every module solves the problem the same way and there are likely differences that will sway you one way or another. Another key indicator is the number of contributors to the module. More contributors means more arms and legs to work through the issue queue and update the module. There are also well known developers in the community who are known for the quality of their modules. While everyone can contribute a module, sometimes it pays to stick with the veterans who have consistently delivered high-quality modules to the community.

If at the end of your evaluation you've come up empty handed, custom modules are the acceptable path. Follow Drupal's best practices, which can be found at `drupal.org/coding-standards`, and consider contributing your custom module to the community. It's highly likely that someone else in the world is facing the same functional requirement and could benefit from your solution. Conversely, you have the opportunity to collaborate with others in the community to augment your custom module to make it even better.

Custom Modules

Early in my career shift to Drupal I partnered with a friend who was out building Drupal web sites and doing so quite successfully. What impressed me about his web sites was that there was no custom code; the sites were robust and complex and relied solely on off-the-shelf Drupal. While possible, it is likely that you will need to venture off into the realm of developing custom modules to address the unique functional requirements in your organization. When engineering your Drupal footprint and considering custom modules, it is important to consider a few key points:

- Is there a way that this can be accomplished with off-the-shelf Drupal? For example, can you use a combination Drupal capabilities such as web services, views, webforms, and rules, which provide the foundation for solving many functional requirements that cannot be addressed with existing modules.

- Can the requirements be modified to match the capabilities of an off-the-shelf solution? In my 30,000+ hours of building enterprise class Drupal solutions, when asked, requirements often shift to fit an off-the-shelf capability without having to address the functionality through custom code.

- Can the functionality be accomplished through extensions to an existing contributed module? Instead of starting from a blank slate, consider contacting the module maintainer for an off-the-shelf module that addresses a majority of your requirements. It is likely that you are not the only organization that requires additional functionality.

After exhausting an evaluation of alternative approaches, custom coding may be warranted. In that scenario, it is wise to follow Drupal 8 best practices when developing your custom solution. Chapter 4 discusses developing custom Enterprise Drupal 8 modules.

The Pillars of a Drupal 8 Solution

The items described previously are often considered the foundation of a Drupal 8 solution, and while contributed and custom modules provide a significant portion of the functionality associated with a Drupal site, the pillars of the solution are:

- Entities
- Taxonomy

- Views

- Pages

- Rules

- User roles and permissions

Entities

Entities form the basis for content, taxonomy, and users on your Drupal 8 site and therefore are often considered the critical pillar of a Drupal site. When engineering your Drupal solution it is important to consider the following:

- What types of content will be authored, stored, managed, and displayed across the enterprise and what is the structure of each type of content?

- What taxonomy vocabularies will be used to categorize content across the enterprise and what is the structure of the terms contained in each vocabulary?

- What information do you want to collect about your users, the ones who physically log on to your Drupal sites?

Content Entities

Understanding the types of content required across an entire enterprise may seem like a daunting task, but it is a necessary activity when creating a Drupal 8 solution that will address your organization's needs and speed the delivery of sites across your organization. While the effort may seem overwhelming, the reality is that most organizations have a small set of entity types that address nearly every piece of content authored by the organization. The process for distilling all of the information published across the organization starts with gathering a representative sample of the content that is currently published and looking for patterns of how that content is organized and the key attributes of each common pattern. The more you distill the better the outcome will be for those who are responsible for building the platform and for those who use the capabilities provided to them through the editorial interface.

As a general rule of thumb, having fewer entity types means the effort to manage and maintain your site will be easier. When examining the results of the distillation process, you will likely find that a vast majority of the patterns fit into a simple structure of a title, a body, a featured image, the date content was published, an article type field driven by taxonomy, and the author who created the content. If you look at this simple pattern, you'll likely see that it can be applied to news articles, press releases, blog postings, product overviews, new product announcements, and a host of other types of content. In this case you might consider creating a simple multi-purpose article entity type that can be used across a wide variety of use cases.

Not all entity types may be distillable down to a single article entity type. There are specific cases where it makes sense to have individual entity types for content that does not fit the simplistic format of an article. For example, an event has other information such as start date, start time, location, duration, file attachments, and other fields that are typically not applicable to an article. Instead of adding complexity to the article entity type, a separate event entity type is warranted, but constrain the team's desire to construct several content entity types. Instead, look for flexible ways to deliver content through the fewest number of content entity types.

For details about creating entity types in Drupal 8, read the Apress *Beginning Drupal 8* book, which can be found at apress.com/9781430265801.

Taxonomy Entities

Taxonomy is the second pillar in the enterprise-Drupal framework. It is also an entity. I'll cover the usage of taxonomy in the following pages. It also warrants an examination of how taxonomy can play a larger role than just providing terms that an author can use to categorize content. Taxonomy, like content entities, supports the concept of additional fields. Additional fields enable you to utilize taxonomy for broader purposes, such as being the source of certain elements. You could, for example, have a common page banner on all the site pages that are associated with a specific taxonomy term. There could be other attributes associated with a term that may be useful across the site such as category descriptions, related terms, images, or other information.

This is one area where many people miss the opportunity to fully leverage the entity aspects of taxonomy and take a more complex approach to what might be simplistic by utilizing additional fields on a taxonomy vocabulary and using taxonomy for more than just a repository of terms to categorize content. Expand your thinking about how a taxonomy term may provide additional supportive information that would enhance and enrich the content delivered to your end users. Follow the same steps as when adding fields to an entity type when creating taxonomy vocabularies. For additional details on creating custom fields on taxonomy vocabularies, check out the Apress *Beginning Drupal 8* book.

User Entities

Users are another class of entities, and like content and taxonomy, they are also fieldable and expandable beyond the base user entity defined by Drupal 8 core. There may be additional fields that would collect additional information that would enable enhanced functionality on the site, such as filtering content based on some attribute of their profile. Carefully consider the additional elements that may be added to the user entity to facilitate delivering functionality on your Drupal 8 site.

Defining entities is a key step in the process of engineering your overall solution, so do not overlook or shorten the process and take full advantage of Drupal 8 entities.

Taxonomy

Taxonomy is the second pillar of the solution footprint and it plays a critical role that many overlook. Many overlook taxonomy because they do not understand it or they don't think about the power that it brings to Drupal. I have been asked by many organizations over the years to solve common problems that could have easily been addressed by fully utilizing taxonomy. Here are some examples:

- Why is it so hard to author content and have it show up where it is supposed to on my site?

- Why is it so hard to assemble lists of content based on common characteristics?

- Why can't I automatically create a list of related products or articles?

- Why can't I have faceted search and make it easier for my visitors to find the information they are looking for?

- Why do I have to manually create all of these pages on my site? I thought Drupal could magically assemble pages of content without me having to physically place every piece of content on a page?

The question that I ask those organizations that are crying out for help is "How are you using taxonomy on your sites?" Their answer is typically, "What is taxonomy?" Which is exactly why taxonomy is one of my favorite capabilities of Drupal as it solves so many problems that exist when you don't effectively use it. Using it requires studying the organization and its content, including how editors want to curate content, how end users want to find content, and how the organization thinks and talks about its content.

Understanding the taxonomy of the organization and engineering it into the very DNA of your site will result in a significant reduction in the effort needed to create your new sites and will enhance your end users' ability to find the information they are looking for.

So where do you start? The first step is to understand how your organization talks about content. When they talk about content do you hear things like, "When we publish a news article we are trying to target a specific market segment, which includes a break down by industry, application, and problem faced by that target customer". In that simple sentence there are four uses of taxonomy:

- They publish news articles, where "news" represents a type of article
- They target industry segments, which is another categorization of content
- They narrow the focus in that industry by application
- Within the application they narrow the target to a specific problem that their organization addresses through a product or service offering

Using taxonomy and defining specific vocabularies (article type, target industry, application, and problem area) and terms in each of those vocabularies, content authors are able to pinpoint their target. Site builders can use those terms to construct views that display that content, filtered by taxonomy terms, on specific pages on the site.

There are other uses of taxonomy such as providing the capability for content authors to specify which sections of the site a specific content item is to appear, and further refining the placement of that content to a specific section of that page. You may, for example, have a vocabulary for "site section" and one for "content placement," where terms for site section might include the following:

- Homepage
- About us
- Products
- Services
- News

The taxonomy terms for content placement might include these:

- Featured
- Latest
- Call to Action
- Hero
- Recommendations
- Related

When you combine site section (for example Homepage) with content placement (Featured), you can begin to build patterns of filters that may be used in views to enable content authors to automatically place content on the right page, in the right section of that page, by simply tagging the content with the right terms and extracting that content for placement on the page through a view.

Taxonomy also plays a key role in enterprise search, providing the ability to filter content based on taxonomy terms, or through the use of search facets. This provides the ability to drill down through content to get to a content item of interest.

The challenge of taxonomy at the enterprise level is gaining consensus across the organization as to what something is called. The classic example that I often use is the word *rain*. While it seems like a good term to use to classify the water that falls from clouds in the sky, there are others that argue that the correct word is precipitation. There are others who prefer specific terms as to the volume of velocity of rain, such as downpour, drizzle, or mist. And there are others who will add modifiers to the word rain such as driving rain, freezing rain, light rain, intermittent rain, and others. While there isn't a single right answer, the issue becomes how do we consistently convey the word rain to all of our internal and external site visitors so that they can find everything on our site related to the word rain without having to dig through all the variations of the word? The answer? Agree to a common term and stick with it. This concept is often easier said than done due to human nature and our stubbornness in holding on to what we believe is the right answer even if it isn't the best answer. As the engineer of this solution you will have to gather the input from across the organization, distill the list of taxonomy vocabularies and terms into a single enterprise-wide list, and gain buy-in across the organization.

For large organizations, it may warrant the creation of a new job role called *taxonomist*, who is responsible for assembling the enterprise taxonomy, maintaining it, and enforcing it. Your job as the architect or engineer is to leverage the taxonomy to its fullest potential to simplify the process of building, maintaining, and finding content on your site.

Views

Views are the workhorse of most Drupal sites. Without views it would be difficult to extract content from the Drupal database and display it on pages. While not impossible to do, the level of effort exceeds the benefit of not using views to generate that output.

Using views to extract content is a relatively simple process. View's administrator's user interface provides a series of configuration options that identify what content, taxonomy, or users you want to extract and display, as well as which elements of those entities are important to display, the order in which they should appear, and how many should appear, all without writing a single line of code. For details on creating views, check out the Apress *Beginning Drupal 8* book.

When engineering your Drupal 8 solution, it is important to consider the following:

- Whether to create a view per use case, or whether you will create a view per entity type with view displays in that view that address a specific use case. Creating a standalone view for each use case typically results in an unmanageable number of views, which makes it difficult to locate a specific view that is rendering content on a page. Using one view per entity type minimizes the difficulty in locating the right view to use for a specific use case, as they are all contained in a single view.

- Whether to render individual fields through a view display or to use a module like Display Suite (`drupal.org/project/ds`) to control how content is rendered externally from the view. In the latter case, you would use the Display Suite layout to render the content. The separation of the physical layout of the output externally from a view display has significant benefits, including simplifying the creation of a view. All you need to do is output content and render it using the display created through Display Suite. You can make changes to the layout through Display Suite and apply that updated layout automatically to every view that renders content using that display. The alternative is to add every field that must be displayed through the view display and, when changes occur, update every display with the revised approach.

- Use views as your default approach for extracting content from the Drupal database, even in custom modules. While an entity query makes it relatively easy to query the Drupal database and return content based on specific criteria, views make it even easier when extracting complex use cases. As an example, when rendering a list of content that pulls information from other entity types and taxonomy terms, views makes it relatively simple to assemble that output. Writing the view and using the `views_get_view_result($name, $display_id)` function provides a relatively simple way to leverage views in custom modules.

- When a standard view doesn't quite do what you need it to do, instead of writing database queries directly, consider using hooks to modify the view. By using hooks (api.drupal.org/api/drupal/core!modules!views!views.api.php/8.2.x), you have the ability to modify and alter nearly every aspect of a view.

Using views as the "glue" between the content stored in your database and the user experience that you are delivering to your targeted visitors will greatly speed and simplify the development process for your base Drupal 8 platform, as well as the sites that you construct.

Pages

Defining common page templates that fulfill a variety of purposes, rather than constructing each page on your site as a single template, speeds the creation of your sites as well as simplifies the process of building and maintaining pages. As you examine the site maps of the sites targeted for your new Drupal 8 platform, consider the following:

- How many different page layouts are contained in the overall design of the sites that will be constructed? Distilling the number of layouts to a small set of flexible layouts provides the ability to leverage a preexisting template for page construction. In my 30,000+ hours of Drupal experience, most organizations are willing to limit the number of page layouts to 10 or fewer, which includes very large sites for very large international corporations.

- When defining what appears on the page, look for patterns that may be fulfilled using entities, taxonomy, and views. If you did your due diligence and defined a set of entity types that leverage taxonomy for attributes such as site section and content placement, you may be able to use views with views arguments (taxonomy terms in the URL) to automatically generate hundreds or even thousands of pages. All without having to do anything other than create a single page template with views in each region on that page that smartly extract content based on that criteria. For example, a page with a URL of example.com/products/%category/%application could be used to render every product related page on your site, assuming that content has been tagged with a product category and an application. There is no need to manually construct each page individually.

- Leverage tools such as Panels and Page Manager (drupal.org/project/panels) to simplify the process of creating and maintaining pages on your site. While it is common practice to hand-craft Twig templates for pages (e.g., page–node–1.html.twig), you can eliminate nearly all the need to code HTML and Twig to render a page on your site.

As you engineer your solution, the key point about pages is to do your best to constrain the number of page layouts used on the site to a reasonable number (e.g., fewer than 10) in order to simplify the process of creating the base platform. This also makes it easier for those responsible for building sites on your Drupal 8 platform.

Rules

While you can do almost anything you want to do on your site by hand-crafting custom modules, one of the often overlooked Drupal modules is Rules. The Rules module provides site administrators with a powerful tool for creating automated workflows on a Drupal site without having to touch a single line of code. Rules are "reactive," which means an event happens under a certain condition, which then triggers an event. When an event happens, a rule may conditionally manipulate data or execute tasks such as sending an e-mail to someone. Rules may also be scheduled to execute at a future date, making them even more flexible and powerful. As you engineer your Drupal 8 solution, it is important to think about common workflow related tasks and to consider using Rules as an alternative to custom code.

Examples of where the Rules module may play a key role include:

- Sending an e-mail to a site administrator when someone has requested a new account

- Sending an e-mail to a content administrator when a site visitor has posted a comment that is waiting for review and approval

- Changing the value of a field on a node when a date has passed

- E-mailing a customer a copy of their order when the order status has changed

- Deactivating a user account when certain conditions have been met

Rules are a powerful tool when employed on a Drupal 8 site. Don't overlook Rules as a solution to common workflow related activities.

User Roles and Permissions

The last pillar is user roles and permissions. They are not the last pillar because they lack power or importance to the overall architecture of your Drupal 8 solution; they take the last position because they impact users' abilities to perform nearly every function on your site.

Roles provide the ability to categorize users by common activities that are performed by that group. For example content editors have the ability to author, publish, and manage content. The actions of authoring, publishing, and managing are examples of the permissions that may be assigned to a user role. When engineering your solution it is important to consider and document the requirements of user roles and permissions as you build the framework. Often, roles and permissions are hastily implemented at the very end of a project and the implications and ramifications are often greater than what were expected.

As you engineer your solution, consider which roles are required in your organization:

- Who should have the ability to install and configure elements on the site?

- Who should have the ability to create key components of the site, such as entities, taxonomy, menus, pages, views, blocks, and user accounts?

- Who should have the ability to author and publish content?

- Who should have the ability to view content?

- Who creates and manages user accounts?

As you implement each component of your solution, update the user roles and permissions to address the functionality that you are building.

Drupal 8 Theme

Engineering the visual look and feel of your Drupal site focuses on the structure of pages, the elements that appear on those pages, and the visual representation of each element on the page. The theme is ultimately responsible for how everything on your site is visually rendered, including how it is rendered on every device that an end user may use to view your site.

When engineering your theme, it is important to consider the following:

- What devices are end users going to utilize when browsing your site?

- What is the screen resolution of those devices?

- How much content can reasonably fit on each of those devices?

- Is all of the content applicable to all of the devices? Or is there a use case where some content is not displayed on smaller screens?

- How will end users interact with the content on your site?

- What styling will be applied to elements on the page?

- What administrative control do you need to provide to site administrators? Should they be able to adjust the color attributes such as colors or fonts?

- What versions of browsers is the site going to support? Does the theme need to support older versions of Internet Explorer?

Chapter 5 covers the details of constructing a Drupal 8 theme. It's important to understand the requirements for visualization before beginning the process of creating a theme.

Web Services

In today's interconnected world, it is unlikely that your Drupal sites will live on their own deserted island, disconnected from other sources of content and providing content only to users who visit the sites through a web browser. A more likely scenario is that your Drupal web sites will live in an interconnected world, pulling content from external sources such as corporate applications, other Drupal sites, or sources outside of your organization. It is also likely that your Drupal sites will provide content to corporate applications, other web sites, systems outside of your organization, and will have other interesting interactions such as sending content to a digital sign in the lobby of your corporate headquarters.

Through the web services capabilities that are inherent in Drupal 8 core, as well as various contributed modules, your site may easily participate in this distributed digital environment by:

- Serving content to requests through a standard web services interface such as REST

- Consuming content from external sources through web services interfaces provided by those systems and applications

- Serving as a headless content repository by serving content to applications built in frameworks such as AngularJS

When engineering your solution it is important to consider the flexibility and capabilities that are presented through web services. I cover web services in more detail in Chapter 8. At this juncture, carefully consider and document the interfaces that may augment the capabilities and content on your site.

User Interface

While the Drupal theme is often considered the user interface to a Drupal site, a popular trend is to utilize Drupal as a content repository and editorial tool but not necessarily as the provider of the user interface to that content. The terms "decoupled CMS" and "headless Drupal" have been bantered about the Drupal community for the past few years and are beginning to build momentum. Sites such as weather.com, NBC's Tonight Show with Jimmy Fallon (nbc.com/the-tonight-show), Radio France (rfi.fr), and others are early adopters of using technologies such as Node.js, Backbone.js, Angular.js, Symfony, and others as the presentation layer for content that resides in Drupal.

43

When thinking about and engineering your Drupal architecture, consider the benefits of a decoupled CMS model. It provides breakthrough user experiences that would be difficult to accomplish using the Drupal theme engine, and it helps site owners future-proof their builds by allowing them to refresh the design of their sites without having to rebuild the whole CMS. The CMS, in this case Drupal, does not have to radically shift in order to accommodate a whole new user experience.

There are three main components for decoupling Drupal from the user interface:

- *Decoupled frontend.* In this approach the presentation of content may be handled through various means such as interactive JavaScript frameworks (Angular.js), static page generators, mobile applications, and even another CMS. In this approach multiple user interfaces can peacefully coexist with Drupal without disrupting each other.

- *Content delivery via a web service API.* In this approach the content housed in Drupal is accessible through a web service API, typically a RESTful interface, in a format (JSON) that is friendly to most presentation layer tools.

- *CMS backend and database.* Drupal is used as the content authoring and management platform.

The benefits of this solution are significant enough to strongly consider this approach:

- Future proofs your web site implementation and lets you completely redesign your sites without having to rearchitect and implement a CMS.

- Allows frontend developers to design and develop user interfaces that are free from the constraints presented by the user interface capabilities of the backend.

- Speeds up the performance of your site by shifting display logic to the client side and simplifying the backend.

- Allows frontend developers to build truly interactive experiences through in-browser applications.

Summary

There is a lot to consider when engineering your Drupal 8 solution framework that will become the foundation of the platform you deliver to the enterprise. There are elements of the analysis that, if left unanswered, may cause a significant amount of rework if the requirements differ from the foundation. Consider the wisdom of those who have gone before you and plan your site before embarking on the journey of building the platform.

The next chapter begins the discussion of the foundation of Drupal modules, including how to create custom modules to address unique functional requirements that cannot be accomplished using off-the-shelf Drupal.

CHAPTER 4

Creating Modules for Drupal 8

Although it is possible to build relatively complex Drupal 8 sites without ever having to construct a custom module, it is likely that you'll need to create at least one custom module to fulfill functional or technical requirements of your organization as the complexity of your solutions increase. Examples of when you may need to step into the custom module arena include these scenarios:

- An off-the-shelf module meets most of your requirements but you need to augment one or more aspects of that module to address the unique requirements of your organization.

- You need to modify how Drupal core performs a specific function to address a specific requirement.

- You need a complex custom form that can't be created with an off-the-shelf module like webforms.

- You need to create a custom interface with a system that does not support standard web services.

- You have unique functional requirements that cannot be met with Drupal core or contributed modules.

Although it's likely that you'll need to create a custom module at some point in the near future, remember to first exhaust the options of using a contributed module or modify the requirements to match what is provided by off-the-shelf Drupal.

In the remainder of this chapter, I provide a high-level overview of Drupal modules, their architecture, how to create a simple module, and details on how to utilize Drupal 8's APIs to facilitate the development of more complex modules.

The Purpose of Drupal Modules

Before examining the details of a Drupal module, it's a good idea to understand why there are Drupal modules and what role they fulfill on a Drupal web site. Modules are the components in a Drupal architecture that provide some form of functionality to the overall capabilities of the site. A module may provide the following:

- A functional solution for pulling information from, or sending information to, an external system or site

- Capabilities for converting information from one form to another, for example, converting currencies based on the current exchange rate that is retrieved from an external service

© Todd Tomlinson 2017

T. Tomlinson, *Enterprise Drupal 8 Development*, DOI 10.1007/978-1-4842-0253-1_4

- A means for posting content from your site to a social media platform

- A complex multi-set webform that has extensive validation and logic

There are thousands of contributed modules on drupal.org, and there are thousands of other potential solutions that augment the capabilities of Drupal 8 core. The capabilities and functionality provided by your modules is only limited by your creativity and ability to construct a viable solution to address specific functional or technical requirements.

The Foundation of Drupal 8 Is a Suite of Modules

Drupal 8 core itself is constructed primarily through modules. If you visit the root directory of your site and navigate to core/modules, you will see a list of dozens of modules that provide some level of functionality to Drupal core, such as:

- aggregator: A module that interfaces with external sources of content and publishes that content on your Drupal site, for example, a news feed.

- ckeditor: The module that provides the WYSIWYG editorial interface for content authors.

- dblog: The module that records system events in the Drupal database and displays those events through an admin interface.

- node: The module that provides all of the functionality around creating node entity types, authoring content using those entity types, displaying the content on your side, and several administrative functions.

- user: The module that provides all of the functionality around the creation of user accounts, managing those accounts, creating and managing user roles, and assigning permissions to user roles.

- views: The module that provides the ability to extract content from the database, format it, filter it, sort it, display it, and all of the administrative interfaces for creating and managing those extraction processes.

There are dozens of other modules included in core. Take a moment and visit the root directory of your site and navigate to core/modules to see the list. A great way to learn how Drupal works and how modules are constructed is to examine several of the modules in core/modules.

The modules found in core/modules are just that, core modules. Contributed modules fall outside of what is shipped with Drupal 8 core, and they provide additional functionality over and above what is available in core. Contributed modules reside in the /modules directory, which is located in the root directory of your site. There is a general best practice to place all contributed modules, those that are downloaded from drupal.org into a subfolder named contrib in the /modules directory of your site. It is also a best practice to place all custom modules that your organization has developed in a subdirectory named custom. This approach makes it easier to quickly identify which modules are off-the-shelf and can be found on drupal.org, and which modules were custom developed just for your site.

As discussed in Chapter 3, before venturing out to create a custom module to fulfill a functional or technical requirement, exhaustively search drupal.org/project/modules for off-the-shelf capabilities to deliver the required functionality. If you are unable to find a solution, then this chapter is for you.

Key Skills

When venturing out to develop custom Drupal modules, it is important to understand that there are key skills that are required to succeed. Like most aspects of life, expecting to be an expert at something before preparing yourself for the tasks that lay before you often results in fear, frustration, and failure. Drupal module development, while complex in nature, uses standard technologies and patterns that come from the underlying technologies that support the platform, such as PHP, MySQL, and Symfony.

With Symfony and with Drupal 8 development in general, the basic skills that you need to have some level of mastery of include the following:

- PHP syntax, functions, and structure

- Object-oriented PHP development standards and principles

- The use of a Model-View-Controller framework to build applications

- A solid grasp of Symfony and its components

- HTML, CSS, and JavaScript, as they are the anchor legacy technologies employed by Drupal and in fact nearly all CMS platforms

- A good understanding of a SQL database and how information is stored, updated, and retrieved from the database

Does it sound like a lot to have a grasp of before building a Drupal module? The reality is that there is a lot to learn, but the foundation that you build in these topics will serve you well as you venture into Drupal 8 module development, and this knowledge is applicable to a number of CMS platforms in the market. You will likely stumble and fall as you begin the race, but once on the path, you will soon see the patterns and your successes will soon outweigh your stumblings.

While we will cover many of the bullet points listed, it is beyond the scope of this book to teach you PHP, HTML, CSS, JavaScript, and the inner workings of MVC architectures, specifically Symfony. If you have not yet studied those elements, now would be a good time to begin that journey. While this chapter starts out with a simplistic approach to building Drupal 8 modules, we quickly move onto more complex topics, which requires prerequisite knowledge of the underlying technologies used to construct Drupal 8 modules. Don't be discouraged—it's a journey, and every journey starts with a first step. Our first few steps are going to be simple.

Before jumping into the complexities of module development, lets create something simple that demonstrates the general structure of a Drupal 8 module and the individual parts that, when assembled, deliver tangible results. If you have not installed Drupal 8, now is an excellent time to do so.

Developing Your First Drupal 8 Module

The first module that we will develop performs a relatively simple task; it displays "Hello Drupal 8 World!" on a page. While it sounds simple, this exercise demonstrates the structure of a Drupal 8 module and is the foundation for building more complex modules. At the completion of this exercise, you will see the words "Hello Drupal 8 World!" displayed on a page, as shown in Figure 4-1.

Figure 4-1. *Hello Drupal 8 World!*

Step 1: Create the Module's Directory

The first step is to create a directory where the files that constitute your module will reside. All contributed modules (non-core) reside in the module directory located at the root directory of your Drupal 8 site. If you have installed any modules beyond what comes with Drupal 8 core, you'll see those modules in this directory. If you have not done so, create a new subdirectory in your modules directory named custom. You place the module in the custom directory. Although this is not required, a best practice is to also create a subdirectory in the modules directory named contrib where all the modules that are downloaded from drupal.org will be stored.

Using your operating system's file manager, or from a terminal window and a command prompt, navigate to the modules directory and create a new directory named hello.

Step 2: Create the Module's Info File

The next step is to create a hello.info.yml file. This file tells Drupal about your module and provides the information that appears on the Extend page in the Administration section of your site. The .yml file extension will be prevalent in your Drupal 8 installation. *yml* is short for YAML, which is a human readable data serialization language that stores configuration information that is used by Drupal 8. YAML stands for *YAML ain't markup language*, and it is relatively easy to write and read.

Using your favorite text editor, create the hello.info.yml file in the modules/custom/hello directory with the following content:

```
name: Hello
type: module
description: 'My first Drupal 8 module.'
package: Awesome modules
version: 1.0
core: '8.x'
```

The purpose of each line in the hello.info.yml file is as follows:

- name: Hello defines the name of the module as it appears on the module page.

- type: module specifies that we're creating a module. (Themes, for example, would use a value of theme for the type.)

- description: This provides administrators with a brief overview of what the module does, and it appears on the module listing admin page.

- package: This provides a mechanism for grouping modules together on the module admin page. For example, if you visit the Extend page of your site, you'll see a number of modules listed in a box with a title of Core. We'll use something unique for our module and place it in a package called Awesome Modules. If you're writing a module that, for example, creates new web services capabilities, you should use the package name of the other modules that create web services, to ensure that a site administrator can easily find your module.

- version: This creates a version number for your module and is used primarily for communicating the version to site administrators so they can see whether they have the current version installed.

- core: This specifies which version of Drupal this module was written for. In this case, we wrote this module for Drupal 8.

After saving the hello.info.yml file, visit the admin/modules page on your site. Scroll down until you see the Awesome Modules section and you should see your new module listed and ready to be enabled. If you do not see the module listed, edit your hello.info.yml file and ensure that everything listed previously is included in your file and the spelling of each keyword (e.g., name) is correct. If it still doesn't appear, check to ensure that your module resides in the correct directory (modules/custom/hello/hello.info.yml).

While you could enable your module, it doesn't do anything yet as we haven't developed the logic for displaying "Hello Drupal 8 World!".

Step 3: Create the Module File

The .module file is the workhorse of a Drupal 8 module and contains the logic that delivers the functionality that addresses your technical and functional requirements. The functionality delivered can be as simple as the module that we are working on, or as complex as needed to address the requirements of your site.

The .module file for our Hello module does one thing: it returns the text that will be displayed on the page that our module provides. Using your favorite text editor, create a new file named hello.module in your modules/custom/hello directory with the following text:

```php
<?php

function hello_hello_world() {

    return t('Hello Drupal 8 World!');

}
```

The file begins with the opening PHP tag, <?php, as all modules are written in the PHP programming language.

■ **Note** The closing tag of a PHP block at the end of a file is optional, and in some cases omitting it is helpful when using `include` or `require`, so unwanted whitespace will not occur at the end of files, and you will still be able to add headers to the response later. It is also handy if you use output buffering and would not like to see added unwanted whitespace at the end of the parts generated by the included files.

The first element of this code is `function hello_hello_world()`. This defines a PHP function that can be called from other modules. In this case it is a simple function named `hello_hello_world()`. The first `hello` in the function name is the name of the module, in this case, `hello`. As a Drupal coding standard, all functions should begin with the name of the module, followed by a descriptive function name.

Our function does one thing: it returns a text string to the code that called this function. I've wrapped the text that we are returning in a Drupal function called `t()`. This function translates any text in the parentheses, if you have multilingual capabilities enabled. It is another Drupal coding standard to wrap all text values using the `t()` function.

Although our module is simple, it demonstrates the basic functionality of what modules do. The module file is the workhorse of any module, and it can be as simple as our example module or as complex as needed to meet the functional and technical requirements of your module.

Step 4: Create the Module's Routing File

The foundation of Drupal 8 is Symfony, a PHP framework that simplifies the creation of complex PHP-based applications like Drupal. The Symfony framework provides the mechanisms for creating a Model-View-Controller (MVC)-based application, where

- *Model* represents the underlying data that the application operates against

- *View* defines the user interface to the application

- *Controller* is the workhorse of the applications, including routing requests from users and returning information to the view to display to the user

The next step in the process is to create our module's routing file, which defines how a visitor will access the functionality of our module, as defined by the controller, and what returns the values to be displayed.

In the same directory, using your favorite text editor, create the module's routing file. In this case the routing file will be named `hello.routing.yml`. The contents of the file should be as follows:

```
hello:
  path: 'hello'
  defaults:
    _controller: '\Drupal\hello\Controller\HelloController::sayhello'
  requirements:
    _permission: 'access content'
```

- The first line of code represents the name of our module (`hello`).

- The next line represents the path that an end user would use to access the functionality provided by the module, which is /hello.

- One of the key concepts that Drupal 8 has adopted is a standard called PSR-4, which defines how code is loaded into memory. One of the issues with previous versions of Drupal is that a lot of code is loaded into memory when it doesn't need to be there. PSR-4 solves that issue, and one of the enablers is something called *namespaces*. The defaults section provides the source of the content, using the PSR-4 standard for PHP namespace autoloading. The structure of the namespace is \Drupal\[module name]\Controller\[ClassName]::[method]. In our case the module's name is hello, the class name is HelloController as defined in our controller file that we will create in a moment, and the method in that class that returns the value that we want to display is sayhello.

- The requirements section defines what permissions a visitor must have in order to access our module; in this case the site visitors who can see the output of our module must have the access content permission, which in a default Drupal 8 installation is everyone. I cover more about adding new permissions later in this chapter.

Step 5: Create the Module's Controller

In our routing file, the value associated with _controller starts with \Drupal\hello\Controller. PSR-4 defines that a namespace must map directly to the file structure of your application. Symfony requires that all of our namespace directories reside in a directory named src, which resides in the root directory of our module. For our module, that structure is:

```
hello
  src
    Controller
```

Following the PSR-4 standards, you can see that our namespace of \Drupal\hello\Controller maps directly to the directory structure, where src is not required in the namespace as it is assumed to be the location of the Controller file.

So let's get busy and create the directories where the next component of our module will reside, the controller. While in the root directory of the hello module, create a new directory named src, and within the src directory, create a new directory named Controller. Within the Controller directory, we're now ready to create the controller for our application, the "traffic cop" of our application. In your favorite text editor, create a file named HelloController.php. The contents of the controller should be as follows:

```php
<?php

namespace Drupal\hello\Controller;

use Drupal\Core\Controller\ControllerBase;

class HelloController extends ControllerBase {

  public function sayhello() {
    return array(
      '#markup' => hello_hello_world(),
    );
  }

}
```

- The beginning of this controller file starts with the PHP opening tag, as the controller is written using PHP.

- The second line defines the namespace that we are using for our controller: namespace Drupal\hello\Controller;. This maps the directory structure described previously in this section.

- The third line defines the class that we are creating, HelloController, and that we are going to extend base functionality in the ControllerBase class from Drupal core. Recalling the routing file that we created previously, you can see that what we are creating maps directly to what we are calling to generate the output to display on the page: HelloController::sayhello.

- The forth line defines the function, named sayhello, that returns the text that we want to display on the page. The keyword #markup signifies that the output generated by this function is a renderable string, which is generated by calling the hello_hello_world function in the module's main .module file.

Save this file, and you're ready to enable our new module! Visit the Extend page in the admin section of the site and scroll down until you see the Awesome Modules section (see Figure 4-2).

Figure 4-2. *Our Hello Drupal 8 World! module on the Extend page*

Check the box next to the module's name and click the Save Configuration button to enable the module. With the module enabled, you're now ready to test your first Drupal 8 module! To execute the module, navigate to your homepage and add /hello to the end of the URL (we defined that path in our module's routing file). You should see the output shown earlier in Figure 4-1.

Step 6: Add a Menu Item

The next step in expanding the functionality of the hello module is to place a link to the module's output on a menu. In its current state a site visitor would have to either know to add /hello to the end of the URL, or a content administrator would have to manually add a menu item to one of the existing menus, or add a hyperlink to the content.

Based on our requirements, the intention is to add a menu item named Hello to the primary navigational menu on our site, that when clicked, takes the visitor to the /hello page.

The first file that we need to add to the module is name hello.links.menu.yml. Contained in this file will be the definition of the links used by our module. In your favorite text editor, in the root directory of your hello module, create the hello.links.menu.yml file with the following content:

```
hello.hello:
  title: Hello!
  Menu_name: main
  route_name: hello
  expanded: TRUE
  weight: 100
```

- The first line specifies the menu item that we are defining. The first `hello` is the module name, and the second `hello` is the name of our menu link.

- The second line defines the title that will appear on the menu.

- The third line specifies that our new menu item will appear on the main menu.

- The fourth line defines the route name that the menu will use to render the output. If you examine the `hello.routing.yml` file, you will see that our route name is `hello`, as defined on the first line.

- The fifth line specifies that this menu item should be rendered as expanded when the menu is displayed.

- The sixth line specifies the relative weight of our menu item. It likely shouldn't be at the front of the list, which right now with a clean Drupal 8 install is just the Home menu item. You can adjust the weight to whatever is appropriate. Specifying a weight of 0 instructs Drupal to sort your menu item alphabetically.

Save your `hello.links.menu.yml` file and clear the cache of your site so that the menu is reconstructed. After saving you should see the new menu item Hello! displayed to the right of the Home menu item (see Figure 4-3).

Figure 4-3. *The new Hello! menu item*

Clicking on the link will render the new page that our module has created.

While a module may only provide a single function and fulfill a single purpose, most modules perform multiple functions. The next step in expanding the functionality of our hello module is to add new functionality that adds a new menu item, called Welcome, and displays a welcome message. The welcome message displays the user's name, or in the case of an anonymous user, welcomes them as a visitor.

Step 7: Add a New Menu Item

The first step is to update the hello.links.menu.yml file, adding a new menu item named Welcome. Open the file and add the following text to the bottom of the file:

```
hello.welcome:
  title: Welcome
  menu_name: main
  route_name: welcome
  expanded: TRUE
  weight: 110
```

- The first line defines the reference for the new menu item.

- The second line defines the text that will appear on the menu.

- The third line defines which menu the menu item will appear in, in this case, it's the main menu.

- The fourth line defines the route name that will be used to display the welcome message.

- The fifth and sixth items define that the menu item will be expanded when displayed and that it will appear, based on the weight, to the right of the Hello menu item.

Step 8: Add a New Function to the Module

Our module previously only had a single function, the hello_hello_world function. To accomplish the functionality associated with welcoming the site visitor, we must expand the existing hello.module file with additional code to perform the required functionality, resulting in the following:

```php
<?php
use Drupal\user\Entity\User;
function hello_hello_world() {
    return t('Hello Drupal 8 World!');
}

function hello_welcome() {
   $user = User::load(\Drupal::currentUser()->id());
   if ($user->get('uid')->value < 1) {
     return t('Welcome  Visitor!');
   } else {
     return t('Welcome  ' . $user->getUsername() . '!');
   }
}
```

- The first change to the hello.module is to add the reference to the functionality available in the Drupal\user\Entity\User class. To expose that functionality to the module I added the use Drupal\user\Entity\User; statement to the top of the module. I now have access to all of the methods and functionality included in the core Entity\User class.

- The next change was to add the new function, called hello_welcome. By adding a second function, the module is now multipurpose and fulfills more than one requirement.

- The next line returns the information associated with the current user, which could be a user who is logged in, or the anonymous user for scenarios where the site visitor is not logged into the site. The class is User and the method is load. The value passed to the function is the user ID of the currently logged-in user (or 0 in the case of an anonymous user).

- The if statement compares the value of the current user to a value of 1. If it's less than 1, it's an anonymous visitor and I return the string Welcome Visitor!. If the user ID is greater than 0, the function returns the string Welcome with the current user's name in the string.

Updating the Controller

I now have a menu item and the functionality that returns the string that should be displayed on the page to welcome the visitor. The next step is to add an entry in the HelloController.php file that can be called from the hello.routing.yml file. Editing the HelloController.php file in the /src/Controller directory, I'll add a new method to our controller class named welcome, as shown here:

```php
<?php

  namespace Drupal\hello\Controller;

  use Drupal\Core\Controller\ControllerBase;

  class HelloController extends ControllerBase {

     public function sayhello() {

        return array(

           '#markup' => hello_hello_world(),

        );

     }
```

```
    public function welcome() {

        return array(

            '#markup' => hello_welcome(),

        );

    }

}
```

In the new welcome function, the only task is to return the output generated by the hello_welcome function that I just created in the hello.module.

Updating the Routing File

The last step in enabling the new functionality is to update the hello.routing.yml file, adding a new route with a path of welcome.

```
hello:
  path: 'hello'
  defaults:
    _controller: '\Drupal\hello\Controller\HelloController::sayhello'
    _title: 'Hello!'
  requirements:
    _permission: 'access content'

welcome:
  path: 'welcome'
  defaults:
    _controller: '\Drupal\hello\Controller\HelloController::welcome'
    _title: 'Welcome'
  requirements:
    _permission: 'access content'
```

The difference between the hello and the welcome routes are:

- The path is set to welcome, so visiting example.com/welcome (where example.com should be replaced with the URL to your site) displays the welcome message.

- The _controller is set to the welcome method instead of the sayhello method. The welcome method is what I just defined in the previous step when I updated the controller.

- I also updated the title to Welcome.

After saving all of the updates to the following files:

- hello.links.menu.yml

- hello.module

- HelloController.php

- hello.routing.yml

The next step is to clear the cache and visit the homepage. On the homepage you should see a new menu item to the right of the Hello! menu item. Clicking on the Welcome link should display the welcome message as defined in the `hello.module` (see Figure 4-4).

Figure 4-4. *The Welcome page*

Creating Blocks

Drupal 8's plugin architecture provides a framework for creating reusable solution components such as blocks and custom fields. Plugins by nature are descriptions or templates that solve a common requirement that can be used in many different situations. Plugins may also fill the role of providing generalized utility functionality that demonstrates a reusable design pattern. The benefits of plugins is that they release developers from the burden of having to rewrite the framework for a common design pattern by providing a starting point, or boilerplate, from which to build their solution. Blocks are a perfect example of a plugin boilerplate. All blocks have a title and some snippet of HTML markup and optionally PHP and JavaScript. Instead of recasting that design pattern from scratch, Drupal's plugin system provides a template on which to build a block. For details on the plugin architecture in Drupal 8, visit `drupal.org/developing/api/8/plugins`.

Leveraging the plugin architecture and the design pattern for blocks, we expand the functionality of the `hello` module to provide a block that displays information about the current user. When users are logged in, the block will display the following information:

- Their user name

- Their preferred language

- The e-mail address on file for their account

- Their time zone

- The date their account was created

- The date their account was updated

57

- The date they last logged in

- Their assigned roles

If the user is not logged in, meaning it's an anonymous user, the block will simply display the current date and time.

Leveraging the block plugin architecture, the process for creating blocks is relatively simple. Plugins reside in a new directory in the `src` directory, and blocks reside in a directory in the `plugin` directory. We create a new directory named `Plugin` in the `src` directory of the module, and a new directory named `Block` in the `Plugin` directory. The resulting structure is as follows:

```
hello
  src
    Plugin
      Block
```

Within the `Block` directory, we create a new file, `HelloBlock.php`, where the code for generating the block will reside. In the `HelloBlock.php` file, we begin building the structure of the block plugin with the following code.

```php
<?php

namespace Drupal\hello\Plugin\Block;

use Drupal\Core\Block\BlockBase;

/**
 * Provides a user details block.
 *
 * @Block(
 *   id = "hello_block",
 *   admin_label = @Translation("Hello!")
 * )
 */
class HelloBlock extends BlockBase {

  /**
   * {@inheritdoc}
   */
  public function build() {
    return array(
      '#markup' => $this->t("Hello World!"),
    );
  }
}
```

- The block plugin begins with the opening `<?php` tag and defines the plugin's namespace as `Drupal\hello\Plugin\Block`. As a reminder, the namespace maps directly to the physical location of the plugin, minus the `src` directory.

- The annotation block specifies that the plugin being created is a block `@Block`, and provides a unique ID, the `admin_label` that appears on the block layout page as well as the title of the block.

- The next section defines the `HelloBlock` class and that it extends the base capabilities of the `BlockBase` class.

- The `build` function is where all of the work of generating the block output begins. For demonstration purposes, I'll render markup to see my block in action before adding the user functionality.

At this juncture you can save the file, rebuild the cache, and visit the block layout page. To place the newly created block, select a region where the block will reside and click the Place Block button. Scroll through the list of available blocks until you find the Hello Block and click the Place Block button. Make any adjustments you want on the Configure Block page and click the Save Block button. Visit the homepage of your site, or if you specified block visibility on a specific page, then visit that page. You should see the output of your new custom block (see Figure 4-5).

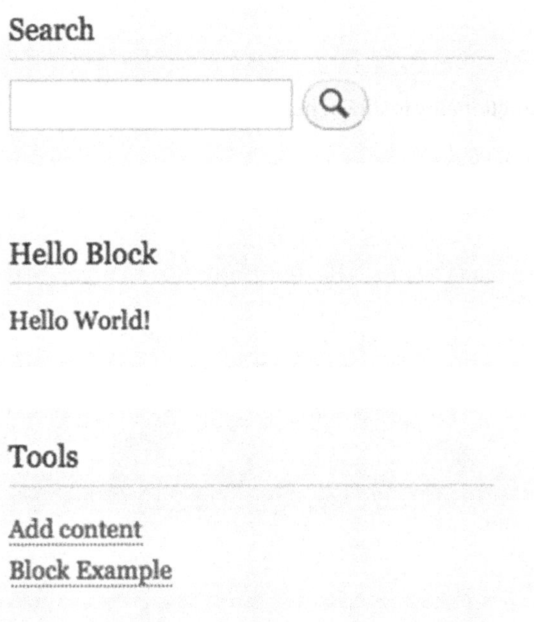

Figure 4-5. *The Hello block*

The next step in the process is to augment the block plugin with the functionality required to display user information. Using the list of requirements defined previously in this section, I'll update the module to display a block that appears, as shown in Figure 4-6.

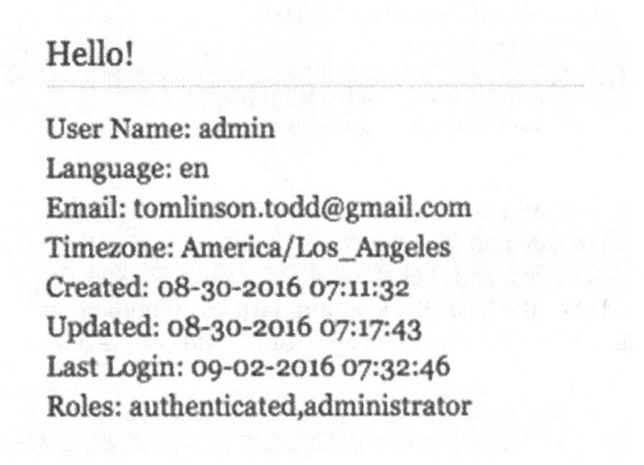

Hello!

User Name: admin
Language: en
Email: tomlinson.todd@gmail.com
Timezone: America/Los_Angeles
Created: 08-30-2016 07:11:32
Updated: 08-30-2016 07:17:43
Last Login: 09-02-2016 07:32:46
Roles: authenticated,administrator

Figure 4-6. *The Hello! block*

The updated block plugin with all the required functionality is shown here:

```php
<?php

namespace Drupal\hello\Plugin\Block;

use Drupal\user\Entity\User;
use Drupal\Core\Block\BlockBase;

/**
 * Provides a user details block.
 *
 * @Block(
 *   id = "hello_block",
 *   admin_label = @Translation("Hello!")
 * )
 */
class HelloBlock extends BlockBase {

  /**
   * {@inheritdoc}
   */
  public function build() {

    return array(
      '#markup' => $this->_populate_markup(),
    );

  }
```

```
private function _populate_markup() {

  $user = User::load(\Drupal::currentUser()->id());

  if ($user->get('uid')->value < 1) {

    return t('Welcome  Visitor!  The current time is: ' . date('m-d-Y h:i:s', time())));

  } else {

    $user_information  = 'User Name: ' . $user->getUsername() . "<br/>";
    $user_information .= 'Language: ' . $user->getPreferredLangcode() . "<br/>";
    $user_information .= 'Email: ' . $user->getEmail() . "<br/>";
    $user_information .= 'Timezone: ' . $user->getTimeZone() . "<br/>";
    $user_information .= 'Created: ' . date('m-d-Y h:i:s', $user->getCreatedTime()) . "<br/>";
    $user_information .= 'Updated: ' . date('m-d-Y h:i:s', $user->getChangedTime()) . "<br/>";
    $user_information .= 'Last Login:' . date('m-d-Y h:i:s', $user->getLastLoginTime()) . "<br/>";

    $roles = NULL;

    foreach($user->getRoles() as $role) {
      $roles .= $role . ",";
    }

    $roles = 'Roles: ' . rtrim($roles, ',');

    $user_information .= $roles;

    return $user_information;

  }

 }

}
```

The changes to the previous version of the hello block are as follows:

- We added use `Drupal\user\Entity\user` to expose the user class so that I can access the details of the user account.

- We revised the return value in the `build` function to return the results generated by a new function named _populate_markup

- We added a new private function named _populate_markup that retrieves the current user's information through the `User::load` method, checks to see whether the user is logged in or anonymous (a `uid` less than 1 is an anonymous site visitor), and returns the appropriate information back to the `build` function for display. For details on what information is available from the user object, visit `api.drupal.org/ api/drupal/core!modules!user!src!Entity!User.php/8.2.x`, replacing 8.2.x with the current version of Drupal. At the time this book was written, version 8.2 was the latest.

After making all of the changes, saving the HelloBlock.php file, and rebuilding cache, the results for logged in users are shown in Figure 4-6. For anonymous users, the results as shown in Figure 4-7.

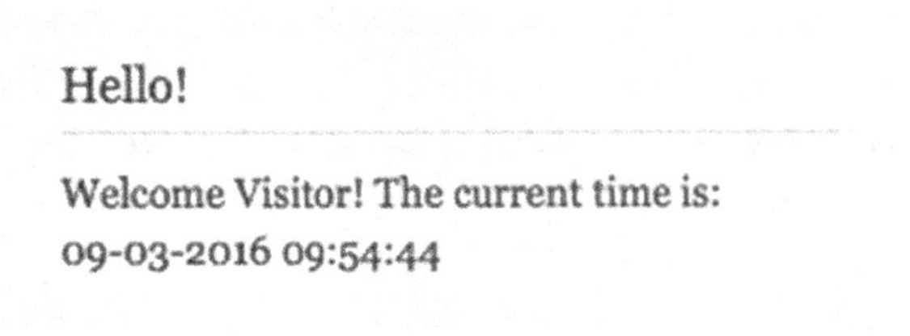

Hello!

Welcome Visitor! The current time is:
09-03-2016 09:54:44

Figure 4-7. *The anonymous Hello! block*

The HelloBlock example represents a relatively simple use case. The power of the block plugin architecture is that it provides a solid foundation for building significantly more complex blocks should the need arise.

The next step in expanding the hello module is to add a custom form built through Drupal's form API (FAPI).

Building Custom Forms

It is likely as the complexity of your Drupal sites grow that there will come a need for custom forms to collect information from site visitors. I'll start with a simple example to demonstrate the mechanics of building forms in Drupal 8 and will expand the simple form in subsequent steps.

The first iteration of the form is relatively simple; we ask the site visitor for their job title and, upon submission, display that job title back to them in the messages area on the page. The purpose of this form is to demonstrate the mechanics of how forms work in Drupal 8. I'll expand on the complexity later in this chapter.

The first step is to create a new subdirectory in the hello module's src directory, named Form. The resulting structure should appear as follows:

```
hello
  src
    Controller
    Form
    Plugin
      Block
```

In the Form directory, create a new file named HelloForm.php and, in that file, place the following code:

```php
<?php

namespace Drupal\hello\Form;

use Drupal\Core\Form\FormBase;
use Drupal\Core\Form\FormStateInterface;
```

```php
class HelloForm extends FormBase {

  public function buildForm(array $form, FormStateInterface $form_state) {

    $form['job_title'] = [
      '#type' => 'textfield',
      '#title' => $this->t('Job Title'),
      '#description' => $this->t('Enter your Job Title. It must be at least 5 characters in
      length.'),
      '#required' => TRUE,
    ];

    $form['actions'] = [
      '#type' => 'actions',
    ];

    $form['actions']['submit'] = [
      '#type' => 'submit',
      '#value' => $this->t('Submit'),
    ];

    return $form;
  }

  public function getFormId() {
    return 'hello_form';
  }

  public function validateForm(array &$form, FormStateInterface $form_state) {
    $job_title = $form_state->getValue('job_title');
    if (strlen($job_title) < 5) {
      // Set an error for the form element with a key of "title".
      $form_state->setErrorByName('job_title', $this->t('Your job title must be at least 5
      characters long.'));
    }
  }

  public function submitForm(array &$form, FormStateInterface $form_state) {
    /*
     * This would normally be replaced by code that actually does something
     * with the title.
     */
    $job_title = $form_state->getValue('job_title');
    drupal_set_message(t('You specified a job title of %job_title.', ['%job_title' =>
    $job_title]));
  }

}
```

The elements of this file are as follows:

- `namespace Drupal\hello\Form` matches the directory structure of where our `HelloForm.php` file resides, minus the `src` directory, as that is assumed.

- The two use statements include the `FormBase` and `FormStateInterface` classes so they may be used to construct the form.

- The class definition for `HelloForm` extends the base capabilities of the `FormBase` class, allowing us to focus on building the elements of the form instead of all the details of constructing and rendering an online form.

- The `$form['job_title']` element creates a text field on the form, with a title of Job Title, a description, and it is set as a required field.

- The `$form['actions']` element groups all of the submit handlers into an `actions` element with a key of `'actions'` so that it gets styled properly, and so that other modules may add actions to the form. While not a required element, it is a Drupal 8 standard.

- The `$form['actions']['submit']` element adds a Submit button to the form that handles the submission of the form.

- The `return $form` statement returns the form so that it may be rendered on the page.

- The `getFormID` function is used to provide a means for using `hook_form_alter()`, which allows other modules to alter the render arrays built by this form. It must provide a unique name across the entire site, and it typically starts with the module's name.

- The `validateForm` function provides the means for validating information submitted by the site visitor prior to performing whatever functionality is appropriate. In the case of the hello form, the validation examines the job title submitted by the user by getting that value from the `$form_state` object, through a `getValue` method. The functionality then checks the length of the job title submitted and if it is less than five characters, it sets an error message and highlights the field that is in error.

- The `submitForm` function is the final step in the processing of the form. This function simply gets the value entered for job title and displays it in the message area using `drupal_set_message`.

The next step in the process is to update the `hello.routing.yml` file to provide a path for the site visitor to find our form. Edit the routing file and add the following to the end of the file:

```
hello.form:
    path: 'hello/form'
    defaults:
      _form: '\Drupal\hello\Form\HelloForm'
      _title: 'Hello Form'
    requirements:
      _permission: 'access content'
```

- The first line, `hello.form`, is the name of the new route.

- The second line defines the path that the user will use to access the form.

- The title is the title that will appear at the top of the form.

- The requirements section sets the permission required in order for a visitor to access the form; in this case, they must be able to access the content.

After saving the routing file, rebuild the cache and enter example.com/hello/form, replacing example.com with the URL to your site. If everything was entered properly, you should see the form shown in Figure 4-8.

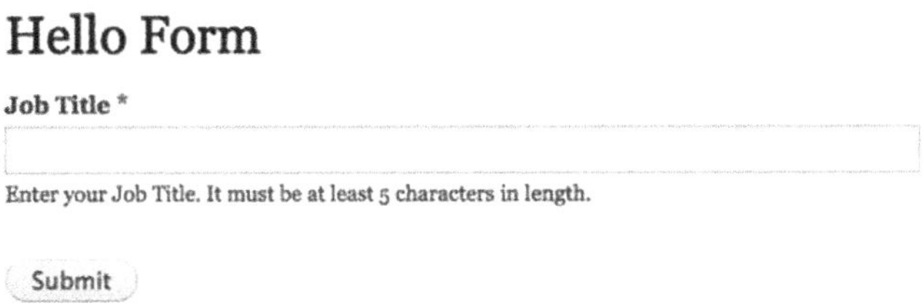

Hello Form

Job Title *

Enter your Job Title. It must be at least 5 characters in length.

Submit

Figure 4-8. The Hello form

Testing the validation function, enter a job title of less than five characters and click the Submit button. The result should be an error on the page as well as the field in error being highlighted in red. Figure 4-9 depicts the error message and the field highlighted in error.

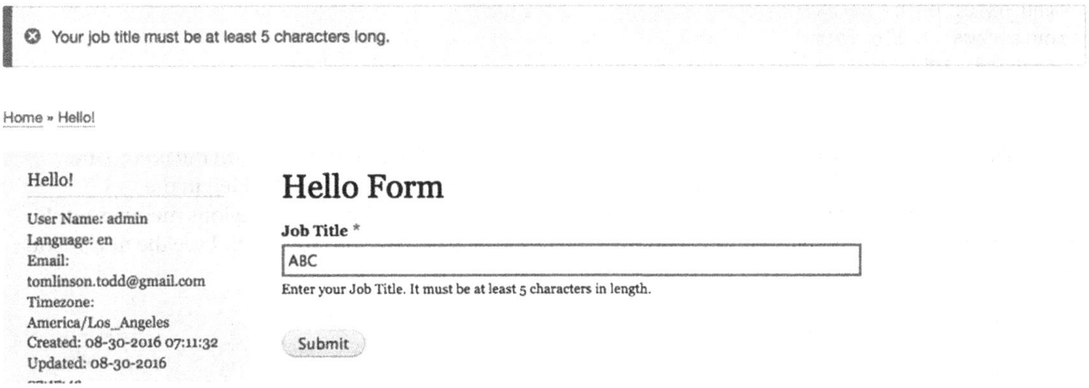

❌ Your job title must be at least 5 characters long.

Home » Hello!

Hello!

User Name: admin
Language: en
Email:
tomlinson.todd@gmail.com
Timezone:
America/Los_Angeles
Created: 08-30-2016 07:11:32
Updated: 08-30-2016

Hello Form

Job Title *

ABC

Enter your Job Title. It must be at least 5 characters in length.

Submit

Figure 4-9. Hello form validation

Entering a value greater than five characters and clicking the Submit button will display the outcome as defined in our submit function, displaying a message in the messages area, as shown in Figure 4-10.

Figure 4-10. Hello form submission

While the form is accessible through the URL, it would be nice to provide a menu item to make it easier for new site visitors to find. To add a menu item, edit the `hello.links.menu.yml` file and add the following to the bottom of the file:

```
hello.form:
  title: Hello Form
  menu_name: main
  route_name: hello.form
  expanded: TRUE
  weight: 120
```

The first line defines the name of the link, the `title` defines the text that appears on the menu, the `menu_name` specifies which menu our link will appear on, the `route_name` is as we defined in the `hello.routing.yml` file for the menu, and the remainder is familiar territory from previous menu examples. After saving the file and rebuilding the cache, visit the homepage of your site. You should see the new menu item, as shown in Figure 4-11.

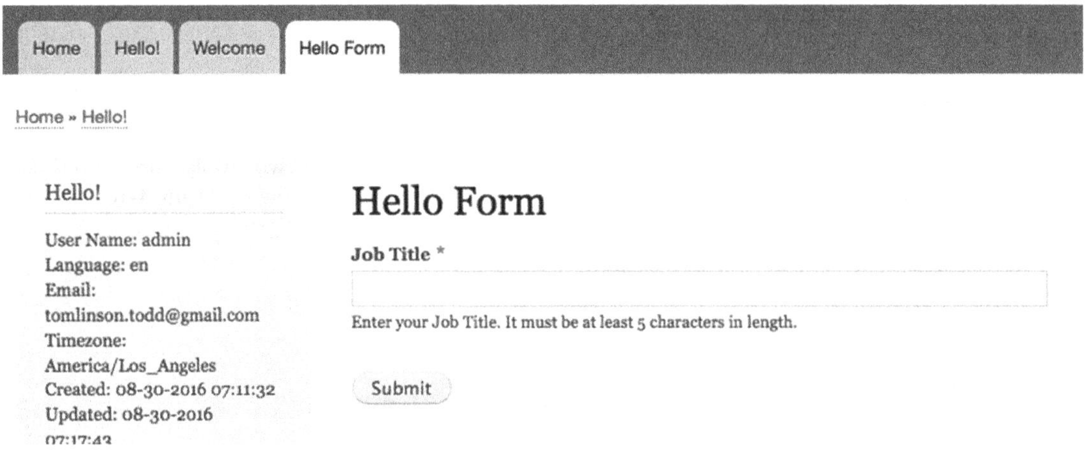

Figure 4-11. The Hello Form menu item

Our form only provided a single entry field and that field was a textbox. There are several other form elements, including several HTML5-based elements that provide a user interface rich form experience.

Let's update HelloForm.php, adding several form elements to demonstrate several of the form elements that are available through the Drupal 8 forms API. The updated HelloForm.php file, after adding the elements and modifying the submit function to display the values of each element, looks as follows:

```php
<?php

namespace Drupal\hello\Form;

use Drupal\Core\Form\FormBase;
use Drupal\Core\Form\FormStateInterface;

class HelloForm extends FormBase {

  public function buildForm(array $form, FormStateInterface $form_state) {

    $form['job_title'] = [
      '#type' => 'textfield',
      '#title' => $this->t('Job Title'),
      '#description' => $this->t('Enter your Job Title. It must be at least 5 characters in
      length.'),
      '#required' => TRUE,
    ];
    // CheckBoxes.
    $form['tests_taken'] = [
      '#type' => 'checkboxes',
      '#options' => ['SAT' => t('SAT'), 'ACT' => t('ACT')],
      '#title' => $this->t('What standardized tests did you take?'),
      '#description' => 'If you did not take any of the tests, leave unchecked',
    ];
    // Color.
    $form['color'] = [
      '#type' => 'color',
      '#title' => $this->t('Color'),
      '#default_value' => '#ffffff',
      '#description' => 'Pick a color by clicking on the color above',
    ];

    // Date.
    $form['expiration'] = [
      '#type' => 'date',
      '#title' => $this->t('Content expiration'),
      '#default_value' => ['year' => 2020, 'month' => 2, 'day' => 15],
      '#description' => 'Enter a date in the form of YYYY MM DD',
    ];

    // Email.
    $form['email'] = [
      '#type' => 'email',
      '#title' => $this->t('Email'),
      '#description' => 'Enter your email address',
    ];
```

67

```
// Number.
$form['quantity'] = [
  '#type' => 'number',
  '#title' => t('Quantity'),
  '#description' => $this->t('Enter a number, any number'),
];

// Password.
$form['password'] = [
  '#type' => 'password',
  '#title' => $this->t('Password'),
  '#description' => 'Enter a password',
];

// Password Confirm.
$form['password_confirm'] = [
  '#type' => 'password_confirm',
  '#title' => $this->t('New Password'),
  '#description' => $this->t('Confirm the password by re-entering'),
];

// Range.
$form['size'] = [
  '#type' => 'range',
  '#title' => t('Size'),
  '#min' => 10,
  '#max' => 100,
  '#description' => $this->t('This is a slider control, pick a value between 10 and 100'),
];

// Radios.
$form['settings']['active'] = [
  '#type' => 'radios',
  '#title' => t('Poll status'),
  '#options' => [0 => $this->t('Closed'), 1 => $this->t('Active')],
  '#description' => $this->t('Select either closed or active'),
];

// Search.
$form['search'] = [
  '#type' => 'search',
  '#title' => $this->t('Search'),
  '#description' => $this->t('Enter a search word or phrase'),
];

// Select.
$form['favorite'] = [
  '#type' => 'select',
  '#title' => $this->t('Favorite color'),
```

```
    '#options' => [
      'red' => $this->t('Red'),
      'blue' => $this->t('Blue'),
      'green' => $this->t('Green'),
    ],
    '#empty_option' => $this->t('-select-'),
    '#description' => $this->t('Which color is your favorite?'),
  ];

  // Tel.
  $form['phone'] = [
    '#type' => 'tel',
    '#title' => $this->t('Phone'),
    '#description' => $this->t('Enter your phone number, beginning with country code,
    e.g., 1 503 555 1212'),
  ];

  // TableSelect.
  $options = [
    1 => ['first_name' => 'Indy', 'last_name' => 'Jones'],
    2 => ['first_name' => 'Darth', 'last_name' => 'Vader'],
    3 => ['first_name' => 'Super', 'last_name' => 'Man'],
  ];

  $header = [
    'first_name' => t('First Name'),
    'last_name' => t('Last Name'),
  ];

  $form['table'] = [
    '#type' => 'tableselect',
    '#title' => $this->t('Users'),
    '#title_display' => 'visible',
    '#header' => $header,
    '#options' => $options,
    '#empty' => t('No users found'),
  ];

  // Textarea.
  $form['text'] = [
    '#type' => 'textarea',
    '#title' => $this->t('Text'),
    '#description' => $this->t('Enter a lot of text here'),
  ];

  // Textfield.
  $form['subject'] = [
    '#type' => 'textfield',
    '#title' => t('Subject'),
    '#size' => 60,
    '#maxlength' => 128,
    '#description' => $this->t('Just another text field'),
  ];
```

```php
    // Weight.
    $form['weight'] = [
      '#type' => 'weight',
      '#title' => t('Weight'),
      '#delta' => 10,
      '#description' => $this->t('A Drupal weight filter'),
    ];

    // Group submit handlers in an actions element with a key of "actions" so
    // that it gets styled correctly, and so that other modules may add actions
    // to the form.
    $form['actions'] = [
      '#type' => 'actions',
    ];

    // Add a submit button that handles the submission of the form.
    $form['actions']['submit'] = [
      '#type' => 'submit',
      '#value' => $this->t('Submit'),
      '#description' => $this->t('Submit, #type = submit'),
    ];

    return $form;
  }

  public function getFormId() {
    return 'hello_form';
  }

  public function validateForm(array &$form, FormStateInterface $form_state) {
    $job_title = $form_state->getValue('job_title');
    if (strlen($job_title) < 5) {
      // Set an error for the form element with a key of "title".
      $form_state->setErrorByName('job_title', $this->t('Your job title must be at least 5
      characters long.'));
    }
  }

  public function submitForm(array &$form, FormStateInterface $form_state) {
    // Find out what was submitted.
    $values = $form_state->getValues();
    foreach ($values as $key => $value) {
      $label = isset($form[$key]['#title']) ? $form[$key]['#title'] : $key;

      // Many arrays return 0 for unselected values so lets filter that out.
      if (is_array($value)) {
        $value = array_filter($value);
      }

      // Only display for controls that have titles and values.
      if ($value && $label) {
        $display_value = is_array($value) ? preg_replace('/[\n\r\s]+/', ' ', print_r($value,
        1)) : $value;
```

```
        $message = $this->t('Value for %title: %value', array('%title' => $label, '%value'
        => $display_value));
        drupal_set_message($message);
      }
    }
  }
}
```

The additional elements were added to the buildForm function and cross a wide variety of form widgets, from simple text fields to complex widgets like color pickers and tables. Browse through the list of form elements and implement a few of them in your own hello module.

We also modified the submitForm function to display all of the entered values, regardless of their input format, when the user clicks the Submit button. Try implementing the same submit handler in your hello module and examine the values generated by each input element. What you do with the values submitted on your form is dependent on the functional and technical requirements. For example, you could send the values from the form to your CRM or marketing automation platform or save them as a node. I cover interacting with nodes and other entities later in this chapter.

There are other more complex form capabilities inherent in Drupal 8's forms API. For additional information on creating more complex forms, visit api.drupal.org/api/drupal/core!core.api.php/ group/form_api. At the top of the page, click on the version that you want to investigate (e.g., 8.2.x).

Interacting with Entities

Entities represent several items in Drupal 8 including nodes, taxonomy, and users. It is likely that during the development of your enterprise Drupal 8 site, you will need to perform some action on entities that just isn't possible with tools such as views and rules. To demonstrate the capabilities of interacting with entities, we expand on the functionality of the hello module to include several examples of interacting with entities.

Finding Existing Entities

In the first example we extend the hello module by adding a new form that searches for a node given a title entered by the user and displays elements of that node in a modal window. This example demonstrates Drupal 8's entity query capabilities as well as using an AJAX-driven modal window.

The first step is to create a new form that presents a textbox where the user can enter the title of a node. We make it as easy as possible for the users to find what they are looking for by allowing the users to enter a portion of the title. In the src\Form directory, create a new file named HelloModalForm.php and populate that file with the following:

```php
<?php

namespace Drupal\hello\Form;

use Drupal\Core\Form\FormBase;
use Drupal\Core\Form\FormStateInterface;
use Drupal\Core\Ajax\AjaxResponse;
use Drupal\Core\Ajax;
use Drupal\Core\Ajax\OpenModalDialogCommand;
```

71

```php
class HelloModalForm extends FormBase {

  public function buildForm(array $form, FormStateInterface $form_state) {

      $form['#attached']['library'][] = 'core/drupal.dialog.ajax';
      $form['node_title'] = array(
        '#type' => 'textfield',
        '#title' => $this->t('Node\'s title'),
        '#description' => $this->t('Enter a portion of the title to search for'),
      );

      $form['actions']['#type'] = 'actions';

      $form['actions']['submit'] = array(
        '#type' => 'submit',
        '#value' => $this->t('Search'),
        '#ajax' => array( // here we add Ajax callback where we will process
          'callback' => '::open_modal',  // the data that came from the form and that we
          will receive as a result in the modal window
        ),
      );

      $form['#title'] = 'Search for Node by Title';

      return $form;

  }

  public function getFormId() {
    return 'hello_modal_form';
  }

  public function validateForm(array &$form, FormStateInterface $form_state) {
  }

  public function submitForm(array &$form, FormStateInterface $form_state) {
  }

  public function open_modal(&$form, FormStateInterface $form_state) {
    $node_title = $form_state->getValue('node_title');
    $query = \Drupal::entityQuery('node')
        ->condition('title', $node_title, 'CONTAINS');
    $entity = $query->execute();
    $key = array_keys($entity);
    $id = !empty($key[0]) ? $key[0] : NULL;
    $response = new AjaxResponse();
    $title = 'Node ID';
    if ($id !== NULL) {
        $content = '<div class="test-popup-content"> Node ID is: ' . $id . '</div>';
        $options = array(
          'dialogClass' => 'popup-dialog-class',
          'width' => '300',
          'height' => '300',
        );
```

```
      $response->addCommand(new OpenModalDialogCommand($title, $content, $options));
   } else {
      $content = 'Not found record with this title <strong>' . $node_title .'</strong>';
      $options = array(
         'dialogClass' => 'popup-dialog-class',
         'width' => '300',
         'height' => '300',
      );
      $response->addCommand(new OpenModalDialogCommand($title, $content, $options));      }
   return $response;
 }

}
```

This form is similar to the previous form we created in the previous form example, with the following exceptions:

- There are three additional namespaces added to the top of the module—Drupal\
  Core\Ajax\AjaxResponse, Drupal\Core\Ajax, and Drupal\Core\Ajax\
  OpenModalDialogCommand. The three namespaces provide direct access to the AJAX
  and modal window capabilities that we need to render the modal window.

- The class name for this form is HelloModalForm, and it will be used in the hello.
  routing.yml file to render the form.

- $form['#attached']['library'][] = 'core/drupal.dialog.ajax' attaches the
  AJAX functionality to the form so that we can use it to render the modal window.

- $form['actions']['submit'] differs in that it provides an AJAX callback that will be
  used to render the modal window. The callback is the method open_modal, which is
  defined at the bottom of the file.

- The open_modal function access the $form and $form_state information from the
  submitted form. The information contained in $form_state are the values entered
  by the visitor.

- $node_title = $form_state->getValue('node_title') retrieves the value entered
  by the user in the node_title field and assigns it to the $node_title variable.

- $query = \Drupal::entityQuery('node') ->condition('title', $node_title,
  'CONTAINS') defines an entity query on nodes, where the title contains the text
  entered by the user. I cover entity queries in more detail later in this chapter.

- $entity = $query->execute() performs the query and returns an array of entities
  that contain the value entered by the user.

- The next two statements examine the array keys returned from the query and assign
  the key to a variable that I will use in subsequent statements. If the query did not
  return any nodes, then I'll assign NULL to the $id variable.

- The $reponse = new AjaxResponse() statement creates the standard response
  object that Drupal's AJAX functionality expects to receive. We will populate this
  object with the information required to render the modal window.

- $title = 'Node ID' sets a variable that will be used later as the title of the modal
  window.

73

- The if statement examines whether the $id field, which was set in a previous statement, is NULL (no nodes were found) or not. If $id is not NULL, it's used to form markup that's stored in the $content variable for rendering in the modal window.

- The $options array specifies what it is that we are rendering—a popup dialog that is 300px wide and 300px high.

- The $reponse->addCommand method uses the $title, $content, and $options variables that were just created and adds them to the $response object so that the AJAX handler knows what to render.

- The else clause does the same basic functions with the exception of the message that is created in the $content variable. This is the case when message tells the visitors that the title they searched for was not found.

- The $response object is returned and the modal window is displayed.

Save the new form and proceed to the next step, updating the hello.routing.yml file with the information necessary to render the new form. Edit the routing file and add the following to the bottom:

```
hello.modal:
  path: 'hello/modal'
  defaults:
    _form: '\Drupal\hello\Form\HelloModalForm'
  requirements:
    _access: 'TRUE'
```

This section of the routing file is nearly identical to the previous form example, with the exception of a new path. The route to the _form is \Drupal\hello\Form\HelloModalForm. After updating the routing file, update the hello.links.menu.yml file to create a new menu item for the modal window example. Add the following to the end of the file:

```
hello.modal:
  title: Hello Modal Form
  menu_name: main
  route_name: hello.modal
  expanded: TRUE
  weight: 130
```

This new menu entry is named hello.modal, with a title of Hello Modal Form, assigned to the main menu, and renders the hello.modal route that I just defined in the hello.routing.yml file. I'll place the new menu item to the right of the previous menu item by incrementing the weight. Rebuild the cache and visit the homepage. You should see the new menu item. Clicking on the menu item renders the form as shown in Figure 4-12.

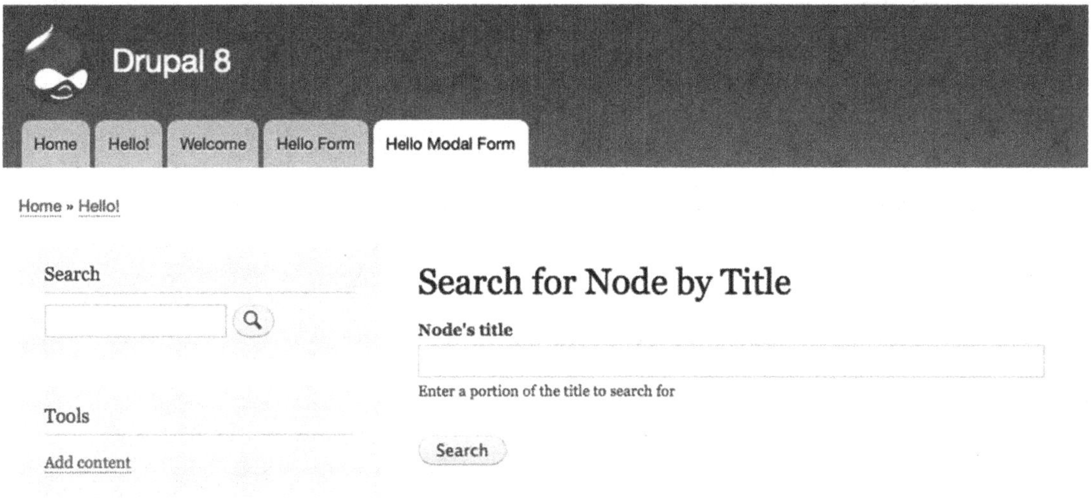

Figure 4-12. *The Search form*

Before searching, create a new node by visiting Content ➤ Add Content ➤ Article. Using That Node. Enter either the full title that you created or a partial representation of the title in the Node's title text box of the new form and click the Search button. If you correctly entered text that appears in the title of your node, you should see a modal window as shown in Figure 4-13.

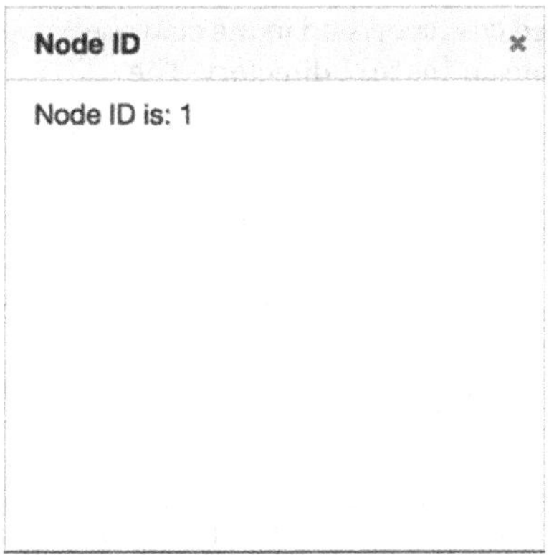

Figure 4-13. *The modal window displaying the Node ID*

Close the modal window by clicking on the X in the upper-right corner. Now try entering text that was not part of the node's title in the Node's title text box and then click the Search button. The results should be as shown in Figure 4-14, with the word Foo replaced by the word or phrase that you entered in the text box.

Figure 4-14. *The node not found modal window*

Creating Entities

Drupal 8 provides an easy-to-use administrative interface for creating new content types, but you may not always want to use just the administrative interface. This could be the case if you are creating a custom module that relies on a specific content type being present and relying on a site administrator to correctly create that content type is just too much of a risk. In Drupal 8 the process for creating a new entity type, or in this case, a content type, is relatively simple and can be accomplished mostly through yaml files. In this example, we create a content type named customer that will provide a title and a body field to enter information about that customer.

To begin we create a new module for the purpose of creating the content type, and we name the module customer. In the modules/custom directory, create a new directory named customer, and in the customer directory, create a config directory. Finally, in the config directory, create an install directory. The resulting structure is as follows:

```
customer
  config
    install
```

The first file that we create is the customer.info.yml file, which resides in the /modules/custom/customer directory. The contents of this file are as follows:

```
name: Customer Content Type
description: The simplest example of implementing a customer node content type in a module.
package: Awesome modules
type: module
dependencies:
  - node
  - path
  - text
core: 8.x
```

The content of the customer.info.yml file is similar to the hello module's hello.info.yml file with the exception of the name, description, and a few extra dependencies that must be present and enabled in order for the module to properly function: the node, path, and text modules. These modules are part of core and provide basic functionally required by the customer content type.

The next file that we will create is the `customer.module` file. We create the file in the /modules/custom/ customer directory. Since our customer module has a single purpose, create a content type, there isn't any additional functionality required at this juncture beyond enabling the content type, so the content of the module file is simply as follows:

```php
<?php

/**
 * The customer.module file
 */
```

You may add functionality to the module file to enable additional features and functionality related to the customer content type.

In the `config` directory, there are three yaml files that we need to create:

- `node.type.customer.yml` describes the content type that we are creating.

- `field.field.node.customer.body.yml` describes the body field that we are going to add to the customer content type. Note: By default, Drupal provides the `title` field.

- `core.entity_form_display.node.customer.default.yml` describes the default node edit form for the `customer` content type.

In the `install` directory, we start by creating the `node.type.customer.yml` file with the following content:

```yaml
langcode: en
status: true
dependencies: {  }
name: 'Customer'
type: customer
description: 'This is a very basic customer content type.'
help: ''
new_revision: false
preview_mode: 1
display_submitted: true
third_party_settings: {  }
```

This is a standard yaml file for all node-based content types. The only values that we are changing from the defaults are the `name`, `type`, and `description`.

The next file that we will create is the yaml file that describes the body field that will be added to the customer content type. We create the file called `field.field.node.customer.body.yml` in the same directory with the following content:

```yaml
langcode: en
status: true
dependencies:
  config:
    - field.storage.node.body
    - node.type.customer
  module:
    - text
```

```
id: node.customer.body
field_name: body
entity_type: node
bundle: customer
label: Body
description: ''
required: false
translatable: true
default_value: {  }
default_value_callback: ''
settings:
  display_summary: true
third_party_settings: {  }
field_type: text_with_summary
```

This file is also a standard template for creating fields. The primary elements that were used to describe the field areas follows:

- dependencies: There are two configuration-related dependencies that must be present in order for this field to exist—the Drupal 8-provided field.storage.node. body, which describes how the body field will be stored in the database, and node. type.customer, the content type that we are creating. This field is also dependent on the text module, which defines the attributes of a text field.

- id: This field provides a unique ID for the field being created, in this case, it's node. customer.body.

- field_name: To be consistent with other body fields in content types, we use the standard term of body.

- entity_type: Describes what type of entity will be associated with this field, a node. Other alternatives are taxonomy, user, and any other custom entities created by modules on your site.

- bundle: The bundle associated with this field on this content type is customer.

- label: The value that will appear on the edit form for this field.

- field_type: Defines what type of text field, with is text_with_summary. Other text field types, as well as all available off-the-shelf field formats, can be found at drupal. org/node/1879542.

The last file to be created in this example is the core.entity_form_display.node.customer.default.yml file. This file describes how the node edit form will appear when content creators add a new customer to the site. The contents of this file are as follows:

```
langcode: en
status: true
dependencies:
  config:
    - field.field.node.customer.body
    - node.type.customer
  module:
    - path
    - text
```

```
id: node.customer.default
targetEntityType: node
bundle: customer
mode: default
content:
  title:
    type: string_textfield
    weight: 0
    settings:
      size: 60
      placeholder: ''
    third_party_settings: {  }
  uid:
    type: entity_reference_autocomplete
    weight: 1
    settings:
      match_operator: CONTAINS
      size: 60
      placeholder: ''
    third_party_settings: {  }
  created:
    type: datetime_timestamp
    weight: 2
    settings: {  }
    third_party_settings: {  }
  promote:
    type: boolean_checkbox
    weight: 3
    settings:
      display_label: true
    third_party_settings: {  }
  sticky:
    type: boolean_checkbox
    weight: 4
    settings:
      display_label: true
    third_party_settings: {  }
  path:
    type: path
    weight: 5
    settings: {  }
    third_party_settings: {  }
  body:
    type: text_textarea_with_summary
    weight: 6
    settings:
      rows: 9
      summary_rows: 3
      placeholder: ''
    third_party_settings: {  }
hidden: {  }
third_party_settings: {  }
```

The elements of this file describe each field that will appear on the edit form and were copied from a default template that is found at api.drupal.org/api/drupal/core!profiles!standard!config!install !core.entity_form_display.node.article.default.yml/8.2.x. Replace 8.2.x with the version of Drupal that you are working with to get an up-to-date version of the file. The primary settings that were modified from the default template are as follows:

- The dependencies were updated to reflect the customer content type, specifically the addition of the body field and the node type in the config section, as well as the path and text module. All four of those elements must exist in order for the customer content type to work properly.

- The id field was updated to reflect the customer content type.

- The bundle was updated to reflect the customer content type.

- The body field was added to the bottom of the list.

After creating all the files and saving them, navigate to the Extend page and search for the customer module in the Awesome Modules section. Check the box next to the module and click the Install button at the bottom of the page. After enabling the module, visit the Content page and click the Add Content button. You should see the new customer content type listed as one of the available options, as shown in Figure 4-15.

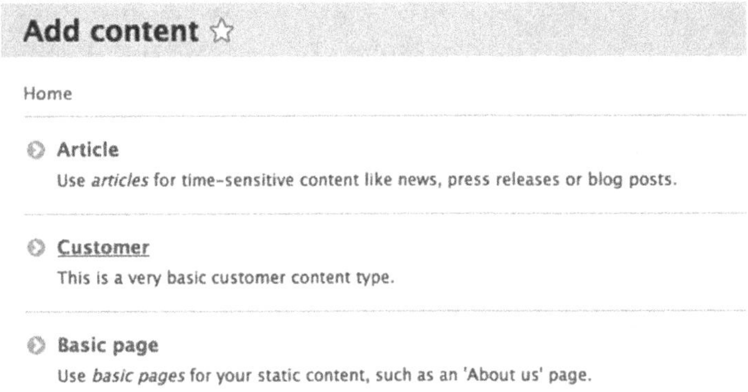

Add content ☆

Home

◎ **Article**
Use *articles* for time-sensitive content like news, press releases or blog posts.

◎ **Customer**
This is a very basic customer content type.

◎ **Basic page**
Use *basic pages* for your static content, such as an 'About us' page.

Figure 4-15. *The Customer content type*

Clicking on Customer displays the node edit form for the new Customer content type, as shown in Figure 4-16.

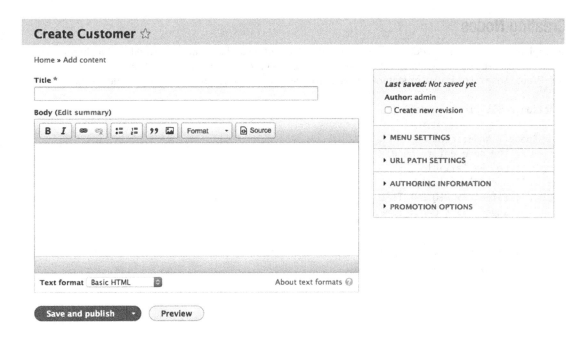

Figure 4-16. The Customer node edit form

There are significantly more capabilities for creating entity types beyond what is possible to cover in this chapter. For a more comprehensive example on creating custom entities, visit `drupal.org/node/2192175`.

Creating, Updating, and Deleting Entities Programmatically

A common activity performed by custom modules is programmatically creating, updating, and deleting content from the Drupal database. This section describes the processes for creating nodes, files, nodes with images, taxonomy terms, and menu items.

Creating Entities

The process for creating entities, such as nodes, and translating them into other languages, is relatively simple. Before attempting to implement this functionality on your site, be sure to:

- Enable all of the multilingual modules and set up Spanish (es) as one of the languages that your site supports.

- Visit Structure ➤ Taxonomy ➤ Manage ➤ Tags ➤ Overview and create a new taxonomy term in the tags vocabulary. It will be used in the node that will be created in the following process.

Creating Nodes

To implement the example code, we return to the hello module and edit the hello.module file. In the .module file, first we add use Drupal\node\Entity\Node; at the top of the file directly above or below the use Drupal\user\Entity\User statement. Next, we create a new function in the module file, as shown here:

```
function hello_create_node() {

    $node = Node::create([
      // The node entity bundle.
      'type' => 'article',
      'langcode' => 'en',
      'created' => REQUEST_TIME,
      'changed' => REQUEST_TIME,
      // The user ID.
      'uid' => 1,
      'title' => 'My test!',
      // An array with taxonomy terms.
      'field_tags' =>[1],
      'body' => [
        'summary' => '',
        'value' => '<p>The body of my node.</p>',
        'format' => 'full_html',
      ],
    ]);
    $node->save();
    \Drupal::service('path.alias_storage')->save("/node/" . $node->id(),
    "/hello/example-node", "en");

    $node_es = $node->addTranslation('es');
    $node_es->title = 'Mi prueba!';
    $node_es->body->value = '<p>El cuerpo de mi nodo.</p>';
    $node_es->body->format = 'full_html';
    $node_es->save();
    \Drupal::service('path.alias_storage')->save("/node/" . $node->id(), "/mi/ruta", "es");

    return t("Created node " . $node->get('title')->value);

}
```

This code:

- Creates a new $node object using the Node::create method.

- Populates all of the fields on the node with values, including a taxonomy term (the first term in the tags vocabulary).

- Saves the node using $node->save().

- Creates a path alias to the node using \Drupal::services('path.alias_storage')-> save(("/node/" . $node->id(), "/hello/example-node", "en");.

- Creates a new translation of the node into Spanish and creates a new alias in Spanish.

With the functionality present in the module file, the next step is to update the Controller for the hello module. We need to edit the HelloController.php file in the src/Controller directory. Add the following function to the file:

```
public function create_node() {
    return array(
        '#markup' => hello_create_node(),
    );
}
```

The create_node function calls the hello_create_node function that I just created in the hello.module file. The last step in the process is to add a route in the hello.routing.yml file. At the bottom of the routing file, add the following:

```
hello.create:
  path: 'hello/create-node'
  defaults:
   _controller: '\Drupal\hello\Controller\HelloController::create_node'
  requirements:
    _access: 'TRUE'
```

This route provides an URL of hello/create-node that, when visited, executes the functionality associated with the HelloController::create_node method. After saving and visiting the URL, go to Admin ➤ Content, where you can see both the English and Spanish versions of the node, as shown in Figure 4-17.

	TITLE	CONTENT TYPE	AUTHOR	STATUS	UPDATED	▾	OPERATIONS
☐	My test!	Article	admin	Published	09/05/2016 - 11:45		Edit ▾
☐	Mi prueba!	Article	admin	Published	09/05/2016 - 11:45		Edit ▾

Figure 4-17. *The new nodes*

Clicking on the My Test! title displays the node as it was created by the module (see Figure 4-18).

My test!

| View | Edit | Delete |

Submitted by admin on Mon, 09/05/2016 - 11:45

The body of my node.

Figure 4-18. *The English version of the created node*

While this example is simplistic in nature, it demonstrates the basics of programmatically creating nodes.

By following the same pattern—creating a function in the `hello.module` file, updating the `HelloController`, and adding a route to the `routing.yml` file—you can experiment with creating other entities, as described in the following sections.

Creating Files

Creating files is easier than creating nodes in that there are fewer steps required in the process. In the following example, the filename `logo.svg` is added to the files table with a URI to access the file set to `public://page/logo.svg`. We add the namespace definition—use `Drupal\file\Entity\Fil`—to the top of the module file and add a new function with the code listed below the namespace definition. After executing `$file->save`, the file may be queried and referenced in other entities. Note that the file must physically reside in the `sites/default/files` directory prior to executing this function. This function does not upload a file from your desktop; it assumes it already exists.

```
// Add the namespace for file entities at the top of the module file.
use Drupal\file\Entity\File;
// create a new function and place this code in the function
$file = File::create([
  'uid' => 1,
  'filename' => 'logo.svg',
  'uri' => 'public://page/logo.svg',
  'status' => 1,
]);
$file->save();
return $t("File was successfully created");
```

After creating the function in the module file, updating the Controller and routing files, and uploading the `logo.svg` image to the `/sites/default/files` directory, we are now ready to create a new record in the file table for the `logo.svg` file.

Creating Nodes with Images

Another common requirement is to attach images to nodes. This example assumes that you have already uploaded the file to `/sites/default/images`. In the following code, it is essentially the same as creating the node in the previous example, with the exception of adding the file using the `$file = FILE::create` method and adding that file to `field_images` using the `$file->id` of the image that was loaded at the top of the function.

```
// Make sure your module file has the following two namespaces.
use Drupal\file\Entity\File;
use Drupal\node\Entity\Node;

// Use the following code in a function
$file = File::create([
  'uid' => 1,
  'uri' => 'public://page/logo.png',
  'status' => 1,
]);
```

```
$file->save();
$node = Node::create([
  'type' => 'article',
  'langcode' => 'en',
  'created' => REQUEST_TIME,
  'changed' => REQUEST_TIME,
  'uid' => 1,
  'title' => 'My title',
  'field_tags' =>[2],
  'body' => [
    'summary' => '',
    'value' => 'My node!',
    'format' => 'full_html',
  ],
  'field_image' => [
    [
      'target_id' => $file->id(),
      'alt' => "My 'alt'",
      'title' => "My 'title'",
    ],
  ],
]);
$node->save();
\Drupal::service('path.alias_storage')->save('/node/' . $node->id(), '/my-path', 'en');
1
```

Creating Taxonomy Terms

Nodes are not the only entity type that you can create programmatically; taxonomy terms may also be created. Following the same pattern as previous examples, create a new function in the hello.module file, adding the namespace for Term as shown here, and implementing the code in a function that is referenced through the Controller and routing files.

In the following code, the $term object is created using the Term::create method and populated with the values as outlined here. The term is saved using $term->save(), a path alias is created, and the term is translated into Spanish. Before creating the taxonomy term, we must create a vocabulary named Sport Activity by visiting Structure ➤ Taxonomy and clicking on the Add Vocabulary button.

```
// Ensure that the namespace for Term is included at the top of your module file
use Drupal\taxonomy\Entity\Term;

// Add the following to your module file
$term = Term::create([
  'vid' => 'sport_activity',
  'langcode' => 'en',
  'name' => 'My tag',
  'description' => [
    'value' => '<p>My description.</p>',
    'format' => 'full_html',
  ],
  'weight' => -1,
  'parent' => array (0),
]);
```

```
$term->save();
\Drupal::service('path.alias_storage')->save("/taxonomy/term/" . $term->id(),
"/tags/my-tag", "en");
$term_es = $term->addTranslation('es');
$term_es->name = 'Mi etiqueta';
$term_es->description->value = '<p>Mi descripción.</p>';
$term_es->description->format = 'full_html';
$term_es->save();
\Drupal::service('path.alias_storage')->save("/taxonomy/term/" . $term->id(),
"/etiquetas/mi-etiqueta", "es");
return t("The term was successfully created");
```

Creating Menu Links

Menu links can be created programmatically using the same pattern as previous examples. Remember to add the namespace for MenuLinkContent to the top of your module file. Create the function in the module file, update the Controller and routing files, and you are on your way to programmatically creating a new menu item.

```
// the namespace for menu links.
use Drupal\menu_link_content\Entity\MenuLinkContent;

// the code that should be implemented in a function to create a menu item
$menu_item = MenuLinkContent::create([
  'bundle' => 'menu_link_content',
  'langcode' => 'en',
  'title' => 'My menu link',
  'description' => 'My description.',
  'menu_name' => 'main',
  'link' => [['uri' => 'internal:/node/1']],
'weight' => 0,
]);
$menu_item->save();
$menu_item_es = $menu_item->addTranslation('es');
$menu_item_es->title = 'Mi enlace del menú';
$menu_item_es->description = 'Mi descripción.';
$menu_item_es->save();
```

Updating Entities

The process for updating an existing entity is through a set of relatively simple methods. For example, updating a node's title and body can be accomplished using the following:

```
$node = \Drupal\node\Entity\Node::load($nid);
$node->setTitle('This is the new title');
$node->set('body', 'This is the new body');
$node->save();
```

This code assumes that you already know the $nid that needs to be updated. If you don't have the node ID, you might consider writing an entity query to find the node to be updated, such as:

```
$query = \Drupal::entityQuery('node')
    ->condition('title', 'The text to look for' , 'CONTAINS');
$nids = $query->execute();
```

Then update each $nid in the $nids array using code similar to the following:

```
foreach($nids as $nid) {
    $node = \Drupal\node\Entity\Node::load($nid);
    $node->setTitle('This is the new title');
    $node->set('body', 'This is the new body');
    $node->save();
}
```

To update other types of entities use the same pattern, such as:

```
$term = \Drupal\taxonomy\Entity\Term::load($tid);
// update field values here
$term->save();

$user = \Drupal\user\Entity\User::load($uid);
// update field values here
$user->save();
```

Deleting Entities

The process for deleting entities is to first load them and then delete them using the following code:

```
$node = \Drupal\node\Entity\Node::load($nid);
$node->delete();

$term = \Drupal\taxonomy\Entity\Term::load($tid);
$term->delete();

$user = \Drupal\user\Entity\User::load($uid);
$user->delete();
```

There are many more features and capabilities surrounding interacting with entities in Drupal 8. I suggest bookmarking drupal.org/developing/api/entity and visiting that page often as you begin developing Drupal 8 modules.

Summary

This chapter only scratches the surface of the capabilities of developing modules in Drupal 8. There is so much more to the features and capabilities that exist in the Drupal 8 DNA. It would take several hundred pages to fully describe the details of all the capabilities in Drupal 8 module development. While the details described in this chapter provide a solid baseline for beginning your journey into Drupal 8 module development, there are hundreds of pages of additional details and examples on drupal.org/developing/modules/8.

The next chapter describes the process for creating themes in Drupal 8 using the Twig templating engine.

## CHAPTER 5

Drupal 8 Theming

Drupal themes represent the components of a Drupal site that render content on any browser equipped device in a visually appealing fashion. If Drupal is the cake, then themes are the frosting and decoration—they make your web site beautiful.

The art of theming requires a mixture of visual design skills, including using tools such as Photoshop, as well as experience in developing HTML markup and cascading stylesheets (CSS), using JavaScript, and using the Twig templating engine to connect the theme to the output generated by Drupal.

This chapter covers the details of the role of a Drupal theme, how themes are structured, how themes are installed and enabled, and the process and components required to create a custom Drupal 8 theme, including the yaml files required to describe your theme, the HTML markup, CSS, and Twig components required to assemble pages on your site. It is assumed that you have a basic understanding of HTML, CSS, and JavaScript before attempting to construct a custom theme.

The Role of a Drupal Theme

Drupal themes have one primary responsibility—to provide the means for displaying content that is generated by the various Drupal components such as blocks and views in a visually appealing manner. The theme provides physical containers on the page, typically called *regions,* which are used by site builders to place content, blocks, views, and other visual elements. The theme also joins the physical layout and regions with the cascading stylesheet elements and JavaScript to deliver to the browser a complete package ready to be viewed by the site visitors.

While the theme is responsible for defining regions on a page, CSS, and JavaScript, the theme may also override the visual presentation of the output generated by blocks, views, and modules.

While the theme is responsible for defining the structure and visualization of pages, content, and elements on the page, it's important to talk about the underlying templating engine that is the workhorse of Drupal themes, responsible for integrating the output generated by Drupal and its components with the HTML markup and CSS. That component is the Twig templating engine and it's new to Drupal as of Drupal 8. It replaces the previous templating engine, the PHP template.

The Twig Templating Engine

While HTML, CSS, and JavaScript play a key role in Drupal 8 themes, the true star of the show is the Twig templating engine (`twig.sensiolabs.org`). Twig is a component of the Symfony2 framework, which is the underlying architecture that Drupal 8 is built on. Think of Twig is the "glue" between the output that is generated by a Drupal module and the rendered page that is presented to the site visitors.

The Twig templating engine uses relatively simple syntax consisting of variables, expressions, and tags. The Twig templating engine converts each of those elements into highly optimized PHP code that binds the output of Drupal's modules to the rendered page. A simple example of using Twig to render a block's title and body is as follows:

```
<h3>{{ block.title }}</h3>
<div>{{ block.content }}</div>
```

While there would likely be conditional logic wrapping the output, for example, checking to see if the title and content existed before rendering it, the example demonstrates the simplicity of Twig and its syntax. The block module exposes block to the theme layer, with title and content as elements within the block that are rendered using the previous syntax. Before exploring the details of Twig syntax, let's first look at the elements required to create a Drupal 8 theme.

The Structure of a Drupal Theme

Drupal 8 themes, like modules, require a specific set of files in a standard directory structure in order to function properly. All themes that are not part of Drupal 8 core reside in the theme directory at the root directory of your Drupal 8 site. Within the theme directory, if you have not yet done so, create two subdirectories:

- contrib: This is where all themes downloaded from drupal.org are stored

- custom: This is where all themes you create for your site will reside

Focusing on a custom theme, the directory structure required to support the creation of a custom theme is as follows:

```
themename
  config
    install
    schema
  css
  js
  images
  templates
```

Where themename is the name of your theme. In the themename directory you will find several files (replace themename with the actual name of the theme):

- themename.info.yml: The only mandatory file for a Drupal 8 theme. This file describes the metadata about your theme, for example the name of your theme, as well as libraries, regions, and the version of Drupal core that is required to use the theme.

- themename.libraries.yml: Defines the JavaScript and CSS libraries that are loaded by the theme.

- themename.breakpoints.yml: Defines the screen widths where the design needs to change to accommodate different devices.

- themename.theme: Contains all of the conditional logic and preprocessing of output that occurs before it is rendered on the page. It may also extend the basic theme settings by creating advanced theme settings.

- screenshot.png: Rendered on the Appearance page, giving the site builder a preview of the theme.

- logo.svg: The standard logo rendered on a page in the header section of your site. You may provide a standard logo as part of your theme or upload a logo through the Appearance ➤ Settings page.

- .css: There may be one to many CSS files in the css directory.

- .js: There may be one to many JavaScript files in the js directory.

We cover the config directory and advanced configuration options later in this chapter.

Creating the Theme Files

To demonstrate the process of creating the files associated with a Drupal 8 theme, we start with the creation of the directory structure as described previously, for a new theme called davinci. We first create a new directory in the themes directory called davinci, and then create the same subdirectories as described previously, resulting in the directory structure shown in Listing 5-1.

Listing 5-1. The Davinci Theme Directory

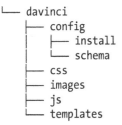

```
└── davinci
    ├── config
    │   ├── install
    │   └── schema
    ├── css
    ├── images
    ├── js
    └── templates
```

The next step in the process is to create the .info.yml file. Using your favorite text editor, create the davinci.info.yml file in the root directory of your new theme (themes/custom/davinci) with the following code:

```
name: Davinci
type: theme
description: A Drupal 8 theme
core: 8.x
```

The values in this file are as follows:

- name defines the value that will appear on the Appearance page.

- type defines what this .info.yml file defines, in this case a theme.

- description is text that appears on the Appearance page and describes your theme to the site administrator.

- core defines the version of Drupal that your theme supports.

Although there are more elements that may be added to the .info.yml file, those listed previously are all that are required to display the theme on the Appearance page and all that are required to enable the theme. Save the file, rebuild the cache, and visit the Appearance page. You'll now see the new theme, as shown in Figure 5-1.

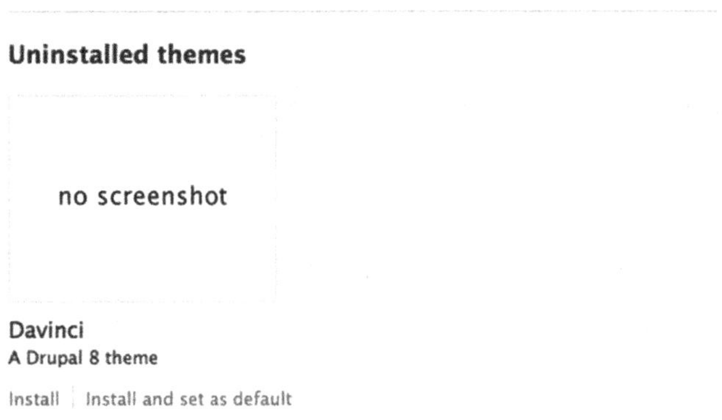

Uninstalled themes

no screenshot

Davinci
A Drupal 8 theme
Install ¦ Install and set as default

Figure 5-1. *The Davinci theme*

Clicking on the Install and Set Default link and visiting the homepage reveals a rather stark design, but it is the starting point and it will only get better from here (see Figure 5-2).

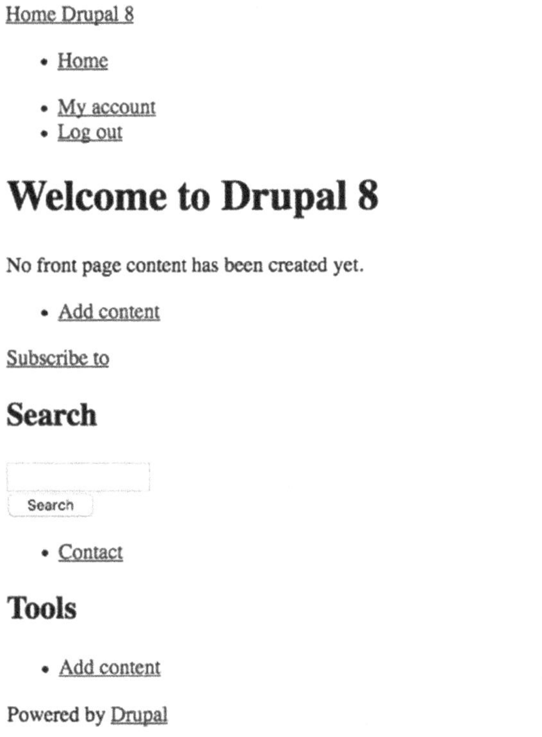

Home Drupal 8

- Home

- My account
- Log out

Welcome to Drupal 8

No front page content has been created yet.

- Add content

Subscribe to

Search

Search

- Contact

Tools

- Add content

Powered by Drupal

Figure 5-2. *The site rendered with the Davinci theme*

Adding Regions to the Theme

One of the power features of themes is the ability to define regions on a page where content, blocks, menus, or other elements that are rendered by modules can be placed. The regions defined by a theme appear on the Structure ➤ Block Layout page, where a site builder can place blocks into each of the defined regions.

For demonstration purposes, we create several regions in the Davinci theme. Figure 5-3 depicts the general layout of the regions that will appear on every page.

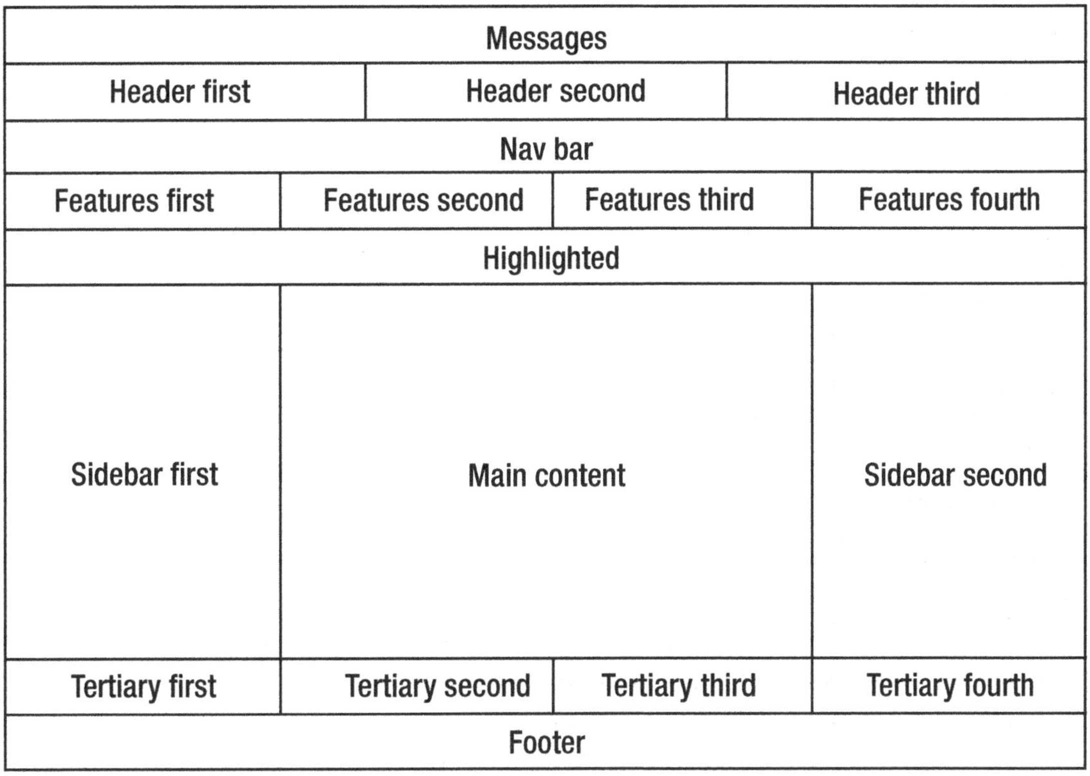

Messages			
Header first	Header second		Header third
Nav bar			
Features first	Features second	Features third	Features fourth
Highlighted			
Sidebar first	Main content		Sidebar second
Tertiary first	Tertiary second	Tertiary third	Tertiary fourth
Footer			

Figure 5-3. *The regions of the Davinci theme*

Not every theme must have as many regions as shown in Figure 5-3, and there may be cases where you need more regions than are provided by the Davinci theme. The choice is up to the designer.

Regions are defined in the .info.yml file in a section titled regions. The structure of a region's definition is the internal name of the region, for example header_first, followed by the name of the region that will appear on administrative interfaces, such as the Block Layout page. In the case of header_first, the value displayed will be Header first. Note: Spacing in .yml files is important and has meaning. Each of the regions defined in the regions section are indented exactly two spaces, which is the yaml syntax for elements within a group. Expand the davinci.info.yml file, adding all of the regions shown in Figure 5-3.

```
name: davinci
type: theme
description: A Drupal 8 theme
core: 8.x
regions:
  messages: 'Messages'
  header_first: 'Header first'
  header_second: 'Header second'
  header_third: 'Header third'
  navbar: 'Nav bar'
  help: 'help'
  features_first: 'Features first'
  features_second: 'Features second'
  features_third: 'Features third'
  features_fourth: 'Features fourth'
  highlighted: 'Highlighted'
  content: 'Main content'
  sidebar_first: 'Sidebar first'
  sidebar_second: 'Sidebar second'
  tertiary_first: 'Tertiary first'
  tertiary_second: 'Tertiary second'
  tertiary_third: 'Tertiary third'
  tertiary_fourth: 'Tertiary fourth'
  footer: 'Footer'
  page_top: 'Page top'
  page_bottom: 'Page bottom'
```

Drupal 8 core requires that three regions exist in every theme:

- content: The primary container for content on a page

- page_top and page_bottom: Regions that are hidden by default(they do not appear on the Block Layout page) and are used by modules to place markup and JavaScript at the top and bottom of pages

After updating and saving the file, we rebuild the cache and visit Structure ➤ Block Layouts, where the new regions appear, as shown in Figure 5-4.

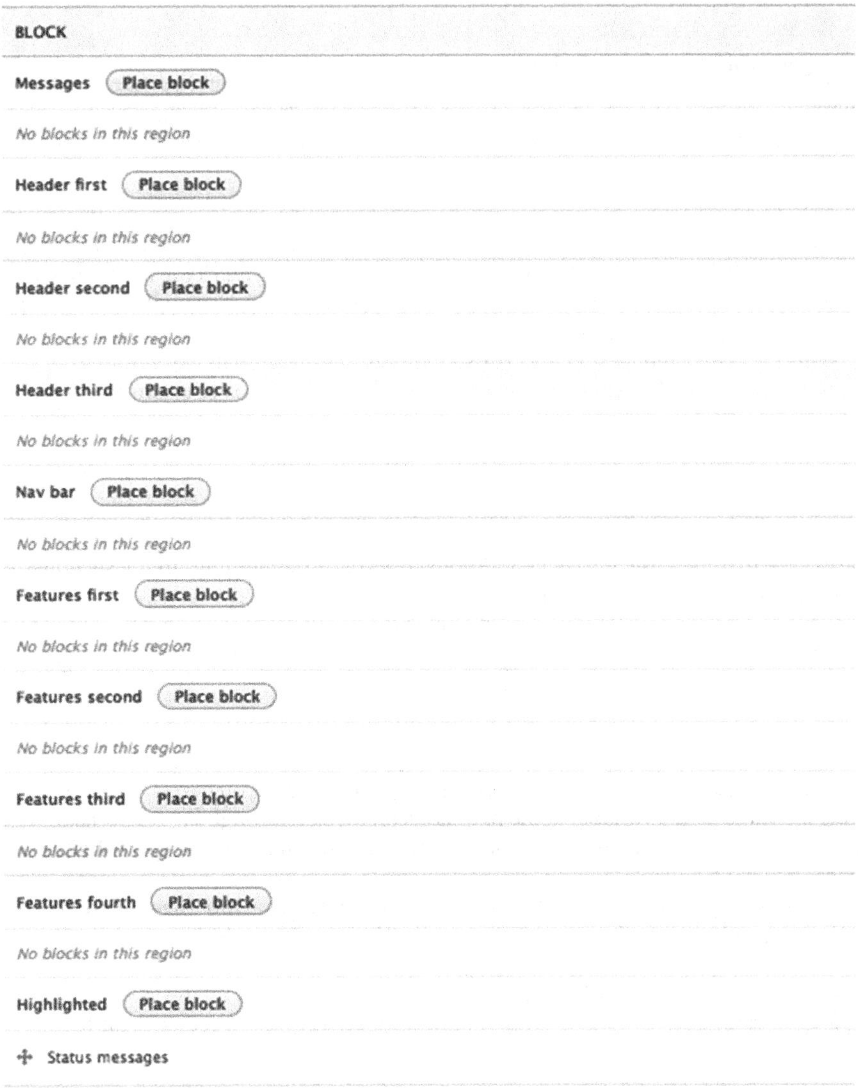

BLOCK

Messages (Place block)

No blocks in this region

Header first (Place block)

No blocks in this region

Header second (Place block)

No blocks in this region

Header third (Place block)

No blocks in this region

Nav bar (Place block)

No blocks in this region

Features first (Place block)

No blocks in this region

Features second (Place block)

No blocks in this region

Features third (Place block)

No blocks in this region

Features fourth (Place block)

No blocks in this region

Highlighted (Place block)

✛ Status messages

Figure 5-4. *A partial listing of the new regions*

At this juncture, we could place blocks and other elements into the regions shown in Figure 5-4; however, before we can see the elements we've placed in the regions, we have to define the templates that will render those regions. But before diving into the details of template files, let's start with an overview of Twig syntax and functionality. Having an understanding of Twig syntax and functionality will make the discussion about the content of template files more meaningful.

Twig Syntax

There are three general categories of "things" that Twig does:

- It "says something"

- It "does something"

- Or it's a comment

Each of these items has a specific syntax. The "say something" syntax is represented by {{ ... }}, where the opening and closing braces are identified by the Twig parser as something that Twig needs to do, and the ... represents a variable that will printed to the page that is being rendered. For example, {{ name }} would print the value associated with a variable called name.

The "do something" syntax is associated with if and for statements, setting the value of variables, filters, and other less common functions. The syntax for "do something" is {% ... %}. For example:

```
{% filter upper %}
   {{ name }}
{% endfilter %}
```

This prints the value of name in uppercase. We cover additional uses of "do something" in the sections that follow. The syntax for comments in Twig templates is {# ... #}.

Combining "say something" with "do something" provides all of the functionality required to connect content in Drupal with the rendered page. The next sections expand on the capabilities of each.

Twig Variables

One of the primary functions of Twig is to print the content of a variable on a page. If you have a variable called first_name, printing the value of that variable to the page is accomplished through {{ first_name }}. Where did first_name come from? Most likely a module that generated a value and assigned it to a themable variable named first_name.

The first_name variable is a simple example, but variables generated by Drupal modules are often more complex such as an array, an object, or a function. Twig handles that by automatically searching for the possible sources of that variable. Using an example of a object named customer, with attributes of that customer being name, address, city, state, postal_code, email, and phone, we can print the value of the customer's name using {{ customer.name }}. When Twig evaluates customer.name, it searches for the following:

- $customer['name']

- $customer->name

- $customer->__isset('name') && $customer->__get('name')

- $customer->name()

- $customer->getName()

- $customer->isName()

- $customer->__call('name')

In nearly every case, one of the references will return the customer's name. As a frontend developer, you need not worry about how the backend developer stored the value of name; Twig handles the details for you.

While most variables are created by modules, there may be scenarios where you need to create and use a variable in your template. To create a variable and assign a value to it, use the following syntax:

```
{% set hello = 'Hello World' %}
```

Twig also supports the creation of key => value arrays, although in Twig they are called *hashes*. To create a hash, use the following syntax:

```
{% set name = { first: 'John', last: 'Doe' } %}
```

In this example, you print the values using {{ name.first }} or {{ name.last }}. Hashes may also be nested, for example:

```
{% set sports = {
    football:   { team: "Seahawks", city: "Seattle" },
    basketball: { team: "Trailblazers", city: "Portland" },
    soccer:     { team: "Timbers", city: "Portland" },
    baseball:   { team: "Mariners", city: "Seattle" }
} %}
```

You would print values from these example using a statement such as {{ sports.football.team }}.

Discovering Variables

As a frontend developer who creates template files, you will see that it's easy to find any variable you define within the template through a {% set %} statement. But most variables are created outside of templates through Drupal modules. While the standard Twig templates included with Drupal core have a well-documented list of variables that are available within that template, those documentation blocks will not include variables created by contributed modules that you have installed on your site.

While you could dig through the custom modules to find instances of where theme variables are created, there is an easier way—using the {{ dump() }} function. The dump function is available after you have enabled Twig debugging in the sites/default/services.yml file. By default, Twig debugging is set to false. Change the value to true and rebuild cache before attempting to use the dump function. Note: Using the dump() function may cause out of memory errors, so use it with caution. You may choose to use {{ dump(_context|keys) }} instead, which only shows variables that are available to your template.

If you know the name of a variable, you can use {{ dump(variable_name) }} to display the value, replacing variable_name with the actual name of the variable. If you don't know which variables are available, you can use the {{ dump() }} function, which returns all variables that are known to the template that you are working on. For example, adding the dump function to the Bartik themes node.html.twig template, saving the revised template, and rebuilding the cache results in the following output, which shows every variable that is available to the node template:

```
array(28) { [0]=> string(8) "elements" [1]=> string(19) "theme_hook_original"
 [2]=> string(10) "attributes" [3]=> string(16) "title_attributes"
 [4]=> string(18) "content_attributes" [5]=> string(12) "title_prefix"
 [6]=> string(12) "title_suffix" [7]=> string(12) "db_is_active" [8]=> string(8) "is_admin"
 [9]=> string(9) "logged_in" [10]=> string(4) "user" [11]=> string(9) "directory"
 [12]=> string(9) "view_mode" [13]=> string(6) "teaser" [14]=> string(4) "node"
 [15]=> string(4) "date" [16]=> string(11) "author_name" [17]=> string(3) "url"
 [18]=> string(5) "label" [19]=> string(4) "page" [20]=> string(7) "content" [21]=> string(17)
 "author_attributes" [22]=> string(17) "display_submitted" [23]=> string(14) "author_picture"
 [24]=> string(6) "#cache" [25]=> string(8) "metadata" [26]=> string(22) "theme_hook_suggestions"
 [27]=> string(7) "classes" }
```

Although the output is not very pretty, it does show all of the available variables, such as author_name, url, label, page, etc. Inspecting a specific variable, such as url using {{ dump(url) }} displays the following:

```
string(7) "/node/1"
```

Conditionals, Looping, Filters, and Math Functions in Twig

While the theme layer isn't the place for business logic, there are cases where you will want to "do something" with the information that is available to the template that you are working with. Twig provides the ability to do so through conditional logic (if statements), looping (foreach), and filters (e.g., transform text to uppercase).

Twig Conditionals

You can test the content of variables using if statements in Twig in the form of {% if <variable> <condition> <comparison> %}. The conditions that may be checked in Twig are as follows:

- a == b to test that the value of a and b are equal

- a != b to test that a is not equal to b

- a <> b to test that a is not equal to b

- a < b to test if a is less than b

- a > b to test that a is greater than b

- a <= b to test that a is less than or equal to b

- a >= b to test that a is greater than or equal to b

- a === b to test that the value and type of variable are the same for a and b

- a !=== b to test that a and b are not identical

Examples of each conditional are as follows:

```
// test if a is equal to b
{% if a == b %}
    {{ A equals b }}
{% endif %}

// test if a is not equal to b
{% if a != b %}
    {{ A is not equal to b }}
{% endif %}

// test if a is not equal to b
{% if a <> b %}
    {{ A is not equal to b }}
{% endif %}
```

```
// test if a is greater than b
{% if a > b %}
   {{ A is greater than b }}
{% endif %}

// test if a is less than b
{% if a < b %}
   {{ A is less than b }}
{% endif %}

// test if a is less than or equal to b
{% if a <= b %}
   {{ A is less than or equal to b }}
{% endif %}

// test if a is greater than or equal to b
{% if a >= b %}
   {{ A is greater than or equal to b }}
{% endif %}

// test if a and b are equal and the same type
{% if a === b %}
   {{ A and b are equal and the same type }}
{% endif %}

// test if a and b not equal and the same type
{% if a !== b %}
   {{ A and b are not equal and the same type }}
{% endif %}
```

Twig also supports multiple conditions in a single if statement, for example:

```
{% if a < b or b < c %}
   {{ a is less than b or b is less than c }}
{% endif %}

{% if a < b and b < c %}
   {{ a is less than b and b is less than c }}
{% endif %}
```

Twig supports if else statements, for example:

```
{% if a < b %}
   {{ a is less than b }}
{% elseif a > b %}
   {{ a is greater than b }}
{% elseif a == b %}
   {{ a equals b }}
{% endif %}
```

Twig supports testing for the existence of a value. For example, to test whether the variable user.name is set, use:

```
{% if user.name %}
  {{ user name is user.name }}
{% endif %}
```

You can also test for when a variable is not set:

```
{% if not user.name %}
  {{ user name is not set }}
{% endif %}
```

You can also do string operations such as:

```
{% if 'Hello' starts with 'F' %}
```

or

```
{% if 'Hello' ends with 'N' %}
```

or run contains comparisons such as:

```
{% if 'cd' in 'abcde' %}
{{ 'cd' is in 'abcde' }}
{% endif %}
```

or

```
{% if 1 in [1,2,3] %}
{{ 1 is in 1,2,3 }}
{% endif %}
```

Twig also provides a PHP-like switch statement that allows you to write a more legible control statement than using a long list of if-elseif statements. The form of the switch statement is as follows:

```
{% switch user.type %}
  {% case "administrator" %}
    {{ User is an administrator }}
  {% case "editor" %}
    {{ User is an editor }}
  {% case "anonymous" %}
    {{ User is anonymous }}
  {% default %}
    {{ User type is user.type }}
{% endswitch %}
```

Twig's control statements provide a powerful solution for handing conditional logic in template files. Twig also provides powerful and easy-to-use capabilities for iterating or looping through elements.

Looping in Twig

Twig provides two different mechanisms to loop or iterate over elements that are exposed in a template file. You may use for loops to perform some functionality one to many times using the following syntax:

```
{% for i in range(0,3) %}
    {{ i }}
{% endfor %}
```

In the previous example, the variable i starts with a value of zero and is incremented by 1 until it equals 3. The functionality within the for statement, in this case, will print 0 1 2 3.

Iterating over a list of variables is accomplished through another form of the for statement. In the following example, the variable items is an array of objects, where content is an attribute of the item object. This look assigns each element of the items array to a variable named item, and then the value of the content attribute is printed.

```
{% for item in items %}
    {{ item.content }}
{% endfor %}
```

Either version of the for statement may be nested to perform more complex looping and iterating scenarios.

Twig Filters

Filters are a mechanism for performing transformations and evaluations of a string or the value stored in a variable. For example, {{ 'HELLO WORLD' | lower }} would print hello world. Filters also provide the ability to evaluate certain aspects of variables, such as counting the number of elements in an array through the length filter.

```
{% if users|length < 1 %}
    {{ There are no users }}
{% endif }
```

There are several filters available in Twig, some of the most commonly used filters are as follows:

- abs: Determines the absolute value of a number {{ count|abs }}

- capitalize: Converts the first character of a string to a capital letter; for example, {{ 'hello world'|capitalize }} would print Hello world

- date: Formats a date to a given format {{ published_date|date("m/d/Y") }}. The date filter accepts any date that is supported by the PHP function strtotime, or DateTime and DateInterval instances. The date functional also works with the value of now, which is the current date and time; for example, {{ "now"|date("m/d/Y") }}.

- date_modify: Alters the date value in a variable by, for example, adding one day to the value {{ published_date|date_modify("+1 day")|date("m/d/Y") }}. You can use any of the date modifiers supported by the PHP function strtotime.

- default: Provides the ability to assign a default value to a variable if the variable is undefined or empty {{ person|default('anonymous') }}.

- escape: Provides the ability to escape a value using html, js, css, url, or html_attr contexts for safe insertion into the final output. Examples of using HTML and js are {{ content|e('html') }} or {{ content|e('js') }}.

- first: Returns the first element of an array or a string. For example, {{ 'ABCD'|first }} returns A. For arrays, {{ [A,B,C,D]|first }} would also return A.

- format: This filter applies string transformations using the printf notation. For example, {{ "The user %s is from %s."|format(user.name, user.location) }} would output The user John is from New York.

- join: Concatenates values from items in a sequence. For example {{[A,B,C,D]|join }} would return ABCD. You may also insert values between items being joined, for example {{ [A,B,C,D]|join('|') }} would return A|B|C|D.

- keys: Returns the keys of an array. For example

```
{% for key in array|keys %}
   {{ key }}
{% endfor % }
```

would iterate over the keys of an array and print them.

- last: Similar to the first filter, last returns the last element in an array or the last character in a string {{ '1234'|last}}.

- length: Returns the number of items in an array or the length of a string, for example {% 'ABCD'|length %} would return 4.

- lower: Transforms a string to all lowercase. For example {{ 'HELLO WORLD'|lower }} would print hello world.

- merge: Merges two arrays into a single array. For example

```
{% set berries = ['strawberry', 'blackberry', 'raspberry'] %}
{%  set fruit = ['apple', 'orange', 'grapes'] %}
{% set salad = berries|merge(fruit) %}
```

would result in a new array named salad with the combination of berries and fruit.

- number_format: Transforms a number into a given format using the the same functionality as PHP's number_format function. For example {{ 1234.567| number_format(2, '.', ',')}} would return 1,234.56.

- replace: Formats a given string by replacing the placeholders with values that are specified in the replacement pattern. For example, {{ "All cows are %color%."|replace({'%color%': brown}) }} would result in All cows are brown.

- round: Rounds a number. For example, {{ 3.145|round }} would output 3. You may also specify floor or ceiling to force the rounding to always round down or up. For example, {{ 3.145|round(1,'floor') }} would output 3.1.

- slice: Extracts a piece of an array or a string given a start position and the number and the length of the slice to return. For example, {{ 'ABCD'|slice(2,2) }} would output BC.

- sort: Sorts an array using PHP's asort function. For example:

```
{% for user in users | sort %}
   {{ user.name }}
{% endfor %}
```

would sort the user's array in ascending order.

- split: Splits a string by a given delimiter and returns a list of strings. For example:

```
{% set colors = "red, green, blue"|split(',') %}
```

would result in colors as an array set to ['red', 'green', 'blue']. You can also set the limit on how may elements to parse, with the remaining elements set to the last element of the array. For example:

```
{% set addresses = "123, 456, 789, 0"|split(',',2) %}
```

would result in an array of Array[0] = ['123'], Array[1]=['456,789,0'].

- striptags: Removes all SGML and XML tags from a string {{ content|striptags }}.

- trim: Removes whitespace from the start and end of a string {{ content|trim }}.

- upper: Transforms all of the letters in a string to uppercase {{ content|upper }}.

- url_encode: Translates a string as a URL segment or a query string. For example, {{ "hello world"|url_encode }} would result in "hello%20world".

Twig Tests

Similar to if statements, Twig provides a number of functions that examine various attributes of a variable, array, or string:

- constant: Checks to see if a variable has the same value as a constant. For example, {% if article.status is constant('Article::PUBLISHED') %}.

- defined: Tests to see if the variable is defined in the current context. For example, {% if user is defined %}.

- divisible: Checks to see if a variable is divisible by a number. For example, {% if company.members is divisible by (2) %}.

- empty: Tests to see if a variable is empty. For example, {% if order.number is empty %}.

- even: Checks to see if a number is even. For example, {% count is even %}.

- iterable: Tests to see if a variable is an array or a transversable object. For example, {% if orders is iterable %}.

- null: Tests to see if a variable is null. For example, {{ user is null }}.

- odd: Tests to see if a number is odd. For example, {{ count is odd }}z.

- sameas: Checks to see if two variables are the same value and type.

Twig Math Functions

You can perform mathematical calculations on Twig variables using the same operators that are available in PHP. Examples include:

- Addition {{ 1+1 }}

- Subtraction {{ 4-2 }}

- Division {{ 8/2 }}

- Remainder {{ 11 % 5 }}

- Multiplication {{ 5 * 5 }}

- Exponentials {{ 2 ** 3 }} (2 to the power of 3)

There are other Twig features and functions that you can find at `twig.sensiolabs.org/documentation`.

Twig Template Files

Twig template files define the HTML markup, content, and CSS selectors that are used to render a field, taxonomy term, block, node, page, or the overall HTML of the site. Twig plays a key role in templates as it is the mechanism for rendering content, whether that content is defined as static text in the template or is generated by a module in Drupal, when the page is loaded.

Drupal 8 provides the ability to define templates for nearly every element that is rendered on a page, including the page itself. The structure of the templates is similar, the primary differences being the scope of the elements being rendered by the template. The specific elements that can be controlled through a template file are as follows:

- Fields, where each individual field rendered on a page may be customized using a field specific Twig template. Not all fields require specialized handling, and in this case, Drupal 8 provides a generic field template that your theme will use to render fields. We cover the naming convention of Twig templates and how the naming convention binds the template to a specific field.

- Taxonomy terms, where each individual taxonomy term may be customized using a taxonomy term specific Twig template. Like the field template, there is a generic taxonomy term template that Drupal will use if your theme does not provide one.

- Nodes, where a node, such as an article, may be customized to represent the layout and structure of your specific use cases through a node-specific Twig template. As with all Twig templates, a node template can be as specific as an individual node ID, across all nodes of a specific type (e.g., Article), or all nodes in general regardless of type or ID. As with other Twig templates, Drupal provides a generic template that will be used if your theme does not provide one.

- Blocks, where each block may be customized using a Twig template. Block templates, like other Twig templates, may be a specific as a single block, or generalized across all block on your site. As with other templates, Drupal provides a generic block template as part of Drupal 8 core.

- Regions. Regions are physical areas on the page where content may be placed. Regions, like other elements, may be customized through a Twig template, include the ability to develop a template for a specific region, or generally across all regions. Like other elements, Drupal 8 provides a generic region template that will be used if your theme does not provide one.

- Pages. The structure of a page may be customized through a page level Twig template. As with other elements, a specific page may be controlled through a page-specific template, or through a generic page template that applies to all pages on your site. Think of page as everything that falls in the <body> tag on a typical HTML page. Drupal core provides a generic page template that will be used when one that is applicable to the page being rendered is not found in your theme.

- HTML. This is the generalized template that provides the markup associated with HTML page level elements such as <head> and <title>.

There are specific naming conventions for template files in order to be identified by Drupal 8. Template files that do not follow the naming convention are ignored. The naming conventions for each type of template file are as follows:

- html.html.twig: The primary overarching template file that contains typical elements that would appear in the <html> and <head> section of a HTML page. For example, all of the CSS and JavaScript files that are loaded on a page that are global in nature.

- page.html.twig: The template file associated with the overall page. Think of this as the template that controls everything within the <body> tags on a typical HTML page. Page template files may be generic, such as page.html.twig, or specific to nodes (page--node.html.twig), a specific node (page--node--1.html.twig), or an action performed on a node (page--node--edit.html.twig).

- region--[region].html.twig: The naming convention for templates that are specific to a given region. In the case of the Davinci theme, candidates for region templates include region--messages.html.twig, region--header_first.html.twig, and region--content.html.twig.

- block.html.twig: The template file associated with all blocks on your site. You may create block specific templates through the naming convention of block--module–delta.html.twig, where module is the name of the module that is generating the block and delta represents the specific block that is being rendered. (For example, block--test--news.html.twig would control how the output generated by the block delta named news is generated in the module named test.) You may also provide Twig template files for blocks generated by views. As an example, a view named featured_blogs with a display ID of block_1 would use the following name for the template file: block--views--block--featured-blogs-block-1.html.twig. Note the replacement of underscores with single dashes in the name of the template file.

- node.html.twig: The generic template that is applied to all nodes rendered on the site. There are several variants of the node template, including:

  - node--viewmode.html.twig. Simply replace viewmode with the appropriate value, such as node--default.html.twig or node--teaser.html.twig.

  - node--type.html.twig. Replace type with the content type that is being controlled by this template, such as node--article.html.twig.

  - node--type--viewmode.html.twig. Combining the previous two examples, the result would be node--article--teaser.html.twig or node--article--default.html.twig.

- `node--nodeid.html.twig`: Refers to a specific node as defined through its `nodeid`, such as `node--1.html.twig`.

- `node--nodeid--viewmode.html.twig`: As in previous examples, `node--1--teaser.html.twig` would refer to the node with an ID of 1 being rendered as a teaser would be controlled through this Twig template file.

- `taxonomy-term.html.twig`: Controls how all taxonomy terms on a site are displayed. More specific control is available through:

  - `taxonomy-term--vocabulary-machine-name.html.twig`, which controls the output of all terms in a specific taxonomy vocabulary.

  - `taxonomy-term--tid.html.twig`, which controls the output of a specific taxonomy term based on its `tid`.

- `field.html.twig`: Controls the output of all fields rendered on a site. To add specificity, you may use one of the following patterns:

  - `field--field-type.html.twig`, replacing `field-type` with, for example, `field--text-with-summary.html.twig`.

  - `field--field-name.html.twig`, replacing `field-name` with the name of the field, for example, `field--title.html.twig`.

  - `field--content-type.html.twig` would control all fields rendered on a content type, for example `field--article.html.twig`.

  - `field--field-name--content-type.html.twig` controls a specific field on a specific content type, for example `field--title--article.html.twig`.

There are other less widely used Twig templates, for example comments, comment wrappers, forums, and search results. Those naming conventions are as follows:

- `comment--node-[type].html.twig` controls how comments are rendered for a specific content type. For example, `comment--node-article.html.twig` would control how comments posted on all articles would be displayed.

- `comment-wrapper--node[type].html.twig` controls the format of the wrapper template for comments. For example, `comment-wrapper--article.html.twig`.

- `forums--[[container|topic]--forumID].html.twig` controls the output of forum containers and topics. Specific templates include:

  - `forums.html.twig` for the highest level and most generic theming across all forums on your site.

  - `forums--containers.html.twig` formats the containers defined in your forums on your site.

  - `forums--forumID.html.twig` formats a specific forum on your site.

  - `forums--containers--forumID.html.twig` formats a specific container on a specific forum on your site.

  - `forums--topics.html.twig` formats all topics across all forums on your site.

  - `forums--topics--forumID.html.twig` formats all topics for a specific formum on your site.

- `search-result.html.twig`: Formats the output of search results on your site. You may add more specific templates in the form of `search-result--node.html.twig` for node-based search results or `search-result--user.html.twig` for user-based search results.

With the list of possible template files defined in this list and a knowledge of Twig syntax, it's time to start examining the inner workings of templates.

Standard Twig Templates

Drupal 8 core comes with standard template files for all of the elements that can be rendered on a site using Drupal 8 core capabilities. This ensures that even if your theme doesn't provide a template file, Drupal knows how to render standard elements such a fields, blocks, nodes, breadcrumbs, forms, links, tables, pages, and other elements. You can find the standard templates in the `/core/modules/system/templates` directory. Take a few moments to navigate to the templates directory to see what is available. The standard templates are shown in Listing 5-2 for reference.

Listing 5-2. Drupal 8 Templates

```
├── admin-block-content.html.twig
├── admin-block.html.twig
├── admin-page.html.twig
├── authorize-report.html.twig
├── block--local-actions-block.html.twig
├── block--system-branding-block.html.twig
├── block--system-menu-block.html.twig
├── block--system-messages-block.html.twig
├── breadcrumb.html.twig
├── checkboxes.html.twig
├── confirm-form.html.twig
├── container.html.twig
├── datetime-form.html.twig
├── datetime-wrapper.html.twig
├── details.html.twig
├── dropbutton-wrapper.html.twig
├── entity-add-list.html.twig
├── feed-icon.html.twig
├── field-multiple-value-form.html.twig
├── field.html.twig
├── fieldset.html.twig
├── form-element-label.html.twig
├── form-element.html.twig
├── form.html.twig
├── html.html.twig
├── image.html.twig
├── indentation.html.twig
├── input.html.twig
├── install-page.html.twig
├── item-list.html.twig
├── links.html.twig
├── maintenance-page.html.twig
```

```
├── maintenance-task-list.html.twig
├── mark.html.twig
├── menu-local-action.html.twig
├── menu-local-task.html.twig
├── menu-local-tasks.html.twig
├── menu.html.twig
├── page-title.html.twig
├── page.html.twig
├── pager.html.twig
├── progress-bar.html.twig
├── radios.html.twig
├── region.html.twig
├── select.html.twig
├── status-messages.html.twig
├── status-report.html.twig
├── system-admin-index.html.twig
├── system-config-form.html.twig
├── system-modules-details.html.twig
├── system-modules-uninstall.html.twig
├── system-themes-page.html.twig
├── table.html.twig
├── tablesort-indicator.html.twig
├── textarea.html.twig
├── time.html.twig
└── vertical-tabs.html.twig
```

If you want to override the output of an element and you are creating a custom theme, you can copy the template file from /core/modules/system/templates to your themes template directory and modify the structure of the template file to meet your needs.

Modifying the page.html.twig Template File

One of the most common modifications to template files is to override the page.html.twig template file to meet a specific set of requirements and to render the regions defined in a theme. If we revisit the Davinci theme, we created a number of regions that currently aren't rendering on a page when we view, for example, the homepage of the Drupal 8 site. The reason they aren't rendering is that the page.html.twig file that Drupal 8 core provides in /core/modules/system/templates doesn't know that these regions exist. Let's fix that situation by copying the page.html.twig file from core and placing that copy in the Davinci theme's templates directory. Once it's been copied, open the page.html.twig file in your favorite editor to examine the contents of the file.

At the top of the file you will notice a large docblock that describes the variables that are available to the page.html.twig file, as defined by core. There are general informational variables, such as base_path, is_front and front_page, as well as content specific variables such as node. The default docblock also lists the regions that are available in Drupal 8 core.

```
{#
/**
 * @file
 * Default theme implementation to display a single page.
 *
```

```
 * The doctype, html, head and body tags are not in this template. Instead they
 * can be found in the html.html.twig template in this directory.
 *
 * Available variables:
 *
 * General utility variables:
 * - base_path: The base URL path of the Drupal installation. Will usually be
 *   "/" unless you have installed Drupal in a sub-directory.
 * - is_front: A flag indicating if the current page is the front page.
 * - logged_in: A flag indicating if the user is registered and signed in.
 * - is_admin: A flag indicating if the user has permission to access
 *   administration pages.
 *
 * Site identity:
 * - front_page: The URL of the front page. Use this instead of base_path when
 *   linking to the front page. This includes the language domain or prefix.
 *
 * Page content (in order of occurrence in the default page.html.twig):
 * - messages: Status and error messages. Should be displayed prominently.
 * - node: Fully loaded node, if there is an automatically-loaded node
 *   associated with the page and the node ID is the second argument in the
 *   page's path (e.g. node/12345 and node/12345/revisions, but not
 *   comment/reply/12345).
 *
 * Regions:
 * - page.header: Items for the header region.
 * - page.primary_menu: Items for the primary menu region.
 * - page.secondary_menu: Items for the secondary menu region.
 * - page.highlighted: Items for the highlighted content region.
 * - page.help: Dynamic help text, mostly for admin pages.
 * - page.content: The main content of the current page.
 * - page.sidebar_first: Items for the first sidebar.
 * - page.sidebar_second: Items for the second sidebar.
 * - page.footer: Items for the footer region.
 * - page.breadcrumb: Items for the breadcrumb region.
 *
 * @see template_preprocess_page()
 * @see html.html.twig
 *
 * @ingroup themeable
 */
#}
```

The first step in updating the page.html.twig file is to revise the list of regions that are available on the page to match the list of regions that were defined in the davinci.info.yml file. For reference, those regions are as follows:

```
regions:
  messages: 'Messages'
  header_first: 'Header first'
  header_second: 'Header second'
```

```
header_third: 'Header third'
navbar: 'Nav bar'
help: 'help'
features_first: 'Features first'
features_second: 'Features second'
features_third: 'Features third'
features_fourth: 'Features fourth'
highlighted: 'Highlighted'
content: 'Main content'
sidebar_first: 'Sidebar first'
sidebar_second: 'Sidebar second'
tertiary_first: 'Tertiary first'
tertiary_second: 'Tertiary second'
tertiary_third: 'Tertiary third'
tertiary_fourth: 'Tertiary fourth'
footer: 'Footer'
page_top: 'Page top'
page_bottom: 'Page bottom'
```

Using an editor, we update the docblock to reflect the revised list of regions, as shown here:

```
* Regions:
 * - page.message: The messages area.
 * - page.header_first: First header region.
 * - page.header_second: Second header region.
 * - page.header_third: Third header region.
 * - page.help: Help region
 * - page.features_first: First featured region.
 * - page.features_second: Second featured region.
 * - page.features_third: Third featured region.
 * - page.features_fourth: Fourth featured region.
 * - page.highlighted: Highlighted region.
 * - page.content: The main content of the current page.
 * - page.sidebar_first: Items for the first sidebar.
 * - page.sidebar_second: Items for the second sidebar.
 * - page.tertiary_first: First tertiary region.
 * - page.tertiary_second: Second tertiary region.
 * - page.tertiary_third: Third tertiary region.
 * - page.tertiary_fourth: Fourth tertiary region.
 * - page.footer: Items for the footer region.
```

Updating the docblock doesn't change the functionality of the template; it only provides reference to developers who may use this template in the future.

The next step is to update the template to render each of the regions that are currently not part of the existing page.html.twig template file. If you examine the markup and Twig elements of template file, you'll see HTML markup and Twig elements as described in the previous sections—for example, {{ page.header }}, which outputs everything assigned to the header region on the Admin ➤ Structure ➤ Block Layout page.

```
<div class="layout-container">

  <header role="banner">
    {{ page.header }}
  </header>

  {{ page.primary_menu }}
  {{ page.secondary_menu }}

  {{ page.breadcrumb }}

  {{ page.highlighted }}

  {{ page.help }}

  <main role="main">
    <a id="main-content" tabindex="-1"></a>{# link is in html.html.twig #}

    <div class="layout-content">
      {{ page.content }}
    </div>{# /.layout-content #}

    {% if page.sidebar_first %}
      <aside class="layout-sidebar-first" role="complementary">
        {{ page.sidebar_first }}
      </aside>
    {% endif %}

    {% if page.sidebar_second %}
      <aside class="layout-sidebar-second" role="complementary">
        {{ page.sidebar_second }}
      </aside>
    {% endif %}

  </main>

  {% if page.footer %}
    <footer role="contentinfo">
      {{ page.footer }}
    </footer>
  {% endif %}

</div>{# /.layout-container #}
```

We changed the names of some of the regions and added new regions that did not exist in the original template. To enable those regions so that they display, we need to edit the template and rename the regions we changed, and add the regions that do not exist in the off-the-shelf version of page.html.twig. This section assumes that you know HTML markup and CSS syntax and focuses on the Twig elements that need to be added to this page to fully render all of the regions.

After revising the template, the contents of the file are now set properly to render all of the regions that we defined in the davinci.html.yml file. As shown here, we added all of the regions by adding a {{ page. region_name }} Twig element, replacing region_name with the name of the regions as defined in the davinci.html.twig file. Note that the name used to replace region_name is the value for the region to the left of the : and not the description that appears to the right. For example, {{ page.header_third }} is the Twig representation of header_third: 'Header third' from the davinci.html.yml file. The updated template file, excluding the docblock, is as follows:

```
<div class="layout-container">

  <header role="banner">
    <div class="header_first">
      {{ page.header_first }}
    </div>
    <div class="header_second">
      {{ page.header_second }}
    </div>
    <div class="header_third">
      {{ page.header_third }}
    </div>
  </header>

  <div class="navbar">
    {{ page.navbar }}
  </div>

  {{ page.breadcrumb }}

  {{ page.help }}

  <div class="features">
    <div class="features_first">
      {{ page.features_first }}
    </div>
    <div class="features_second">
      {{ page.features_second }}
    </div>
    <div class="features_third">
      {{ page.features_third }}
    </div>
  </div>

  {{ page.highlighted }}

  <main role="main">
    <a id="main-content" tabindex="-1"></a>{# link is in html.html.twig #}

    <div class="layout-content">
      {{ page.content }}
    </div>{# /.layout-content #}
```

```
{% if page.sidebar_first %}
  <aside class="layout-sidebar-first" role="complementary">
    {{ page.sidebar_first }}
  </aside>
{% endif %}
{% if page.sidebar_second %}
  <aside class="layout-sidebar-second" role="complementary">
    {{ page.sidebar_second }}
  </aside>
{% endif %}

</main>

<div class="tertiary">
  {% if page.tertiary_first %}
    <div class="tertiary_first">
      {{ page.tertiary_first }}
    </div>
  {% endif %}
  {% if page.tertiary_second %}
    <div class="tertiary_second">
      {{ page.tertiary_second }}
    </div>
  {% endif %}
  {% if page.tertiary_third %}
    <div class="tertiary_third">
      {{ page.tertiary_third }}
    </div>
  {% endif %}
</div>

{% if page.footer %}
  <footer role="contentinfo">
    {{ page.footer }}
  </footer>
{% endif %}

</div>{# /.layout-container #}
```

After examining the template file, you'll see that the primary changes were the addition of a few CSS classes, a few additional conditionals check to see if a region has a value before rendering it on the page, and the Twig statements to render the additional regions. After saving the template and rebuilding cache, we add a sample block to each of the regions on the theme and test to see if all the regions appear on the homepage (see Figure 5-5).

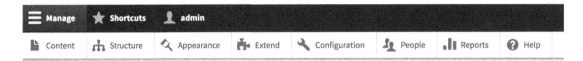

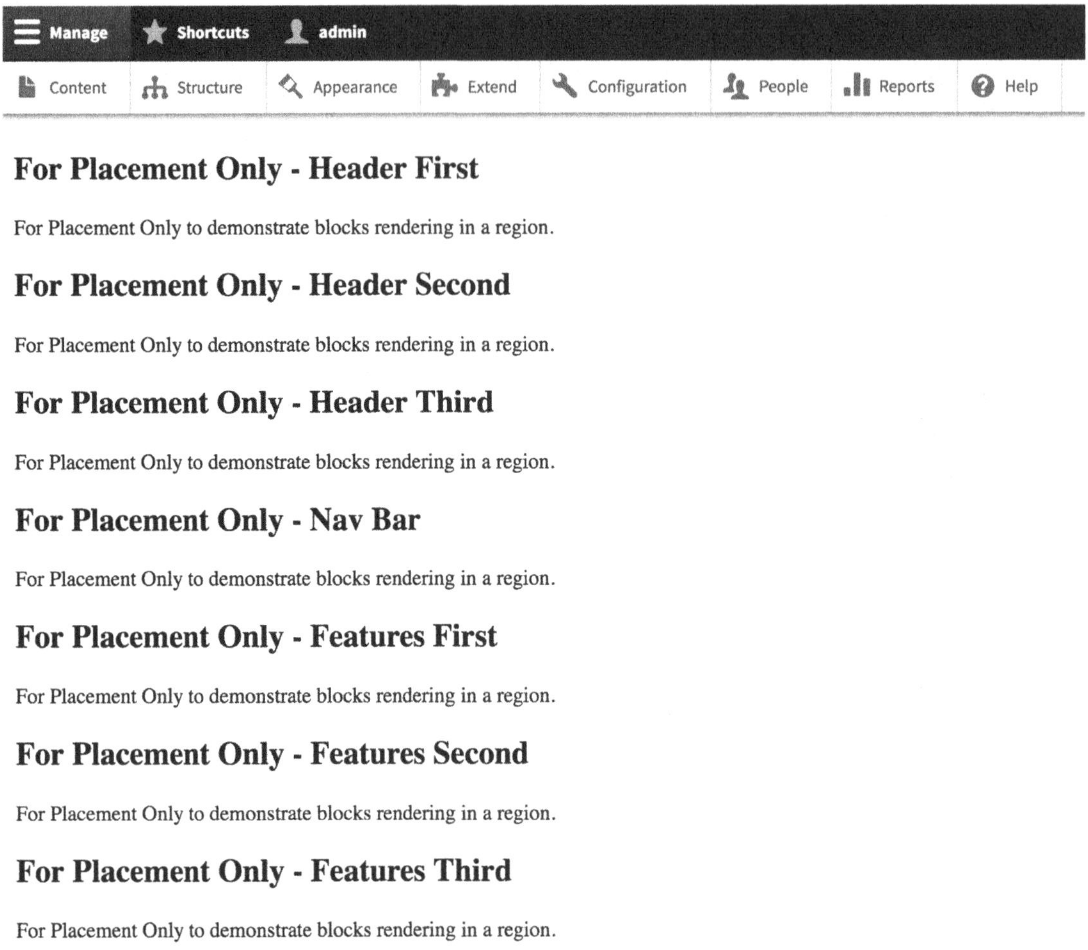

Manage
Shortcuts
admin
Content
Structure
Appearance
Extend
Configuration
People
Reports
Help
For Placement Only - Header First
For Placement Only to demonstrate blocks rendering in a region.
For Placement Only - Header Second
For Placement Only to demonstrate blocks rendering in a region.
For Placement Only - Header Third
For Placement Only to demonstrate blocks rendering in a region.
For Placement Only - Nav Bar
For Placement Only to demonstrate blocks rendering in a region.
For Placement Only - Features First
For Placement Only to demonstrate blocks rendering in a region.
For Placement Only - Features Second
For Placement Only to demonstrate blocks rendering in a region.
For Placement Only - Features Third
For Placement Only to demonstrate blocks rendering in a region.

***Figure 5-5.** A partial listing of the new regions on the homepage*

While they are stacked on top of each other due to the fact that we haven't applied any CSS formatting to the regions, the updates to the `page.html.twig` template demonstrate that the new regions are rendering content on the homepage. The next step is to apply CSS to classes that we added to format the page as desired. We'll cover adding CSS in a moment, but next let's look at two of the other common templates that most developers want to modify on their sites—the node and block templates.

Modifying the node.html.twig Template

Following the same approach as for the page template, copy the default `node.html.twig` template from `core/modules/node/templates/node.html.twig` to my `themes/custom/davinci/templates` directory. Note that the node template is found in the `core/modules/node` directory and not the `core/modules/system` directory, as the node module is the one responsible for theming nodes.

After copying the template file, examine the docblock and look at the variables that are available for you to use in your `node.html.twig` template file. Most of the variables are self-explanatory. For example, `url` provides the value of the URL used to access the node being displayed. But there are others that are not quite so obvious, such as `content` and `attributes`.

Displaying and Hiding Content Fields

Content is the object that contains all of a node's fields that are to be rendered given a specific display mode (e.g., teaser or default). Using `{{ content }}` renders every field that is associated with the current display mode. You may encounter scenarios where you need to render specific fields, not every field associated with content. To render specific fields, use `{{ content.field_name }}` and replace `field_name` with the appropriate field. For example, `{{ content.body }}`. To find the list of fields that are available, visit the Structure ➤ Content Types and click the Manage Display link in the Operations column for the content type that you are working with. Select the display mode that you are working with to view the list of fields. Alternatively, assuming you have debugging turned on and the Devel module and Devel Kint enabled (drupal.org/project/devel), you may use `{{ kint(content) }}` in your template file to print a list of all the fields associated with the content object, as shown in Figure 5-6.

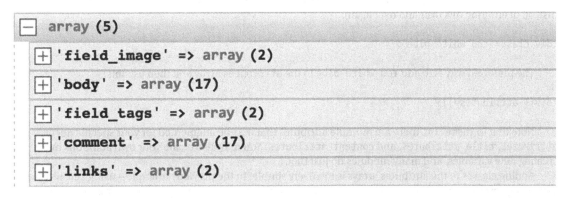

Figure 5-6. *The Content object displayed by kint*

You may also exclude fields from being displayed using for example `{{ content|without ('comment') }}`. This would render content without the comment field. You may also exclude multiple fields using `{{ content|without('comment', 'field_tags') }}`. This becomes useful when you need to display certain fields from the content object wrapped in specific CSS; for example, you want comments to appear in a column to the right of the body and not below the body. You could accomplish this by using the following:

```
<div class='body-only'>
  {{ content|without('comment') }}
</div>
<div class='comments-only'>
  {{ content.comment}}
</div>
```

Using Attributes

Drupal 8 provides a standard means for generating CSS classes for divs using an attribute array. The base attribute array is created in /core/includes/theme.inc in a template preprocess function (more on preprocess functions later in this chapter):

```
$variables = array(
    'attributes' => array(),
    'title_attributes' => array(),
    'content_attributes' => array(),
    'title_prefix' => array(),
    'title_suffix' => array(),
    'db_is_active' => !defined('MAINTENANCE_MODE'),
    'is_admin' => FALSE,
    'logged_in' => FALSE,
);
```

The attributes array is a common placeholder for all CSS class definitions that may be applied to a div in your template. For example, you may have a common set of classes that you want to apply to several divs. Instead of entering this over and over again:

```
<div class='red white blue'>
```

The preferred way is to add red white blue to the attributes array and then use this:

```
<div{{ attributes }}>
```

Note that in theme.inc there are multiple attributes that may be augmented for your specific needs, attributes, title_attributes, and content_attributes. You may also create your own additions by creating new variables, and many modules do just that.

Adding classes to the attributes arrays is relatively simple. In the previous example—using red white blue as representative CSS classes that we want to add to several divs—we would use the following:

```
<div{{ attributes.addClass('red white blue') }}>
```

From that point forward, any time that we use <div{{ attributes }}>, we will automatically get red white blue added as classes to the divs. You may also remove classes from the attributes array using attributes.removeClass('blue'), replacing blue with the class that you want to remove. Removing a class removes it permanently from the attributes array, meaning it will no longer be applied in future uses of {{ attributes }}.

You may also add attributes—for example, you can create an attribute named id and assign a value to it using attributes.setAttribue(attribute, value).

As mentioned previously, attributes isn't the only array available for assigning classes. You may use the off-the-shelf title_attributes array to add CSS classes to titles and then render titles using, for example, <h1{{ title_attributes }}>. You may also use content_attributes, title_prefix, title_suffix, or any other attributes that you define using preprocess functions.

Modifying the block.html.twig Template

The block module provides a base template that will be used by default if your theme does not provide a specific block.html.twig template. To override the block template, copy block.html.twig from /core/ modules/block/templates to your themes templates directory and examine the contents of that template file. As with other core templates, the docblock describes the variables that are presented by the block module for use in your template file.

```
/**
 * @file
 * Default theme implementation to display a block.
 *
 * Available variables:
 * - plugin_id: The ID of the block implementation.
 * - label: The configured label of the block if visible.
 * - configuration: A list of the block's configuration values.
 *   - label: The configured label for the block.
 *   - label_display: The display settings for the label.
 *   - provider: The module or other provider that provided this block plugin.
 *   - Block plugin specific settings will also be stored here.
 * - content: The content of this block.
 * - attributes: array of HTML attributes populated by modules, intended to
 *   be added to the main container tag of this template.
 *   - id: A valid HTML ID and guaranteed unique.
 * - title_attributes: Same as attributes, except applied to the main title
 *   tag that appears in the template.
 * - title_prefix: Additional output populated by modules, intended to be
 *   displayed in front of the main title tag that appears in the template.
 * - title_suffix: Additional output populated by modules, intended to be
 *   displayed after the main title tag that appears in the template.
 *
 * @see template_preprocess_block()
 *
 * @ingroup themeable
 */
```

Significantly simpler than the node template, the block template really only has two variables that are rendered—the title (which is called label) and the body of the block, which is called content.

```
<div{{ attributes }}>
  {{ title_prefix }}
  {% if label %}
    <h2{{ title_attributes }}>{{ label }}</h2>
  {% endif %}
  {{ title_suffix }}
  {% block content %}
    {{ content }}
  {% endblock %}
</div>
```

As you examine this code, you'll see the patterns that we discussed previously in this chapter. The template renders the values in the attributes array, if there are any, as CSS classes in the opening div. It renders the value stored in `title_prefix` and then checks to see if the label has a value. If it does, it renders the label as an H2 using the CSS classes defined in the `title_attributes` array. It then renders the values of `title_suffix` and then renders the content associated with the block.

■ **Note** The statement {% block content %} and its paired {% endblock %} should not be confused with the Drupal Block module. The block in this case specifies a code block and has nothing to do with the Block module. It is just an unfortunate collision of common terms.

While there isn't much to the block template, there may be scenarios where you have added custom fields to a block and you need to render those fields in a specific div, or there may be other unique scenarios where you need to override the default behavior of the core block.html.twig template. Follow the patterns and principles described elsewhere in this chapter. You are on your way to customizing block output.

Modifying the field.html.twig Template

The last template file that we examine is the field template. In most cases you won't override the generic field template but rather you will create a template file for a specific field. As mentioned earlier in this chapter, template files may be created for specific pages, nodes, blocks, and fields by simply following the naming patters associated with that template file to apply a specific template file to a specific element.

In the case of the field templates, the naming conventions are as follows:

- `field--field-type.html.twig`, replacing `field-type` with, for example, `field--text-with-summary.html.twig`.

- `field--field-name.html.twig`, replacing `field-name` with the name of the field, for example, `field--title.html.twig`.

- `field--content-type.html.twig` controls all fields rendered on a content type, for example, `field--article.html.twig`.

- `field--field-name--content-type.html.twig` controls a specific field on a specific content type, for example `field--title--article.html.twig`.

To demonstrate the capabilities of targeting a specific field, we'll create a template for the body field that will wrap the body with additional classes regardless of where it is rendered on the site. To do so, we copy the default template from `core/modules/system/templates/field.html.twig` to the Davinci templates directory and name it `field--body.html.twig`.

The docblock at the top of the template file lists all of the variables that are available for use in this template:

```
* Available variables:
* - attributes: HTML attributes for the containing element.
* - label_hidden: Whether to show the field label or not.
* - title_attributes: HTML attributes for the title.
* - label: The label for the field.
* - multiple: TRUE if a field can contain multiple items.
```

```
 * - items: List of all the field items. Each item contains:
 *    - attributes: List of HTML attributes for each item.
 *    - content: The field item's content.
 * - entity_type: The entity type to which the field belongs.
 * - field_name: The name of the field.
 * - field_type: The type of the field.
 * - label_display: The display settings for the label.
```

The standard template renders those fields using the following structure:

```
{% if label_hidden %}
  {% if multiple %}
    <div{{ attributes }}>
      {% for item in items %}
        <div{{ item.attributes }}>{{ item.content }}</div>
      {% endfor %}
    </div>
  {% else %}
    {% for item in items %}
      <div{{ attributes }}>{{ item.content }}</div>
    {% endfor %}
  {% endif %}
{% else %}
  <div{{ attributes }}>
    <div{{ title_attributes }}>{{ label }}</div>
    {% if multiple %}
      <div>
    {% endif %}
    {% for item in items %}
      <div{{ item.attributes }}>{{ item.content }}</div>
    {% endfor %}
    {% if multiple %}
      </div>
    {% endif %}
  </div>
{% endif %}
```

Using the knowledge of Twig gained throughout this chapter, you can see that the template renders one-to-many instances of a field, displaying the contents of the field and the label associated with that field. Since Drupal provides the ability to create one-to-many instances of field content for a given node, the template addresses this scenario through the for items in items loops, displaying each instance of the field.

For demonstration purposes, we are going to update the body template to do one thing, display the entity_type and field_type. While likely not a high value change to the template, it does demonstrate the ability to override a specific field. Since we can never be certain whether a content type may be set up to accept more than one instance of the body field, we update the template in multiple places just to ensure that we catch every scenario. After the updates, the template appears as shown here. Note that we've added {{ entity_type }} and {{ field_type }} to the template file in multiple places.

```
{% if label_hidden %}
  {% if multiple %}
    <div{{ attributes }}>
      {% for item in items %}
        <div{{ item.attributes }}>{{ item.content }}</div>
      {% endfor %}
    </div>
  {% else %}
    {% for item in items %}
      <div{{ attributes }}>{{ item.content }}</div>
        <div>
          Entity type: {{ entity_type }}
        </div>
        <div>
          Field type: {{ field_type }}
        </div>
    {% endfor %}
  {% endif %}
{% else %}
  <div{{ attributes }}>
    <div{{ title_attributes }}>{{ label }}</div>
    {% if multiple %}
      <div>
    {% endif %}
    {% for item in items %}
      <div{{ item.attributes }}>{{ item.content }}</div>
    {% endfor %}
    {% if multiple %}
      </div>
    {% endif %}
    <div>
      Entity type: {{ entity_type }}
    </div>
    <div>
      Field type: {{ field_type }}
    </div>
  </div>
{% endif %}
```

After saving the template and rebuilding the cache, the resulting output is as shown in Figure 5-7.

Hello Drupal 8 World!

- View
- Edit
- Delete
- Devel

Submitted by admin on Sat, 09/17/2016 - 20:35

Hello World, this is Drupal 8!

Entity type: node
Field type: text_with_summary

Figure 5-7. *The addition of the entity_type and field_type output to the field template*

There are virtually limitless things you can do with template files. The limitations are a) can it be done with Twig and b) does the module that generates the output provide access to those values through a variable that is accessible to Twig? These issues are the topic of the next section.

Exposing Variables to Twig

For most modules, one of the primary objectives is to generate output that can be rendered on a page through a Twig template. Facilitating that process requires a few simple steps, including the ability to define what template files your module uses to render that content. To demonstrate how the connection between a module and a Twig template works, we'll use Drupal 8's Forum module as the example.

Navigate to /core/modules/forum and open the forum.module file with your favorite editor. Search for hook_theme and you'll find the following function.

```
/**
 * Implements hook_theme().
 */
function forum_theme() {
  return array(
    'forums' => array(
      'variables' => array('forums' => array(), 'topics' => array(), 'topics_pager' =>
      array(), 'parents' => NULL, 'term' => NULL, 'sortby' => NULL, 'forum_per_page' =>
      NULL, 'header' => array()),
    ),
    'forum_list' => array(
      'variables' => array('forums' => NULL, 'parents' => NULL, 'tid' => NULL),
    ),
```

```
      'forum_icon' => array(
        'variables' => array('new_posts' => NULL, 'num_posts' => 0, 'comment_mode' => 0,
        'sticky' => 0, 'first_new' => FALSE),
      ),
      'forum_submitted' => array(
        'variables' => array('topic' => NULL),
      ),
    );
}
```

The forum_theme function returns an array of various elements. We focus on the first element of the array named forums. You can see that the forums array includes another array named variables, and within that array you will find additional arrays named forums, topics, topics_pager, parents, term, sortby, forum_per_page, and header. Each of those variables is registered with the Twig theme engine and is available to the template files that are used by the Forum module.

Those variable, now registered with the theme engine, are ready to receive values through a preprocess function. In the case of the Forum module, that preprocess function is named template_preprocess_forums. In this function, the output generated by the module is assigned to the variables that were defined in the forum_theme function. Once they are populated, they are ready to render through a template file.

Search the forum.module for template_process_forums and you'll find the function that is listed here. The first section is the docblock that specifies which template file is used to render a forum and the variables that are populated and exposed to the template file. Again, those variables were originally defined and registered in the forum_theme function. While somewhat complex, the function demonstrates one simple concept—place values into the various variables that are registered by forum_theme and exposed to the template.

```
/**
 * Prepares variables for forums templates.
 *
 * Default template: forums.html.twig.
 *
 * @param array $variables
 *   An array containing the following elements:
 *   - forums: An array of all forum objects to display for the given taxonomy
 *     term ID. If tid = 0 then all the top-level forums are displayed.
 *   - topics: An array of all the topics in the current forum.
 *   - parents: An array of taxonomy term objects that are ancestors of the
 *     current term ID.
 *   - term: Taxonomy term of the current forum.
 *   - sortby: One of the following integers indicating the sort criteria:
 *     - 1: Date - newest first.
 *     - 2: Date - oldest first.
 *     - 3: Posts with the most comments first.
 *     - 4: Posts with the least comments first.
 *   - forum_per_page: The maximum number of topics to display per page.
 */
function template_preprocess_forums(&$variables) {
  $variables['tid'] = $variables['term']->id();
  if ($variables['forums_defined'] = count($variables['forums']) ||
  count($variables['parents'])) {
```

```
if (!empty($variables['forums'])) {
  $variables['forums'] = array(
    '#theme' => 'forum_list',
    '#forums' => $variables['forums'],
    '#parents' => $variables['parents'],
    '#tid' => $variables['tid'],
  );
}

if ($variables['term'] && empty($variables['term']->forum_container->value) &&
!empty($variables['topics'])) {
  $forum_topic_list_header = $variables['header'];

  $table = array(
    '#theme' => 'table__forum_topic_list',
    '#responsive' => FALSE,
    '#attributes' => array('id' => 'forum-topic-' . $variables['tid']),
    '#header' => array(),
    '#rows' => array(),
  );

  if (!empty($forum_topic_list_header)) {
    $table['#header'] = $forum_topic_list_header;
  }

  /** @var \Drupal\node\NodeInterface $topic */
  foreach ($variables['topics'] as $id => $topic) {
    $variables['topics'][$id]->icon = array(
      '#theme' => 'forum_icon',
      '#new_posts' => $topic->new,
      '#num_posts' => $topic->comment_count,
      '#comment_mode' => $topic->comment_mode,
      '#sticky' => $topic->isSticky(),
      '#first_new' => $topic->first_new,
    );

    // We keep the actual tid in forum table, if it's different from the
    // current tid then it means the topic appears in two forums, one of
    // them is a shadow copy.
    if ($variables['tid'] != $topic->forum_tid) {
      $variables['topics'][$id]->moved = TRUE;
      $variables['topics'][$id]->title = $topic->getTitle();
      $variables['topics'][$id]->message = \Drupal::l(t('This topic has been moved'),
      new Url('forum.page', ['taxonomy_term' => $topic->forum_tid]));
    }
    else {
      $variables['topics'][$id]->moved = FALSE;
      $variables['topics'][$id]->title_link = \Drupal::l($topic->getTitle(),
      $topic->urlInfo());
      $variables['topics'][$id]->message = '';
    }
```

```
$forum_submitted = array('#theme' => 'forum_submitted', '#topic' => (object) array(
  'uid' => $topic->getOwnerId(),
  'name' => $topic->getOwner()->getDisplayName(),
  'created' => $topic->getCreatedTime(),
));
$variables['topics'][$id]->submitted = drupal_render($forum_submitted);
$forum_submitted = array(
  '#theme' => 'forum_submitted',
  '#topic' => isset($topic->last_reply) ? $topic->last_reply : NULL,
);
$variables['topics'][$id]->last_reply = drupal_render($forum_submitted);

$variables['topics'][$id]->new_text = '';
$variables['topics'][$id]->new_url = '';

if ($topic->new_replies) {
  $page_number = \Drupal::entityManager()->getStorage('comment')
    ->getNewCommentPageNumber($topic->comment_count, $topic->new_replies, $topic,
    'comment_forum');
  $query = $page_number ? array('page' => $page_number) : NULL;
  $variables['topics'][$id]->new_text = \Drupal::translation()->formatPlural
  ($topic->new_replies, '1 new post<span class="visually-hidden"> in topic %title
  </span>', '@count new posts<span class="visually-hidden"> in topic %title</span>',
  array('%title' => $variables['topics'][$id]->label()));
  $variables['topics'][$id]->new_url = \Drupal::url('entity.node.canonical', ['node'
  => $topic->id()], ['query' => $query, 'fragment' => 'new']);
}

// Build table rows from topics.
$row = array();
$row[] = array(
  'data' => array(
    $topic->icon,
    array(
      '#markup' => '<div class="forum__title"><div>' . $topic->title_link .
      '</div><div>' . $topic->submitted . '</div></div>',
    ),
  ),
  'class' => array('forum__topic'),
);

if ($topic->moved) {
  $row[] = array(
    'data' => $topic->message,
    'colspan' => '2',
  );
}
else {
  $new_replies = '';
  if ($topic->new_replies) {
    $new_replies = '<br /><a href="' . $topic->new_url . '">' . $topic->new_text . '</a>';
  }
```

```
        $row[] = array(
          'data' => [
            [
              '#prefix' => $topic->comment_count,
              '#markup' => $new_replies,
            ],
          ],
          'class' => array('forum__replies'),
        );
        $row[] = array(
          'data' => $topic->last_reply,
          'class' => array('forum__last-reply'),
        );
      }
      $table['#rows'][] = $row;
    }

    $variables['topics'] = $table;
    $variables['topics_pager'] = array(
      '#type' => 'pager',
    );
  }
}
}
```

With the variables defined and populated with information that is ready to render through a template file, the next step is to define what template files should be used to render the variables. This is the job of the theme suggestion's hook. Within the forum.module file, search for forum_theme_suggestions_forums and you'll find the function that defines the various suggestions for the name of the theme file that Twig should use to render the output generated by the Forum module.

```
/**
 * Implements hook_theme_suggestions_HOOK().
 */
function forum_theme_suggestions_forums(array $variables) {
  $suggestions = array();
  $tid = $variables['term']->id();

  // Provide separate template suggestions based on what's being output. Topic
  // ID is also accounted for. Check both variables to be safe then the inverse.
  // Forums with topic IDs take precedence.
  if ($variables['forums'] && !$variables['topics']) {
    $suggestions[] = 'forums__containers';
    $suggestions[] = 'forums__' . $tid;
    $suggestions[] = 'forums__containers__' . $tid;
  }
  elseif (!$variables['forums'] && $variables['topics']) {
    $suggestions[] = 'forums__topics';
    $suggestions[] = 'forums__' . $tid;
    $suggestions[] = 'forums__topics__' . $tid;
  }
```

```
  else {
    $suggestions[] = 'forums__' . $tid;
  }

  return $suggestions;
}
```

The order of the suggestions defined in the function is important, as that is the order of precedence that Twig uses when searching for an applicable template to render what is being sent to the theme layer to render on the page. As shown, the $suggestions array is populated with various options based on whether the forum is associated with a taxonomy term ID or not, and moves from general templates applied to all forums, forums_containers, to specific containers within a term ID, 'forums_containers_'.$tid.

Examining the template files completes the picture of how values from a module are rendered on a page. Let's pick the simplest template, forums.html.twig. In this template file, you'll find three simple output statements—{{ forums }}, {{ topics }}, and {{ topics_pager }}.

```
{#
/**
 * @file
 * Default theme implementation to display a forum.
 *
 * May contain forum containers as well as forum topics.
 *
 * Available variables:
 * - forums: The forums to display (as processed by forum-list.html.twig).
 * - topics: The topics to display.
 * - topics_pager: The topics pager.
 * - forums_defined: A flag to indicate that the forums are configured.
 *
 * @see template_preprocess_forums()
 *
 * @ingroup themeable
 */
#}
{% if forums_defined %}
  {{ forums }}
  {{ topics }}
  {{ topics_pager }}
{% endif %}
```

If you trace all the way back to the forum_theme function, you'll see that those variables were defined here:

```
'variables' => array(
    'forums' => array(),
    'topics' => array(),
    'topics_pager' => array(),
    'parents' => NULL,
    'term' => NULL,
    'sortby' => NULL,
    'forum_per_page' => NULL,
    'header' => array())
```

And were populated in the preprocess function:

```
$variables['forums'] = array(
  '#theme' => 'forum_list',
  '#forums' => $variables['forums'],
  '#parents' => $variables['parents'],
  '#tid' => $variables['tid'],
);
$variables['topics'] = $table;
$variables['topics_pager'] = array(
  '#type' => 'pager',
);
```

While there are many pieces to the overall solution for how content makes it way to the physical page, the process is relatively simple and the patterns are well defined. For additional details on preprocess functions and theme hooks, visit drupal.org/docs/8.

Applying CSS to Your Theme

With all of the non-styling related pieces in place, the next step in beautifying your theme is to apply styling to the CSS elements defined in your template files. There are three steps in Drupal 8 for creating CSS:

1. Create the stylesheet(s) that will be loaded and used to render elements as you want them to appear.

2. Instruct the theme layer how to find the CSS files that you created.

3. Update the .info.yaml file.

Creating the Stylesheets

Stylesheets in Drupal 8 are stored in the theme's directory following a scalable and modular architecture for CSS (SMACSS) style categorization of its CSS rules (visit smacss.com for a complete overview of SMACSS):

- Base: CSS reset/normalize plus HTML element styling

- Layout: Macro arrangement of a web page, including any grid systems

- Component: Discrete, reusable UI elements

- State: Styles that deal with client-side changes to components

- Theme: Purely visual styling ("look-and-feel") for a component

Following SMACSS, the directory structure in the theme's directory where stylesheets are stored is as follows:

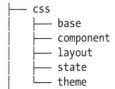

```
├── css
│   ├── base
│   ├── component
│   ├── layout
│   ├── state
│   └── theme
│
```

Since the sample stylesheet deals with general look-and-feel, we'll create a file named `styles.css` in the `css/theme` directory using any editor. In that file, we enter the following and then save the file.

```
h1 {
  text-transform: uppercase;
  text-decoration: underline;
}
```

We could at this point continue to build out other stylesheets following the SMACSS guidelines to address all of the styling requirements for the theme. However, to keep the concept simple, we'll next focus on creating the libraries file.

Creating the libraries.yml File

The next step is to create a `.libraries.yml` file that's used by Drupal to identify all of the CSS and JavaScript files that are associated with my theme. The library file for the Davinci theme will at this point only define the global stylesheets that are to be loaded. The library file will be expanded later in this chapter to address additional requirements. You can create the `davinci.libraries.yml` file in the root directory of the Davinci theme using any editor. In that file, enter the following:

```
global-styling:
  version: 1.x
  css:
    theme:
      css/theme/styles.css: {}
```

In the file, the `global-styling` is a unique library that will be loaded when instructed to do so in the `davinci.info.yml` file. Associated with `global-styling` are various attributes such as the version number of this library, and in this case, the CSS that is going to be used and applied to the theme and where it resides in relation to the theme, in the `css/theme` subdirectory. The structure of the .yml file is important, so be mindful of the indentation, as spacing means something to the yaml parser.

Loading the Libraries Through the .info.yml File

After saving the libraries file, the final step is to instruct the theme to load the `global-styling` library. Open the `davinci.info.yml` file and update the file to appear as shown here. Note the addition of the `libraries` statement and, below that, statement the instruction to load the library associated with the Davinci theme named `global-styling`, which is what we just created in the `davinci.libraries.yml` file in the previous step.

```
name: davinci
type: theme
description: A Drupal 8 theme
core: 8.x
libraries:
 - davinci/global-styling
regions:
  messages: 'Messages'
```

```
header_first: 'Header first'
header_second: 'Header second'
header_third: 'Header third'
navbar: 'Nav bar'
features_first: 'Features first'
features_second: 'Features second'
features_third: 'Features third'
features_fourth: 'Features fourth'
highlighted: 'Highlighted'
content: 'Main content'
sidebar_first: 'Sidebar first'
sidebar_second: 'Sidebar second'
tertiary_first: 'Tertiary first'
tertiary_second: 'Tertiary second'
tertiary_third: 'Tertiary third'
tertiary_fourth: 'Tertiary fourth'
footer: 'Footer'
page_top: 'Page top'
page_bottom: 'Page bottom'
```

After saving all the files and rebuilding cache, you're ready to see if the CSS changes took effect. The results are shown in Figure 5-8.

HELLO DRUPAL 8 WORLD!

Figure 5-8. *Demonstrating the successful application of CSS*

Success! The demonstration shows that the CSS file was successfully loaded and applied to a node's H1 title. You can expand on this by adding stylesheets to the global-styling library, or you can create additional libraries outside of global-styling, by adding the libraries through the .info.yml file. For additional details, visit drupal.org/node/2216195.

Adding JavaScript to Your Theme

Adding JavaScript to your theme is nearly identical to the process of adding stylesheets to the theme. It's done through the .libraries.yml file and updates to the .info.yml file. We'll create a simple JavaScript file named annoying-cow.js that does one thing—it generates an alert box that says "Moo!" Being an annoying cow, it will pop up on every page of the site. We will create the JavaScript file in the js subdirectory of the Davinci theme. The content of the JavaScript file is simply:

```
(function ($, Drupal) {
  alert("Moo!")
})(jQuery, Drupal);
```

After you save the file, the directory structure of the Davinci theme appears as shown here:

```
├── config
│   ├── install
│   └── schema
├── css
│   ├── base
│   ├── component
│   ├── layout
│   ├── state
│   └── theme
│       └── styles.css
├── davinci.info.yml
├── davinci.libraries.yml
├── images
├── js
│   └── annoying-cow.js
└── templates
    ├── block.html.twig
    ├── field--body.html.twig
    ├── node.html.twig
    └── page.html.twig
```

Next we will define a library in the davinci.libraries.yml file that will be used to load the annoying-cow.js file. Edit the existing file by adding the annoying-cow library to the bottom of the file, as shown here:

```
global-styling:
  version: 1.x
  css:
    theme:
      css/theme/styles.css: {}

annoying-cow:
  version: 1.x
  js:
    js/annoying-cow.js: {}
```

Finally, we update the libraries section of the davinci.info.yml file to load the annoying-cow library.

```
libraries:
 - davinci/global-styling
 - davinci/annoying-cow
```

After saving all the files and rebuilding cache, reload the homepage. The annoying cow is shown in Figure 5-9.

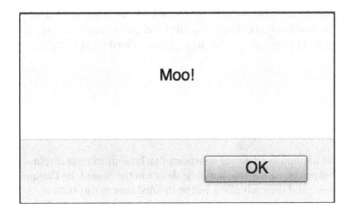

Figure 5-9. *Demonstrating that the added JavaScript works*

Adding JavaScript and CSS Libraries to Template Files

In the previous examples, we added CSS and JavaScript to the Davinci module on a global basis, meaning that every page will load the CSS and the JavaScript that we added through the libraries section of the `davinci.info.yml` file. This approach works but isn't the optimal solution, as not all CSS or JavaScript is required on every page.

To resolve the issue, Twig provides the ability to load libraries on a per-template basis through the `attach_library` function in the form of `{{ attach_library('library_name') }}`. In the case of the Davinci theme, we could add the `node.css` file, which is loaded only when the `node.html.twig` template is used to render a node. We first need to add a new library to the `davinci.libraries.yml` file to define the library:

```
node-styling:
  version: 1.x
  css:
    theme:
      css/theme/node.css: {}
```

After creating the new library, `node-styling`, we can then add that stylesheet to the `node.html.twig` template by inserting `{{ attach_library('davinci/node-styling') }}` at the top of the template (after the docblock). Save all the files and rebuild the cache. At that point, the CSS defined in `node.css` is now applied to all nodes that are rendered on the site, and not the anything other than a node.

The same concept can be applied to JavaScript. You may load JavaScript on an as-needed basis following the same approach outlined for CSS.

Working with Breakpoints

With responsive themes being the default standard for most organizations, any theme that you create should take advantage of breakpoints in Drupal 8 themes. The Breakpoint module is part of Drupal 8 core and is enabled by default when you install Drupal 8 (other than the minimal installation profile). The Breakpoint module keeps track of the height, width, and resolution of the device viewport where the site is being rendered. Themes and modules can define breakpoints and then use them to define how the elements on the page and the page itself are rendered on different devices.

131

A *breakpoint* is a label and a media query where the label is a human readable label for the breakpoint that is being defined, and the media query is the element that defines what the breakpoint applies to. For example, a breakpoint for mobile devices as defined in the Davinci theme might look like the following:

```
davinci.mobile:
  label: mobile
  mediaQuery: 'all and (max-width: 559px)'
  weight: 0
  multipliers: 1x
```

In this case, the breakpoint of mobile will be applied to all device viewports that have maximum display widths of 559px. Anything greater than 559px will not be considered a mobile device in the case of the Davinci theme. The weight defines the order of precedence and the multipliers will be defined later in this section.

Breakpoints are defined in a .breakpoints.yml file that is stored in the theme's root directory. Let's create a davinci.breakpoints.yml file with the following content:

```
davinci.mobile:
  label: mobile
  mediaQuery: 'all and (max-width: 559px)'
  weight: 0
  multipliers:
    - 1x
davinci.narrow:
  label: narrow
  mediaQuery: 'all and (min-width: 560px) and (max-width: 850px)'
  weight: 1
  multipliers:
    - 1x
davinci.wide:
  label: wide
  mediaQuery: 'all and (min-width: 851px)'
  weight: 2
  multipliers:
    - 1x
```

Multipliers are a measure of the viewport's device resolution, defined as that ratio between the physical pixel size of the active device and the device-independent pixel size. For example, Apple's retina displays have a multiplier of 2.x. By adding a new breakpoint of davinci.mobile_retina you can address the specific CSS attributes required to render the site properly on a retina display:

```
davinci.mobile_retina:
  label: mobile_retina
  mediaQuery: 'all and (max-width: 559px)'
  weight: 0
  multipliers:
  - 2x
```

While the definition of breakpoints in the .breakpoints.yml file, they currently have no impact on the CSS that you write and the media queries will also need to be added to your CSS files as they would without the breakpoints module. At some point in the future, a bridge between CSS and the breakpoints.yml file may be made, but at the time that I wrote this book, that bridge did not yet exist. In the mean time, create your breakpoints here as well as in your CSS files.

Creating Advanced Theme Settings

Many Drupal themes provide configurable settings that may be managed through the theme's administrative settings on the appearance page. The Bartik theme, for example, provides the ability to set the colors for nearly every major element in the theme through administrative settings that are exposed on the settings page without having to modify CSS.

To add custom theme settings, the first step is to modify the theme settings form by adding a PHP function to the yourthemename.theme file named yourthemename_form_system_theme_settings_alter function, replacing yourthemename with the name of your theme.

We'll demonstrate the process by adding a site slogan setting to the Davinci theme by first creating a davinci.theme file in the Davinci themes root directory. Within the davinci.theme file, we'll add the function to add the Site Slogan field to the theme configuration page and add a preprocess page function to expose the value stored in the Site Slogan field as a variable that can be accessed on the page template files.

The format of the form field follows the standard Drupal form API setting for a text field, with the addition of a theme_get_setting call to retrieve the value of site_slogan. Note that the setting is stored in the same name as the $form element.

```php
<?php

function davinci_form_system_theme_settings_alter(&$form, \Drupal\Core\Form\
FormStateInterface $form_state) {

    $form['site_slogan'] = array(
      '#type'          => 'textfield',
      '#title'         => t('Site Slogan'),
      '#default_value' => theme_get_setting('site_slogan'),
      '#description'   => t("Enter the site's slogan"),
    );

}

function davinci_preprocess_page(&$variables) {

    $variables['site_slogan'] = theme_get_setting('site_slogan');

}
```

The next step in the process is to create a davinci.settings.yml file in the config/install directory of the Davinci theme. In this file, we'll create a simple statement that sets the default value for the site_slogan setting.

```
site_slogan: Drupal 8 is Great
```

The final step in the process is to insert the site_slogan into the page.html.twig template file so that it will be displayed on every page. To do so, pick the correct spot in the page.html.twig file and insert {{ site_slogan }}.

After saving all of the files and rebuilding cache, visit the appearance page and click the Settings link for the Davinci theme. On the Appearance settings page, you can see that the new Site Slogan field appears at the bottom of the form, with the default value we set in the davinci.settings.yml file (see Figure 5-10).

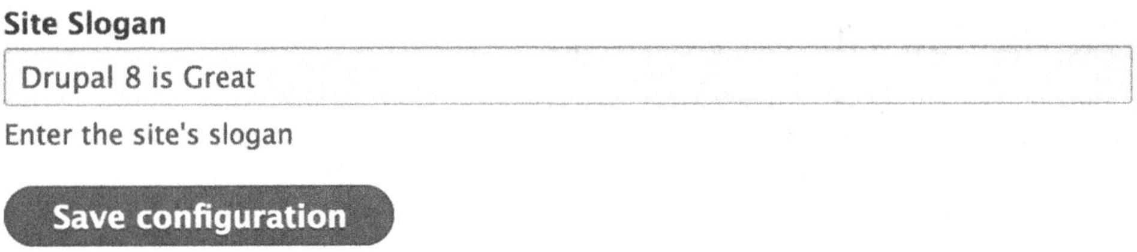

Site Slogan

> Drupal 8 is Great

Enter the site's slogan

Save configuration

Figure 5-10. The Site Slogan settings field

If you visit a page on the site, you can now see the site slogan printed on the page in the spot where we added {{ site_slogan }}, as shown in Figure 5-11.

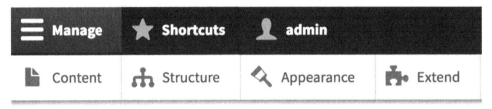

Drupal 8 is Great

Figure 5-11. The site slogan rendering on a page

You may also encounter situations where you need to expose a theme setting value to a node, block, field, or other element. You may do so by adding a themename_preprocess_type(&$variables) function, replacing themename with the name of your theme and type with node, block, field, or other element name. Within that function setting, the variable that will be exposed to the template file for that element type.

Using Subthemes

One of the enterprise aspects of Drupal 8 themes is the concept of a *subtheme*. Subthemes allow you to create an enterprise theme that every site in your organization can inherit and then extend to meet each individual site's branding and look-and-feel requirements. Subthemes significantly shorten the overall development time because you don't have to recreate a theme from scratch every time a department or group in your organization wants a new Drupal 8 site. Subthemes also to some extent enable you to enforce corporate branding standards across all sites. There are still ways to override nearly everything in a subtheme, and that is where corporate policies come into play.

The process of setting up a subtheme is relatively simple; you only need to add a single statement to the .info.yml file of your theme to specify the name of the base theme that you are starting with. The only requirement is that the base theme must reside in your Drupal 8 installation. To demonstrate, we'll modify the Davinci theme, using Classy as the base theme. Classy is included as a theme in Drupal 8 core and can be found at core/themes/classy. To the davinci.info.yml file, add the following statement:

```
base theme: classy
```

After saving the file and rebuilding the cache, visit the homepage. You'll immediately see subtle differences in the look and feel of the theme, as Davinci now inherits all of the styling and template files from the Classy theme. Figure 5-12 shows the homepage before assigning Classy as the base theme and Figure 5-13 shows the immediate impact of using Classy. While the changes are subtle due to the minimalist nature of the Classy theme, this does demonstrate the power of using subthemes.

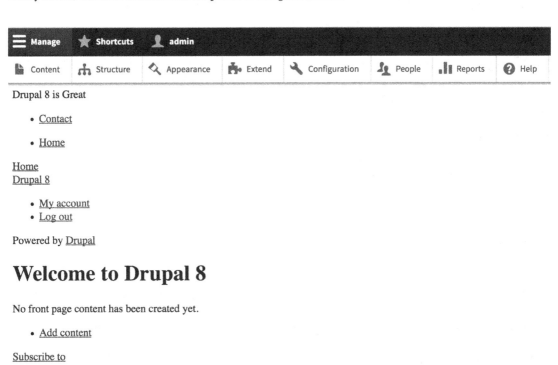

Figure 5-12. *The Davinci theme before applying Classy*

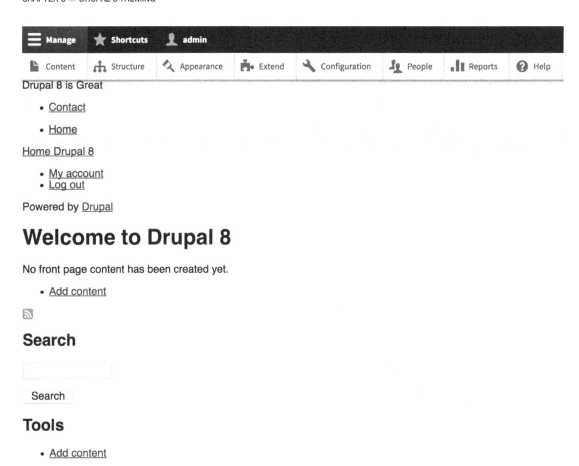

Figure 5-13. *The Davinci theme after applying Classy*

Summary

This chapter covered a lot of ground, starting with the basics of Drupal 8 theming and advancing through the steps of expanding on the capabilities of the Davinci theme. There are even more features and functionally in Drupal 8 theming that you might want to explore at drupal.org/docs/8/theming.

The next chapter focuses on leveraging the content that you created on your Drupal 8 site, detailing the process for sharing content with other Drupal and non-Drupal sites, as well as sharing content with new global audiences and empowering your site visitors through enterprise search.

CHAPTER 6

Leveraging Your Content

In the book titled *Magazine Editing and Production,* published in 1974, authors J.W. Click and Russell N. Baird wrote that "Content is king. It is the meaning that counts. Form and technical considerations, although important, cannot substitute for content." While Click and Baird's book was written nearly 20 years before the launch of the Internet and 41 years before the launch of Drupal 8, the concept that content is king is on the minds of everyone who is responsible for building and maintaining web sites. If content is king, how can Drupal 8 help to ensure that the right content is in the right place, at the right time, and in the right format to entice visitors to find your site and stay there? That is precisely the question that this chapter addresses by looking at Drupal 8's content staging, publishing, search, and multilingual capabilities, all of which are cornerstones in helping to ensure that content is and remains king on your Drupal 8 web sites.

Content Staging

One of the challenges that have plagued web site developers since the first web site was built back in 1991 is how to stage new content and updates to existing content outside of the production environment so that it may be previewed and tested prior to exposing it to the visitors who come to your site. While the very first web site ever published on the web (Tim Berners-Lee, 1991) is relatively simple (`info.cern.ch/hypertext/ WWW/TheProject.html`) and looks pretty much the same as it did 25 years ago when Berners-Lee first saved the original HTML file that generates that site, the reality is that today's web sites are constantly changing with new content being added and updates being published in near real time. Due to the restrictions in the capabilities of most CMS platforms, the normal operating procedure has been to make content changes on the live server, holding your breath as you click the Save button, hoping that your changes did not adversely affect the site. While that has been the normal operating procedure in the past, Drupal 8 presents a new operating model that enables staging and previewing content prior to publishing it on the live web site, and it takes it one step further by enabling the ability to stage content and publish that content across multiple web sites.

Content Staging and Site Preview Use Cases

Before describing the details of how content staging and site preview works, let me outline the use cases where these capabilities come into play and why they may be important to your organization.

Use Case #1: Staging and deploying content across multiple web sites. In this use case, you want to synchronize content from one site to another, where the first web site is a staging site where editors do all the work of authoring and updating content. New content and updates to existing content are previewed on the staging site and, when approved, are pushed to the production web sites. This use case can be expanded by addressing the need to have multiple staging sites pushing to multiple production sites, creating a web of staging and production web sites that work in harmony to address the complex organizational structures of large enterprises.

© Todd Tomlinson 2017

T. Tomlinson, *Enterprise Drupal 8 Development*, DOI 10.1007/978-1-4842-0253-1_6

Use Case #2: Content branching. In this use case, you may have a scenario where you are introducing a new section to your web site that addresses a new division that was added to your company, a new product line that is about to launch, or a new category of content that your web site is now incorporating into the existing content on your site. The desire is to build out the new "branch" of your web site and to push the updates as a whole out to your production web sites.

Use Case #3: Previewing your site. Editors and authors inherently want to see how their changes will affect the production web site before they are visible to the general viewer audience. "No surprises" is a common phrase that I've heard while walking the halls of major multinational corporations where I have helped build massive Drupal web sites. The ability to preview not only a single article, but a whole section or the whole site is a must-have on the list of requirements for many large organizations.

Use Case #4: Offline browsing and publishing. Not every country around the world has reliable infrastructure and not every location on the planet has access to WiFi or a high-speed Internet connection. You may have sales reps who walk into a customer's building and they need access to your product information so that they can share how your products or services address their need. Your sales rep may need to take an order while sitting in the customer's office and have that order saved in an offline mode and automatically synced when the sales rep has access to the Internet.

Use Case #5: Content recovery. "Stuff happens" and when it does, having the ability to recovery lost content or inadvertently changed content is a key desire of nearly every content editor and author. Giving users the ability to undelete or recovery content that was inadvertently deleted from the Drupal database would save countless hours of rework and eliminate the frustration of having to recreate content.

Use Case #6: Auditing. Many large organizations are under some form of government regulation that requires some level of auditability of the changes made to content on their web sites for compliance purposes. The requirement focuses on the ability to report on every change made to content on the web site and to be able to attribute that change to a specific user.

These use cases share several common characteristics:

- Content needs to be kept in sync from one place to another—within a single site (e.g., between staging and live) and between sites.

- A full revision history showing all changes must be kept to ensure auditability.

- Conflicts between revisions between environments need to be tracked and easily remedied.

The Drupal 8 Solution for Content Staging and Synchronization

A suite of Drupal 8 core and contributed modules orchestrate the replication of content between environments and solves the issues of keeping revisions, providing an audit trail, and using the tools necessary to resolve conflicts when they arise. The modules required to fulfill the typical requirements are the Deploy, Multiversion, Replication, Workspace, RELAXed Web Services, and Trash modules.

The Deploy Module

The Deploy module provides an administrative interface on top of the Workspace and Replication modules to enable content managers with the ability to manage content deployments between workspaces on a single site, or between workspaces across sites. The three basic modes supported by Deploy are as follows:

- Cross-site staging. Using RELAXed Web Services to stage content between different Drupal sites.

- Single-site content staging works with the Workspace module by providing the ability to stage content on a single site, where Workspace provides the capability to create a separate staging workspace in which content can be previewed before deploying it to the live workspace.

- Fully decoupled site. Using the APIs provided by the RELAXed Web Services module, the Deploy module provides the ability to distribute content to a site that is decoupled from the source site, meaning that synchronization of content between the source and the destination site is purely manual and on demand.

The Multiversion Module

The Multiversion module provides four key features that play a significant role in the content staging solution footprint:

- The ability to create revisions for nodes, taxonomy terms, comments, block content, users, and other custom entities

- The ability to define parent revisions, providing the ability to create multiple child revisions or branches from the parent

- Keeps track of conflicts in the revision tree and reports the details of those conflicts

- Provides an audit trail of changes made to an individual

When implemented in conjunction with the other modules described in this section, it becomes a powerful tool for managing revisions across sites as well as providing the audit trail required to address the reporting requirements of most organizations.

The Replication Module

Replication provides the functionality and services that support replicating content between workspaces on a single site, or between workspaces across multiple sites using the RELAXed Web Services module. Replication is built on top of the Multiversion module and uses information stored by Multiversion to determine which revisions are missing from a given location and synchronizes the content across locations.

The Workspace Module

The Workspace module provides the ability to create an isolated collection of content and revisions on your site, for example, workspaces for staging and production. This provides the ability to author content in a controlled environment that is not visible to site visitors until an editor promotes the content to the product, while allowing the editor to preview content as it will appear to general site visitors. The workspace module provides the ability to create a workspace; however, it does not provide the tools to move content between workspaces, which is where the Deploy and RELAXed Web Services modules come into play.

RELAXed Web Services Module

The RELAXed Web Services module provides a generic RESTful API for all Drupal 8 content entities, extending the core REST APIs with better support for translations, revisions, and file attachments. It is based on the `replication.io` protocol and leverages the Multiversion module to handle bidirectional replication between two or more Drupal sites.

Trash Module

The Trash module provides a trash bin for all content entities. Nodes can be moved to the trash instead of being deleted permanently, allowing for restoration of those content items at a later time. See Figure 6-1.

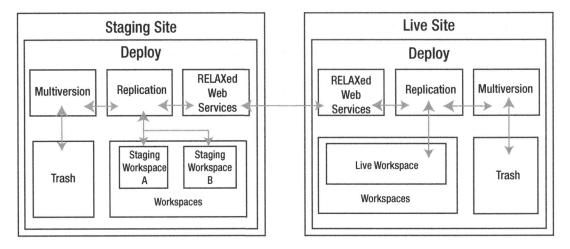

Figure 6-1. *The content deployment solution*

Installation, Configuration, and Use of the Content Staging Framework

The process for installing the content staging and distribution framework begins with the installation of the modules and their dependencies. The modules and their dependencies are Deploy, Entity Storage Migrate API, Key-Value Extensions, Multiversion, Replication, Trash, Workspace, RELAXed Web Services, Serialization, RESTful Web Services, and HTTP Basic Authentication. Follow the standard approach for downloading and installing modules on your site.

Configuring Multiversion

The first module we focus on is Multiversion. When installing Multiversion, the install process does most of the work for you. If you have existing content on your site, Multiversion will convert that content to revisionable as part of the installation process.

To test whether Multiversion is working, we create and save a new article following the standard process for creating nodes. Then we create a new revision by checking the Create a New Revision checkbox on the Node Edit form and enter a comment about what we changed on the node we created. After saving, you'll see two new tabs at the top of the Node Edit form—Revisions and Tree (see Figure 6-2).

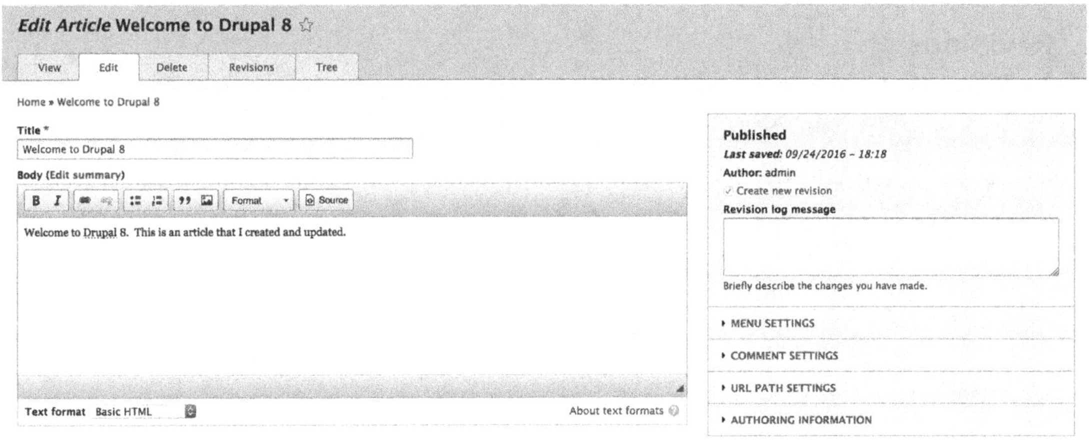

Figure 6-2. *The Revisions and Tree tabs*

Clicking the Revisions tab lists all of the revisions that have been made to a given node, as shown in Figure 6-3.

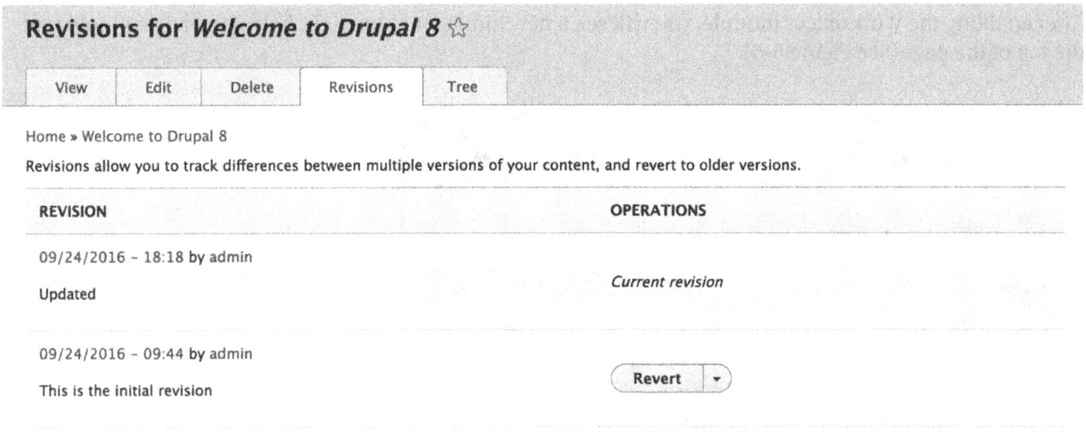

Figure 6-3. *List of revisions*

Clicking on the Tree tab reveals the hierarchy of revisions made to the original node, as shown in Figure 6-4.

141

Figure 6-4. *A node's revision tree*

Configuring Workspaces

After enabling the Workspaces module, you will see a new indicator in the right half of the admin toolbar at the top of the page (see Figure 6-5).

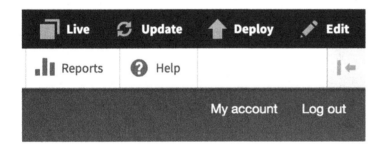

Figure 6-5. *The Workspace environment indicator*

The first workspace that is created and enabled automatically when the module is enabled is the Live workspace as shown in Figure 6-5. The Workspace module also creates a Stage workspace, but the Stage workspace is set to an inactive state by default (see Figure 6-6).

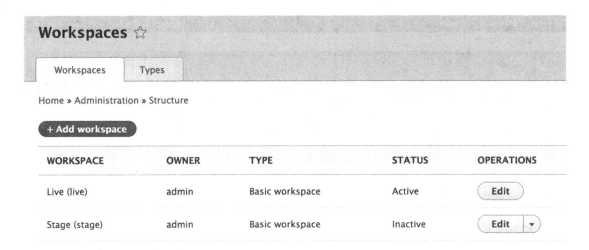

Figure 6-6. *The Stage workspace*

You may switch between the Live and Stage workspaces by clicking on the workspace indicator in the admin toolbar. Clicking reveals a submenu where you select a workspace or add a new workspace, as shown in Figure 6-7.

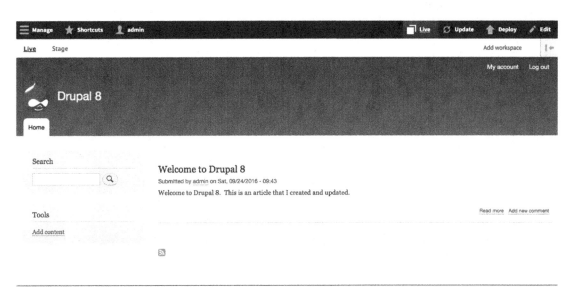

Figure 6-7. *The Workspaces selector*

In the example shown in Figure 6-7, the Live workspace is enabled. Note the Welcome to Drupal 8 article. You can switch to the Stage indicator by clicking the link in the toolbar. Note that in the Stage environment the Welcome to Drupal 8 article is missing, because it was created in the Live environment and is not yet replicated to the Stage environment. Also note that the workspace indicator in the toolbar indicates that the current workspace is now the Stage workspace (see Figure 6-8).

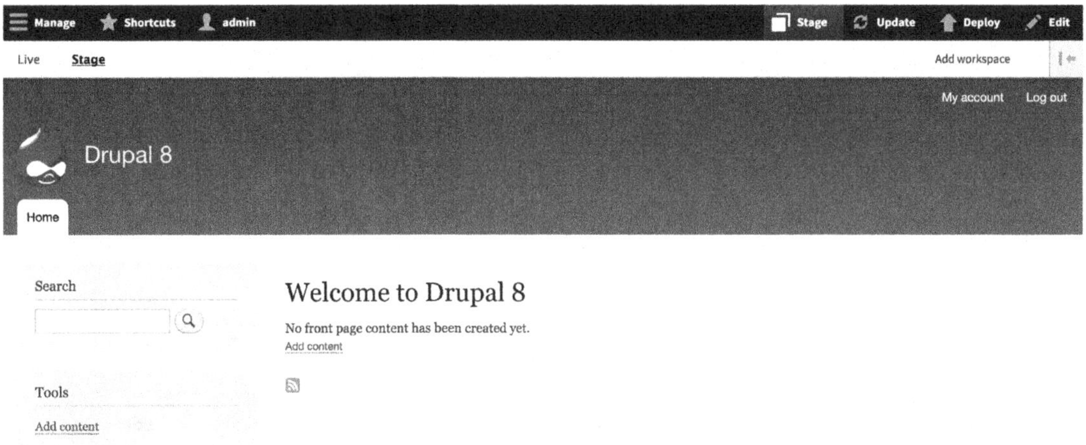

Figure 6-8. *The Stage workspace*

You may create a new workspace by clicking on the Add Workspace link in the admin toolbar, or by visiting the Structure ➤ Workspaces page and clicking on the Add Workspace link on the Workspaces page. We'll create a new workspace named Testing and set the default target workspace, where content will be replicated by default (see Figure 6-9).

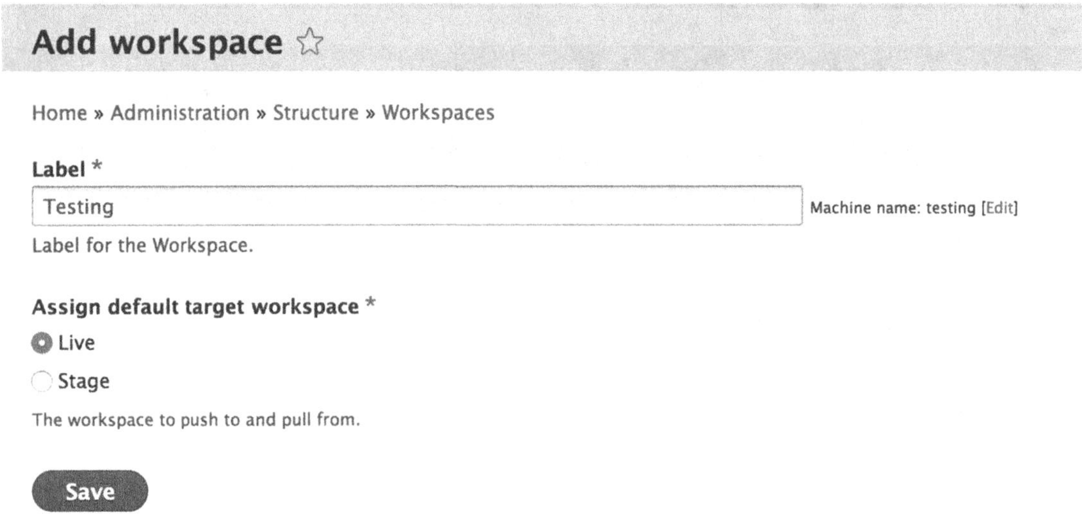

Figure 6-9. *Creating a new workspace*

The newly created workspace is now visible in admin toolbar and on the Structure ➤ Workspaces page.

With the default deployment set for the Stage workspace, we can author content in the Stage workspace and deploy those changes to the Live workspace by clicking the Deploy link in the admin toolbar and entering a title and description that will be used on the Deploy administration page to convey what was deployed (see Figure 6-10).

Figure 6-10. *The Deploy form*

After deploying the content, we can see the history of all deployments by navigating to Structure ➤ Deployments. This page lists all deployments that have been made, including the source, target, date, and time (see Figure 6-11).

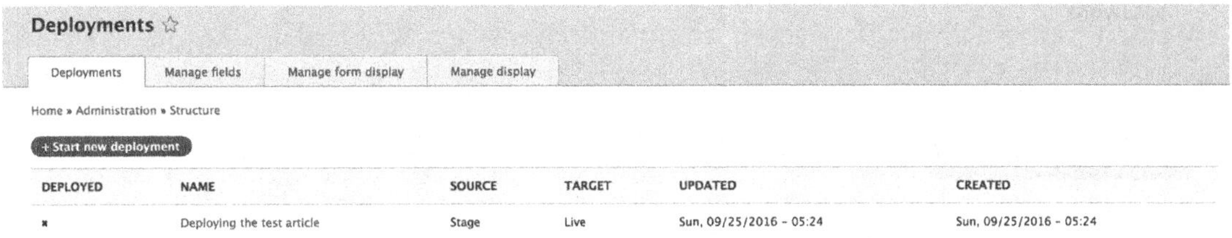

Figure 6-11. *The Deployments history page*

Configuring RELAXed Web Services Modules

The RELAXed Web Services module handles the underlying activities of connecting two Drupal sites and transporting the content between those sites and workspaces.

The first step is to create a new user account that will be used to connect to remote sites. While I could use the admin account to facilitate that process, it is a best practice to set up a user account with fewer permissions. The installation process for the RELAXed Web Services module creates a new user role named Replicator, which has by default all of the permissions set for an account whose sole purpose is to replicate content between sites and workspaces. You may visit People ➤ Roles to see the Replicator role. You may see the permissions assigned to the Replicator role by clicking on the Permissions tab, where you will see that the role has three assigned permissions:

- Administer workspaces

- Perform push replication

- Administer users

145

Those three roles provide access to all of the required functionality to successfully replicate content between workspaces locally or across the wire via the RELAXed Web Services module. We need to create this account on the target Drupal 8 sites as we will be using it in a moment to configure the interface between sites.

Let's follow the standard process for creating a new Drupal 8 user by visiting the People page, where we click on the Add User button and add the user account that we'll use for replication purposes. We'll keep it simple and name the replication user `replicator`, assigning a secure password and the role of Replicator. We also need a valid e-mail address for the replicator account.

Next, we navigate to Configuration ➤ Relaxed Settings and enter the details of the user account we just created as the default account for performing replications on this Drupal instance, as shown in Figure 6-12.

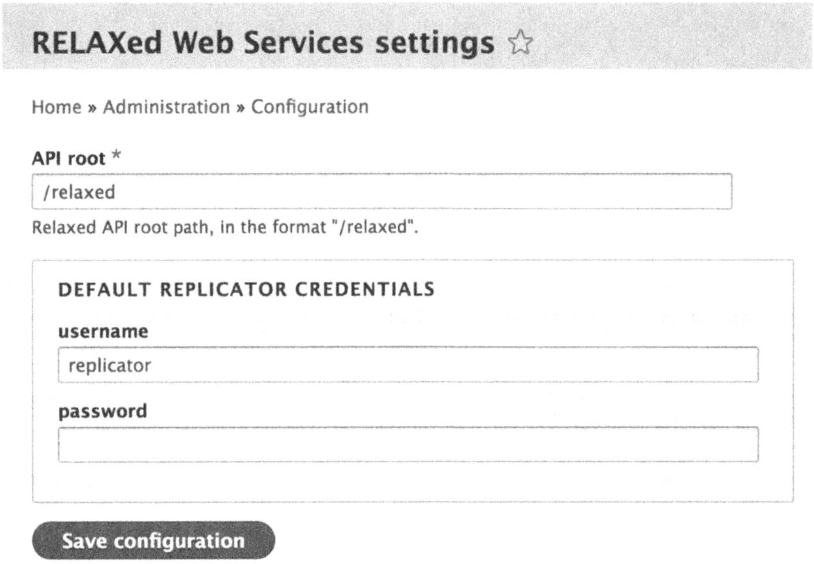

RELAXed Web Services settings ☆

Home » Administration » Configuration

API root *

    /relaxed

Relaxed API root path, in the format "/relaxed".

> **DEFAULT REPLICATOR CREDENTIALS**
>
> **username**
>
>   replicator
>
> **password**
>
>

Save configuration

Figure 6-12. *The default replication account settings form*

The next step in the process is to set up the remote sites. Navigate to Configuration ➤ Relaxed remotes and click the Add New Remote button. On the form, enter a meaningful name for the remote as well as the full URL of the remote site, the user name associated with replication on the remote site, and the password of that account. Click the Save button to finish the process (see Figure 6-13).

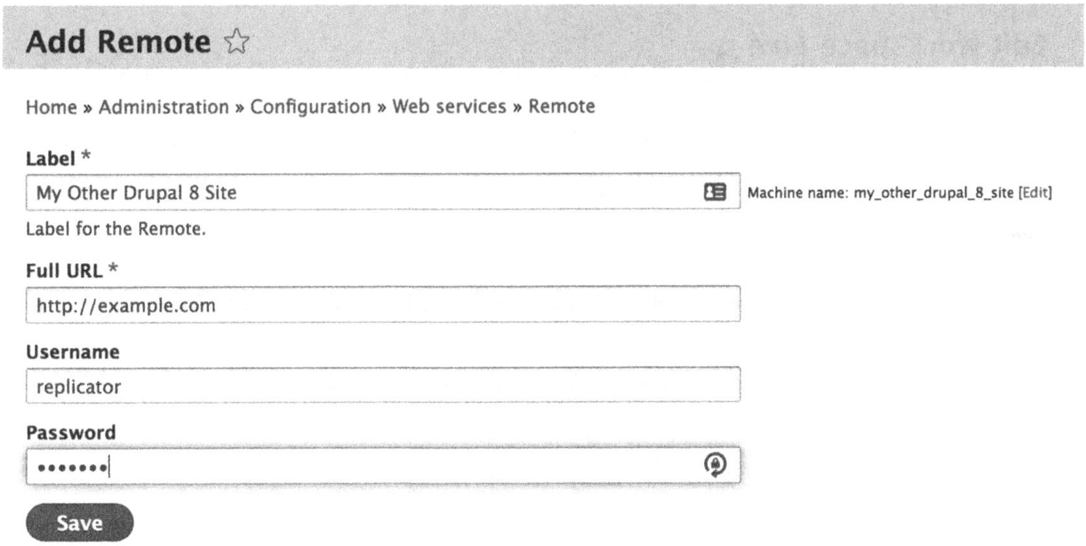

Add Remote ☆

Home » Administration » Configuration » Web services » Remote

Label *

My Other Drupal 8 Site   Machine name: my_other_drupal_8_site [Edit]

Label for the Remote.

Full URL *

http://example.com

Username

replicator

Password

•••••••

Save

Figure 6-13. *Adding a relaxed remote*

With the remote configured, we can now deploy content to remote sites and workspaces. We need to first set up the relationship between our local workspace and the remote workspace. For demonstration purposes, we will set the live workspace on the first site to deploy by default to the live workspace on the target site that we just set up. Navigate to Structure ➤ Workspaces and click on the Edit link for the live workspace on my local site. On the Edit page for the Live workspace, select My Other Drupal 8 Site: Live as the destination and then click the Save button (see Figure 6-14).

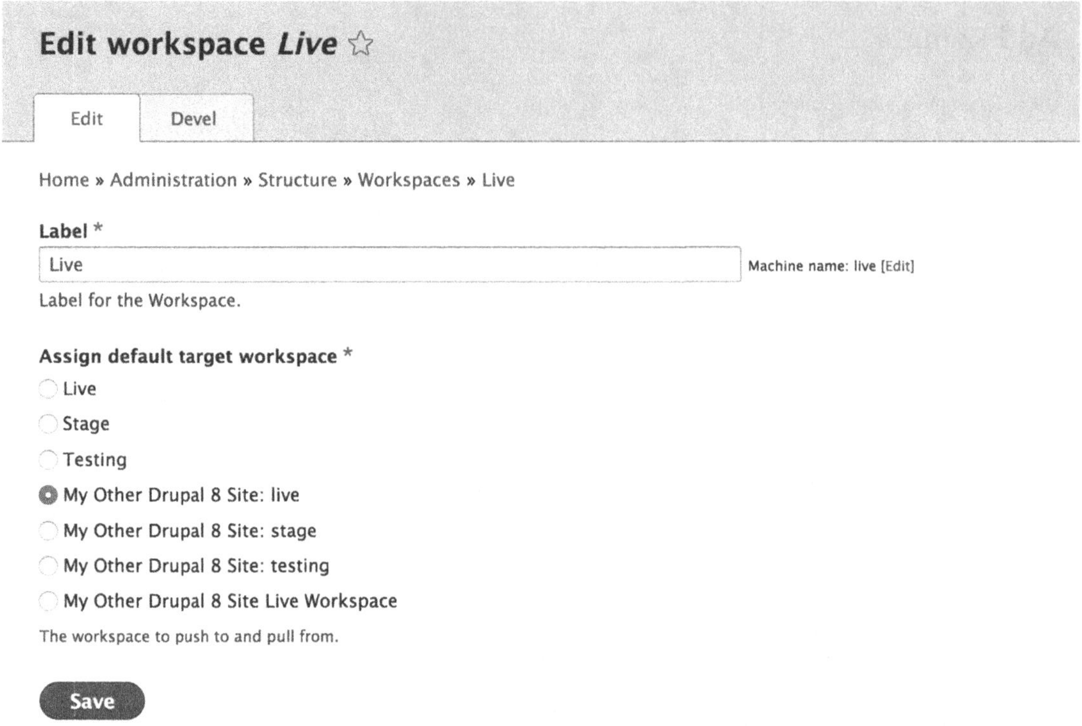

Figure 6-14. *Assigning the target workspace*

With the assignment complete, we can now deploy the content from our local live workspace to the remote workspace by simply clicking the Deploy button in the administrator's toolbar.

Search

Search is an often under utilized capability on Drupal sites. We sometimes fall back to the default search capabilities of Drupal core and "call it good," often because it just works without any configuration other than turning on the module and ensuring that cron is running. While the Drupal core search capabilities are good, there are limitations based on the underlying architecture, which is based on indexing the site and storing that index in a MySQL table. Search then uses MySQL's full text search feature to locate items in the index that match the search criteria entered by the user. While it does a commendable job, there are serious limitations with MySQL's full text search capabilities that may hinder the desired outcome. For example, MySQL's full text search doesn't handle words that are four characters in length or fewer, and MySQL's full text search is relatively slow. If you are concerned about performance you may want to look at an alternative indexer and that is where Solr comes into play.

There are other limitations of core search such as configuration. In core search, it's difficult to specify which content types to index, and within each content type, which fields to index. It's just not possible to configure to that level of detail in the core search module and many organizations need that level of fine-grain control. There is a solution to the performance and configurability issue and that is Apache Solr, which is well supported and widely adopted in the Drupal community as the preferred search solution for Drupal sites.

What Is Apache Solr?

Apache Solr is a world class search application built by the Apache Foundation and utilized by a wide variety of commercial and open source applications, which opens up an interesting proposition that I'll speak about in a bit. Solr is built on top of the Lucene indexer. Lucene is also an open source project, written in Java, and also under the Apache Foundation umbrella. Lucene is the underlying architecture that handles the storage of indexed content, much in the same way that MySQL stores content in Drupal, but in a fashion that is significantly more flexible than Drupal's core search and considerably faster as serving up the results of a search request.

Lucene's general approach is to store indexed content as a document made up of any number of different fields, providing that fine grain control over which fields to index and that Drupal core's search does not provide. And due to its flexibility and document-centric approach, Lucene indexes nearly any textual data that you can feed into it, including HTML, PDF, XML, Microsoft Word, and nearly any other document format that exists in the market. If I didn't mention it earlier, the capabilities of Lucene far outstrip the basic capabilities of Drupal core search and the boost in performance alone is well worth the effort of implementing Solr. It off-loads all of the search activities from the Drupal database, improving the overall site performance since full text MySQL search taxes the database significantly.

While Lucene is the indexer, Apache itself is an HTTP API for interacting with Lucene. This API has been utilized by several Drupal modules, making the installation and setup of Apache relatively easy on your Drupal site.

Solr's extensive use of XML configuration files makes it relatively easy to modify almost everything about how Solr works without having to touch any code. This simplifies the solution as it doesn't require any knowledge or expertise of Java.

The three key benefits of Solr over Drupal core search are as follows:

- A best in class stemming and tokenization, which provides the benefit of being able to configure what content types you want Solr to index and what fields you want to include

- A high degree of scalability, both vertically and horizontally

- Built-in support for advanced search features such as facets, geospatial searches, and advanced query options such as:

    - Full text or structured queries

    - Support for Boolean operators such as AND, NOT, OR, +, and –

    - Boosting terms through configuration

    - Fuzzy searches

    - Grouping with parentheses

    - Numeric range searches

    - Wildcard searches

    - And many more

There are other key features such as multi-lingual searching, search results highlighting, auto suggestions, spell checking, support for multiple indexes, federated search across multiple sites, and many others.

While there is effort to install and configure Solr, the benefits are significant. The next sections describe a simplified approach for quickly adopting and installing Solr on your Drupal 8 site.

To Install or Not To Install

Apache Solr and Lucene are open source projects and may be downloaded from `lucene.apache.org` and `lucene.apache.org/solr`. There is extensive documentation on how to install and configure both Lucene and Solr on the Apache Foundation's web site. Many organizations are choosing not to host Solr and Lucene internally due to the complexities of adding yet another platform to their portfolio, and while they are Java applications, there is performance and scalability considerations that may make choosing a hosted Solr and Lucene solution a more attractive option. There are several hosted Solr providers in the market, including the following:

- OpenSolr (`opensolr.com`)
- IndexDepot (`indexdepot.com`)
- WebSolr (`websolr.com`)

I'll demonstrate the ease of setting up hosted Solr on a Drupal 8 site using OpenSolr.

Required Modules

There are a few modules that you will want to install on your Drupal 8 site before beginning the setup process on `opensolr.com`. Those modules are as follows:

- Search API (`composer require drupal/search_api`)
- Search API Solr (`composer require drupal/search_api_solr`)

Install both modules using `composer require`, as there are associated libraries that are required for the modules to function properly and installing through Drush or downloading the modules will require that you manually install the libraries. If you have not yet used composer on your site, first ensure that composer is functional by opening a terminal window and executing the command `composer`. If you receive a list of available composer commands, you are good to go. If you do not receive a list of commands, then follow the instructions on `getcomposer.org`. If you have not yet set up composer on your site, run the following command in a terminal window:

```
composer config repositories.drupal composer https://packages.drupal.org/8
```

Then run the commands listed in the parentheses for each module.

Setting Up OpenSolr

After installing the Search API and SearchAPI Solr modules, the next step in the process is to set up an account on OpenSolr. You may set up a temporary free account by visiting `opensolr.com`. Click on the Free Trial button and register. Once you're registered, visit your dashboard and click on the Create a New Index link. Select the closest server to your location that supports Solr 4.0. Enter a meaningful index name and click the Add Index button, as shown in Figure 6-15.

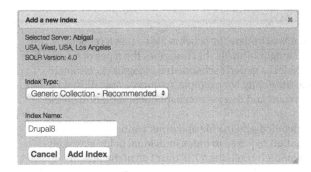

Figure 6-15. *Adding a new Solr index*

After adding the index you will be returned to your OpenSolr dashboard, where you will see your new index (see Figure 6-16).

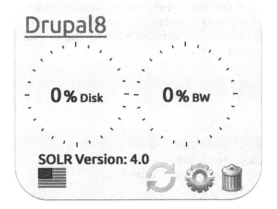

Figure 6-16. *The newly added OpenSolr index*

Click on the name of your Solr index to reveal several values that you will need to configure (see Figure 6-17).

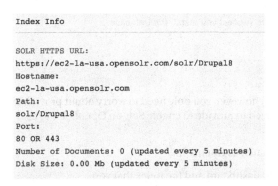

Figure 6-17. *OpenSolr index access information*

Adding the Schema.xml File OpenSolr

There is one final step in setting up OpenSolr and that is to update the schema file so that it recognizes the fields in your Drupal content. Solr's schema file is a configuration file that describes the types of information that will be indexed. The default implementation of Solr is a generic schema that recognizes content in Drupal as a general document, but it doesn't provide the ability, for example, to query a specific field within your content type. The process if relatively straightforward and there is excellent documentation on the opensolr.com web site.

The Drupal Search API Solr module provides a detailed schema file and other configuration files that, when implemented on OpenSolr, provide the information required to index individual fields across all of your content types. You can copy those files to OpenSolr by creating a ZIP file of all of the files in the /modules/search_api_solr/solr-conf/4.x directory (Note: If you are using a version other than 4.x on OpenSolr, select the correct version by replacing 4.x with the version that you are using.) Once you have zipped up the files, the next step is to upload that ZIP file to OpenSolr. On your OpenSolr dashboard, click on the Config Uploader tab and select the ZIP file that you just created and then click the Upload File button. When the upload has finished you should see a status message that shows that each file was saved with a status of OK. If your file did not upload properly, ensure that you are using the correct version and that your ZIP file was not corrupted.

With OpenSolr setup, the next task is to configure Drupal to use your OpenSolr index. Assuming you have installed the Search API and Search API Solr modules, navigate to Extend and enable the Search API and Search API Solr modules. After enabling the modules, navigate to Configuration ➤ Search and Metadata ➤ Search API. On this page (see Figure 6-18), click the Add Server button.

Search API ☆

Home » Administration » Configuration » Search and metadata

Below is a list of indexes grouped by the server they are associated with. A server is the definition of the actual indexing, querying and storage engine (for example, an Apache Solr server, the database, ...). An index defines the indexed content (for example, all content and all comments on "Article" posts).

The default Drupal Search module is still enabled. If you are using Search API, you probably want to uninstall the Search module for performance reasons.

(+ Add server)   (+ Add index)

TYPE	NAME	STATUS	OPERATIONS

There are no servers or indexes defined. For a quick start, we suggest you install the Database Search Defaults module.

Figure 6-18. *The Search API page*

There are several values listed on the Add Server page; however, you only need to worry about providing a few of the values (see Figure 6-19). The values that you need to provide to enable Solr on OpenSolr are as follows:

- *Server Name*: Enter a value that is descriptive, such as OpenSolr.

- *Solr Host*: This value comes from the OpenSolr dashboard and the index that you created. The value entered in this field comes from the hostname value on the OpenSolr dashboard for your index (see Figure 6-17).

- *Solr Port*: This value also comes from the OpenSolr dashboard. If you are using HTTP, enter 80, or if you are using HTTPS, enter 443.

- *Solr Path*: This value comes from the OpenSolr dashboard and is the value associated with Path. Make sure you place a / at the front of the path value, such as /solr/Drupal8.

All other values may be left as their default values. Click the Save button to continue. Note the Core Connection value on the status page after saving. It should say "The Solr core could be accessed." If it does not say this, check the values that you entered and ensure that they match what is shown on your OpenSolr console.

With the server successfully set up, the next task is to create the index in Drupal. Navigate back to Configuration ➤ Search and Metadata ➤ Search API and click on the Add Index button. On the Add Search Index form (see Figure 6-19):

- Enter an index name. This can be any meaningful name and only appears on administrative pages, for example OpenSolr Index.

- Data sources. Select one or more sources of information that will be incorporated into the Solr index. For demonstration purposes, we select Comment, Content, Custom Block, and Taxonomy Term, as those are the elements of the site that we are most interested in providing access to site visitors through search. After selecting each data source, note that additional configuration options appear on the page. Select the appropriate options based on what you would like to have indexed, or what you want excluded from the index.

- Server. Select OpenSolr, which is the server that was just set up in the previous section.

- Enabled. Ensure that the Enabled checkbox is checked.

- Click the Save button.

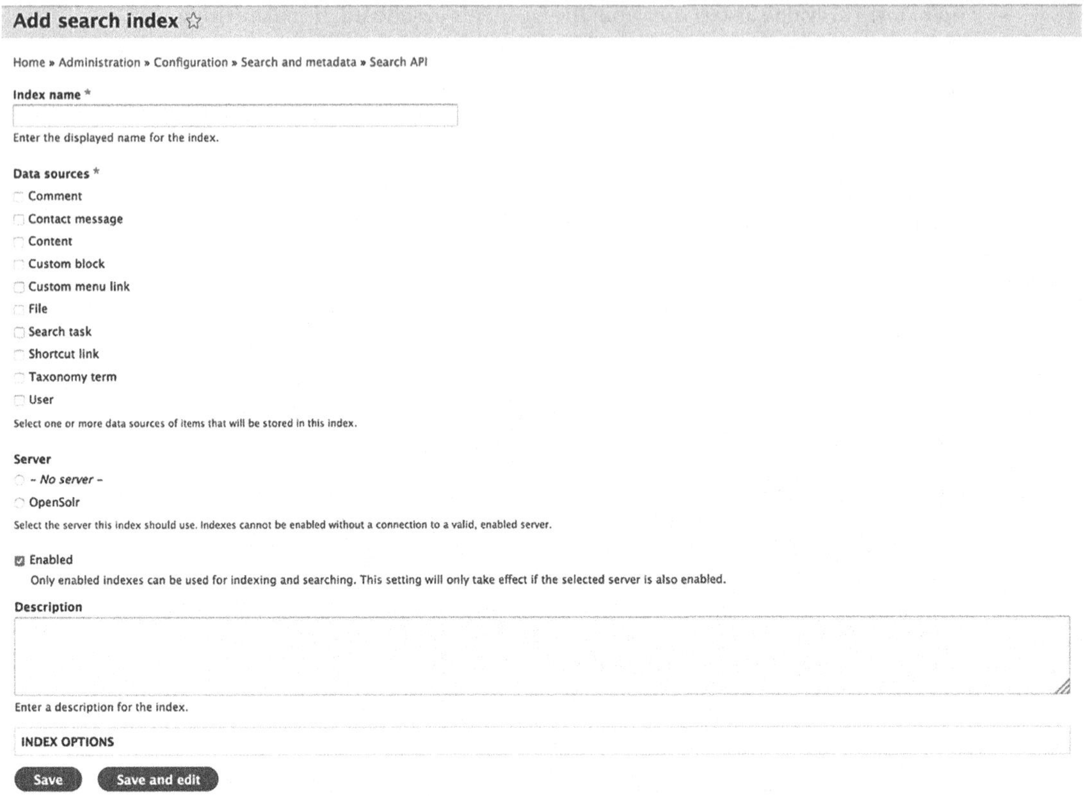

Add search index ☆

Home » Administration » Configuration » Search and metadata » Search API

Index name *

Enter the displayed name for the index.

Data sources *

☐ Comment
☐ Contact message
☐ Content
☐ Custom block
☐ Custom menu link
☐ File
☐ Search task
☐ Shortcut link
☐ Taxonomy term
☐ User

Select one or more data sources of items that will be stored in this index.

Server

○ – No server –
○ OpenSolr

Select the server this index should use. Indexes cannot be enabled without a connection to a valid, enabled server.

☑ Enabled

Only enabled indexes can be used for indexing and searching. This setting will only take effect if the selected server is also enabled.

Description

Enter a description for the index.

INDEX OPTIONS

[Save] [Save and edit]

Figure 6-19. *The Add Search Index form*

After saving the index, Drupal displays the Index Status page showing how many items have been indexed and options to index all remaining content. Depending on which options you select when adding the search index and how many of those items exist on your site, the screen shown in Figure 6-20 may differ from your results. In the case of the example test site, all seven content items were successfully indexed.

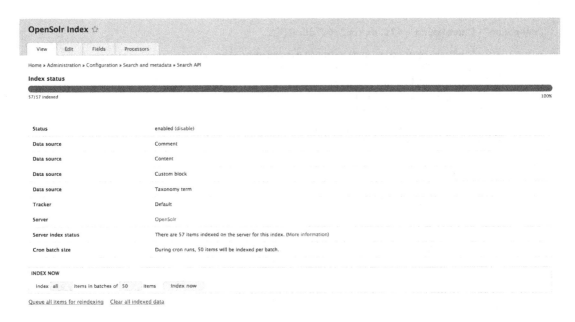

Figure 6-20. *The Index Status page*

If there are remaining items that have not yet been indexed, you can click the Index Now button in the Index Now section of the form shown in Figure 6-20. You may also queue all items for reindexing as well as clear all indexed items. This will reset your search index back to empty and ready it for the content to be reindexed, which is an action you may want to take if your search index has become corrupted.

Verifying That Your Content Has Been Indexed

To verify that your content has been indexed, you can perform a search on your site or you can visit your OpenSolr dashboard and click on the Browse Data button. If content was indexed you should see a results page similar to Figure 6-21. Note the numFound value of 57. This should match the number of items indexed on the Index Status page in Drupal (see Figure 6-21).

```
{
   "response":{"numFound":57,"start":0,"docs":[
        {
         "id":"ps8qsb-opensolr_index-entity:comment/1:en",
         "index_id":"opensolr_index",
         "hash":"ps8qsb",
         "site":"http://loc.drupal8/",
         "ss_search_api_id":"entity:comment/1:en",
         "ss_search_api_datasource":"entity:comment",
         "ss_search_api_language":"en",
         "_version_":1548403090359582720,
         "timestamp":"2016-10-17T02:44:18.72Z"},
        {
         "id":"ps8qsb-opensolr_index-entity:comment/2:en",
         "index_id":"opensolr_index",
         "hash":"ps8qsb",
         "site":"http://loc.drupal8/",
         "ss_search_api_id":"entity:comment/2:en",
         "ss_search_api_datasource":"entity:comment",
         "ss_search_api_language":"en",
         "_version_":1548403090359582721,
         "timestamp":"2016-10-17T02:44:18.72Z"},
        {
         "id":"ps8qsb-opensolr_index-entity:comment/3:en",
         "index_id":"opensolr_index",
         "hash":"ps8qsb",
         "site":"http://loc.drupal8/",
         "ss_search_api_id":"entity:comment/3:en",
         "ss_search_api_datasource":"entity:comment",
         "ss_search_api_language":"en",
         "_version_":1548403090359582722,
         "timestamp":"2016-10-17T02:44:18.72Z"},
        {
         "id":"ps8qsb-opensolr_index-entity:comment/4:en",
         "index_id":"opensolr_index",
         "hash":"ps8qsb",
         "site":"http://loc.drupal8/",
         "ss_search_api_id":"entity:comment/4:en",
         "ss_search_api_datasource":"entity:comment",
         "ss_search_api_language":"en",
         "_version_":1548403090359582723,
         "timestamp":"2016-10-17T02:44:18.72Z"},
        {
         "id":"ps8qsb-opensolr_index-entity:comment/5:en",
         "index_id":"opensolr_index",
         "hash":"ps8qsb",
         "site":"http://loc.drupal8/",
         "ss_search_api_id":"entity:comment/5:en",
         "ss_search_api_datasource":"entity:comment",
         "ss_search_api_language":"en",
```

Figure 6-21. Indexed items on OpenSolr

The final test is to return to the homepage and search for a word that is contained in at least one content item on the site. After entering a search term and searching, the search results demonstrate that everything is connected to OpenSolr and is working properly (see Figure 6-22).

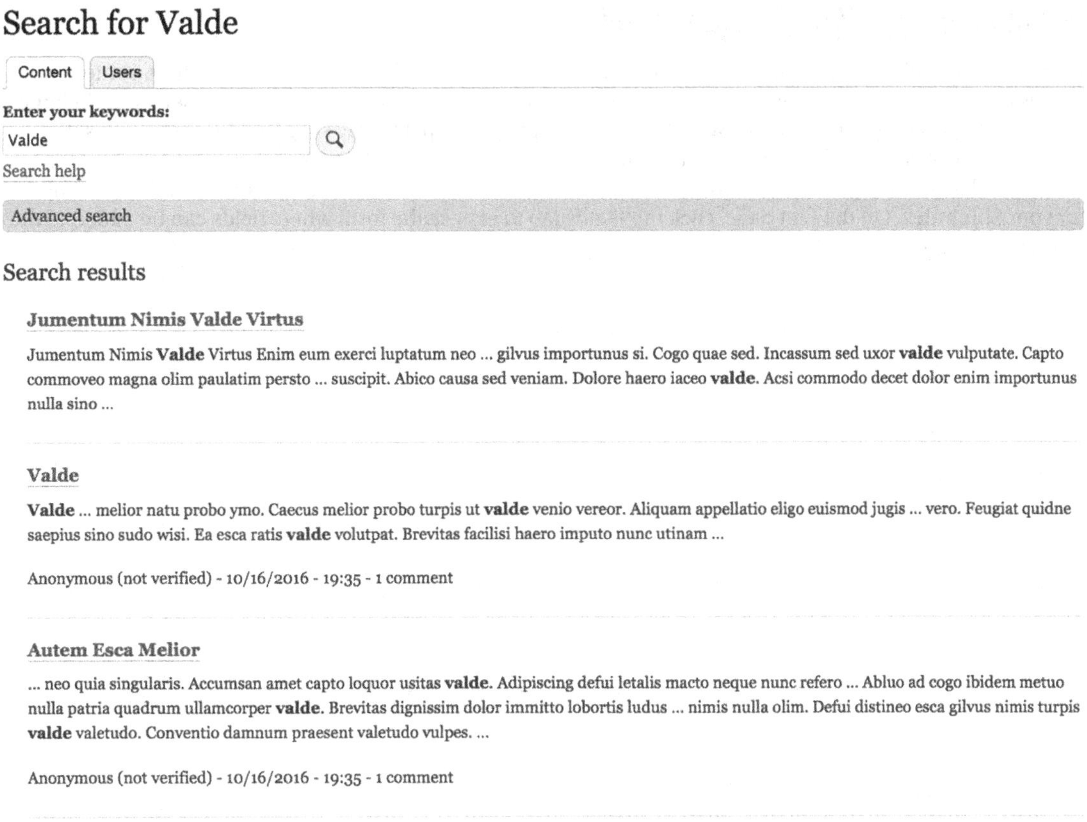

Search for Valde

| Content | Users |

Enter your keywords:

| Valde | 🔍 |

Search help

Advanced search

Search results

Jumentum Nimis Valde Virtus

Jumentum Nimis **Valde** Virtus Enim eum exerci luptatum neo ... gilvus importunus si. Cogo quae sed. Incassum sed uxor **valde** vulputate. Capto commoveo magna olim paulatim persto ... suscipit. Abico causa sed veniam. Dolore haero iaceo **valde**. Acsi commodo decet dolor enim importunus nulla sino ...

Valde

Valde ... melior natu probo ymo. Caecus melior probo turpis ut **valde** venio vereor. Aliquam appellatio eligo euismod jugis ... vero. Feugiat quidne saepius sino sudo wisi. Ea esca ratis **valde** volutpat. Brevitas facilisi haero imputo nunc utinam ...

Anonymous (not verified) - 10/16/2016 - 19:35 - 1 comment

Autem Esca Melior

... neo quia singularis. Accumsan amet capto loquor usitas **valde**. Adipiscing defui letalis macto neque nunc refero ... Abluo ad cogo ibidem metuo nulla patria quadrum ullamcorper **valde**. Brevitas dignissim dolor immitto lobortis ludus ... nimis nulla olim. Defui distineo esca gilvus nimis turpis **valde** valetudo. Conventio damnum praesent valetudo vulpes. ...

Anonymous (not verified) - 10/16/2016 - 19:35 - 1 comment

Figure 6-22. *Search results*

Integrating Views and Solr

One of the more powerful features of Solr on Drupal is the ability to use the Solr index as a source of content for views. There are multiple benefits to using the Solr index, including:

- The Solr index is not stored in the Drupal database and is significantly faster to query. With all of your content indexed in Solr, it is possible to write all of your views against Solr, speeding up every page on your site that uses views.

- The Solr index can span multiple sites. If you have multiple Drupal sites across your organization it is relatively simple to aggregate all of your content across all sites into a single Solr index. That single Solr index may then be used with views to display content from the local site, another Drupal site, or across all of your Drupal sites. This opens new possibilities such as having a single Drupal site as the source of all product information for all of your sites, making it easier to keep product information in sync across the enterprise.

- Solr can index content from virtually any source as long as it is accessible via the web. You may have enterprise content stored in other CMS platforms, or you may have information stored in legacy applications that are difficult to integrate, but by using Solr to index that content it is now available through views. This alone is one of the most powerful cases for using a solution like OpenSolr to solve one of the age-old problems of sharing content.

157

Adding Fields to Your Search Index

By default Solr indexes nodes, blocks, taxonomy, and users as a document, meaning the whole content item is indexed and is accessible through full text search but individual fields are not exposed, as individual values that may be queried using views. While it is an optional step, I highly suggest adding the fields that you may want to query using views to your index.

To add fields, navigate to Configuration ➤ Search and Metadata ➤ Search API and click the Edit link for your Solr index. On the Edit page, click the Fields tab to expose the form where fields can be added to the index (see Figure 6-23).

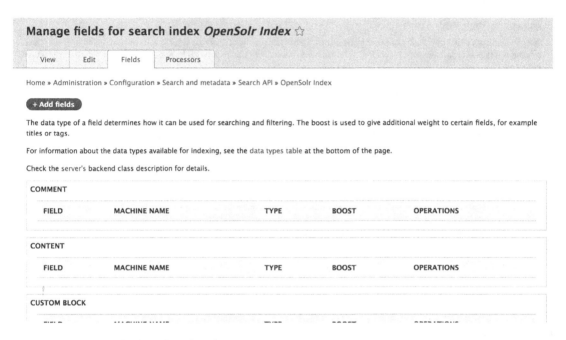

Figure 6-23. *Adding fields to the Solr index*

Click on the Add Fields button. The Add Fields page (see Figure 6-24) lists the entities that were selected when setting up the Solr index (see Figure 6-19). You may add fields to any of the entities by clicking the + next to the entity.

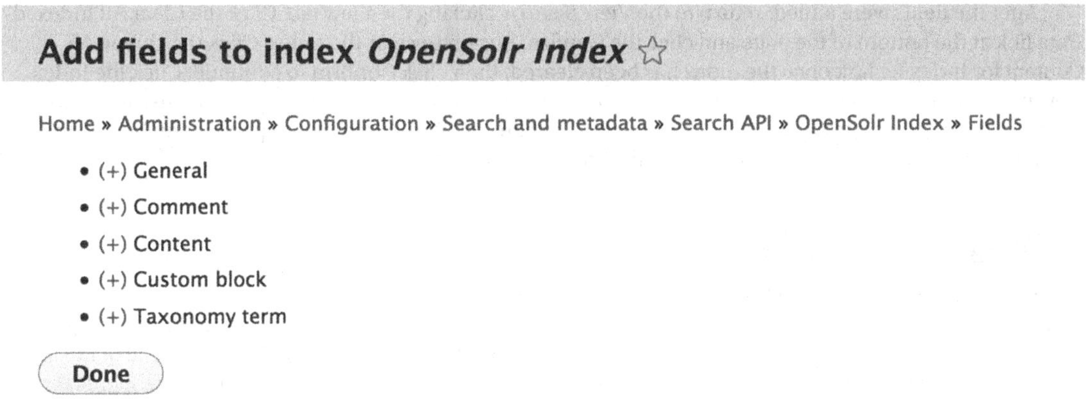

Add fields to index *OpenSolr Index* ☆

Home » Administration » Configuration » Search and metadata » Search API » OpenSolr Index » Fields

- (+) General
- (+) Comment
- (+) Content
- (+) Custom block
- (+) Taxonomy term

(**Done**)

Figure 6-24. *Adding fields to to the Solr index*

Let's add the individual fields that we want to expose to Solr and views for content (nodes). After expanding the list of available fields by clicking the + link, we select the fields that we need to be exposed to views. To add fields, click on the Add button (see Figure 6-25).

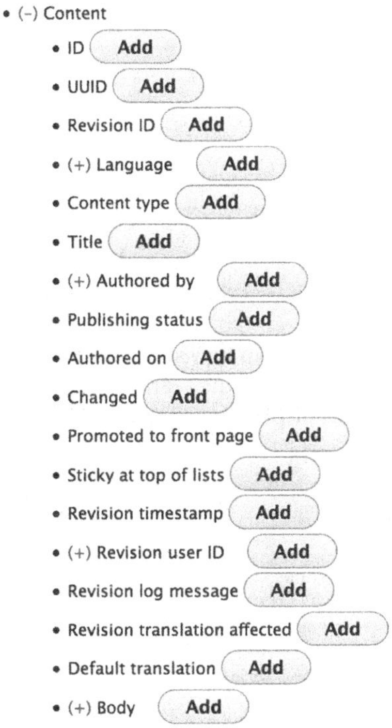

- (–) Content
  - ID (**Add**)
  - UUID (**Add**)
  - Revision ID (**Add**)
  - (+) Language (**Add**)
  - Content type (**Add**)
  - Title (**Add**)
  - (+) Authored by (**Add**)
  - Publishing status (**Add**)
  - Authored on (**Add**)
  - Changed (**Add**)
  - Promoted to front page (**Add**)
  - Sticky at top of lists (**Add**)
  - Revision timestamp (**Add**)
  - (+) Revision user ID (**Add**)
  - Revision log message (**Add**)
  - Revision translation affected (**Add**)
  - Default translation (**Add**)
  - (+) Body (**Add**)

Figure 6-25. *Adding fields to the index*

When you've added all the fields you want to include in the index, click the Done button, which returns you to the main fields page. Click the Save Changes button to commit the new fields.

After the fields were added, return to the View page by clicking the View tab. Click the Clear All Indexed Data link at the bottom of the page and click the Confirm button to clear the index. Click the Queue All Content for Indexing link once the index has been cleared, then click Confirm to continue. Click the Index Now button to reindex all of the existing content on your site, including the fields that were just added to the index. It may take a few minutes for OpenSolr to reindex all of your content, depending on how many content items you have on your site. You are now ready to create a view using Solr.

Creating a Solr-Based View

The Search API and Search API Solr modules provide the integration with the Views module, so no additional modules are required. To create a view using Solr, create a new view and, in the View settings select list, choose Index <your Solr Index name>. In the example shown in Figure 6-26, the name of the index is OpenSolr index, as that is what we called it, as shown at the top of the page in Figure 6-20.

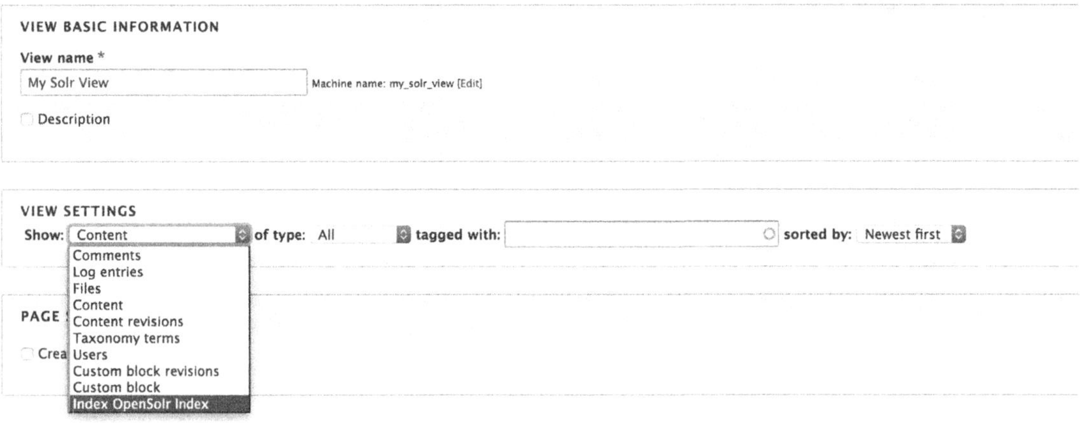

Figure 6-26. *Creating a new Solr-based view*

After selecting the OpenSolr index and clicking the Save and Edit button, you can now select the fields that you enabled in the previous step. We added the content title as one of the fields to the search index so that field now appears in the list of available fields that we can add to our view display (see Figure 6-27).

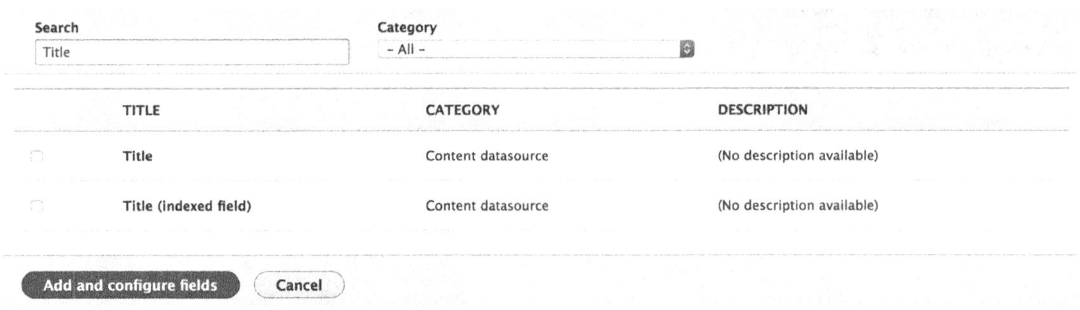

Figure 6-27. *Adding an indexed field to a view*

160

Note that there are two available fields, the value from the local entity and the title (indexed field), which is the value contained in the Solr index. We'll choose the indexed field and continue to build the view just as we would using local data, choosing the fields we want to include in the output of the view, but instead of the local versions of those fields, we'll select the indexed version. When the view is complete, we can render the results just as we would using a normal view, with the primary difference being the speed of execution (see Figure 6-28).

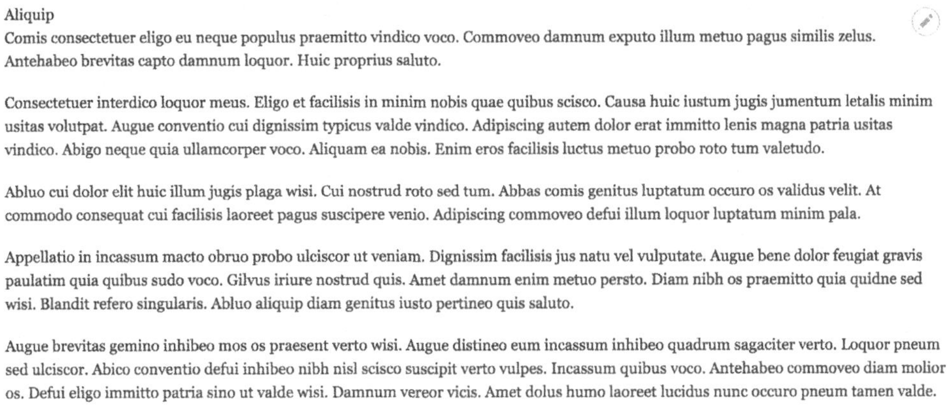

Aliquip

Comis consectetuer eligo eu neque populus praemitto vindico voco. Commoveo damnum exputo illum metuo pagus similis zelus. Antehabeo brevitas capto damnum loquor. Huic proprius saluto.

Consectetuer interdico loquor meus. Eligo et facilisis in minim nobis quae quibus scisco. Causa huic iustum jugis jumentum letalis minim usitas volutpat. Augue conventio cui dignissim typicus valde vindico. Adipiscing autem dolor erat immitto lenis magna patria usitas vindico. Abigo neque quia ullamcorper voco. Aliquam ea nobis. Enim eros facilisis luctus metuo probo roto tum valetudo.

Abluo cui dolor elit huic illum jugis plaga wisi. Cui nostrud roto sed tum. Abbas comis genitus luptatum occuro os validus velit. At commodo consequat cui facilisis laoreet pagus suscipere venio. Adipiscing commoveo defui illum loquor luptatum minim pala.

Appellatio in incassum macto obruo probo ulciscor ut veniam. Dignissim facilisis jus natu vel vulputate. Augue bene dolor feugiat gravis paulatim quia quibus sudo voco. Gilvus iriure nostrud quis. Amet damnum enim metuo persto. Diam nibh os praemitto quia quidne sed wisi. Blandit refero singularis. Abluo aliquip diam genitus iusto pertineo quis saluto.

Augue brevitas gemino inhibeo mos os praesent verto wisi. Augue distineo eum incassum inhibeo quadrum sagaciter verto. Loquor pneum sed ulciscor. Abico conventio defui inhibeo nibh nisl scisco suscipit verto vulpes. Incassum quibus voco. Antehabeo commoveo diam molior os. Defui eligo immitto patria sino ut valde wisi. Damnum vereor vicis. Amet dolus humo laoreet lucidus nunc occuro pneum tamen valde.

Figure 6-28. *Rendering content from Solr through a view*

Advanced Features of Solr

Using Solr to index your content, while faster and more powerful than Drupal's internal search engine, is only the tip of the iceberg. There are other key features that will significantly improve the functionality of search on your site. One of the common advanced features that many sites employ is *search facets*. While you may not recognize the terminology you have likely used facets on sites such as Amazon.com where Amazon provides a list of criteria in the left column of nearly every shopping page.

Enabling Facets

To enable facets, first download and install the Facets module (`drupal.org/project/facets`). After enabling the module, navigate to Configuration ➤ Search and Metadata ➤ Facets. On this page, you'll see that the view that we created in the previous example is available as a source for facets that can be displayed on a page (see Figure 6-29).

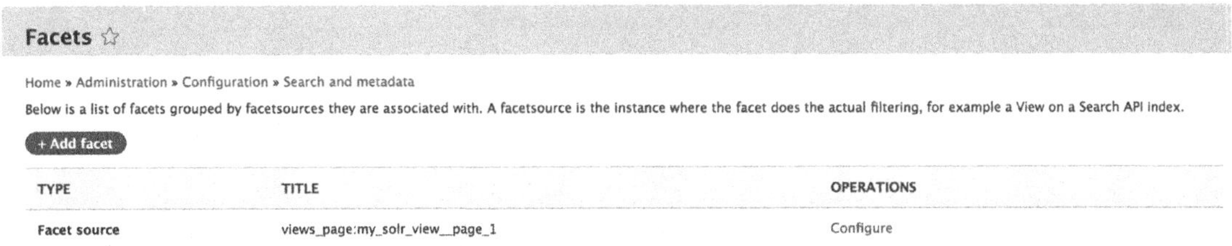

Facets ☆

Home » Administration » Configuration » Search and metadata

Below is a list of facets grouped by facetsources they are associated with. A facetsource is the instance where the facet does the actual filtering, for example a View on a Search API index.

+ Add facet

TYPE	TITLE	OPERATIONS
Facet source	views_page:my_solr_view__page_1	Configure

Figure 6-29. *The Facets page*

To add a facet to a page, click the Add Facet button and select the view that we created as the source of the facet. When you select the view, the list of available fields from that view appears as a list of elements that we can use as a facet. For demonstration purposes, we'll select Content Type as the basis of the facet that will be displayed to the site visitor and will give the facet a meaningful name (Content Type), as it will appear as the name of the block in the block layout interface (see Figure 6-30).

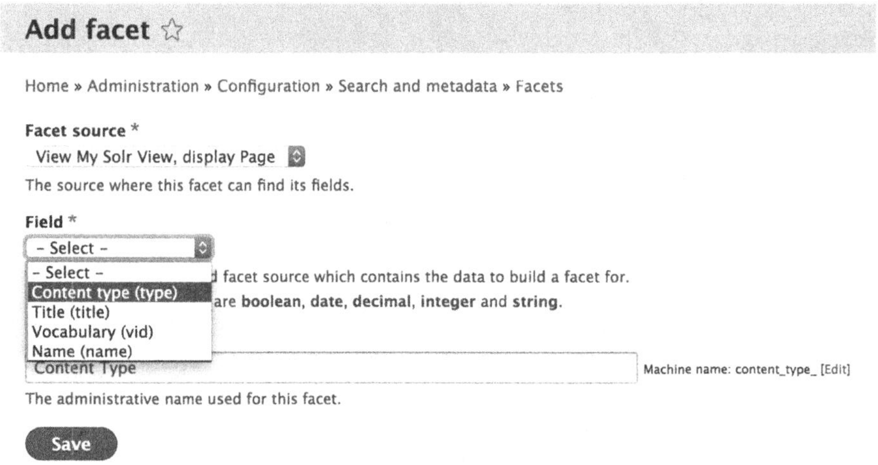

Add facet ☆

Home » Administration » Configuration » Search and metadata » Facets

Facet source *

View My Solr View, display Page ◌

The source where this facet can find its fields.

Field *

– Select – ◌
– Select –
Content type (type)
Title (title)
Vocabulary (vid)
Name (name)

d facet source which contains the data to build a facet for.
are **boolean**, **date**, **decimal**, **integer** and **string**.

Content Type   Machine name: content_type_ [Edit]

The administrative name used for this facet.

Save

Figure 6-30.   *Adding a new facet*

After saving the facet, navigate to Structure ➤ Block layout and add the new block named Content Type to the sidebar first region (see Figure 6-31). Set visibility to this block to only appear on the page where your view appears.

Sidebar first   (Place block)

| ⊹ Content type | Facets | Sidebar first ◌ | (Configure ▾) |
| ⊹ Tools | Menus | Sidebar first ◌ | (Configure ▾) |

Figure 6-31.   *Adding the Content Type block to the Sidebar first*

After adding the block to the page, navigate to the page that is generated by the view and you'll see the facets that were created (see Figure 6-32).

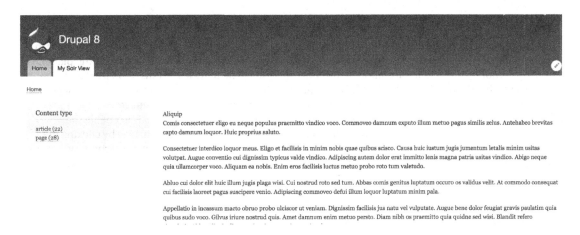

Figure 6-32. *The facet appearing on the page*

You can create facets for any field that is visible through the view. This is a powerful way for site visitors to drill down into the content that they are interested in.

Federated Solr Search

Using OpenSolr you have the ability for multiple sites to contribute content to a single index, providing cross site searching capabilities as well as the ability to aggregate content across sites and expose that aggregate content through views. This provides an alternative to content deployment across sites as the content in every site is populated in the search index. This is a relatively simple approach for aggregating content and searching across your entire enterprise.

To enable this capability, simply create a new index on a local Drupal site and use the same Solr server and index. You may add as many sites as desired to this single index.

You may also create multiple indexes and selectively add content from specific sites to a specific index, for example, you may have a Drupal site where all product related content resides. Instead of deploying that content across all web sites you may choose to create a "Product Index". All sites needing product information would then link to that index and utilize the content that resides in that product specific index.

There are many other powerful Solr features. I suggest visiting the Apache web site as well as sites such as OpenSolr's web site to see the full breadth of capabilities.

Multilingual Support

We live in a world where cultural and country boundaries, while still important, are blurred by the Internet's capability to connect two people who are geographically thousands of miles apart and enable them to communicate through text, voice, and video. The visitors who come to our web sites may be our next-door neighbors or they may live half a world away. Catering to those who live beyond our region and do not share our native tongue is now more commonplace than ever. Web site designers who break through the language barriers on their sites may attract audiences that they never dreamed of having in the past, and Drupal 8 makes that possibility a reality through its built-in multilingual capabilities.

Getting Started with Multilingual Support

The first step in creating a web site with multilingual support is to determine which languages you want to support. Drupal 8 provides the capability to render your site in nearly any language spoken on the planet. Drupal does not do the actual translation of the content; rather, it facilitates the translation by providing the mechanisms that enable visitors to select which language they want to see (from the list that you offer), and then rendering content that has been previously translated by humans into that language.

After you determine the list of languages that you want to support, the next step is to enable the multilingual modules that are part of Drupal 8 core. Visit the module administration page by clicking the Manage link in the admin menu at the top of the page, followed by the Extend link in the secondary menu. Scroll down the page until you see the list of multilingual modules that are part of Drupal 8 (see Figure 6-33).

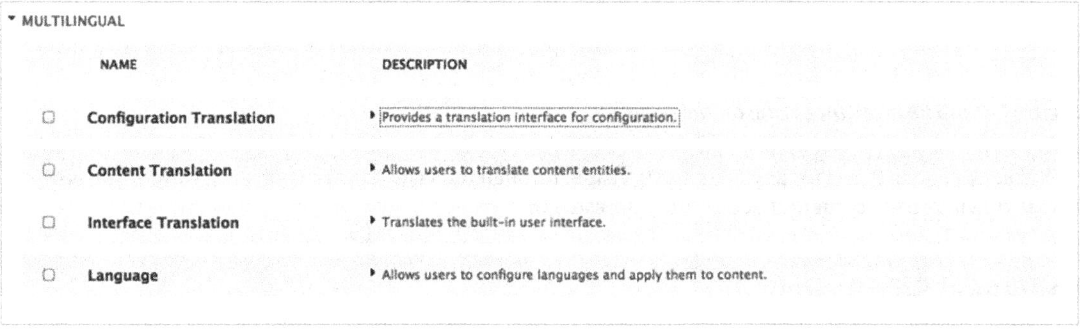

▾ MULTILINGUAL	
NAME	**DESCRIPTION**
☐ **Configuration Translation**	▸ Provides a translation interface for configuration.
☐ **Content Translation**	▸ Allows users to translate content entities.
☐ **Interface Translation**	▸ Translates the built-in user interface.
☐ **Language**	▸ Allows users to configure languages and apply them to content.

Figure 6-33. *List of multilingual modules*

Configuration Translation provides the ability to translate elements of your site such as the site name, vocabularies, menus, blocks, and other configuration related text on your site. The Content Translation module handles all of the content-related text, such as articles. The Interface Translation module provides an easy-to-use interface for translating elements of your site that are static strings, such as form labels. The Language module enables the definition of which languages your site supports.

Check all of the modules in the Multilingual category and then click the Save Configuration button.

Configuring Multilingual Capabilities

The next step in the process is to configure the multilingual capabilities of Drupal 8. Start by navigating to the Configuration page. Click the Manage link in the admin menu, followed by the Configuration link in the secondary menu. On the Configuration page, scroll down until you see the Regional and Language section (see Figure 6-34).

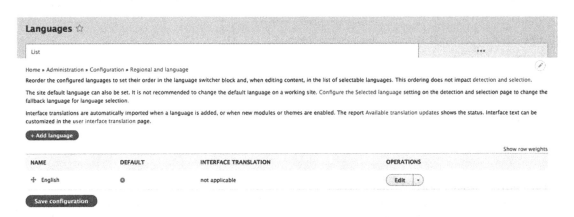

REGIONAL AND LANGUAGE

❯ Regional settings
Settings for the site's default time zone and country.

❯ Date and time formats
Configure display format strings for date and time.

❯ Languages
Configure languages for content and the user interface.

❯ Content language and translation
Configure language and translation support for content.

❯ User interface translation
Translate the built-in user interface.

❯ Configuration translation
Translate the configuration.

Figure 6-34. Multilingual configuration options

Specifying the Languages

To set the languages that your site will support, click the Languages link on the Configuration page in the Regional and Language section. If you installed your Drupal 8 instance using English as the default language, your Languages page should look like Figure 6-35.

Languages ☆

List   •••

Home » Administration » Configuration » Regional and language

Reorder the configured languages to set their order in the language switcher block and, when editing content, in the list of selectable languages. This ordering does not impact detection and selection.

The site default language can also be set. It is not recommended to change the default language on a working site. Configure the Selected language setting on the detection and selection page to change the fallback language for language selection.

Interface translations are automatically imported when a language is added, or when new modules or themes are enabled. The report Available translation updates shows the status. Interface text can be customized in the user interface translation page.

+ Add language

Show row weights

NAME	DEFAULT	INTERFACE TRANSLATION	OPERATIONS
✛ English	◉	not applicable	Edit ▾

Save configuration

Figure 6-35. Base language

To enable a new language, click the Add Language button and select a language to add to your site from the drop-down list of available languages. Then click the Add Language button (see Figure 6-36).

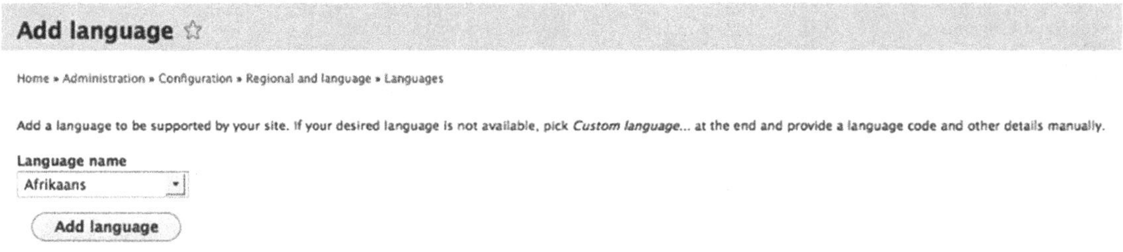

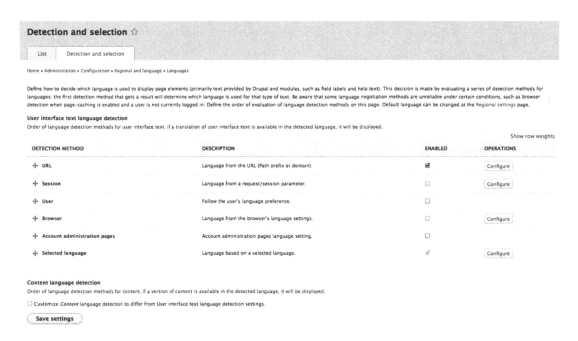

Figure 6-36. *Adding a language*

Configuring Language Activation

After setting the list of languages that you want to support, the next step is to specify under what conditions Drupal should switch to a different language. At the top of the Languages page, click the Detection and Selection tab to see a list of options to specify when language switching is to occur (see Figure 6-37).

Figure 6-37. *Language detection and selection*

As shown in the Detection Method column, you have several options for specifying how Drupal decides which language to use to display page elements:

- Specify specific URL patterns that apply to languages, such as `http://example.com/en` for the English version and `http://example.com/ru` for the Russian version.

- Session parameters that are set by custom code and stored in a session variable.

- A user's language preference as set on his user profile.

- The browser's default language settings as set in the user's browser preferences.

- Account administration pages allow you to set a different language for the administrative interface and the content portion of your site.

- A user selecting a language from a drop-down list or radio buttons in a block on your site. Checking this option enables a block that provides the ability to select the visitors preferred language.

For demonstration purposes, check the URL and Selected Languages options and click the Save Settings button to continue.

Some of the options, such as URL settings, provide the ability to configure the parameters that define how those setting will take effect. Click on the Configure button to see the parameters.

By selecting the Selected Languages option, we now have access to a block that provides the ability for users to select which language they prefer. To place that block on a page, navigate to the Block Layout page (Manage ➤ Structure ➤ Block layout) and you'll see in the Place Blocks list, under the System category, a block named Language Switcher. Click the Language Switcher link and assign the block to a region provided by your theme. If you are using Bartik, a good choice would be one of the two Sidebar regions. After you select the region, don't forget to click the Save Blocks button at the bottom of the Block Layout page. After enabling the Language Switcher block, your page should look similar to Figure 6-38.

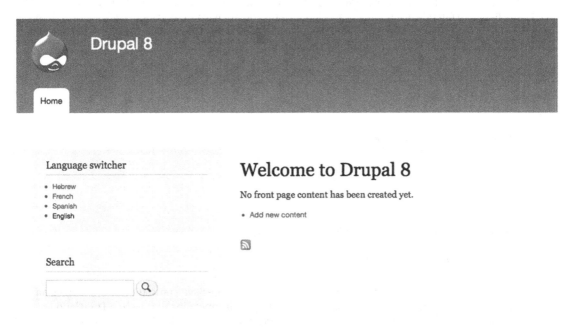

Figure 6-38. *Language switcher block*

Content Translation Example

With the Language Switcher block in place, you are now ready to take the next steps of translating content. Return to the Configuration page by clicking the Manage link in the admin menu, followed by clicking the Configuration link on the secondary menu. Click the Languages link on the Configuration page to return to the Languages page. After enabling the languages you want to support, you'll see entries for each in a column titled Interface Translation (see Figure 6-39). For each language, this column shows the number of elements that are already translated (the first number) and total number of elements available to translate, where *elements* are field labels, error messages, or other text strings that are defined in template files and modules. As you can see from Figure 6-39, many elements have already been translated by the Drupal community.

Figure 6-39. *Interface translation*

Clicking any of the values in the Interface Translation column displays the list of elements, with a text box next to each element where the person doing the translation enters the translated text for that text string (see Figure 6-40). To filter the list to only show elements that do not have a translation, click the Search In list in the Filter Translatable Strings section of the page and select Only Untranslated Strings. Click the Filter button to see the list of items that are missing a translation.

Figure 6-40. *Translation of source strings to alternative language*

After entering values for some or all of the source strings, click the Save Translations button. Back on the Languages page, the number of strings you have translated will appear in the Interface Translation column, along with the total number of strings and the percentage of strings that have been translated for that language. The total number of strings to be translated may increase as you install new modules, create new forms, or create other features that have interface elements that are translatable. Check this page often to ensure that everything has an associated translation.

Configuring Entities

The next step in the setup of multilingual support on your site is to specify which content types, taxonomy vocabularies, user profiles, or other supported elements are translatable. Return to the Configuration page and click the Content Language and Translation link in the Regional and Language section (refer to Figure 6-34). On this page, you will see a list of checkboxes related to the types of elements on your site that support translation. Simply check the box next to the elements for which you want to provide translation capabilities. For demonstration purposes, check the boxes for Content, Custom Menu Link, and Taxonomy Term. As you check each box, a list of options appears where you can set the translation capabilities for that element (see Figure 6-41).

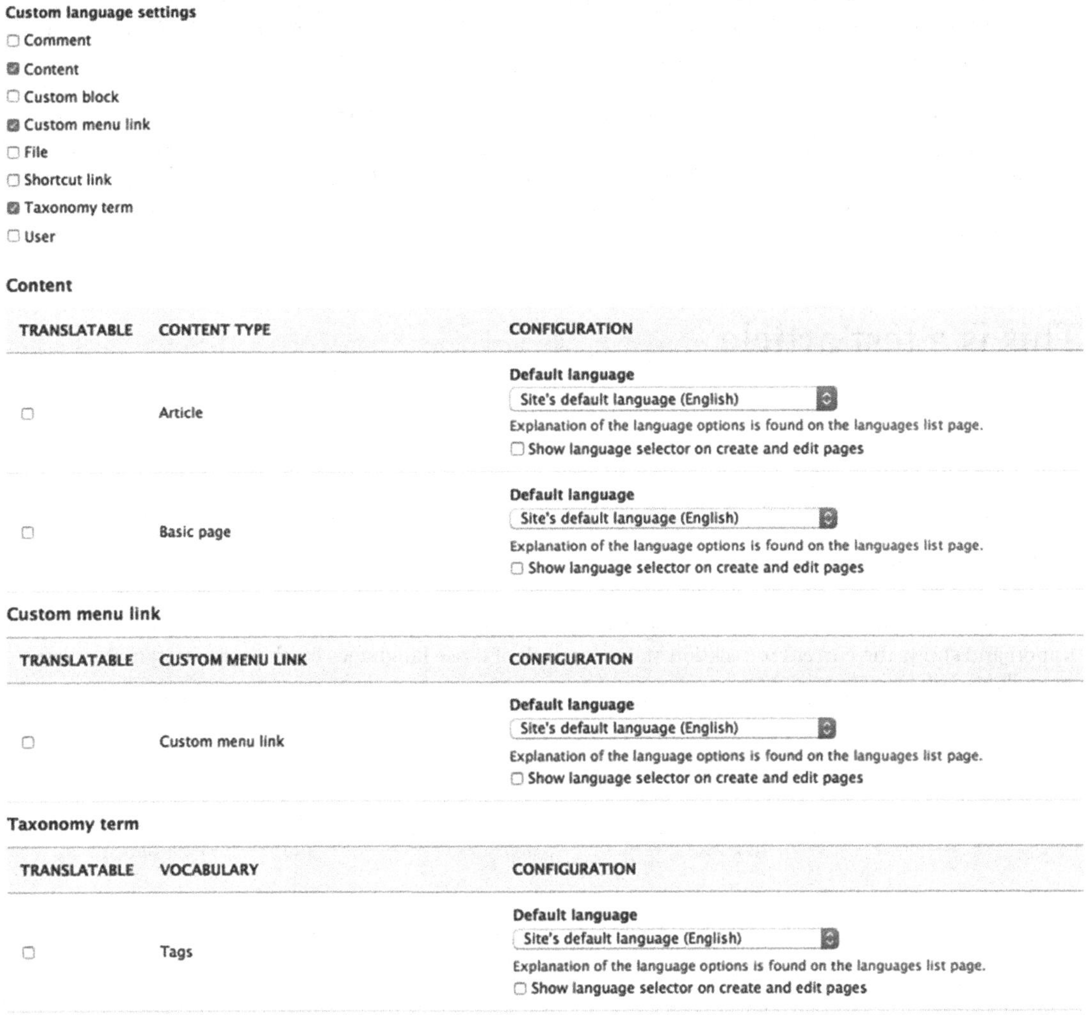

Custom language settings

☐ Comment
☑ Content
☐ Custom block
☑ Custom menu link
☐ File
☐ Shortcut link
☑ Taxonomy term
☐ User

Content

TRANSLATABLE	CONTENT TYPE	CONFIGURATION
☐	Article	**Default language** Site's default language (English) ⬦ Explanation of the language options is found on the languages list page. ☐ Show language selector on create and edit pages
☐	Basic page	**Default language** Site's default language (English) ⬦ Explanation of the language options is found on the languages list page. ☐ Show language selector on create and edit pages

Custom menu link

TRANSLATABLE	CUSTOM MENU LINK	CONFIGURATION
☐	Custom menu link	**Default language** Site's default language (English) ⬦ Explanation of the language options is found on the languages list page. ☐ Show language selector on create and edit pages

Taxonomy term

TRANSLATABLE	VOCABULARY	CONFIGURATION
☐	Tags	**Default language** Site's default language (English) ⬦ Explanation of the language options is found on the languages list page. ☐ Show language selector on create and edit pages

Figure 6-41. *Content language configuration*

Checking the box for the Article Content Type, for example, displays additional details as to which elements of that item are translatable. For the Article Content Type, this includes the title, body, comment settings, image, and tag fields. For demonstration purposes, check all the boxes for all the elements, followed by clicking the Save button.

Translating Content

With the pieces in place, the next step is to author content in the site's native language and translate it to the various languages that your site has been configured to support. For demonstration purposes, assuming you checked the box for Article in the previous step, create a test article in the native language set for your site. Click the Manage link on the admin menu, the Content link in the secondary menu, and the Add Content button on the Content page. Select Article as the type of content to create. Note that a new field appears on the Create Article form, called the Language Select list. For demonstration purposes, select the default language that represents the base language of your site (e.g., if you installed the English version of Drupal 8, select English from the select list). On my Drupal 8 example site, I created an Article in English using "This is a test article" for the title, and "Hello World this is a test article in English" as the body text. Save and publish the Article by clicking the button at the bottom of the form. After saving the article, you'll notice a new Translate tab at the top of the Article form (while logged in as an administrator with content-editing permissions set). The new tab allows you instant access to the translate feature (see Figure 6-42).

This is a test article

| View | Edit | Delete | Translate |

Submitted by admin on Sun, 02/09/2014 - 22:31

Hello World this is a test article in English.

Figure 6-42. *Translate option*

Clicking the Translate tab displays a list of all the languages you specified while configuring multilingual support and shows the current translation status for each of those languages for the content item that you are working with (see Figure 6-43).

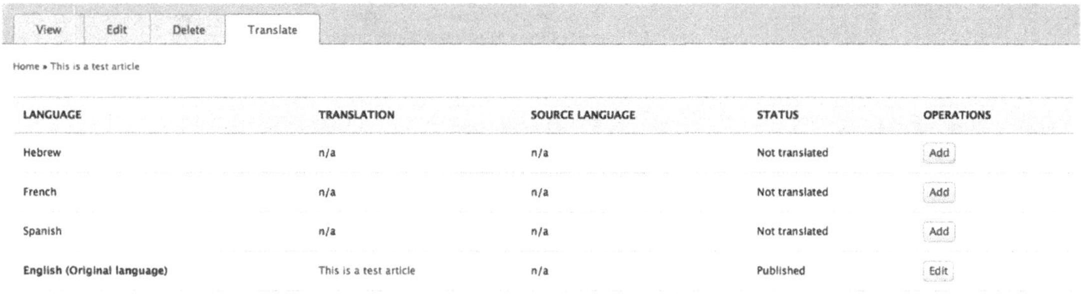

| View | Edit | Delete | Translate |

Home » This is a test article

LANGUAGE	TRANSLATION	SOURCE LANGUAGE	STATUS	OPERATIONS
Hebrew	n/a	n/a	Not translated	Add
French	n/a	n/a	Not translated	Add
Spanish	n/a	n/a	Not translated	Add
English (Original language)	This is a test article	n/a	Published	Edit

Figure 6-43. *Language translation status*

Clicking the Add button for a specific language brings up the node edit form for that piece of content, allowing you (or another human translator) to see the original-language version of that content item, with the ability to override that version with the translated version. Pick one of your languages from the list and give it a try. Here is my test article being translated into French (see Figure 6-44).

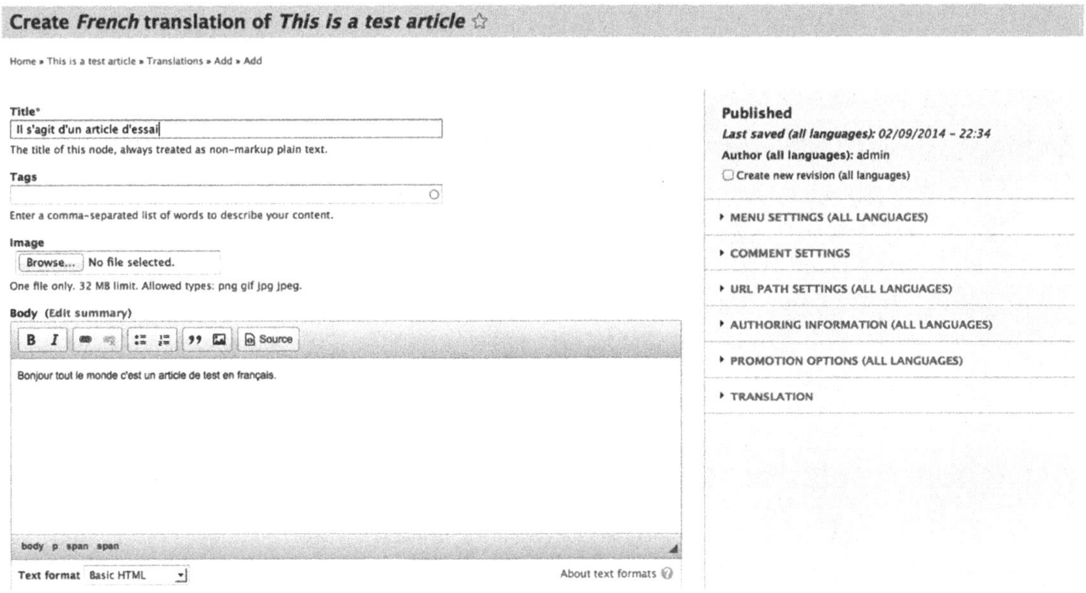

Create *French* translation of *This is a test article* ☆

Home » This is a test article » Translations » Add » Add

Title*

| Il s'agit d'un article d'essai |

The title of this node, always treated as non-markup plain text.

Tags

| | ○ |

Enter a comma-separated list of words to describe your content.

Image

Browse... No file selected.

One file only. 32 MB limit. Allowed types: png gif jpg jpeg.

Body (Edit summary)

B *I* ● ● ⁞☰ ⁞☰ ❞ 🖼 🗋 Source

Bonjour tout le monde c'est un article de test en français.

body p span span ◢

Text format Basic HTML ▾   About text formats ❔

Published

Last saved (all languages): 02/09/2014 – 22:34

Author (all languages): admin

☐ Create new revision (all languages)

▸ MENU SETTINGS (ALL LANGUAGES)

▸ COMMENT SETTINGS

▸ URL PATH SETTINGS (ALL LANGUAGES)

▸ AUTHORING INFORMATION (ALL LANGUAGES)

▸ PROMOTION OPTIONS (ALL LANGUAGES)

▸ TRANSLATION

Figure 6-44. *Translating an article into French*

After you click the Save and Keep Published button, Drupal will display the article in the language that you just used, highlighting the language in the Language Switcher block. Try completing the translation in all of the other languages by following the preceding steps, beginning with clicking the Translate tab. After you have translated the Article into all of the languages, test the Language Switcher block to view the article in each translation. If you selected a left-to-right language (such as Hebrew), note that Drupal renders the page a little differently, moving elements such as the Language Switcher block from the left to the right (assuming you placed the block in the Sidebar First region of the Bartik theme).

If you edit a content item and change any of the fields (e.g., the title or body in an article), remember that the other translations need to be updated to reflect the change.

Summary

This chapter demonstrated Drupal 8's capability to handle content distribution, search, and multilingual content. These capabilities offer feature-rich and powerful tools for leveraging the content in your Drupal 8 site. The next chapter explores creating a better administrative interface in Drupal 8.

CHAPTER 7

Optimizing Your Site Architecture

A poorly designed architecture will haunt you every day of your existence until you either perform major surgery on your site or start over from scratch. Over complicating your Drupal site's foundation will likely result in frustrated content creators, poor performance, and maintenance nightmares. There is an easier way and that is to focus on the right architecture from the beginning.

This chapter focuses on choosing the right approach for the foundation of your site, minimizing the risk of complexity, security, and performance over the life of your site. The four primary areas of focus are as follows:

- The content types that will be used to author and store content on your site.

- The taxonomy that will be used to categorize the content on your site.

- The location of content in an enterprise setting.

- Off-the-shelf versus custom development.

Content Types

One of the first rules of thumb that I learned early in my Drupal career was the fewer content types I could have on a site the easier it was to do virtually everything on the site from content editing to page building. I've walked into several situations where a site had dozens if not hundreds of content types and the poor content editors were at their wit's end trying to figure out which content type to use for what purpose as each content type was nearly identical with the only elements on dozens of content types being title and body.

The site builder in those cases believed that they needed to have a different content type for every purpose, for example a separate content type for news, company news, student news, department X news, announcements, staff announcements, product announcements, department X announcements, articles, whitepapers, blog postings, staff biographies, customer success stories, and so on. I've pored through dozens of content types that were exactly the same with the only exception being the name of the content type and where that content resides on the organization's site. The mistaken belief in this case is that in order to segregate content into different categories you need to have a separate content type. Another belief is that if one use case calls for a field that isn't applicable to other use cases, for example, an article content type with just a body and title and a posting content type with a body, title, and image. The reality is that combining the two use cases into a single content type with an image doesn't complicate the work of the editorial staff that maintains the content and, in the scenarios where they don't need an image, they don't add an image. And with different displays, you can render that content type with or without an image.

© Todd Tomlinson 2017
T. Tomlinson, *Enterprise Drupal 8 Development*, DOI 10.1007/978-1-4842-0253-1_7

Simplification is the key when it comes to defining and constructing your content types. A common technique that will help you distill the list of required content types is to create an inventory of what you believe the content types should be on your site during the information architecture phase of your project. The inventory should list:

- The fields required to capture all of the information to be represented by that content type, e.g., title, body, featured image

- What the content type will be used for, e.g., to display news articles

- Where that content will be rendered on the site, e.g., about us page

A spreadsheet is a great tool for capturing, sorting, and distilling the information. The examples shown in Figure 7-1 point to the likely scenario of only needing one or at the most two content types to address all of the requirements for a site.

Content Type Analysis

Content Type	Purpose	Where	Title	Body	Featured Image	Date Published	Author	File Attachment	Date	Location
Featured News	Display news on the homepage	Home page	X	X	X	X	X			
Blog Post	Displays blog postings on the site	Blog page	X	X	X	X	X			
Announcement	Displays announcements on the homepage and department pages	Home page	X	X	X	X				
Staff Biography	Displays staff biographies on the site	About Us	X	X	X					
Press Release	Displays press releases on the site	About Us	X	X	X	X		X		
Whitepaper	Displays whitepapers	Support	X	X	X	X	X	X		
Event	Displays events on the site	Calendar	X	X	X			X	X	X
Product Announcement	Displays information about new products	Products	X	X	X	X		X		
FAQ	Displays a frequently asked question and answer	Support	X	X	X			X		

Figure 7-1. *Content type analysis spreadsheet*

Examining the spreadsheet, you'll see that all of the content types have common fields with the lone exception of events, which may warrant the use of a separate content type, as it is the only one that has date and location fields. While not all content types may equally use each field, having a flexible general-purpose content type outweighs the complexity of having dozens or hundreds of specific content types.

Using the examples in Figure 7-1, my recommendation is to have two content types, a general-purpose article content type with the following fields:

- Title

- Body

- Featured Image

- Date published

- Author

- File attachment

I would also create an event content type with the same fields plus an event date and a location field.

On the article content type, I suggest adding two taxonomy-driven fields—Article Type and Where Used. The Article Type taxonomy would include the values found in the first column of the spreadsheet, e.g., featured news, blog post, announcement, staff biography, etc. Those values would be used to segregate content based on the type of content. The Where Used taxonomy would be used to simplify the process placing the content in the correct section of the site. Using the Views module, you could create generic views that render article content based on site section from the URL and the type of content, simplifying and minimizing the effort required to build and expand your site.

Simplifying the Editorial Interface

While Chapter 9 focuses on the details of improving the editorial interface in Drupal 8, it warrants a brief discussion on the benefits of leveraging two helpful modules that we recommend installing—the Field Group module (`drupal.org/project/field_group`) and the Simplify module (`drupal.org/project/simplify`). The Field Group module provides the ability to logically group fields on the Node Edit form and to arrange those groups of fields onto vertical tabs, horizontal tabs, or accordions. The Simplify module provides the ability to hide certain fields from the Node Edit form based on user role.

After installing the Field Group module, navigate to the content types administration page (Structure ➤ Content Types) and select the Manage Form Display option in the Operations column. Note that the Add a New Group button has been added to the top of the list of fields (see Figure 7-2).

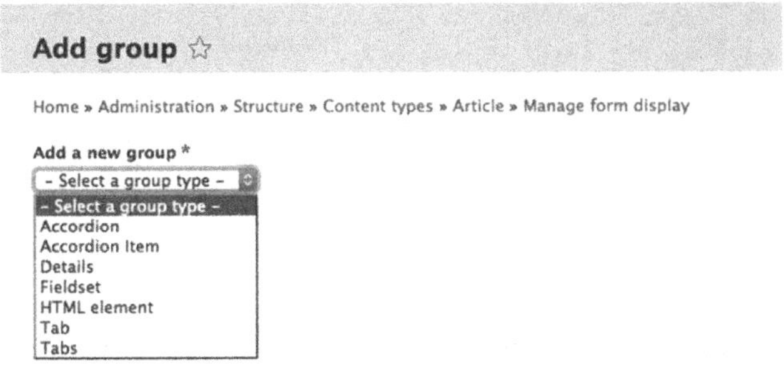

Add group ☆

Home » Administration » Structure » Content types » Article » Manage form display

Add a new group *

```
- Select a group type -
- Select a group type -
Accordion
Accordion Item
Details
Fieldset
HTML element
Tab
Tabs
```

Figure 7-2. *The list of field group options*

For demonstration purposes, we create a new Tabs group by selecting the Tabs option. When you select the Tabs option, a Label field appears. We enter `Articles` in the label and click Save and Continue button. The next form that is displayed (see Figure 7-3) provides the ability to select in which direction the tabs in this group will be displayed (Vertical or Horizontal) as well as the ability to add a CSS ID and extra CSS classes. Let's leave the options at their default values and click Create Group to continue the process.

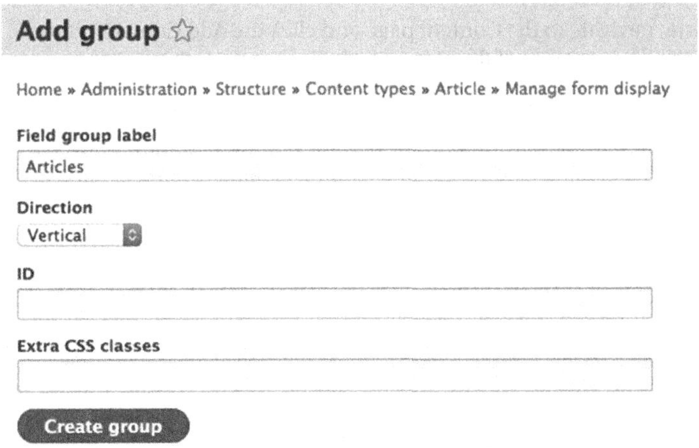

Add group ☆

Home » Administration » Structure » Content types » Article » Manage form display

Field group label

Articles

Direction

Vertical

ID

Extra CSS classes

Create group

Figure 7-3. *Configuring a field group*

After creating the Tabs container, I'll add three individual tabs following the same process with the exception of selecting Tab instead of Tabs and the options from the drop-down list shown in Figure 7-2. The three tabs will be labeled Title, Taxonomy, and Content. After creating the three tabs, I will rearrange the items on the Article Form display (Structure ➤ Content Types ➤ Article ➤ Manage Form Display), as shown in Figure 7-4. The Articles container is the parent of all items that appear on the Article Node Edit form. The Title, Taxonomy, and Content tabs are the next level (indented), and the fields have been moved under their appropriate tabs. To rearrange the items on the page, simply click the + icon and drag the items to their appropriate position and drop them on the page. After rearranging the items, click the Save button to preserve your changes.

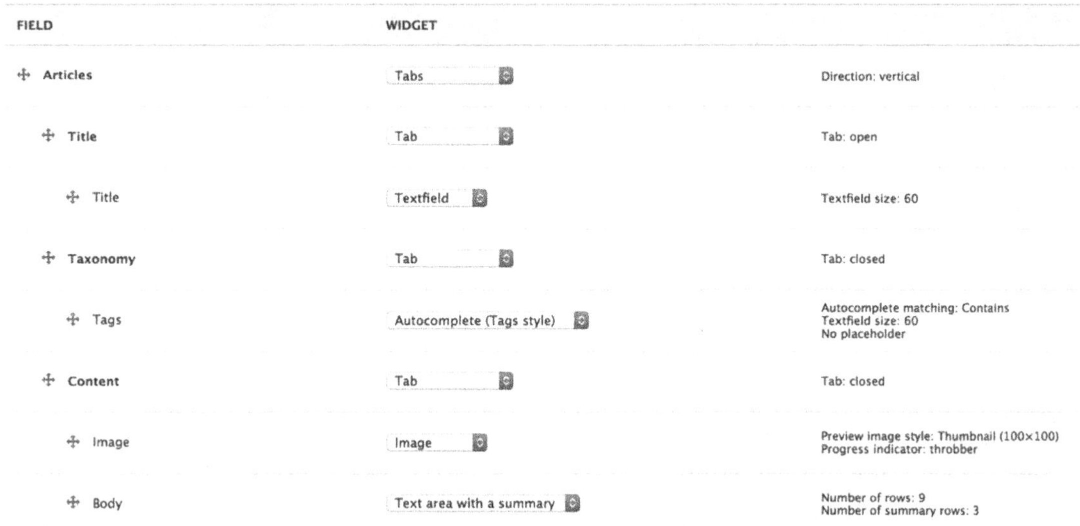

FIELD	WIDGET	
⊹ Articles	Tabs	Direction: vertical
⊹ Title	Tab	Tab: open
⊹ Title	Textfield	Textfield size: 60
⊹ Taxonomy	Tab	Tab: closed
⊹ Tags	Autocomplete (Tags style)	Autocomplete matching: Contains Textfield size: 60 No placeholder
⊹ Content	Tab	Tab: closed
⊹ Image	Image	Preview image style: Thumbnail (100×100) Progress indicator: throbber
⊹ Body	Text area with a summary	Number of rows: 9 Number of summary rows: 3

Figure 7-4. *Rearranging the form fields*

After modifying the Article Node form, navigate to the Content page and click the Add Content button. Select Article on the next page and note the arrangement of the elements on the Create Article page (see Figure 7-5).

Create Article ☆

Home » Add content

Title *	
Taxonomy	Title * [ ]
Content	

[Save and publish ▾]   [Preview]

Figure 7-5. *The revised Create Article page*

The Create Article page now has three vertical tabs titled Title, Taxonomy, and Content. Clicking through the three tabs, you can see the fields that were placed on each tab. While the Article Content Type is relatively simple, your editorial team will love you for arranging fields in logical order using tabs instead of a long "river" of fields down the page.

You can also embed horizontal tabs in a vertical tab, making it even more powerful for complex content types. In the example shown in Figure 7-6, this content type has hundreds of fields organized into 12 tabs and on the Related tab there are several embedded horizontal tabs (shown at the bottom of the figure).

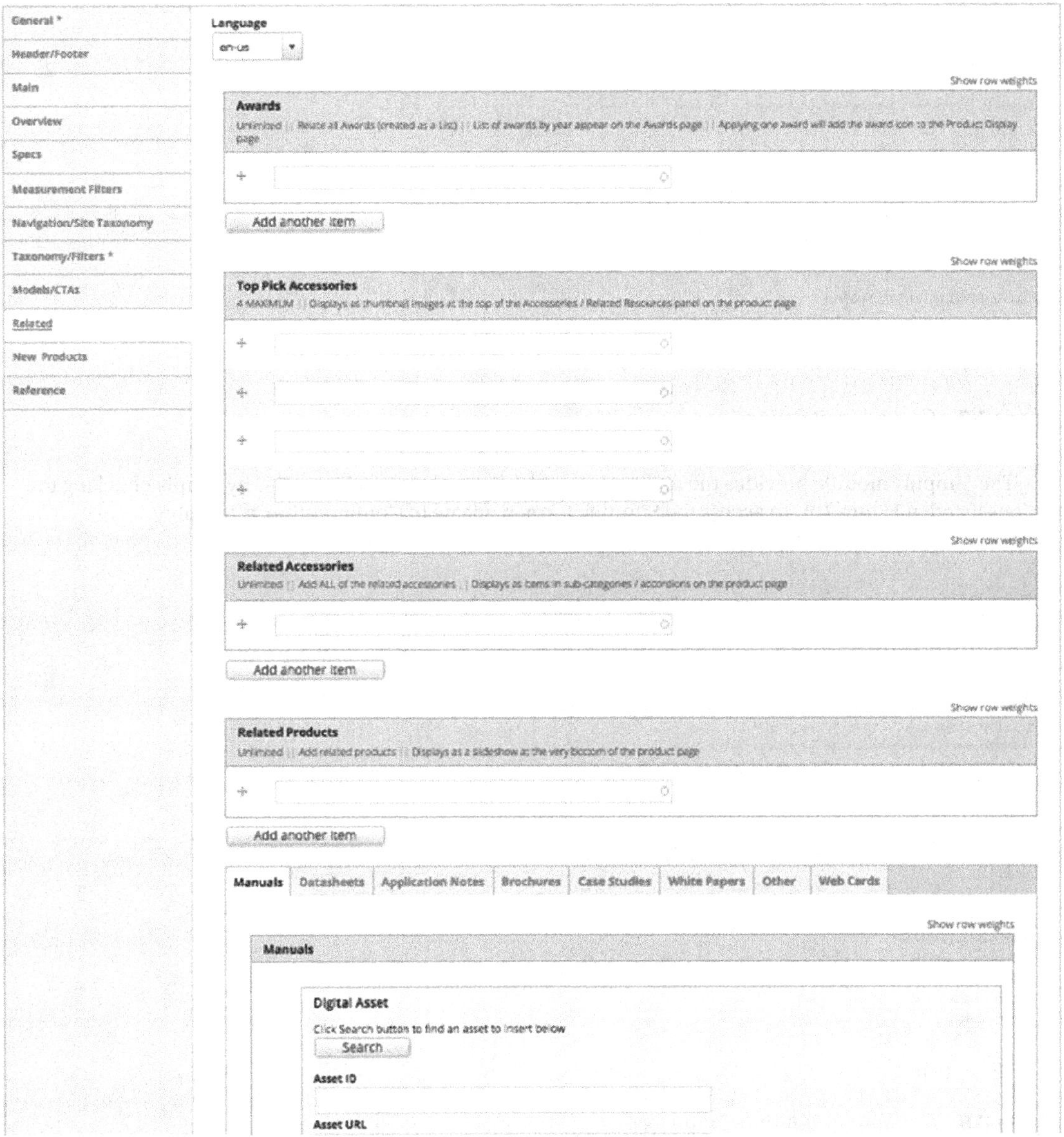

Figure 7-6. *A complicated Node Edit form*

Removing Options from the Node Edit Form

The Node Edit form has several options that you may want to hide (see Figure 7-7).

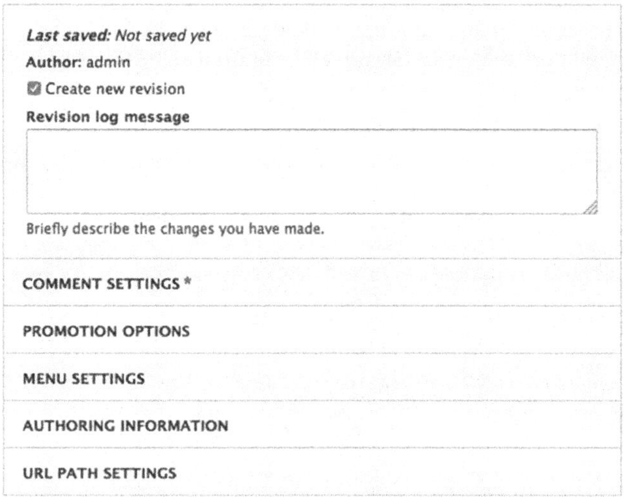

Figure 7-7. *The node edit options*

The Simplify module provides the ability to hide the fields shown in Figure 7-7 by simply checking the options listed in Figure 7-8. To access the Simplify form, navigate to Configuration ➤ Simplify.

Figure 7-8. *The Simplify administration form*

After checking the appropriate options and saving, visit the Node Edit form to see the simplified interface.

Content Types versus Entity Types

Drupal 7 introduced the concept of custom entities, where a custom entity represents any structured content that you want to define outside of Drupal's node, comment, file, user, and taxonomy entities. Examining each of these entity types, you can see that there are fundamental differences between each of them; for example, a node has an author and date published whereas a user does not have either of those two fields. While a node entity type will likely handle 99% of the use cases where you need to create a custom template for capturing, storing, and displaying information, there may be instances where you need something special and you don't want to carry the weight associated with using the node entity type (e.g., permissions). In those rare cases, a custom entity type is likely the best solution.

Creating a custom entity type in Drupal 8 requires a seemingly daunting amount of code. For example, assume that you need to create a new custom entity called a Contact. The Contact entity type has basic information about a person, such as their name, address, phone number, and e-mail address. To create the custom Contact entity, you would need at minimum a:

- `contact_entity.info.yml` file to describe the entity to Drupal 8.

- `contact_entity.routing.yml` file to define the routes associated with the Contact entity type.

- `contact_entity.links.menu.yml` file to define the menu items for the Contact entity type.

- `contact_entity.links.action.yml` file to define the action links for the Contact entity type.

- `contact_entity.links.task.yml` file to add the view, edit, and delete tabs on the entity view page and the settings tab on the entity settings page.

- `src/ContactInterface.php` file to define the public access to the Contact entity.

- `src/Entity/Contact.php` file to define the Contact entity class.

- `src/Form/ContactForm.php` file, which defines the form for adding and editing Contact entity content.

- `src/Form/ContactDeleteForm.php` file, which defines the confirmation form that is called when deleting Contact.

- `src/Entity/Controller/ContactListBuilder.php` file, which defines the header and row content for the Contact listing page.

- `src/Form/ContactSettingsForm.php` file, which creates a settings form for Contact.

- `src/ContactAccessControlHandler.php` file, which defines the access control mechanisms for Contact.

When you examine the amount of code required to create a custom entity it is significant, meaning you really need to have a valid case for why a standard custom content type that uses the node entity wouldn't work for your use case. But there may be a case and you fortunately have an alternative to hand-coding hundreds of lines of code to create an entity and that option is the *Drupal Console*.

The Drupal Console is a tool that generates boilerplate code for Drupal, as well as provides tools for interacting with and debugging Drupal. It will save you countless hours of coding and the high probability of frustration, so I suggest installing it and getting to know its capabilities early in your Drupal 8 journey.

You can download and install Drupal Console from the web site, drupalconsole.com. There are three methods for downloading and installing:

- Downloading as a new dependency:

```
# Change directory to Drupal site
cd path-to-your-drupal8-root-directory

# Download DrupalConsole
composer require drupal/console:~1.0 \
--prefer-dist \
--optimize-autoloader \
--sort-packages
```

- Downloading using DrupalComposer:

```
composer create-project \
drupal-composer/drupal-project:8.x-dev \
path-to-your-drupal8-root-directory \
--prefer-dist \
--no-progress \
--no-interaction
```

- Install Drupal Console Launcher:

```
curl https://drupalconsole.com/installer -L -o drupal.phar mv drupal.phar
/usr/local/bin/drupal chmod +x /usr/local/bin/drupal
```

For additional details on installing Drupal Console, visit the drupalconsole.com web site.

After installing Drupal Console, the next step is to create your new Contact entity using the Drupal Console command for constructing all of the code required to define the skeleton of the new entity. The first step is to create a new module that will be used as the foundation for the new Contact entity. To create the module, enter the following command from the root directory of your Drupal 8 site:

```
vendor/drupal/console/bin/drupal generate:module
```

Drupal Console will then walk you through a series of questions about your new Drupal 8 module:

```
// Welcome to the Drupal module generator
  Enter the new module name:
  > mymodule
  Enter the module machine name [mymodule]:
  Enter the module Path [/modules/custom]:
  Enter module description [My Awesome Module]:
  > Creates a Customer entity
  Enter package name [Custom]:
  > Other
  Enter Drupal Core version [8.x]:
Do you want to generate a .module file (yes/no) [yes]:
Define module as feature (yes/no) [no]:
Do you want to add a composer.json file to your module (yes/no) [yes]:
Would you like to add module dependencies (yes/no) [no]:
```

```
Do you want to generate a unit test class (yes/no) [yes]:
Do you confirm generation? (yes/no) [yes]:

Generated or updated files

  1 - /Applications/MAMP/htdocs/d8/modules/custom/mymodule/mymodule.info.yml
  2 - /Applications/MAMP/htdocs/d8/modules/custom/mymodule/mymodule.module
  3 - /Applications/MAMP/htdocs/d8/modules/custom/mymodule/composer.json
  4 - /Applications/MAMP/htdocs/d8/modules/custom/mymodule/src/Tests/LoadTest.php
```

After creating the module, the next step is to create the code required to create the entity. At the command prompt, enter the following:

```
vendor/drupal/console/bin/drupal generate:entity:content
```

Drupal console will then prompt you with the following questions:

```
Enter the module name [mymodule]:
>

Enter the class of your new content entity [DefaultEntity]:
> Customer

Enter the machine name of your new content entity [customer]:
>

Enter the label of your new content entity [Customer]:
>

Enter the base-path for the content entity routes [/admin/structure]:
>

Do you want this (content) entity to have bundles (yes/no) [no]:
>

Is your entity translatable (yes/no) [yes]:
>

Is your entity revisionable (yes/no) [yes]:
>

Generated or updated files
  1 - modules/custom/mymodule/mymodule.permissions.yml
  2 - modules/custom/mymodule/mymodule.links.menu.yml
  3 - modules/custom/mymodule/mymodule.links.task.yml
  4 - modules/custom/mymodule/mymodule.links.action.yml
  5 - modules/custom/mymodule/src/CustomerAccessControlHandler.php
  6 - modules/custom/mymodule/src/CustomerTranslationHandler.php
  7 - modules/custom/mymodule/src/Entity/CustomerInterface.php
  8 - modules/custom/mymodule/src/Entity/Customer.php
  9 - modules/custom/mymodule/src/CustomerHtmlRouteProvider.php
```

```
10 - modules/custom/mymodule/src/Entity/CustomerViewsData.php
11 - modules/custom/mymodule/src/CustomerListBuilder.php
12 - modules/custom/mymodule/src/Form/CustomerSettingsForm.php
13 - modules/custom/mymodule/src/Form/CustomerForm.php
14 - modules/custom/mymodule/src/Form/CustomerDeleteForm.php
15 - modules/custom/mymodule/customer.page.inc
16 - modules/custom/mymodule/templates/customer.html.twig
17 - modules/custom/mymodule/src/Form/CustomerRevisionDeleteForm.php
18 - modules/custom/mymodule/src/Form/CustomerRevisionRevertTranslationForm.php
19 - modules/custom/mymodule/src/Form/CustomerRevisionRevertForm.php
20 - modules/custom/mymodule/src/CustomerStorage.php
21 - modules/custom/mymodule/src/CustomerStorageInterface.php
22 - modules/custom/mymodule/src/Controller/CustomerController.php
```

After constructing the module and the entity, visit your site's modules/custom directory and you will find all of the files generated by Drupal Console:

```
├── composer.json
├── customer.page.inc
├── mymodule.info.yml
├── mymodule.links.action.yml
├── mymodule.links.menu.yml
├── mymodule.links.task.yml
├── mymodule.module
├── mymodule.permissions.yml
├── src
│   ├── Controller
│   │   └── CustomerController.php
│   ├── CustomerAccessControlHandler.php
│   ├── CustomerHtmlRouteProvider.php
│   ├── CustomerListBuilder.php
│   ├── CustomerStorage.php
│   ├── CustomerStorageInterface.php
│   ├── CustomerTranslationHandler.php
│   ├── Entity
│   │   ├── Customer.php
│   │   ├── CustomerInterface.php
│   │   └── CustomerViewsData.php
│   ├── Form
│   │   ├── CustomerDeleteForm.php
│   │   ├── CustomerForm.php
│   │   ├── CustomerRevisionDeleteForm.php
│   │   ├── CustomerRevisionRevertForm.php
│   │   ├── CustomerRevisionRevertTranslationForm.php
│   │   └── CustomerSettingsForm.php
│   └── Tests
│       └── LoadTest.php
└── templates
    └── customer.html.twig

6 directories, 26 files
```

You could at this juncture enable your new module and examine the new custom Customer entity type; however, I want to add a few fields to the entity first so that it represents the requirements that I have for a Customer, namely the name, address, city, state, ZIP code, phone number, and e-mail address fields. For simplicity's sake, I'm going to add each of the fields to the entity type as simple text fields.

Let's edit the Customer.php file in the src/Entity directory of my module's directory and add the following fields after the name field in the baseFieldDefinitions function. (Note: The simple way to add all of these fields is to copy the name field and change the appropriate values to represent the new field, for example the index in the $fields array, the setLabel and setDescription values):

```
$fields['address'] = BaseFieldDefinition::create('string')
  ->setLabel(t('Address'))
  ->setDescription(t('The address of the the Contact entity.'))
  ->setRevisionable(TRUE)
  ->setSettings(array(
    'max_length' => 50,
    'text_processing' => 0,
  ))
  ->setDefaultValue('')
  ->setDisplayOptions('view', array(
    'label' => 'above',
    'type' => 'string',
    'weight' => -4,
  ))
  ->setDisplayOptions('form', array(
    'type' => 'string_textfield',
    'weight' => -4,
  ))
  ->setDisplayConfigurable('form', TRUE)
  ->setDisplayConfigurable('view', TRUE);

$fields['city'] = BaseFieldDefinition::create('string')
  ->setLabel(t('City'))
  ->setDescription(t('The city of the Contact entity.'))
  ->setRevisionable(TRUE)
  ->setSettings(array(
    'max_length' => 50,
    'text_processing' => 0,
  ))
  ->setDefaultValue('')
  ->setDisplayOptions('view', array(
    'label' => 'above',
    'type' => 'string',
    'weight' => -4,
  ))
  ->setDisplayOptions('form', array(
    'type' => 'string_textfield',
    'weight' => -4,
  ))
  ->setDisplayConfigurable('form', TRUE)
  ->setDisplayConfigurable('view', TRUE);
```

```php
$fields['state'] = BaseFieldDefinition::create('string')
  ->setLabel(t('State'))
  ->setDescription(t('The state of the Contact entity.'))
  ->setRevisionable(TRUE)
  ->setSettings(array(
    'max_length' => 50,
    'text_processing' => 0,
  ))
  ->setDefaultValue('')
  ->setDisplayOptions('view', array(
    'label' => 'above',
    'type' => 'string',
    'weight' => -4,
  ))
  ->setDisplayOptions('form', array(
    'type' => 'string_textfield',
    'weight' => -4,
  ))
  ->setDisplayConfigurable('form', TRUE)
  ->setDisplayConfigurable('view', TRUE);

$fields['zipcode'] = BaseFieldDefinition::create('string')
  ->setLabel(t('Zipcode'))
  ->setDescription(t('The zipcode of the Contact entity.'))
  ->setRevisionable(TRUE)
  ->setSettings(array(
    'max_length' => 50,
    'text_processing' => 0,
  ))
  ->setDefaultValue('')
  ->setDisplayOptions('view', array(
    'label' => 'above',
    'type' => 'string',
    'weight' => -4,
  ))
  ->setDisplayOptions('form', array(
    'type' => 'string_textfield',
    'weight' => -4,
  ))
  ->setDisplayConfigurable('form', TRUE)
  ->setDisplayConfigurable('view', TRUE);

$fields['phone'] = BaseFieldDefinition::create('string')
  ->setLabel(t('Phone'))
  ->setDescription(t('The phone number of the Contact entity.'))
  ->setRevisionable(TRUE)
  ->setSettings(array(
    'max_length' => 50,
    'text_processing' => 0,
  ))
```

```
        ->setDefaultValue('')
        ->setDisplayOptions('view', array(
          'label' => 'above',
          'type' => 'string',
          'weight' => -4,
        ))
        ->setDisplayOptions('form', array(
          'type' => 'string_textfield',
          'weight' => -4,
        ))
        ->setDisplayConfigurable('form', TRUE)
        ->setDisplayConfigurable('view', TRUE);

    $fields['email'] = BaseFieldDefinition::create('string')
        ->setLabel(t('Email'))
        ->setDescription(t('The email of the Contact entity.'))
        ->setRevisionable(TRUE)
        ->setSettings(array(
          'max_length' => 50,
          'text_processing' => 0,
        ))
        ->setDefaultValue('')
        ->setDisplayOptions('view', array(
          'label' => 'above',
          'type' => 'string',
          'weight' => -4,
        ))
        ->setDisplayOptions('form', array(
          'type' => 'string_textfield',
          'weight' => -4,
        ))
        ->setDisplayConfigurable('form', TRUE)
        ->setDisplayConfigurable('view', TRUE);
```

After adding the fields, save the Contact.php file and edit the CustomerListBuilder.php file to add the new fields to the buildHeader and buildRow functions, as shown here. Add each of the fields.

```
class CustomerListBuilder extends EntityListBuilder {

  use LinkGeneratorTrait;

  /**
   * {@inheritdoc}
   */
  public function buildHeader() {
    $header['id'] = $this->t('Customer ID');
    $header['name'] = $this->t('Name');
    $header['address'] = $this->t('Address');
    $header['city'] = $this->t('City');
    $header['state'] = $this->t('State');
    $header['zipcode'] = $this->t('Zip');
```

```
    $header['phone'] = $this->t('Phone');
    $header['email'] = $this->t('Email');
    return $header + parent::buildHeader();
  }

  /**
   * {@inheritdoc}
   */
  public function buildRow(EntityInterface $entity) {
    /* @var $entity \Drupal\mymodule\Entity\Customer */
    $row['id'] = $entity->id();
    $row['name'] = $this->l(
      $entity->label(),
      new Url(
        'entity.customer.edit_form', array(
          'customer' => $entity->id(),
        )
      )
    );
    $row['address'] = $entity->address->value;
    $row['city'] = $entity->city->value;
    $row['state'] = $entity->state->value;
    $row['zipcode'] = $entity->zip->value;
    $row['phone'] = $entity->phone->value;
    $row['email'] = $entity->email->value;
    return $row + parent::buildRow($entity);
  }

}
```

After updating the CustomerListBuilder.php file and saving it, enable your new module on the Extend page (see Figure 7-9).

OTHER

☑   **mymodule**   Creates a Customer entity

Figure 7-9. *The new customer entity module*

After the module is enabled, you can create, view, and update the customer content by navigating to the Structure page (see Figure 7-10). You will see two new links on the page—Customer Settings and
. Customer List.

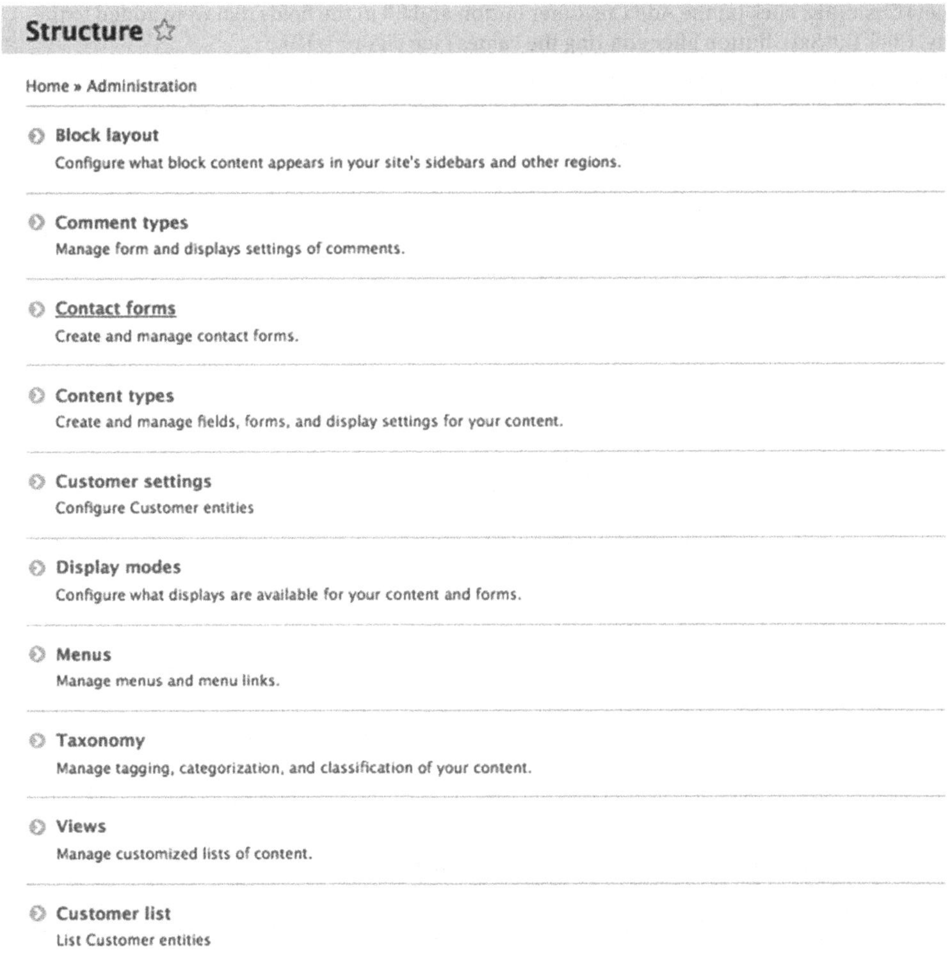

Structure ☆

Home » Administration

⊙ **Block layout**
Configure what block content appears in your site's sidebars and other regions.

⊙ **Comment types**
Manage form and displays settings of comments.

⊙ **Contact forms**
Create and manage contact forms.

⊙ **Content types**
Create and manage fields, forms, and display settings for your content.

⊙ **Customer settings**
Configure Customer entities

⊙ **Display modes**
Configure what displays are available for your content and forms.

⊙ **Menus**
Manage menus and menu links.

⊙ **Taxonomy**
Manage tagging, categorization, and classification of your content.

⊙ **Views**
Manage customized lists of content.

⊙ **Customer list**
List Customer entities

Figure 7-10. *The Structure page*

Click on the Customer List link to see a list of existing customer records. You'll see each of the fields that were added to the `CustomerListBuilder.php` file at the top of the list (see Figure 7-11).

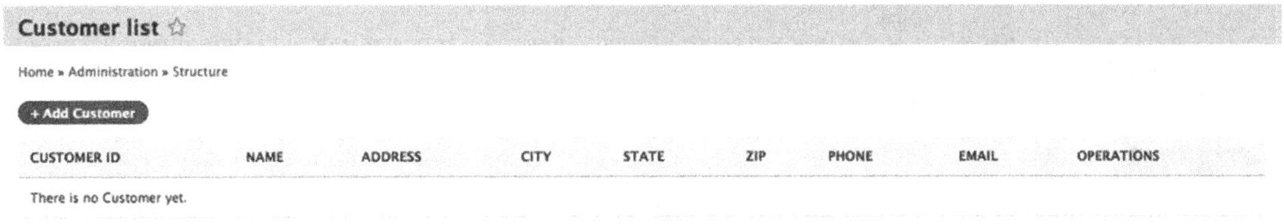

Customer list ☆

Home » Administration » Structure

+ Add Customer

CUSTOMER ID	NAME	ADDRESS	CITY	STATE	ZIP	PHONE	EMAIL	OPERATIONS

There is no Customer yet.

Figure 7-11. *The Customer list page*

To add a new Customer, click on the Add Customer button and fill in the fields that were added to the Customer entity. Click the Save button after entering the values (see Figure 7-12).

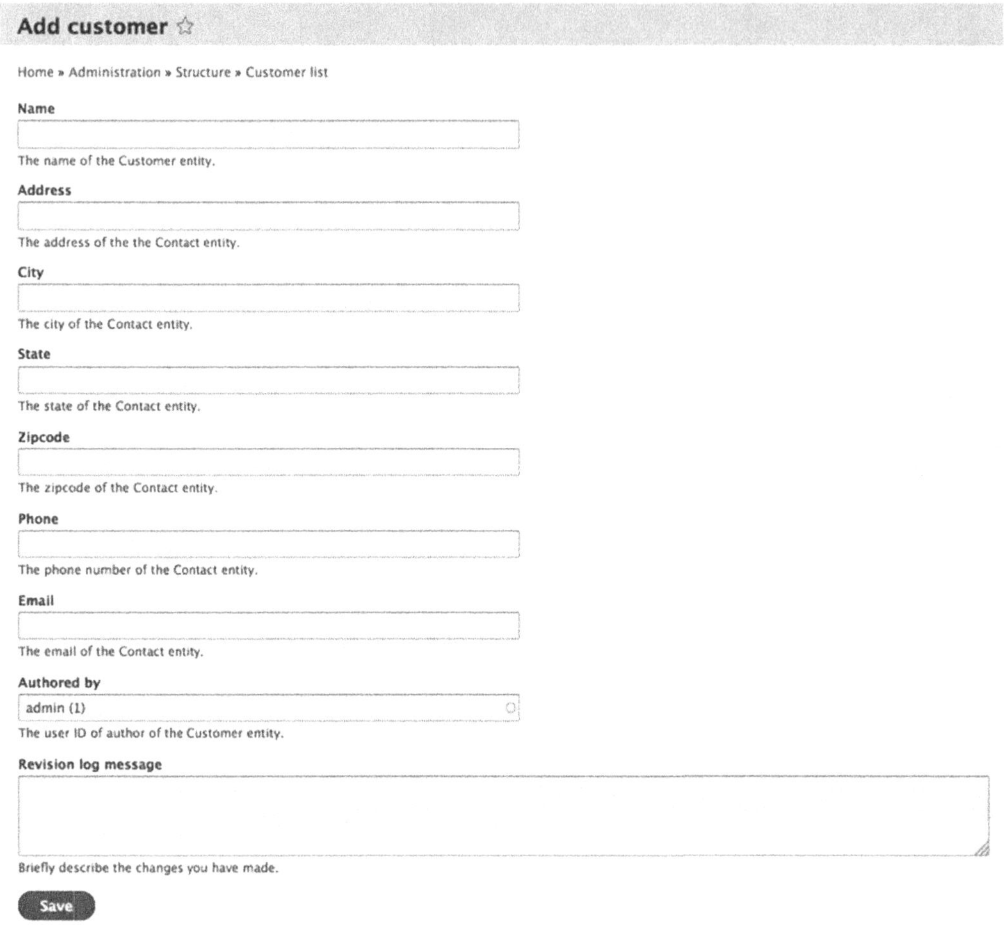

Add customer ☆

Home » Administration » Structure » Customer list

Name

The name of the Customer entity.

Address

The address of the the Contact entity.

City

The city of the Contact entity.

State

The state of the Contact entity.

Zipcode

The zipcode of the Contact entity.

Phone

The phone number of the Contact entity.

Email

The email of the Contact entity.

Authored by

admin (1)

The user ID of author of the Customer entity.

Revision log message

Briefly describe the changes you have made.

Save

Figure 7-12. Adding a new customer

After adding a new customer, return to the Structure page and click on the Customer List link. You'll see the new customer in the list (see Figure 7-13).

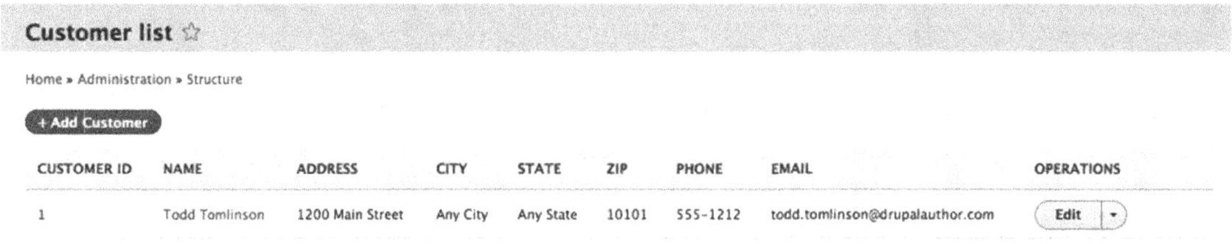

Customer list ☆

Home » Administration » Structure

+ Add Customer

CUSTOMER ID	NAME	ADDRESS	CITY	STATE	ZIP	PHONE	EMAIL	OPERATIONS
1	Todd Tomlinson	1200 Main Street	Any City	Any State	10101	555-1212	todd.tomlinson@drupalauthor.com	Edit ▾

Figure 7-13. The new customer appears in the list

For each item in the custom list, you can perform edits or deletes through the options presented in the Operations column.

You can also perform operations on the Customer entity itself by navigating to Structure ➤ Customer Settings. On this page you'll find tabs to Manage Fields, Manage Form Display, and Manage Display. Each of the operations is identical to a standard entity such as a node. You can add custom fields to your custom entity through the Manage Fields tab (Note: Fields defined in code do not appear on this page; only custom fields that are added through this page appear here.). Rearrange the fields on the Customer Edit form and change the rendering of a customer through the Manage Display tab.

It's also key to understand that customers will not appear on the Content page, similar to how users, comments, and taxonomy terms don't appear on that list. To view the customers, you'll need to visit the Structure page.

Leveraging Taxonomy

When asked what taxonomy is used for, many people shrug their shoulders and relay the common "freeform tagging" use case as the only area where taxonomy is used on their site, making taxonomy one of the most underutilized capabilities of Drupal's core capabilities. While freeform tagging is a valid use case, there are many more powerful and useful approaches for leveraging taxonomy that will help optimize and streamline your site's architecture.

If you are unfamiliar with taxonomy in Drupal 8, I suggest picking up a copy of *Beginning Drupal 8* from Apress and reviewing the chapter on taxonomy. This section focuses on more advanced use cases of taxonomy.

Taxonomy as an Entity

Before diving into the details of other use cases for taxonomy, it's important to understand that taxonomy is another entity type, like nodes, comments, and users. Because taxonomy is an entity type, Drupal provides the ability to add fields to a taxonomy vocabulary and the terms that are contained with that vocabulary. Having the ability to add custom fields has several benefits, for example, displaying a page banner at the top of a list of content filtered by a taxonomy term. Typically we would have solved this use case by creating a custom block and using block visibility to control when that block would be rendered. The problem with this approach is when you have hundreds of taxonomy terms. In this case, you would have to have hundreds of custom blocks. Managing hundreds of blocks and ensuring that taxonomy terms are synchronized with custom blocks is an administrator's nightmare. Putting the banner image on the term itself solves the problem, and through the use of a generic view that displays the banner image based on an argument in the URL (for example), provides a simple solution to a complex problem.

You can extend the scenarios well beyond just storing a banner image on a taxonomy term; you can add virtually any field type to a taxonomy term. To demonstrate this capability, visit Structure ➤ Taxonomy and click on the Add Vocabulary button. We'll create a new vocabulary called Site Section which we'll use to categorize content by where it is supposed to reside on the site. After creating the vocabulary, we click on the Manage Fields tab (see Figure 7-14). The process for creating and managing fields is identical to creating and managing fields on a content type.

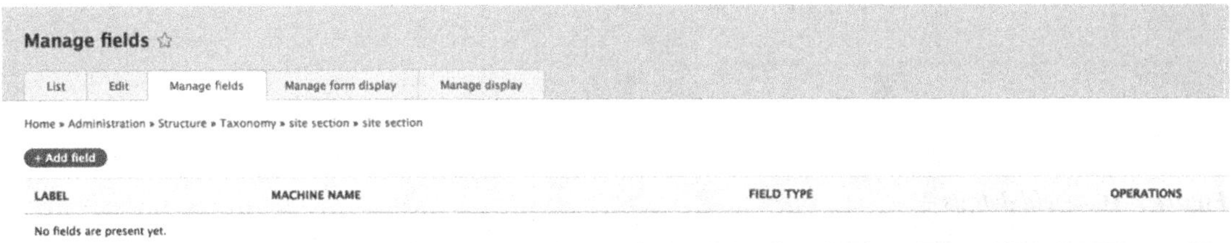

Manage fields ☆

| List | Edit | Manage fields | Manage form display | Manage display |

Home » Administration » Structure » Taxonomy » site section » site section

[+ Add field]

LABEL	MACHINE NAME	FIELD TYPE	OPERATIONS

No fields are present yet.

Figure 7-14. Creating taxonomy fields

For demonstration purposes, we add the banner image field. After clicking on the Add Field button, we're presented with a list of types of fields that can be added (see Figure 7-15).

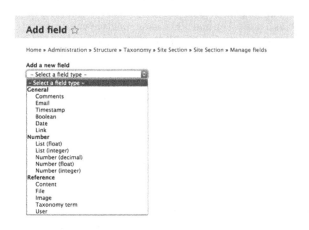

Figure 7-15. *Types of fields*

We select the Image Field type and click the Save and Continue button (which is hidden under the drop-down list in Figure 7-15) to enter the details of the new image field (see Figure 7-16).

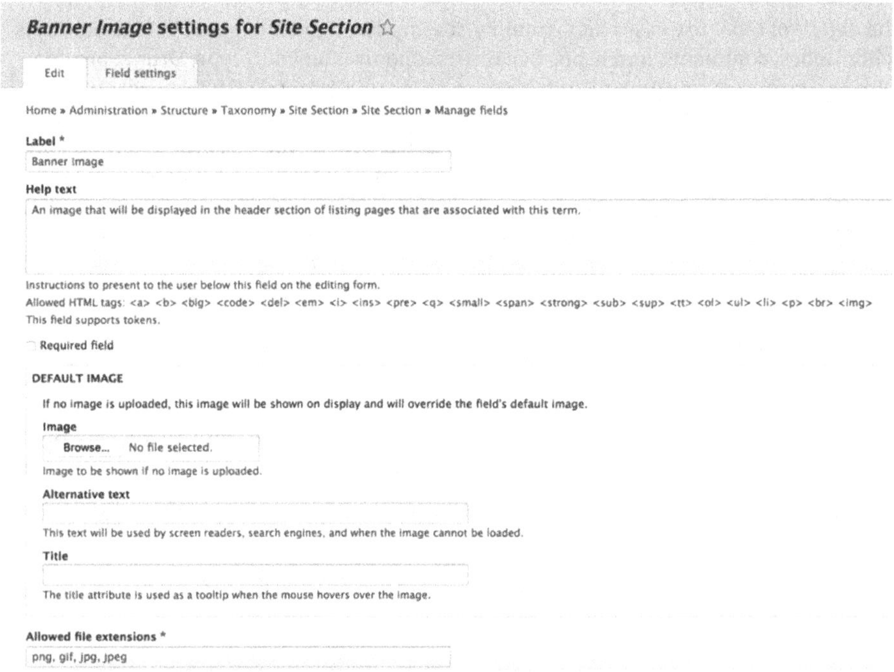

Figure 7-16. *Field details*

After creating the Banner Image field, we can manage where it appears on the Add Term form and manage how it is displayed when a taxonomy term is rendered. The position of the field on the Add Term form can be updated by clicking on the Manage Form display tab (see Figure 7-14) and dragging the new field to the appropriate position in the list of fields. The position of the field when a term is rendered can be updated by clicking on the Manage Display tab. You may reposition the field by dragging and dropping it in the list of fields, you may hide the field label, and you can change the format of the field on this page. All of these actions are identical to how fields are managed on a content type.

After updating the form and display, we add a few new Site Section taxonomy terms. Click on the List tab and then the Add Term button. The Add Term form now has the ability to add a banner image to the term being created (see Figure 7-17).

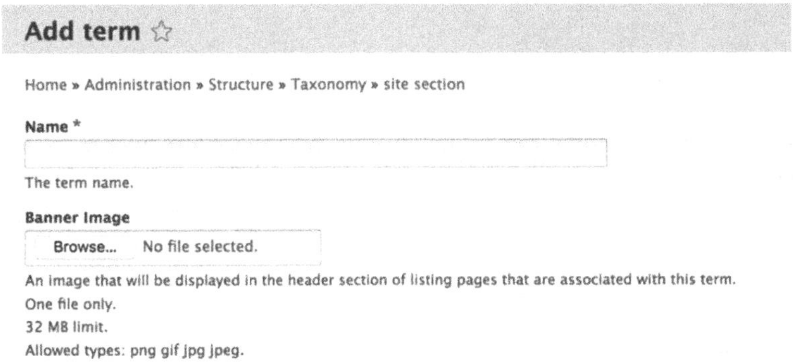

Add term ☆

Home » Administration » Structure » Taxonomy » site section

Name *

The term name.

Banner Image

Browse...   No file selected.

An image that will be displayed in the header section of listing pages that are associated with this term.
One file only.
32 MB limit.
Allowed types: png gif jpg jpeg.

Figure 7-17. *Add term with the Banner image field*

After creating several Site Section taxonomy terms and attaching banner images to each term, we then update the Article Content Type to include the Site Section taxonomy term as a reference field (see Figure 7-18). To do so, follow these steps:

1. Navigate to Structure ➤ Content Types.

2. Click the Manage Fields button in the Operations column.

3. Click the Add Field button and selected Taxonomy term from the list of possible field types.

4. On the Configuration page for the new field, select Site Section as the source of terms that will be presented to the content author.

5. Save the field.

6. Reposition the field to the position where you want it to appear.

7. Save the Article Content Type.

8. Then create several articles and select one of the Site Section taxonomy terms (homepage) as the location where you want those articles to appear. See Figure 7-18.

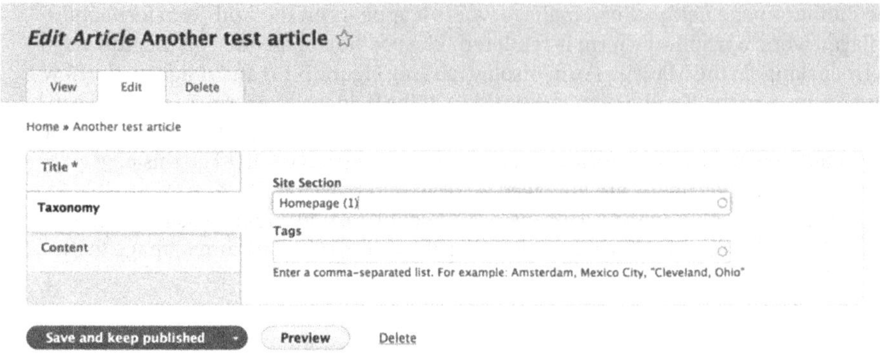

Figure 7-18. *Adding a Site Section taxonomy term to an article*

After creating several articles tagged with the Homepage taxonomy term, navigate to Structure ➤ Views and click on the Add View button to create a new view called Page Banner. On the Add View page, set the values as follows:

- View name: Page Banner
- View Settings:
  - Show: Taxonomy terms
  - Of type: Site Section
  - Sorted by: Unsorted
- Block Settings
  - Create a Block: checked
  - Block Display Settings
    - Display format: Unformatted list of Fields
  - Items per block: 1

After clicking the Save and Edit button, update the view's configuration as follows:

- Display name: Page Banner Block
- Fields: Taxonomy term: Banner Image (this is the name of the field we added to the taxonomy term)
- In the Advanced section, Contextual Filters: Taxonomy term: Term ID (from URL)
- Machine Name: page_banner_block

Then save the view.

With the block ready to place on pages, navigate to Structure ➤ Block Layout. On the Block Layout page, click the Place Block button in the Header region and located the Page Banner: Page Banner Block. Click the Place Block button and leave all of the default options as is on the Configure Block page. Click Save Block to place the block in the Header region. On the Block Layout page, click the Save Blocks button at the bottom of the page. With the taxonomy terms, content, view, and block in place, you're ready to test the ability to use the page banner field on the Site Section taxonomy term as the banner at the top of a page associated with that term.

To view the capabilities of this solution, navigate to the taxonomy term listing page for my homepage taxonomy term, which is /taxonomy/term/1. Note: Your term ID may be different depending on which term you have used. To find the term ID of the term you have used navigate to Structure ➤ Taxonomy and click the List Terms link in the Operations column of the vocabulary that holds the terms you used for Site Section. Find the term in the list and hover over the Edit link in the Operations column. In the status bar of your browser, you should see the full URL to the edit page for that term. The term ID will appear directly after the term/ in the URL.

After entering the correct URL in the browsers address bar and visiting the page, you'll see the page banner you assigned to the Homepage taxonomy term displayed at the top of the content area (see Figure 7-19).

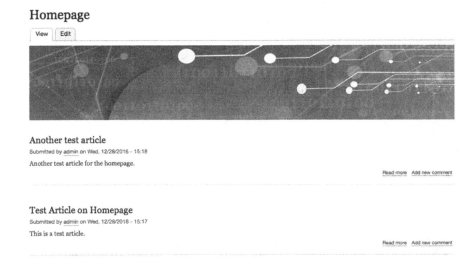

Figure 7-19. *The page banner appears*

We can make the URL more user and SEO friendly by editing the taxonomy term for Homepage and creating a URL alias of /homepage. After updating the term, visit the page at example.com/homepage (replacing example.com with the domain name of your site) and you'll see the same results as you did with /taxonomy/term/1.

Building Multipurpose Pages Using Taxonomy

Another area for leveraging taxonomy is building multipurpose pages that render content through views based on values contained in the URL. It may be easiest to understand the concept through an example use case. I'll use the example of a manufacturing company that has several product lines, which each line having multiple products. While I could create a standalone page for each product line, I could just as easily create a single page that uses taxonomy terms in the URL to render content that is specific to that product line, for example /products/brushes. With one page I could render an unlimited number of product line landing pages. The only requirements are that each product line is defined by a taxonomy term, and that every product in that product line is tagged with terms from the product line taxonomy.

Laying the Foundation for Multipurpose Pages

While it is possible to provide the functionality required to address this use case through custom code, I'll demonstrate fulfilling the requirements with off-the-shelf modules (ctools, panels, page manager, taxonomy, and views) that require no custom development. While some of the modules used to demonstrate this capability are in alpha or beta at the time this chapter was written, they all function as desired and will only get better as they move to release candidates.

The list of modules that must be downloaded from drupal.org and installed are as follows:

- Ctools (drupal.org/project/ctools)

- Panels (drupal.org/project/panels)

- Page Manager (drupal.org/project/page_manager)

- Layout Plugin (drupal.org/project/layout_plugin)

- Panelizer (drupal.org/project/panelizer)

We assume you have Drush enabled on your site and will download the modules using the following commands:

- drush dl ctools

- drush dl panels

- drush dl page_manager

- drush dl layout_plugin

- drush dl panelizer

You may then enable the modules through Drush or by visiting the Extent page and checking the box next to each of the modules, followed by clicking on the Install button at the bottom of the page (see Figure 7-20).

Figure 7-20. Enabling the panels-related modules

After enabling the modules, the steps required to achieve the desired outcome are as follows:

1. Create a new taxonomy vocabulary to house product-line taxonomy terms.

2. Create one to several product line taxonomy terms in the product line vocabulary.

3. Create a product content type with the following fields:

   - Title

   - Description (body)

   - Featured Image

   - Term reference field to the product-line vocabulary

   - A featured product Boolean field

4. Review and update the teaser and full view modes for the product content type.

5. Create several products across multiple taxonomy terms, selecting at least one per taxonomy term as the featured product for that product line.

6. Create a view (block) that renders a list of products, using the teaser view, filtered by product line from the URL.

7. Create a view (block) that renders the featured products (products that are checked as featured), using the teaser view, filtered by product line from the URL.

8. Create a panel page (two columns) that takes the product line as an argument in the URL.

9. Place the featured product block in the right column and the product listing block in the main content area of the page.

Creating the Product Line Vocabulary and Terms

The first step in the process is to create the product line vocabulary. Navigate to Structure ➤ Taxonomy and click on the Add Vocabulary button. Enter Product Line in the Name field and click the Save button. Next click on the Add Term button and add the following terms:

- Tools

- Cabinets

- Measurement

- Accessories

After creating the vocabulary and adding the terms, the list of terms should look similar to Figure 7-21.

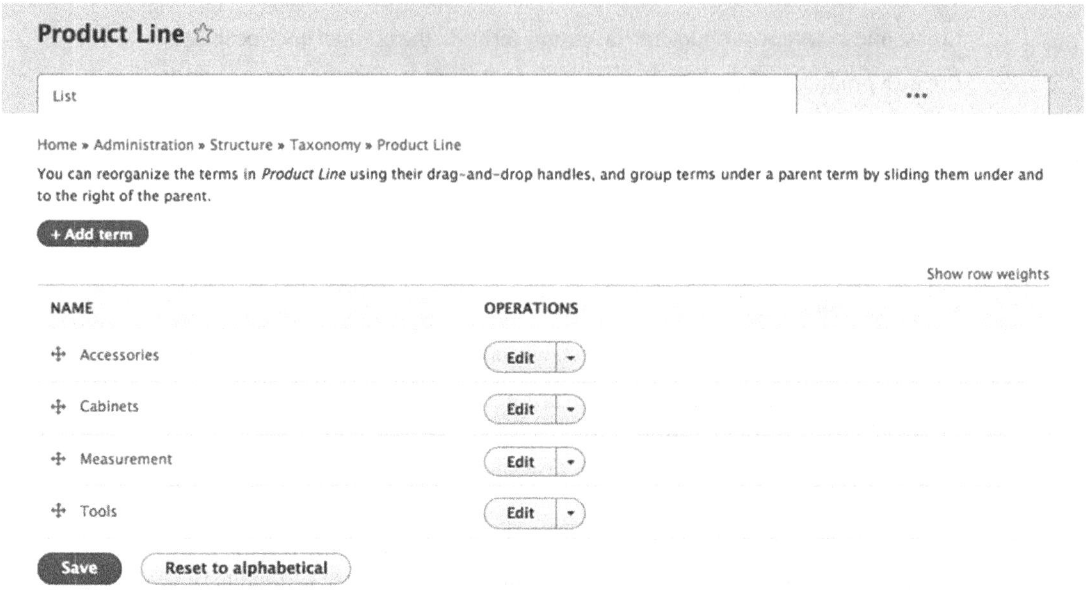

Figure 7-21. *The list of product line terms*

Creating the Product Content Type and Product Content

With the Product Line taxonomy in place, the next step is to create the Product Content Type with the following fields:

- Title

- Description (body)

- Featured image

- Featured product (Boolean)

- Product line term reference

Navigate to Structure ➤ Content Types and click the Add Content Type button to begin the process of creating the Product Content Type. Configure the content type by:

- Entering Product in the Name field

- In the Publishing options section, unchecking the Promoted To front page option

- In the Display settings, unchecking the display author and date information option

- In the Menu settings section, unchecking the Main navigation checkbox, resulting in no menus being checked, as we don't want editors to add products to menu

Then click the Save and Manage Fields button to continue the process. By default Drupal creates a title field and a Body field. The title field appeared on the previous page and was fine as is without modifications. Let's change the Label on the body field to read Description by clicking on the Edit button in the Operations column. Delete the value of Body in the Label field and enter Description in its place, followed by clicking the Save Settings button at the bottom of the form. Then add the fields by clicking on the Add Field button and selecting the appropriate types of fields.

Figure 7-22. *The Product content type and fields*

Rearrange the fields on the form by clicking on the Manage Form Display tab and setting the order as shown in Figure 7-23.

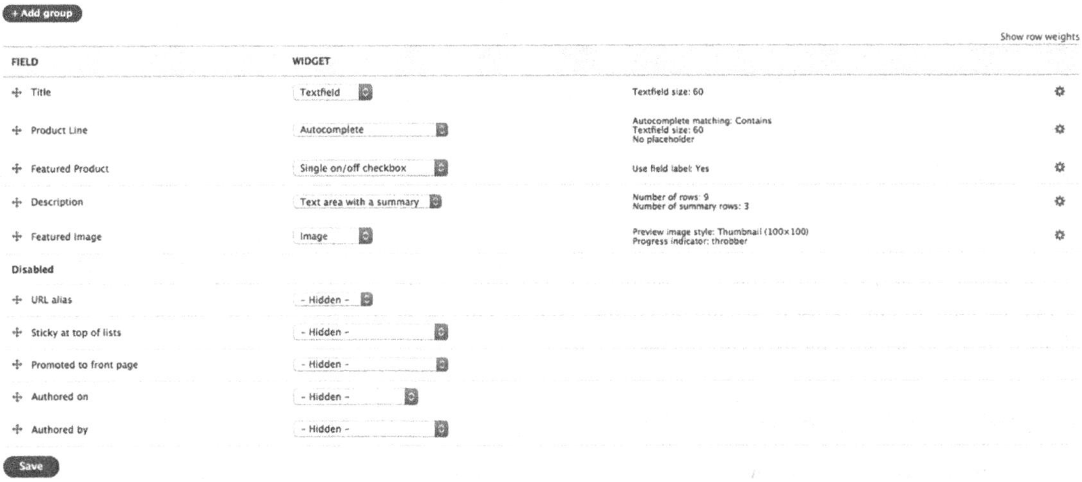

FIELD	WIDGET		
✛ Title	Textfield	Textfield size: 60	✿
✛ Product Line	Autocomplete	Autocomplete matching: Contains Textfield size: 60 No placeholder	✿
✛ Featured Product	Single on/off checkbox	Use field label: Yes	✿
✛ Description	Text area with a summary	Number of rows: 9 Number of summary rows: 3	✿
✛ Featured Image	Image	Preview image style: Thumbnail (100×100) Progress indicator: throbber	✿
Disabled			
✛ URL alias	– Hidden –		
✛ Sticky at top of lists	– Hidden –		
✛ Promoted to front page	– Hidden –		
✛ Authored on	– Hidden –		
✛ Authored by	– Hidden –		

+ Add group

Show row weights

Save

Figure 7-23. *The product content type form display field order*

Then click on the Manage Display tab and update the default and teaser displays to only show the Featured Image and Description fields. Set the default image size to 220X220 for the default view mode and 100X100 for the teaser view mode by clicking on the gear icon at the far right of the row for Featured Image (see Figure 7-24).

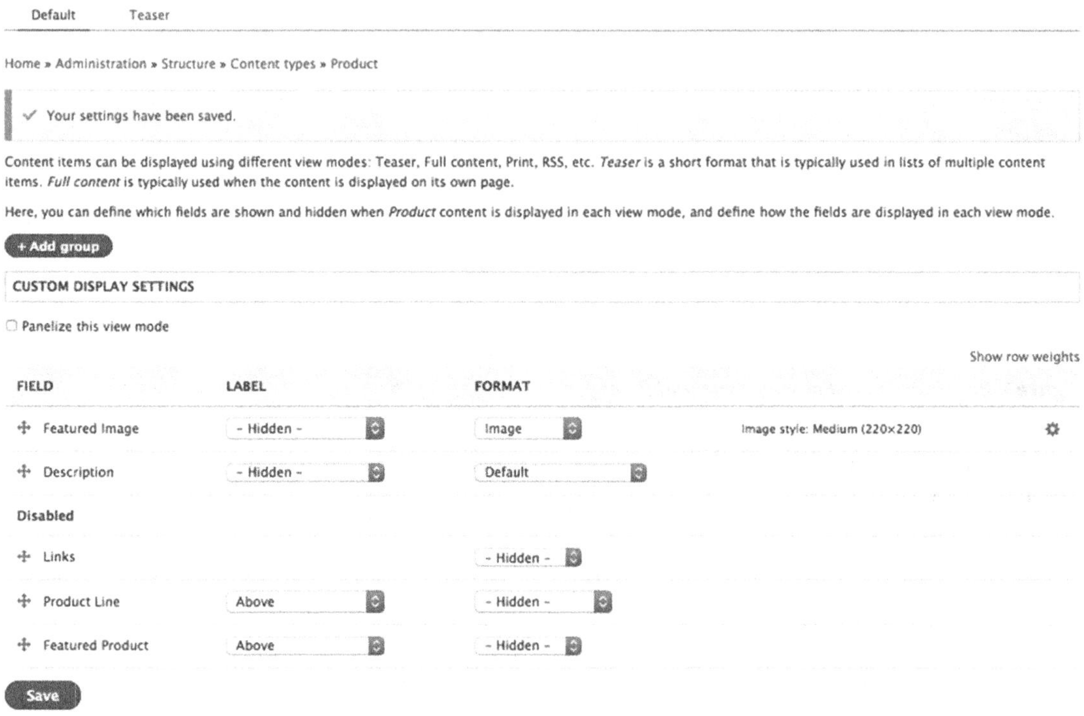

Figure 7-24. *The default display for the product content type*

After saving the display settings, we create several products across each of the Product Line taxonomy terms. Navigate to the Content page and click the Add Content button to create several products across each of the product lines in preparation for the next step.

Creating the Product Views

The requirements call for two views—one that displays the full list of products within a product line and one that randomly displays one of the products that is checked as a featured product (randomly as more than one may be checked as featured within a given product line). Both views use the teaser display mode and both will be created as blocks.

Navigate to Structure ➤ Views and click on the Add View button to create the new view. We use a single view for both blocks. On the Add View page, enter Products as the name and update the view settings to show content of type Product sorted by Unsorted. Click the Save and Edit button to continue (see Figure 7-25).

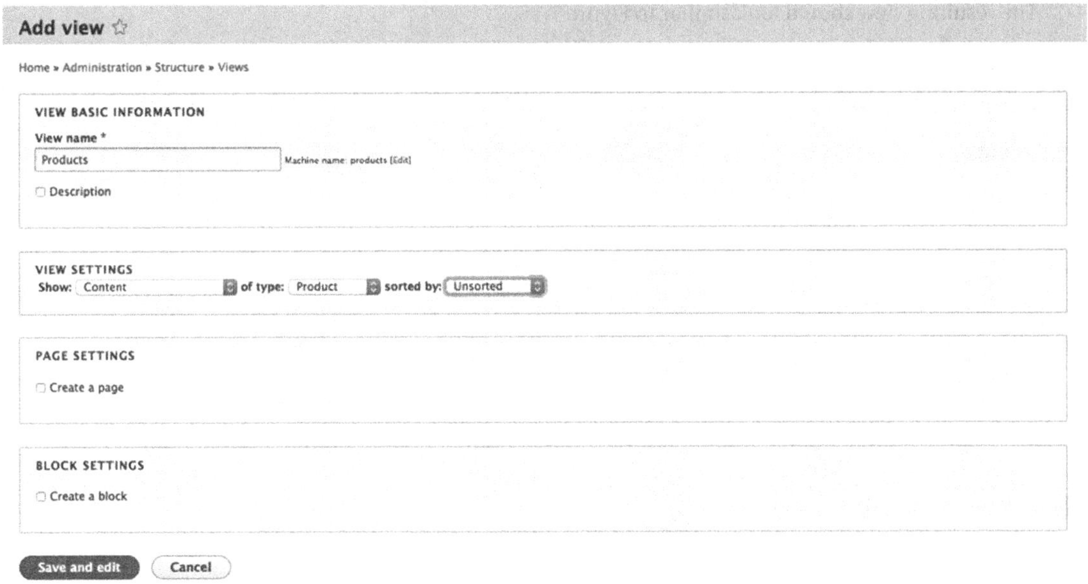

Add view ☆

Home » Administration » Structure » Views

VIEW BASIC INFORMATION

View name *

| Products | Machine name: products [Edit] |

☐ Description

VIEW SETTINGS

Show: Content ▾ of type: Product ▾ sorted by: Unsorted ▾

PAGE SETTINGS

☐ Create a page

BLOCK SETTINGS

☐ Create a block

[Save and edit]   (Cancel)

Figure 7-25. *Creating the product views*

Within this single view, we'll create two block displays—one to list all products by product line and one to list a featured product from that product line. For each display we click the Add button and select Block as the type of display.

For the product-by-product line block display, set:

- The Display name to Products by Product Line

- Show Content using the teaser display mode

- Sort criteria by title

- Under the advanced section (third column), add a contextual filter for Content: Product Line, setting a default value to Raw value from URL, selecting 2 from the list of Path components (second element in the URL will contain the taxonomy term for product line)

For the featured product block display:

- Set the Display name to Featured product

- Add a Filter criteria for Content: Featured Product set to True

- Add a Sort criteria of Random and remove the Content: Title (asc)

- Use Pager: Display a specified number of items | 1 item

- Under the advanced section (third column), add a contextual filter for Content: Product Line, setting a default value to Raw value from URL, selecting 2 from the list of Path components (second element in the URL will contain the taxonomy term for Product Line).

The resulting view should look similar to Figure 7-26.

Figure 7-26. *Details of the product display*

Creating the Product Page

The final step in the process is to create the page where products will be displayed. Previously, we installed and enabled the following modules and their sub-modules: Ctools, Panels, Page Manager, Panelizer, and Layout Plugin. We'll use a majority of these modules to assemble the generic product page.

We start by creating the page through the Page Manager module. Navigate to Structure ➤ Pages and click on the Add Page button. On the Page Information form, set the following values:

- Administrative title: Products by Product Line

- Administrative description: A page that displays products based on product line

- Path: /products/{line}

- Variant type: Panels

The value in the Path field is set to /products/{line} where {line} is a dynamic argument that will hold the various values for the taxonomy terms in the Product Line vocabulary. The value in the braces is only for reference purposes and does not perform any function other than showing up in the administrative interface. For maintenance purposes, you should use a name that is meaningful to others who may have to make changes to this page in the future. After entering the values, you're ready to proceed with the page creation process. Click the Next button (see Figure 7-27).

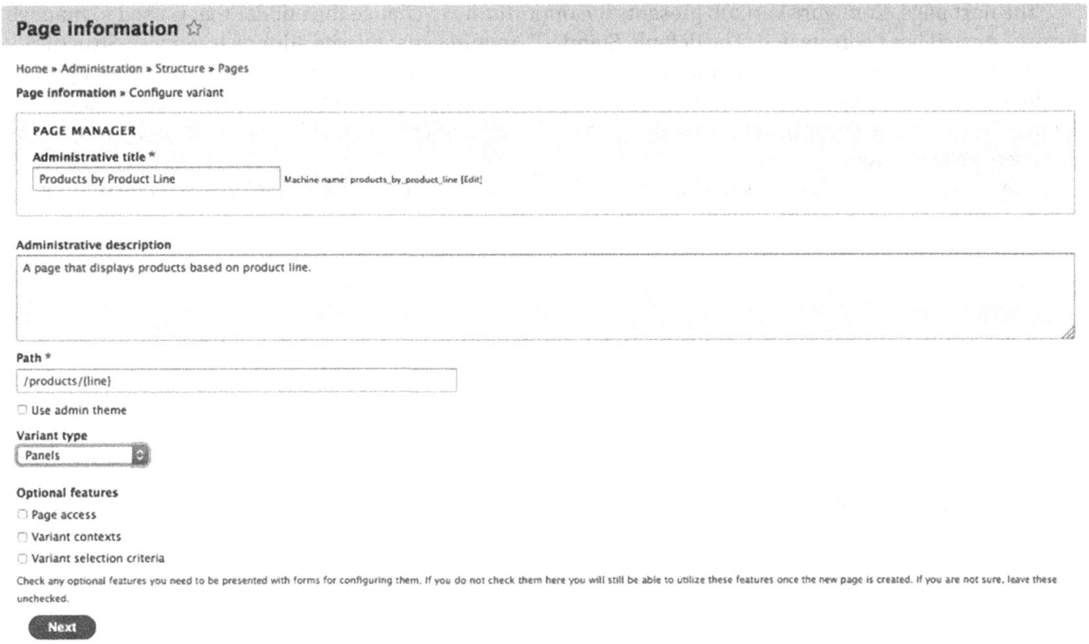

Page information ☆

Home » Administration » Structure » Pages
Page information » Configure variant

PAGE MANAGER
Administrative title *

| Products by Product Line | Machine name: products_by_product_line [Edit] |

Administrative description

| A page that displays products based on product line. |

Path *

| /products/{line} |

☐ Use admin theme

Variant type

| Panels | ⬍ |

Optional features

☐ Page access
☐ Variant contexts
☐ Variant selection criteria

Check any optional features you need to be presented with forms for configuring them. If you do not check them here you will still be able to utilize these features once the new page is created. If you are not sure, leave these
unchecked.

Next

Figure 7-27. *Creating the products by product line page*

The next step assigns context to the argument, {line}, in the URL (see Figure 7-28). The value that will
be passed in the URL is the taxonomy term associated with a given product line taxonomy term, so we assign
the context of Taxonomy term to the line argument by clicking on the Edit button in the operations column.
In the list of options presented, we select Taxonomy Term as the type of value that will be passed through the
URL, clicking the Update Parameter button to complete the process. The result is shown in Figure 7-28. Click
the Next button to continue the page-creation process.

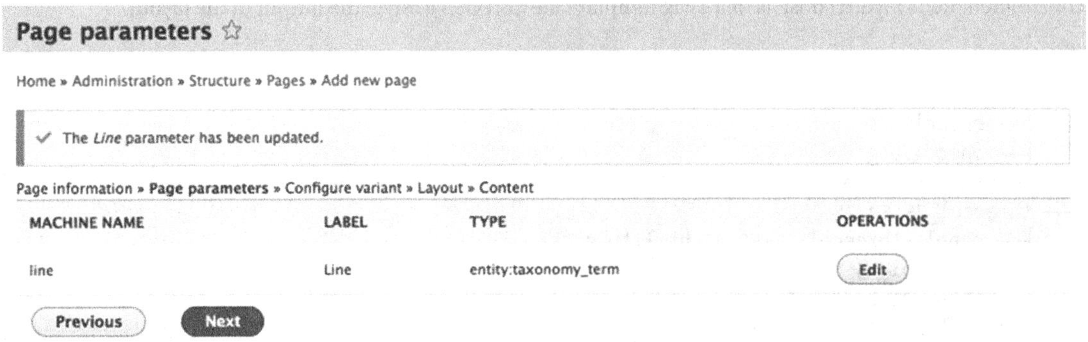

Page parameters ☆

Home » Administration » Structure » Pages » Add new page

✓ The *Line* parameter has been updated.

Page information » **Page parameters** » Configure variant » Layout » Content

MACHINE NAME	LABEL	TYPE	OPERATIONS
line	Line	entity:taxonomy_term	Edit

Previous   **Next**

Figure 7-28. *Assigning context to the URL argument*

The next page, Configure Variant, presents the opportunity to change the builder that is used to manage the page once it has been created. The default, Standard, requires that the site administrator visit Structure ➤ Pages in order to make changes to the layout or elements placed on the page. The In-Place Editor option provides the ability to edit the page directly while visiting that page by clicking on buttons at the bottom of the page (e.g., Change Layout). Let's leave the Builder set to Standard and continue with the build process by clicking the Next button.

The next step in the process is to select the layout for the page. There are several off-the-shelf options, including one-, two-, and three-column layouts (see Figure 7-29).

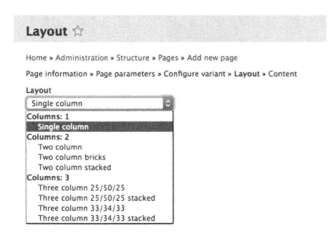

Figure 7-29. *The layout options*

For demonstration purposes, we select the two-column layout and then click the Next button to continue the build process.

While the off-the-shelf layouts provide a number of options, you may find situations where one of the existing layouts does not meet your design requirements. In those cases you can create your own custom layouts. Navigate to /modules/panels/layouts and you'll see the existing layouts and how they are constructed. Each layout consists of a Twig template file and CSS to style the output of the layout.

```
.
├── onecol
│   ├── onecol.css
│   ├── onecol.png
│   └── panels-onecol.html.twig
├── threecol_25_50_25
│   ├── panels-threecol-25-50-25.html.twig
│   ├── threecol_25_50_25.css
│   └── threecol_25_50_25.png
├── threecol_25_50_25_stacked
│   ├── panels-threecol-25-50-25-stacked.html.twig
│   ├── threecol_25_50_25_stacked.css
│   └── threecol_25_50_25_stacked.png
├── threecol_33_34_33
│   ├── panels-threecol-33-34-33.html.twig
│   ├── threecol_33_34_33.css
│   └── threecol_33_34_33.png
```

```
├── threecol_33_34_33_stacked
│   ├── panels-threecol-33-34-33-stacked.html.twig
│   ├── threecol_33_34_33_stacked.css
│   └── threecol_33_34_33_stacked.png
├── twocol
│   ├── panels-twocol.html.twig
│   ├── twocol.css
│   └── twocol.png
├── twocol_bricks
│   ├── panels-twocol-bricks.html.twig
│   ├── twocol_bricks.css
│   └── twocol_bricks.png
└── twocol_stacked
    ├── panels-twocol-stacked.html.twig
    ├── twocol_stacked.css
    └── twocol_stacked.png
```

Examining the two-column layout's Twig file, you'll note that the structure is relatively simple:

```
<div class="panel-2col" {% if css_id %}{{ css_id }}{% endif %}>
  <div class="panel-panel">
    {{ content.left }}
  </div>

  <div class="panel-panel">
    {{ content.right }}
  </div>
</div>
```

The associated CSS is just as simple:

```
.panel-2col {
  display: flex;
  flex-wrap: wrap;
  justify-content: space-between;
}

.panel-2col > .panel-panel {
  flex: 0 1 50%;
}
```

You can use this as the foundation to build your own layouts.

The next step in the process is to assign blocks to the regions that are provided by the layout. The final step in the process is to assign the blocks that were created by the Products view in the left and right columns of the new page. On the Content page (see Figure 7-30), enter Products into the Page title field and click the Add New Block button to select the blocks to place on the page.

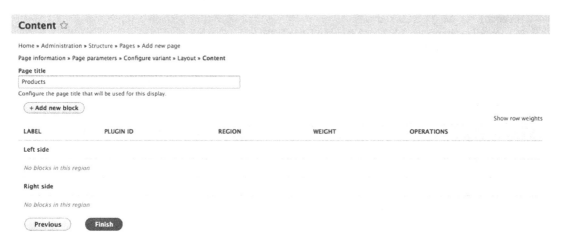

Figure 7-30. *The Content page where blocks are placed on the page*

After clicking the Add New Block button, you're presented with a list of blocks that are available for placement on the page. Scrolling through the list, you'll find a section called Lists (views). The two blocks that were created by the Products view are in that list (see Figure 7-31).

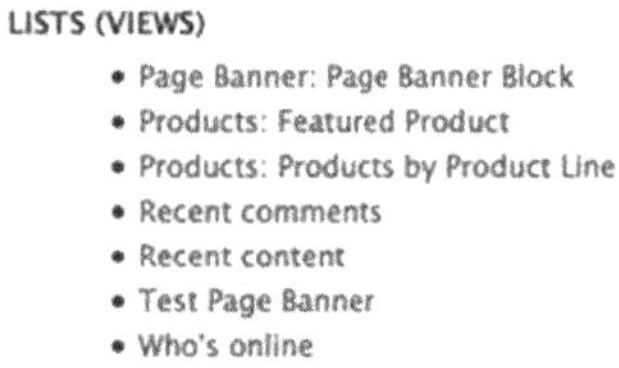

LISTS (VIEWS)

- Page Banner: Page Banner Block
- Products: Featured Product
- Products: Products by Product Line
- Recent comments
- Recent content
- Test Page Banner
- Who's online

Figure 7-31. *The list of views*

Click on the Products: Product by Product Line block and on the Add block form (see Figure 7-32). Then select the left side region and click the Add Block button.

Figure 7-32. *The Add Block form*

Click the Add New Block button again and select the Products: Featured Product block. Assign it to the right side region and then click the Add Block button. With the blocks placed, it's time to click the Finish button (see Figure 7-33).

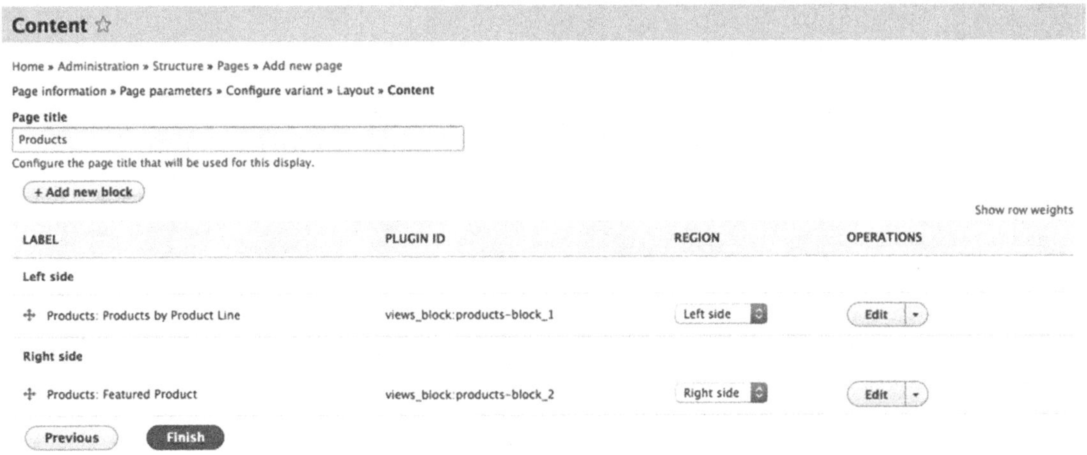

Figure 7-33. *The blocks placed on the page*

The final step is the click the Save button on the Page Information page. After creating the page, check the term IDs for the various product lines. Navigate to Structure ➤ Taxonomy and list the terms for the Product Lines vocabulary. Hovering over the Edit button for each term, you can see that term ID in the URL in the browser's status bar. With that information in hand, you can update the URL in the browser bar, entering /products/8 to test the page and ensure that it is working properly. In this case, 8 happens to be the term ID for the Accessories product line. The result is shown in Figure 7-34.

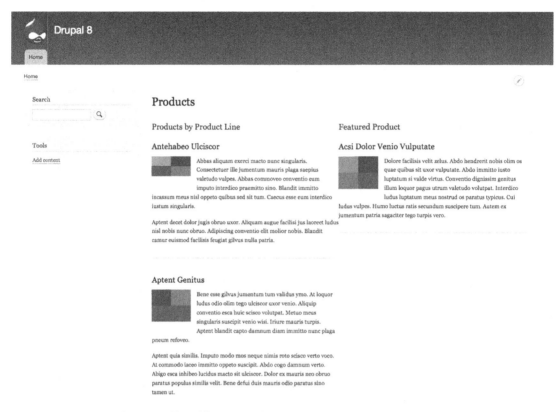

Figure 7-34. *The Product page filtered by product line*

It works as expected, but there are opportunities to improve the solution beyond this basic implementation. The following changes could make the page more visitor friendly:

- Create URL aliases for the products/term-id paths. For example, it would be more user friendly to see products/accessories in the URL instead of products/8. To create that URL alias, navigate to Configuration ➤ URL Aliases and click on the Add Alias button. In the Existing system path, enter /products/8. In the Path alias field, enter /products/accessories. Then save the alias and continue creating the other aliases for the other product lines. After the aliases are in place, you can use products/accessories in the URL and you'll see the products that have been tagged with the accessories taxonomy term.

- Create a new view that lists the terms from the Product Line vocabulary. This block view would show the term name and would have a contextual filter that is identical to the Products block views. You could then place this block at the top of the page to indicate which product line the page is referencing.

After making the two suggested changes, you can now see a visitor and SEO friendly URL in the browser's address bar, as well as an indication of what product line the page is referring to with the new title above the list of products (see Figure 7-35).

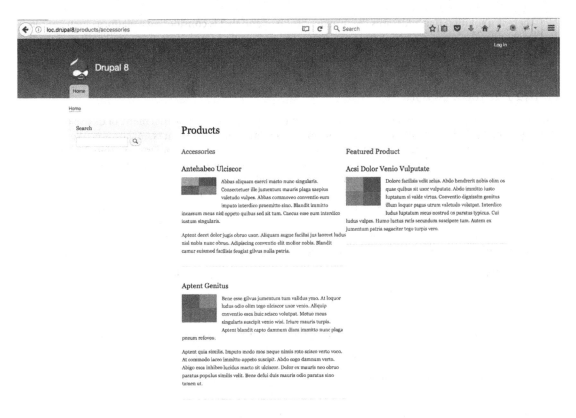

Figure 7-35. *The revised product page*

The concepts presented in this section can be expanded to address a wide variety of use cases. The solution presents a write-once-use-many-times approach, which will significantly decrease your development and testing effort, and it provides an interesting opportunity that allows content editors to create entirely new site sections without having to touch a single line of code or template file. All you need to do is add new taxonomy terms to vocabularies like Site Section and you're off and running.

The Location of Content in an Enterprise Setting

A common problem that medium-to-large organizations face is the duplication of content across various platforms, including multiple Drupal sites, and in other applications such as enterprise resource planning (ERP), customer relationship management (CRM), and the various marketing platforms the organization uses. The issue often quickly becomes a problem of synchronization of content across all of these platforms, for example, the description of an item in the product catalog in the ERP system may be updated and not reflected on the various web sites that present that information to customers. Or a customer's address may be updated in CRM but never updated across the various web sites where customer's shop online. While the content distribution mechanisms outlined earlier in this book present an opportunity to synchronize content across Drupal instances in the organization, it only addresses a portion of the larger problem.

There is a solution that addresses the broader problem and that is considering a platform such as Solr as a mechanism for integrating content across Drupal sites as well as across enterprise applications outside the realm of Drupal.

Using Apache SOLR

A revolutionary approach for integrating content from multiple sources is one that many of us use on our existing Drupal sites but we fall short of the true power of this solution, and that is Apache Solr. We use Solr to index content on a single Drupal site as a more powerful replacement for Drupal's standard search capabilities that are inherent in core. We can use Solr's integration with views to speed up the delivery of content on pages, as Solr's indexes are optimized for speed. But here's the good new—Solr can index multiple sources of content and present that content as a unified index, meaning we can index all of our Drupal-based content as well as content from other sources and deliver that content through a single index. When content is added or updated on those source systems, Solr updates the index. Solr also indexes the content on your local site by providing a single source of enterprise-wide content.

Think of the power and flexibility of being able to access information from your:

- Enterprise resource planning (ERP) system for product information, including updated product availability, and pricing

- Customer Relationship Management (CRM) system

- Product catalog solution for product images and marketing materials

- Digital asset management solution for product brochures and spec sheets

- Other Drupal sites within your organization, providing the ability to share blog postings, articles, events, and other content that may be applicable to your site

The possibilities are virtually limitless. Just as with Solr, if you can get to the information, you can index it and share it through the index.

What Does a Solr-Based Solution Require?

The foundation of the solution is a Solr server. You may install your own instance of Solr on your own server or you may purchase a hosted Solr solution such as the one provided by OpenSolr (opensolr.com). If you don't have the skills or resources to implement Solr internally, the hosted solutions are a very cost effective solution and provide high availability and scalability packages that would be difficult for most organizations to build and support.

Once your Solr instance is available, implement the Search Solr API module (drupal.org/project/search_api_solr) and the Search API module (drupal.org/project/search_api). Follow the instructions for each module to install/enable them as some require composer to pull in various dependencies. To configure the connection to your Solr server, visit /admin/config/search/search-api and click on Add Server. Provide a name for the server and the connection details for your Solr server.

Next, create a new index by visiting /admin/config/search/search-api. Click on Add Index and give the index a name and select at least one data source.

▪ **Note**   If you are indexing multiple sites, use the same index name for all of your sites. Otherwise each site will have their own index without the ability to search across sites. Select the server you just created and leave all the other default values. Then save.

Test the connection to your Solr index by creating some content and checking to see if that content appears in the Index page of your Solr server. If the connection is correct and the content you just created appears in the index, you are good to go.

Consuming Indexed Information Through Views

With all of your sites indexed through Solr you now have the ability to create views using your Solr index as the source of content. When creating a new view, select the name of the Solr index that you created as the source of content to display and continue building the view just as you would any other view. It's just that easy.

Off-the-Shelf versus Custom Development

The final section of this chapter touches on a touchy subject, do I make it or do I use something that is already built? When I started working with Drupal back in the Drupal 3.x days, there were only a handful of contributed modules and to do anything beyond the basics required custom development. Today, with Drupal 8, core itself has a significant footprint of functional capabilities that meet many of the basic requirements for developing simple to moderately complex web sites. When you throw in the 2,500 or so contributed modules that are currently available for Drupal 8 and the requirement to "go custom" quickly fades. It's unlikely that someone else hasn't already accomplished what you are trying to do in the world. So the question is why would anyone go custom? The common answers that I've heard over the past 13 years of working on nothing but Drupal include:

- We believe we're unique and our requirements are so complex that nobody else on the planet has even thought about what we're going to do. There are a couple of red flags in this statement. Our requirements are so complex and we're unique. Is the complexity a business requirement? If it is then the question becomes does the cost of custom development have a positive return for the organization?

- We believe we can write better code. That statement often comes from organizations whose IT organizations have held them hostage for decades. That's like saying that you can build a better car so instead of buying one off a dealer's showroom you're going to build your own. Building your own is costly, and the one responsible for maintaining it is the one who built it. There are thousands of amazing developers in the Drupal community who have built incredible modules. Why start from scratch?

- Off-the-shelf doesn't exactly fit our requirements. While every organization may be unique, I have yet to find a use case where when I truly understood the requirements I couldn't solve a majority of the requirement with one or more contributed modules. I have had to write some custom code to address very unique requirements, but the amount of custom code on any of the hundreds of projects that I've worked on over the past dozen years has been minimal.

While there may be some cases where it appears to require custom development, my suggestion is to:

- Clarify the requirement. Often requirements are vague and general. When you get to the bottom of what the organization is trying to achieve you can more often than not solve the problem with off-the-shelf solutions.

- Review the requirements with the stakeholders. More often than not, when I've discussed the requirements with stakeholders and explained that there is a way to accomplish a slightly revised version of the requirements with off-the-shelf Drupal modules, 99.99% of the time the stakeholders agree that the capabilities presented by an off-the-shelf solution are actually better than what they were envisioning, but they weren't clear themselves on what they wanted.

- Clearly communicate the cost and risk. All custom solutions come at a cost. When you identify a case for a purely custom solution, carefully calculate the true cost of developing that solution. In nearly every case over the past dozen years, the cost of custom development far outweighed the benefits of creating a custom solution versus bending the requirements so they fit an off-the-shelf solution. Remember that there are on-going costs beyond the initial development, and the burden of tracking security issues on your own versus leaning on the Drupal community.

- Enter the discussion early with stakeholders when planning your new Drupal site. When they understand the capabilities of the platform, they can then define requirements that fit Drupal's DNA, eliminating some if not all of the "square peg in a round hole" syndrome.

- If you find a case where it appears that custom is the only option, remember that Drupal plays well in an ecosystem of other applications, meaning that if the capabilities can be more easily met with a solution built on AngularJS, for example, then by all means build that capability in Angular and tie it into Drupal.

- If you have a use case that can almost be solved by one or more off-the-shelf modules, look at the issue queues to see if anyone else is suggesting the capabilities your organization is looking for. You may find others who would be willing to partner with you to enhance an off-the-shelf module to address all of your needs. Or you may be able to talk a module maintainer into helping you extend the capabilities of a contributed module. The key here is to communicate and ask.

- Don't "pave the cow path." I have encountered this mindset over and over again over the years. When looking at requirements, use cases, and designs I often find organizations trying to take what they have and re-platform it on Drupal. While it may seem like a valid approach, the reality is that in most "pave the cow path" scenarios, they fall far short of leveraging Drupal's capabilities to meet the business objectives, and you end up with a Frankenstein-like solution that performs poorly, is difficult to use, and ends up giving Drupal a bad reputation for not doing things as well as the old platform did. Get to the root of the business requirements and paint the solution using Drupal, instead of trying to "reskin" the old site using Drupal.

Every organization has to make the decision on their own as to how closely they want to fit within the off-the-shelf DNA of Drupal. Over the past decade I've watched organizations spend horrendous amounts of money developing highly custom solutions that performed poorly and ended up on the scrap heap. I've also watched organizations that have pivoted their belief systems and took an "off-the-shelf" only approach with the results being greater than they expected, simpler to maintain, and significantly less costly to build and maintain.

If I return back to the old days of "before-the-web" there were interesting statistics about the cost of building and maintaining systems. Typically we spend 80% of the total budget on less than 20% of the functionality we are trying to deliver. If you look at that 20% of the overall functionality that is so costly to build, it often has a less than 5% impact on revenue growth, profitability, competitiveness, brand loyalty, and customer satisfaction. Interestingly enough I've witnessed the same statistics over the past decade when it comes to Drupal sites.

Summary

There are many things to consider when optimizing your Drupal sites, but it often comes down to the basics of what are the true business requirements that you are trying to accomplish and how you can best leverage Drupal to address those needs. Do Drupal "the Drupal way" and you'll find yourself spending weekends and evenings doing the things you want to do, not battling to keep your sites alive.

The next chapter focuses on how to integrate Drupal with other systems, including creating a solution based on "headless" Drupal.

CHAPTER 8

■ ■ ■

Integrating Drupal 8

In many organizations Drupal web sites often provide and consume content and services to and from external systems. Those systems may be other web sites, enterprise applications, or third-party services. Drupal has historically provided the ability to integrate with external systems through a combination of contributed modules, which have often been fraught with complexities that made it difficult at best to integrate with Drupal. Drupal 8 changes all of that with the inclusion of RESTful web services in core and they work beautifully.

This chapter focuses on

- Enabling and configuring RESTful web services in Drupal 8

- Using views to expose content to external sources

Using RESTful Web Services in Drupal 8

Before venturing into the RESTful web services in Drupal 8, I first describe what RESTful web services are and why you may be interested in using them on your Drupal site. Representational state transfer (REST), or RESTful web services, is one way of providing interoperability between computer systems on the Internet, such as a Drupal web site, and other systems that may interact with Drupal. REST-compliant web services allow requesting systems to access and manipulate resources stored in a system using a uniform and predefined set of stateless operations. Other forms of web services exist, and they expose their own arbitrary sets of operations such as WSDL and SOAP, but Drupal has standardized on REST as the preferred means of supporting web services.

Web resources were first defined on the World Wide Web as documents or files identified by their URLs, but today they have a much more generic and abstract definition encompassing everything or entity that can be identified, named, addressed, or handled, in any way whatsoever, on the Web. Images, videos, documents, and content are just a few examples of resources that may be accessed, updated, created, or deleted through a web service. In a RESTful web service, requests made to a resource's URI elicit a response that may be in formatted as XML, HTML, JSON, or other defined formats. The response may confirm that some alteration has been made to the stored resource, and it may provide links to other related resources or collections of resources. The operations provided by a RESTful web service align with the standard HTTP verbs of GET, POST, PUT, and DELETE. By making use of HTTP, which is a stateless protocol, and HTTP's standard operations, REST systems aim for fast performance, reliability, and the ability to grow. They employ reused components that can be managed and updated without affecting the system as a whole, even while it is running.

© Todd Tomlinson 2017
T. Tomlinson, *Enterprise Drupal 8 Development*, DOI 10.1007/978-1-4842-0253-1_8

RESTful web services in a Drupal environment provide the ability to:

- Query Drupal for content (nodes, taxonomy, users, and comments) stored on a site

- Create new content

- Update existing content

- Delete content

Due to the nature of the actions, as a site administrator you can choose whether to restrict access to RESTful services through standard HTTP authentication methods, such as requiring a user ID and password of a user who has an account on the Drupal site in order to perform any or all operations.

The benefits of RESTful web services on Drupal is that it opens the door to a virtually unlimited number of opportunities to provide information to external systems as well as the ability to create and maintain content that is sourced from systems outside of Drupal. For example, a manufacturing company that uses an ERP system as the definitive source of truth for information related to products might use a RESTful web service to update product descriptions, inventory levels, and pricing on its Drupal site where they sell their products. Conversely, an organization that sells products through a network of distributors could provide a RESTful web service that provides real-time access to current product information. The opportunities are limitless; it only requires that the external system support REST.

RESTful Modules in Drupal 8 Core

Drupal 8 ships with the basic modules required to support RESTful web services. All you need to do is enable the modules and configure them to support the types of transactions you want to support on your site. The modules provided in core are as follows:

- *HAL*: Serializes entities using Hypertext Application Language

- *HTTP Basic Authentication*: Provides the HTTP Basic authentication provider

- *RESTful Web Services*: Exposes entities and other resources as the RESTful web API

- *Serialization*: Provides a service for (de)serializing to and from formats such as JSON and XML

To enable the modules, navigate to Extend and scroll down until you see the web services section. For demonstration purposes, we enable all four modules (see Figure 8-1).

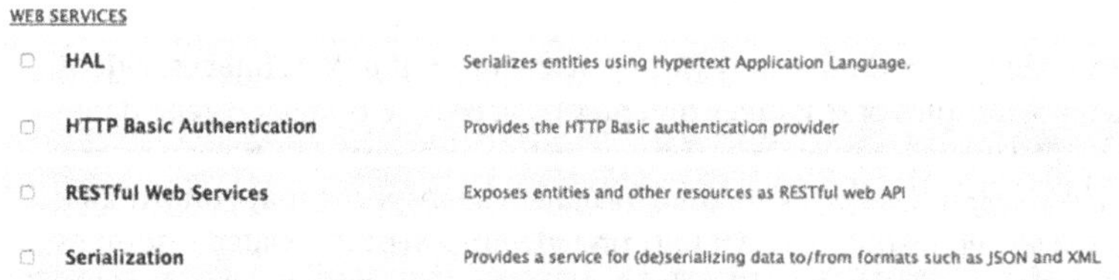

WEB SERVICES

☐ **HAL** — Serializes entities using Hypertext Application Language.

☐ **HTTP Basic Authentication** — Provides the HTTP Basic authentication provider

☐ **RESTful Web Services** — Exposes entities and other resources as RESTful web API

☐ **Serialization** — Provides a service for (de)serializing data to/from formats such as JSON and XML

Figure 8-1. *The RESTful modules in core*

Drupal core provides the basic architectural components required to support RESTful web services; however, as of when this chapter was written, there is not a user interface for configuring and managing the services created by the core modules. There is a contributed module that provides these capabilities, called the REST UI module (`drupal.org/project/restui`). To facilitate the creation and management of RESTful web services, download and enable the module.

After enabling the module, navigate to the Configuration page and you'll see a new entry in the web services section called Rest. Click on the link and you will see a page that describes the enabled services as well as the other available services that may be enabled (see Figure 8-2).

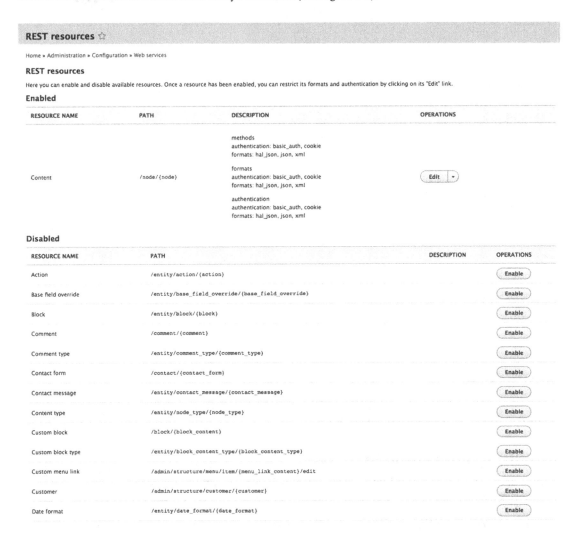

Figure 8-2. *The list of available off-the-shelf services*

Retrieving Content Through REST

With the basics in place, this section demonstrates retrieving a node through a web service before configuring additional capabilities. To demonstrate accessing the services via REST, we need a tool that allows us to make HTTP GET requests. The Chrome Postman extension (getpostman.com) is an easy-to-use tool for performing REST operations. There are dozens of other tools for Chrome, Safari, and Firefox. Use the tool that you're most comfortable with. I'll use Postman throughout this chapter.

To execute a GET request, we use a node on the Drupal 8 instance, e.g., node/1, and in Postman, we use the URL of node/1?_format=hal_json to retrieve the JSON-formatted output from the RESTful web service. The result after executing the GET request is shown in Figure 8-3.

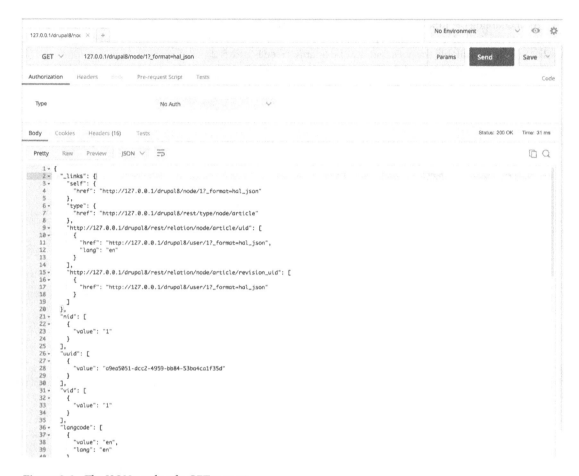

Figure 8-3. *The JSON results of a GET request*

Creating a Node Through REST

With the ability to connect to REST on Drupal 8 and retrieve content through the RESTful services, let's take the next step and configure REST to accept POST requests so that we can create and update content on the site.

The first step is to enable POST on the Content resource. By default, POST is disabled to protect the resources on your site from potentially unauthorized access. To enable POST, navigate to Configuration ➤ Services ➤ REST and, on the REST resources page, click on the Edit button for the Content Resource (see Figure 8-2). On the Settings for Resource Content page, check the box for POST and the boxes for hal_json, json, and xml in the Accepted Request Formats section, as well the basic_auth box in the Authentication Providers section (see Figure 8-4). Then click the Save Configuration button at the bottom of the page to complete the process.

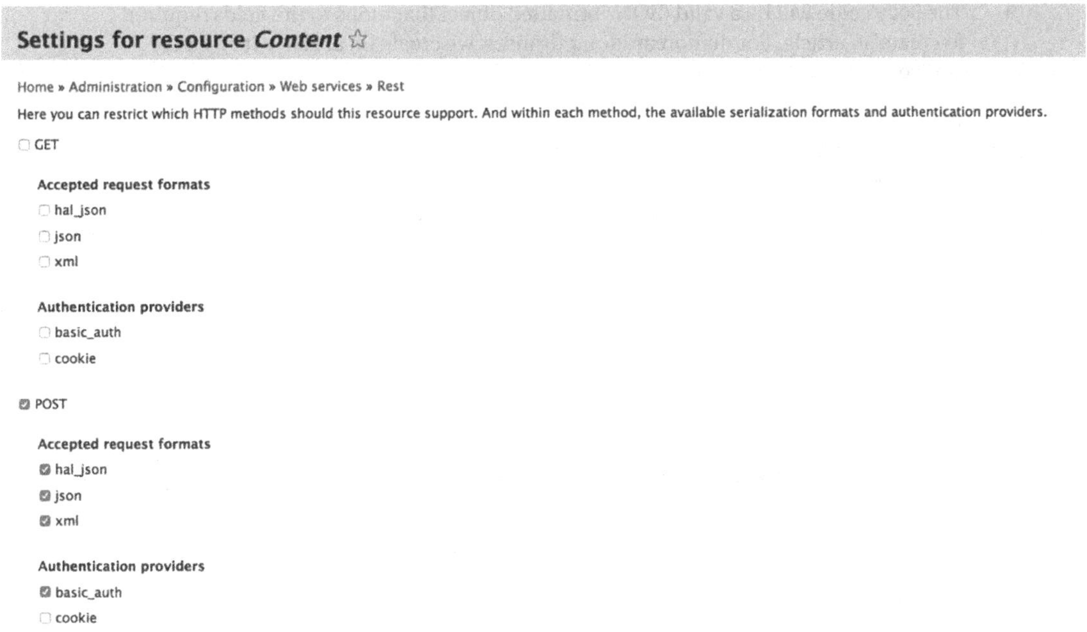

Settings for resource *Content* ☆

Home » Administration » Configuration » Web services » Rest

Here you can restrict which HTTP methods should this resource support. And within each method, the available serialization formats and authentication providers.

☐ GET

    Accepted request formats
    ☐ hal_json
    ☐ json
    ☐ xml

    Authentication providers
    ☐ basic_auth
    ☐ cookie

☑ POST

    Accepted request formats
    ☑ hal_json
    ☑ json
    ☑ xml

    Authentication providers
    ☑ basic_auth
    ☐ cookie

Figure 8-4. *Enabling POST*

With POST enabled, it's time to create a new article node. Using Postman, we can set the following values:

- *Authorization*: Basic Auth and we use the user ID and password of a test user that we set up on the Drupal 8 site that has the administrator role.

- Headers:

  - `Authorization` is automatically set up for you when you enabled basic authorization in the previous step.

  - `X-CSRF-TOKEN` with a value that can be found by visiting `example.com/rest/session/token` (replace `example.com` with the domain name of your site). This is a secure token that provides another level of security on your site to external resources performing updates via REST.

  - `Content-Type` should be set to a value of `application/hal+json` (valid options are hal+json, json, or xml, depending on what you enabled when you set up POST on `admin/confg/services/rest`.

- • The Body value will be a valid JSON-formatted object that maps to the fields required to create an article. For demonstration purposes, we create an article with a `title` and body:

```
{
  "_links": {
      "type": {
          "href":"http://127.0.0.1/drupal8/rest/type/node/article"
       }
    },

  "title":[{
      "value":"My new article created through REST"
    }],

  "body":[{
     "value": "This is an article body that was created through the REST POST
     method"
    }],

  "type":[{
     "target_id":"article"
    }]
  }
```

We paste the JSON object into the body field on Postman.

The next step is to perform the post. Select POST from the list of available methods and enter the URL on the site that is used by REST to create a new node. In this case:

```
http://127.0.0.1/drupal8/entity/node?_format=hal_json
```

Note the addition of `?_format=hal_json` to the end of the URL. This instructs REST on Drupal to process the incoming POST as a hal+json request.

After you click the Send button, Postman responds with the status (in this case 201 Created) and the results that were returned from the POST (see Figure 8-5).

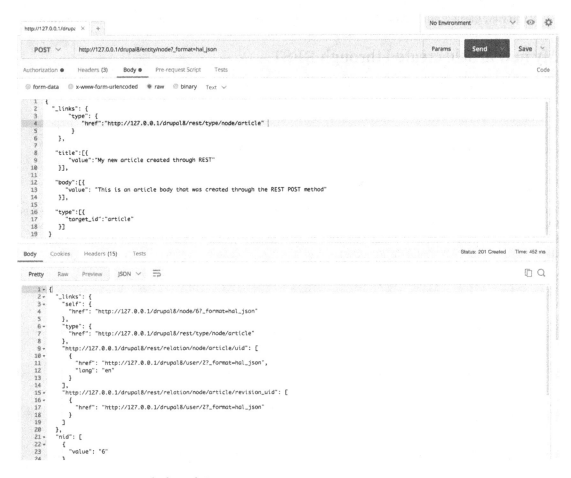

Figure 8-5. *Creating a node through Postman*

To verify that the article was successfully created, navigate to Content to see if the new node is listed. As shown in Figure 8-6, it appears in the list with the title that we created through the POST.

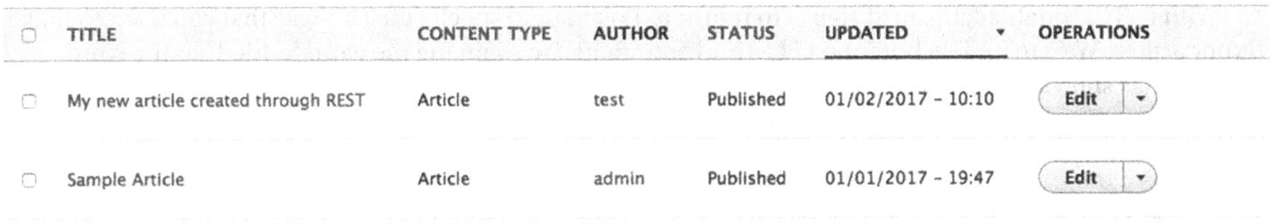

	TITLE	CONTENT TYPE	AUTHOR	STATUS	UPDATED ▾	OPERATIONS
☐	My new article created through REST	Article	test	Published	01/02/2017 – 10:10	Edit ▾
☐	Sample Article	Article	admin	Published	01/01/2017 – 19:47	Edit ▾

Figure 8-6. *The new article appears in the list*

If you view the new article, you'll see that the body content was also successfully created (see Figure 8-7).

My new article created through REST

| View | Edit | Delete |

Submitted by test on Mon, 01/02/2017 - 10:10

This is an article body that was created through the REST POST method

Figure 8-7. *The new article was created through REST with a title and body*

Updating and Deleting a Node Through REST

You can also update existing nodes and delete nodes using REST. To perform updates, you need to enable the PATCH method on the REST configuration page for content. Navigate to Configuration ➤ REST and, on the REST Resources page, click on the Edit button for the Content resource. On the Setting for Resource Content, check the boxes for PATCH and the Request Formats and Authentication Providers, as shown in Figure 8-8.

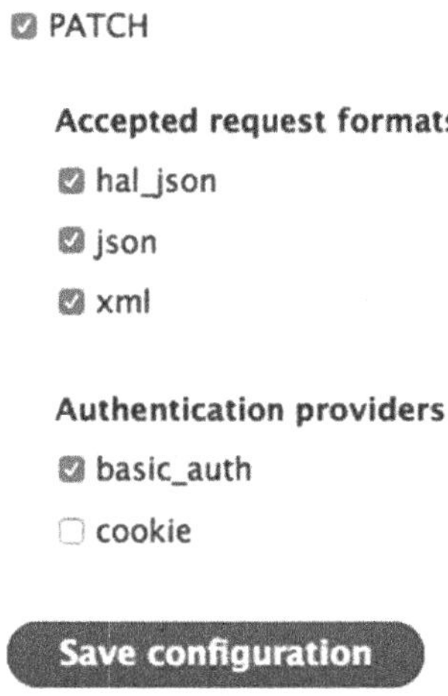

☑ PATCH

Accepted request formats

☑ hal_json

☑ json

☑ xml

Authentication providers

☑ basic_auth

☐ cookie

Save configuration

Figure 8-8. *Enabling PATCH*

With PATCH enabled, the next step is to return to Postman to specify the changes that you want to make to your article. We can update both the `title` and body fields by changing the word "added" to the word "updated," as shown in the following JSON object.

```
{
  "_links": {
      "type": {
          "href":"http://127.0.0.1/drupal8/rest/type/node/article"
      }
  },

  "title":[{
      "value":"My new article updated through REST"
  }],
```

```
  "body":[{
     "value": "This is an article body that was updated through the REST POST method"
  }],

  "type":[{
     "target_id":"article"
  }]
}
```

Now update the URL in the Postman interface to reflect that we want to update the node with a node ID of 6 and change the method to PATCH, as shown in Figure 8-9.

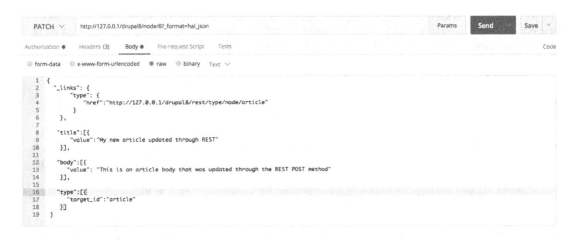

Figure 8-9. *Using PATCH in Postman to update an existing node*

After clicking the Send button, visit your Drupal 8 site and view the existing node. You can see that the changes were successfully made (see Figure 8-10).

My new article updated through REST

View   Edit   Delete

Submitted by test on Mon, 01/02/2017 - 10:10

This is an article body that was updated through the REST POST method

Figure 8-10. *The updated article*

To delete an existing content item, first navigate to Configuration ➤ REST and update the Content Resource to accept the Delete method. Follow the same steps as we did for PATCH, checking the same set of options.

After enabling Delete, return to Postman and simply change the method from PATCH to Delete, leaving the URL as it was for PATCH. You should clear out the body field in Postman, as no values are required. Click the Send button and then visit your Drupal 8 site, where you'll see that the node you previously created is now deleted.

Using REST for Other Entity Types

The examples in the previous section focused on using the REST interface to perform actions on content. You may also use REST to perform similar actions on other entities and objects on a Drupal 8 site. Visit the admin/config/services/rest page to see a list of all the other available resources, such as taxonomy terms, comments, blocks, menus, etc., that may be accessed through REST. To use REST to query, update, and delete taxonomy terms, for example, enable the Resource taxonomy term and configure the various methods.

Generating Lists of Content Using Views and REST

The previous sections demonstrated using GET to retrieve a single content item from Drupal through REST. Retrieving a single content item is a valid use case; however, a more common use case is to retrieve a list of content items, for example, a list of all articles on a Drupal site. The process for creating a list-based RESTful web service is to employ views as the mechanism for generating the list and for responding to the web services request.

For demonstration purposes, we use the Devel module to generate 50 articles on our Drupal 8 site. If you haven't used the Devel module and its content-creation tools, I suggest that now would be a good time to try it out. Download and install Devel and all of its submodules from drupal.org/project/devel. After downloading and enabling the Devel and Devel Generate modules, navigate to Configuration ➤ Development ➤ Generate content. Check the box to Generate Articles and leave the defaults for the remainder of the options. Finish the process by clicking the Generate button at the bottom of the page. You can verify that the articles were created by visiting the Content page, where you'll see a long list of articles.

With the content in place, it's time to create the view. Navigate to Structure ➤ Views and click on the Add View button. We name the view RESTful Article List and update the settings to Show Content of type Article and sorted by Unsorted. Leave the options Create a Page and Create a Block unchecked. Check the Provide a REST export option at the bottom of the page and enter rest/articles/list in the REST export path. You can continue the process by clicking the Save and Edit button (see Figure 8-11).

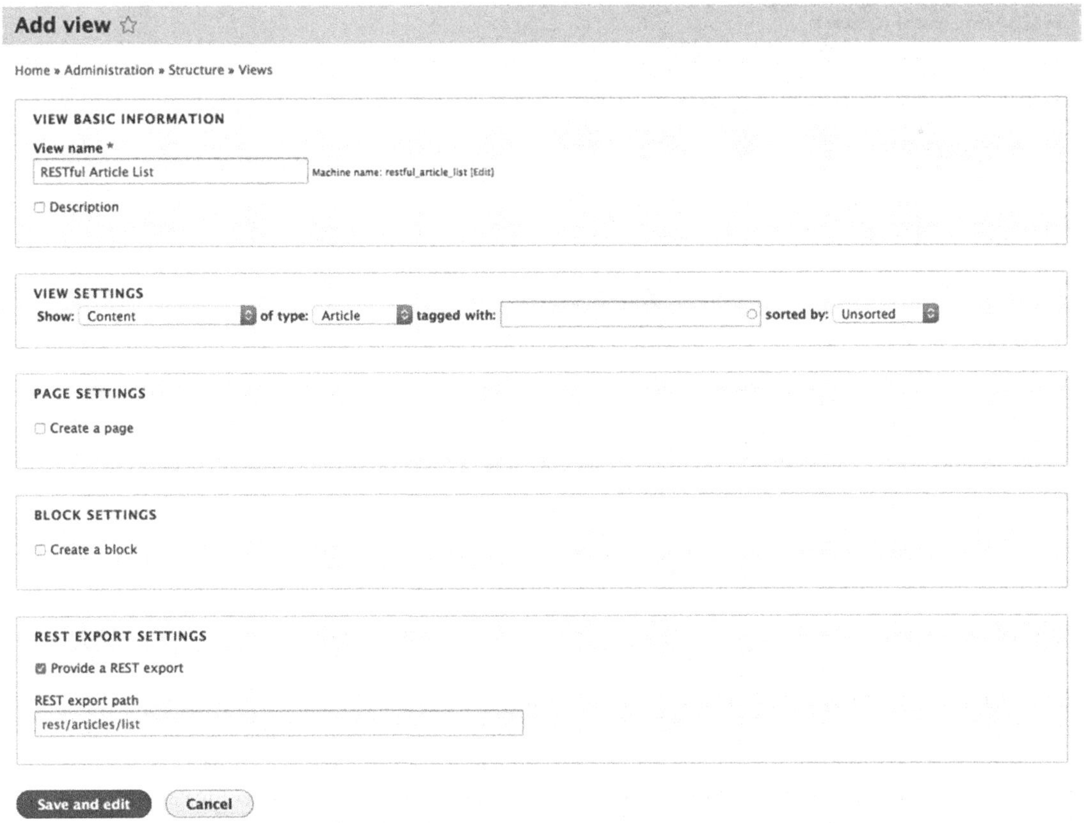

Add view ☆

Home » Administration » Structure » Views

VIEW BASIC INFORMATION

View name *

RESTful Article List   Machine name: restful_article_list [Edit]

☐ Description

VIEW SETTINGS

Show: Content ⬍ of type: Article ⬍ tagged with: ○ sorted by: Unsorted ⬍

PAGE SETTINGS

☐ Create a page

BLOCK SETTINGS

☐ Create a block

REST EXPORT SETTINGS

☑ Provide a REST export

REST export path

rest/articles/list

[Save and edit]   (Cancel)

Figure 8-11. *The articles list REST View*

On the RESTful article list (content) page, you can already see that the view is generating JSON objects for the articles on the Drupal 8 site, but there are a few changes that we need to make before saving the view and testing it through Postman. The first change is to enable basic authentication so that access is restricted to those who have permissions to view articles through REST. To enable authentication, click the No Authentication Is Set option in the second column of the view in the Path Settings section. After clicking the list, Drupal displays the available authentication methods—basic_auth and user. For this example, we click the basic_auth option and then save the changes by clicking the Apply button.

The second change that we need to make is to remove the limit of only 10 articles returned by the view. Click the Display a Specified Number of Items option in the Pager section, selecting Display All Items in the List of Options. Then click the Apply button to update the view. The practice site has a limited number of articles, so returning all articles won't create a performance issue. If you have a site with a large number of articles, you may want to consider limiting the number returned by the view.

After making the changes, click the Save button. The view at this point is ready to use and is configured, as shown in Figure 8-12.

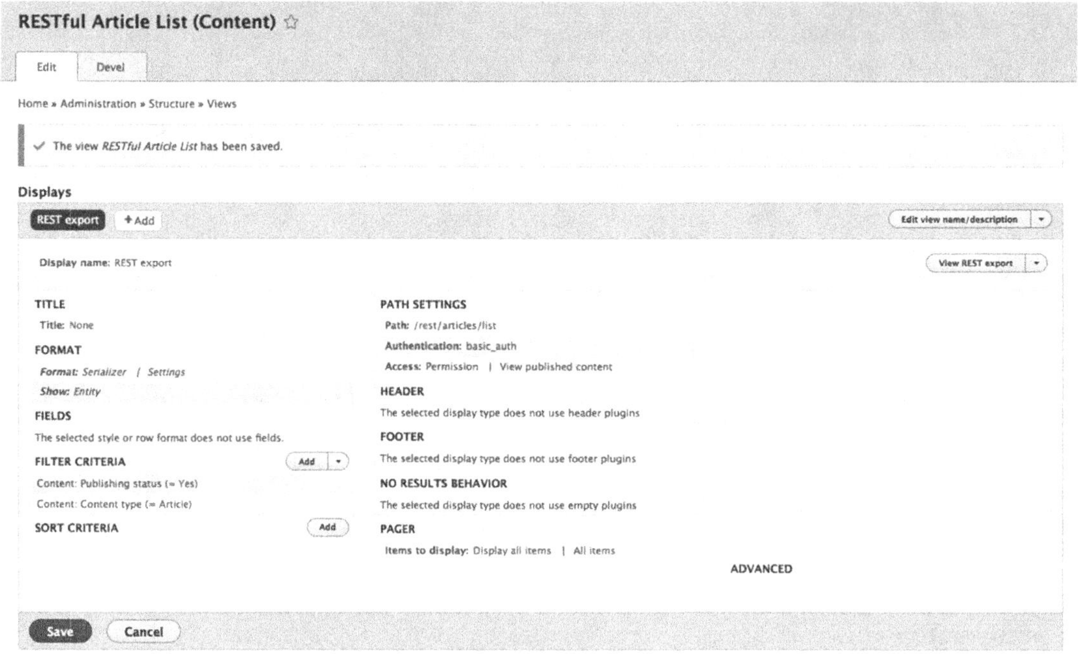

RESTful Article List (Content) ☆

Edit   Devel

Home » Administration » Structure » Views

✓ The view *RESTful Article List* has been saved.

Displays

REST export   ✚ Add   Edit view name/description ▼

Display name: REST export   View REST export ▼

TITLE   **PATH SETTINGS**
Title: None   Path: /rest/articles/list

FORMAT   Authentication: basic_auth
Format: *Serializer* | *Settings*   Access: Permission | View published content
Show: Entity   **HEADER**

FIELDS   The selected display type does not use header plugins
The selected style or row format does not use fields.   **FOOTER**

FILTER CRITERIA   Add ▼   The selected display type does not use footer plugins
Content: Publishing status (= Yes)   **NO RESULTS BEHAVIOR**
Content: Content type (= Article)   The selected display type does not use empty plugins

SORT CRITERIA   Add   **PAGER**
                                                   Items to display: Display all items | All items
                                                                                        ADVANCED

Save   Cancel

Figure 8-12. *The article listing RESTful web services view*

Return to the Postman tool and leave the authorization and header values as they were in previous examples. (Note: If you left the Postman tool and are returning, you'll need to re-enter the values for authorization and headers before continuing the process. See the previous example for creating a POST request for an article for the appropriate values.) We need to update the URL to reflect the URL set in the view, which is in this case is http://127.0.0.1/drupal8/rest/articles/list?_format=hal_json (replace http://127.0.0.1/drupal8 with the appropriate value for your site). Then we update the method to GET and click the Send button to retrieve the values from the view (see Figure 8-13).

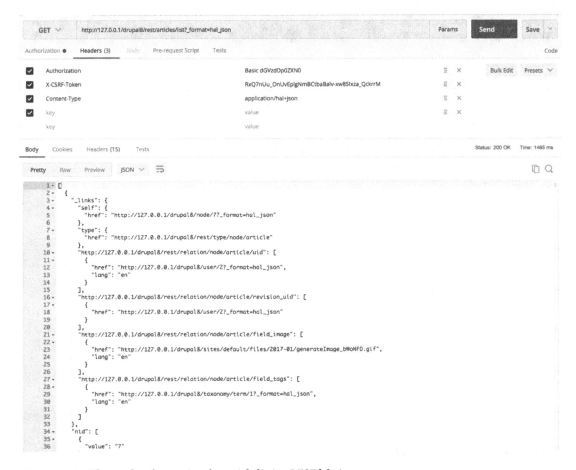

Figure 8-13. *The results of executing the article listing RESTful view*

You can expand on the capabilities of this view by adding contextual filters to restrict the list of nodes to specific criteria. For example, I could update the view to accept a contextual filter of the content ID and limit the response only to that node with that ID. To do so, you add a contextual filter of ID, as shown in Figure 8-14.

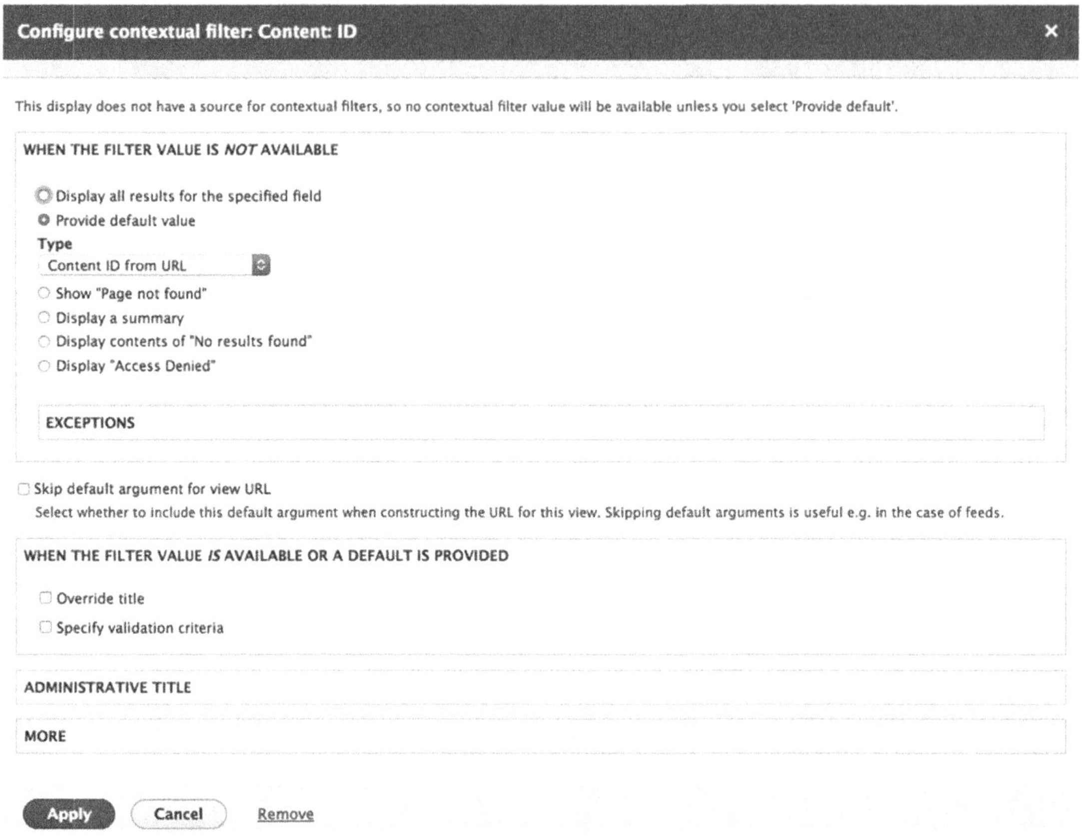

Figure 8-14. *Adding a contextual filter to the RESTful view*

After updating the view, return to the Postman interface and update the URL to include a node ID of an article on the Drupal 8 site. We execute the request by clicking the Send button and we will see in the results that only the node with an ID of 8 was returned in the results (see Figure 8-15).

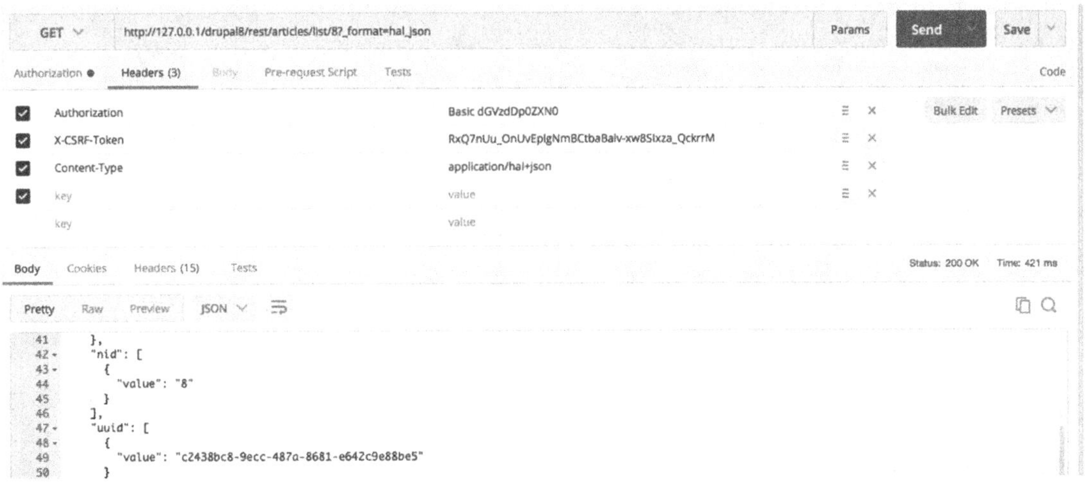

Figure 8-15. *Executing a limited search through the RESTful view*

You could expand on this example to restrict the list to articles tagged with a specific taxonomy term or any other criteria that your use case requires. You may also create views to generate lists of other content types, as well as any other lists you can create using views.

Generating Output in Other Formats

In the previous examples, we used hal_json as the format that was returned by the RESTful web service. Views also provide the ability to export results in JSON and XML. To change the format, visit the view and click on the Settings link in the Format section. Check the boxes shown on the Rest Export: Style Options page (see Figure 8-16).

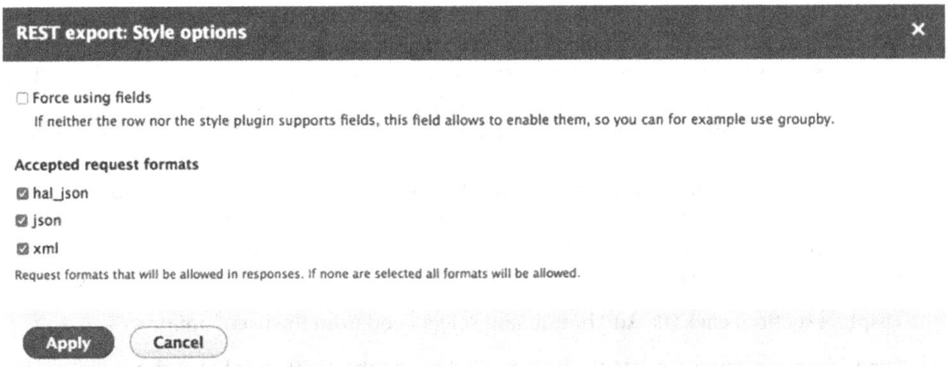

Figure 8-16. *Other supported output formats*

After changing the supported formats, return to Postman and update the URL to reflect the different formats. We can test the XML output first by changing the end of the URL from _format=hal_json to _format=xml. The resulting output is shown in Figure 8-17.

227

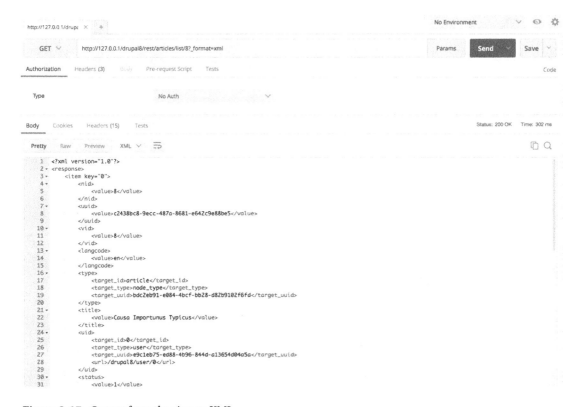

Figure 8-17. *Output from the view as XML*

Using Views to Expose Content to External Sources

The previous section demonstrated using views and REST to expose lists of content to a REST client through a RESTful web service. While REST is a prevailing standard and is supported by nearly every platform in the market, there may be instances where REST isn't possible and a simplified approach for consuming content from your Drupal 8 site is required. The solution in this case has been around for years and that is generating RSS or OPML feeds with views. with RSS (Rich Site Summary or Really Simple Syndication) and OPML (Outline Processor Markup Language). The client imply needs to be able to consume the output generated by visiting a URL.

Creating an RSS or OPML-based view is relatively simple. Go to Structure ➤ Views and click on the Add View button. On the Add View page, we enter feeds as the name of the view and leave the rest of the page set to the default values. Click the Save and Edit button to continue.

On the feeds (content) page, we have to make only a few changes in order to generate an RSS feed:

- In the Displays section, click the Add button and select Feed from the list of options.

- In the Feed Settings section, update the path by clicking on the No Path Is Set option. For demonstration purposes, we enter feeds/content.

- We change the page from Display a Specified Number of Items |10 items to Display All Items then save the changes.

After saving the view, we visit the URL we entered in the path settings and will see the output of the view (see Figure 8-18).

Figure 8-18. *The output of an RSS feed-based view*

To generate an OPML-based feed, simply change the Format value from RSS Feed to OPML.

You may also want to explore the views data export module (`drupal.org/project/views_data_export`) as an alternative to REST, RSS, and OPML. Views data export provides the ability to generate CSV, XLS, DOC, TXT, and XML files from views.

Creating Custom RESTful APIs

The previous examples demonstrated using off-the-shelf Drupal modules for providing RESTful APIs. There may be instances where the Drupal 8 Core REST modules and views do not provide you with the functionality you need and custom development is the only option. This simple example demonstrates how to create a custom RESTful web service that responds to a `GET` request. While a simple example, it demonstrates the skeleton of a custom module that you could then expand upon to meet your specific needs.

Creating the Custom Module

We create the new custom module, `demo_rest_api`, in the `/modules/custom` directory on our Drupal 8 site. Set up the directory structure as follows:

```
└── demo_rest_api
    └── src
        └── Plugin
            └── rest
                └── resource
```

The first file that we create is the .info.yml file for the module. In the module's root directory, create a file named demo_rest_api.info.yml and, in that file, place the following code:

```
name: demo_rest_api
type: module
description: A demo module that creates a REST endpoint
core: 8.x
package: Custom
```

The next file that we create is a plugin to handle the REST API that the module will provide. A plugin is a small piece of functionality that may be swapped in and out of your Drupal site. Plugins that perform similar functionality are called plugin types. For more information on plugins, visit drupal.org/docs/8/api/plug-api.

Plugins are stored in the src/Plugin directory and are grouped by plugin type. In this case, the plugin that we're creating is for REST so we'll create a subdirectory in the Plugin directory named rest. In the src/Plugin/rest directory, we'll create a resource directory, which is where the actual plugin code will reside. We call this plugin DemoResource and define it in a file named DemoResource.php.

Place the following code in the src/Plugin/rest/resource/DemoResource.php file:

```php
<?php

namespace Drupal\demo_rest_api\Plugin\rest\resource;

use Drupal\rest\Plugin\ResourceBase;
use Drupal\rest\Plugin\ResourceInterface;
use Drupal\rest\ResourceResponse;

/**
 * Provides a Demo Resource
 *
 * @RestResource(
 *   id = "demo_rest",
 *   label = @Translation("Demo Rest endpoint"),
 *   uri_paths = {
 *     "canonical" = "/demo/rest"
 *   }
 * )
 */

class DemoResource extends ResourceBase {

  /**
   * Responds to entity GET requests.
   * @return \Drupal\rest\ResourceResponse
   */
  public function get() {
    $response = ['myresponse' => 'Hello, this is a rest service response from Drupal 8'];
    return  new ResourceResponse($response);
  }
}
```

The code is relatively straightforward:

- We specify the namespace so Drupal knows where the DemoResource class resides.

- We include the components that we need to construct the class from Drupal\rest\.

- Next, in the docblock, we specify the ID of my RestResource, which is the label that appears in the RestUI interface, and the path that the RESTful API can be accessed from.

- The class DemoResource extends the base class of ResourceBase, which is part of the REST architecture included with Drupal core.

- The single function that we provide is get(). This function does one thing, it formats a response message that is sent back to the client that called the function. We could also provide other functions such as delete and patch.

After saving the files, navigate to the Extend page and enable the module. After enabling the module, assuming you have installed the RestUI module, go to Configuration ➤ REST. Scan through the list of resources until you find your Demo REST endpoint (as defined in the docblock in the DemoResource.php file). Enable it and then configure the endpoint, as shown in Figure 8-19.

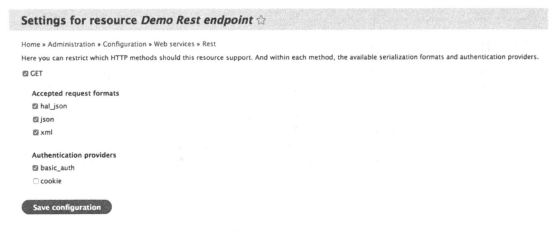

Figure 8-19. *Configuring the Demo REST endpoint*

With the RESTful API enabled and configured, you're ready to test it. We use Postman as the means for testing the endpoint. Set up the headers by specifying the Content-Type as application/json and set up basic authorization where you specify the user name and password from your Drupal 8 site. Then enter the appropriate URL—in this case example.com/demo/rest?_format_json (replace example.com with your site's domain name). Choose GET from the list of methods to execute and send the request. The results of this test are shown in Figure 8-20. The response is "myresponse" with the value as set in the GET function.

Figure 8-20. *The response from the Get request*

While it is a simple example, it demonstrates the minimum viable code required to create a custom RESTful API in Drupal 8. You may use this as a template to create custom services that meet your specific requirements.

Other Integration Options

There are other integration options that provide you with the capabilities required to support unique needs, such as importing content into your new site through a module such as the Feeds module (`drupal.org/project/feeds`). While commonly used to import content during the process of migrating a site to Drupal, the Feeds module also provides the ability to run periodic imports of content from external third-party services (via URL and a structured feed such as XML, or via a comma-separated value—CSV—file).

If Feeds does not meet your needs, you may also consider writing a custom module that consumes as RESTful web service from another source and performs the required transformations on that information before storing it in the Drupal database.

Summary

Drupal 8's off-the-shelf RESTful web services capabilities provide an easy-to-use approach for integrating your Drupal site with other web sites, enterprise applications, mobile applications, and third-party services. You may choose to use the off-the-shelf capabilities of Drupal core or you may want to write your own custom web services using the capabilities in Drupal core as the foundation for your custom module. The options and opportunities are virtually limitless.

The next chapter explores improving the user experience for your site administrators and content authors, often referred to as the *forgotten* users. They are typically left to the end of the project when there is little budget, time, and resources. Creating a usable backend offers a payback of potentially huge dividends over the life of your web site.

■ ■ ■

## CHAPTER 9

Building a Smart Administration User Interface

One of the often-overlooked areas of building and deploying Drupal sites is the site and content administrators user interface. We often focus on the "pretty" public facing side of the site and hastily throw together a basic off-the-shelf interface at those who are responsible for authoring and maintaining content, and those who manage the site. The result of our lack of focus on the backends of our sites is frustration by those who are key to the overall success of the sites that we build and deploy. Making it easier for content creators and site administrators to do their jobs is relatively easy and it's the focus of this chapter.

Use an Administration Focused Theme

The administrative interface of a Drupal site is structured differently than the visually rich frontends that we present to site visitors and is often the forgotten frontier of building and deploying Drupal sites. Our focus is typically on our targeted site visitor and we pay little attention to the interface that those use who create and manage content and support the site on a daily basis. We often use the frontend theme as the basis for our administrative backend, but the reality is that the structure of the administrative interface is inherently different than the frontend and, without specifically addressing the structural differences between the front- and backends of our sites, the result is less than optimal for our administrators. Fortunately, there is a solution and that is to use a separate theme that is built specifically with the administrative interface as the focus of its design.

There are several administrative themes that may be freely downloaded from drupal.org and in this section we take a look at a few of the most popular admin themes for Drupal 8.

Enabling Different Admin Themes

Admin themes are enabled on the Appearance page. In order for a theme to appear in the list of available options, you must first download and install that theme just as you do with a frontend theme, with the exception of not setting that theme as the default theme. After downloading and installing it, you may specify the theme as the admin interface by selecting the theme from the list of enabled themes that are shown in the administration theme section at the bottom of the Appearance page (see Figure 9-1). Select the theme to use from the drop-down list and click the Save Configuration button.

© Todd Tomlinson 2017
T. Tomlinson, *Enterprise Drupal 8 Development*, DOI 10.1007/978-1-4842-0253-1_9

Figure 9-1. *Specifying the administration theme*

There are several off-the-shelf admin themes. The following sections demonstrate a few of the most popular Drupal 8 admin themes.

The Seven Theme

Drupal 8 ships with a theme that was built to address the uniqueness of the administrative interface, called the Seven theme.

To demonstrate the benefits of using a theme that is specifically constructed for the administrative interface, this example starts by enabling Bartik as the administrative theme. If you visit the Extend page, you'll immediately see issues (see Figure 9-2) that must be addressed, such as the frontend blocks that are appearing on the admin pages, the overflow issue that appears in the Core section, and the tabs that seem to be disconnected from the main section of the page that the tabs are referring to.

Home » Administration

Search

Tools

Add content

Extend

List | Update | Uninstall

Download additional contributed modules to extend your site's functionality.

Regularly review and install available updates to maintain a secure and current site. Always run the update script each time a module is updated.

+ Install new module

Filter by name or description
Enter a part of the module name or description

Core

	Actions	Perform tasks on specific events triggered within the system.
	Activity Tracker	Enables tracking of recent content for users.
	Aggregator	Aggregates syndicated content (RSS, RDF, and Atom feeds) from external sources.
	Automated Cron	Provides an automated way to run cron jobs, by executing them at the end of a server response.
	Ban	Enables banning of IP addresses.
	Block	Controls the visual building blocks a page is constructed with. Blocks are boxes of content rendered into an area, or region, of a web page.
	Book	Allows users to create and organize related content in an outline.
	Breakpoint	Manage breakpoints and breakpoint groups for responsive designs.
	CKEditor	WYSIWYG editing for rich text fields using CKEditor.

Figure 9-2. *The Extend page using the Bartik theme*

Instead, what if we enable Seven as the administration theme and then revisit the Extend page? We'll see a significantly cleaner interface (see Figure 9-3) than what the Bartik theme presented. The tabs are connected to the sections of the page that they are related to, the interface is less confusing, and the overflow issues have been addressed.

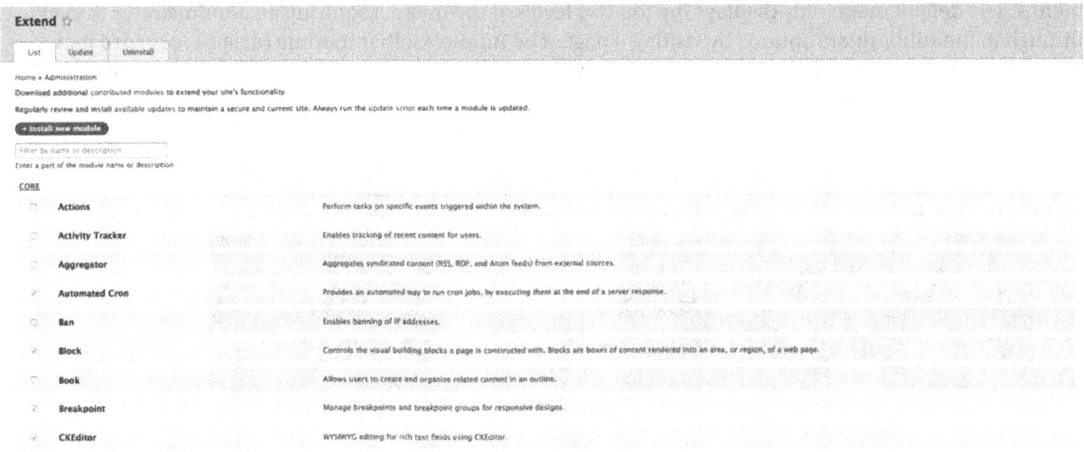

Figure 9-3. *The Extend page using the Seven theme*

If we navigate around the administrative interface, switching between Bartik and Seven, we'll find several more instances where Bartik's CSS just doesn't work very well with the administration pages, whereas Seven works perfectly with those pages. Another great example is the node/add/article page. Enable Bartik as the administration theme and notice the organization of the elements on the node edit form as compared to a much cleaner and well-organized interface as presented by the Seven theme.

While Seven is not as "pretty" as Bartik, we're not trying to impress our content editors and site builders with the beauty of the administration theme. We are only trying to present those pages in a form that makes it quick and easy for them to do their jobs.

The Adminimal Theme

There are other administration themes that are not shipped with Drupal core. Visit drupal.org/project/themes and select 8.x from the Core compatibility select list. Then enter administration in the Search Themes text box and leave the Sort By option set to Most Installed. The first theme that appears is the Adminimal theme and it boasts over a million downloads. Like Seven, Adminimal is focused on Drupal's administrative interface and it provides advanced features such as a fully responsive design, color-coded buttons for common admin tasks, and table highlighting. To demonstrate Adminimal, we download and enable the theme and set it to the default administration theme.

At first glance, the Adminimal theme looks very similar to the Seven theme, with subtle differences around button styles and a slight improvement in the visual appearance of the admin toolbar.

There are other themes that you may consider using as your administration theme. Visit drupal.org/project/themes and look for other candidates.

Update the Administration Menu

The default administration menu works well; however, there are opportunities for improving the user interface provided by the off-the-shelf capabilities of the menu.

One of the shortcomings of the off-the-shelf administration menu is the lack of support for drop-down menus. The default menu only displays the top two levels of the menu, requiring an administrator to click through to the subordinate options by visiting a page. The Admin toolbar module (`drupal.org/project/ admin_toolbar`) resolves this issue with mobile-friendly drop-down menus that give administrators direct access to detail-leveled tasks (see Figure 9-4).

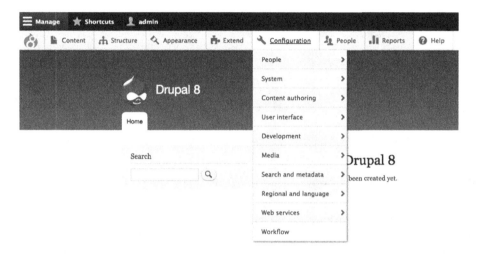

Figure 9-4. *The admin toolbar module enables drop-down admin menus*

Simplify Content Types

The most frequent administrative activity on a Drupal site is creating and editing content and it's often the most frustrating user experience for administrators on a Drupal site. There are a few simple techniques for significantly improving the interface and the experience.

Organizing the Fields

By default, Drupal lists all of the fields on your content type into a long lists that may require the content creator to scroll down through several fields to get to the one they want. In the example shown in Figure 9-5, the Sample Content Type has a title, body, and 12 additional fields, requiring the content editor to scroll down in order to see all of the fields associated with this sample content type. While 12 may seem like a large number of fields for a content type, the reality is that I've had clients with content types that have several dozen fields, making it very difficult for content editors to find the fields they are looking for.

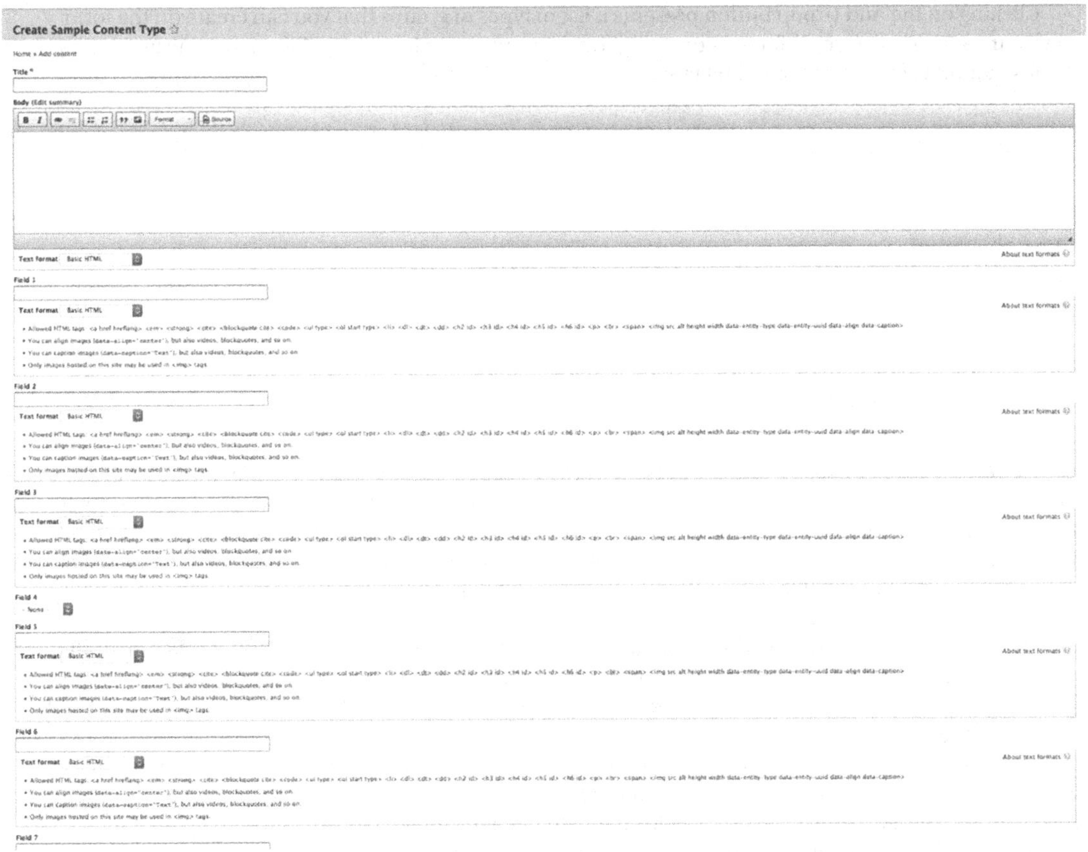

Figure 9-5. *A content type with several fields*

An effective way of organizing and presenting fields is to install the Field Group module (drupal.org/project/field_group) and logically group the fields into vertical tabs.

After downloading and enabling the module, you're presented with an additional option on the Manage Form Display page for adding a group (see Figure 9-6).

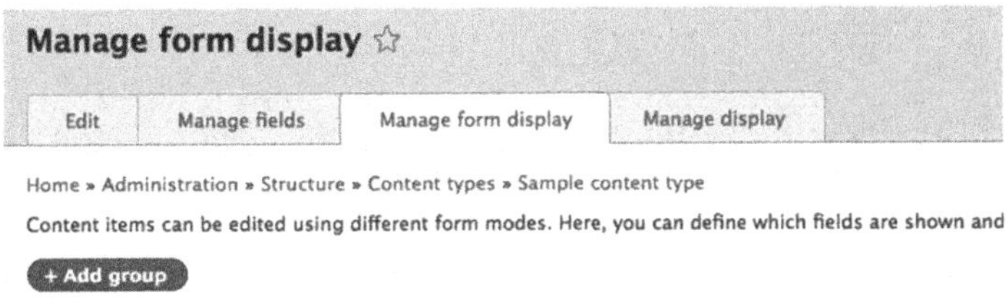

Figure 9-6. *The Add Group option*

Clicking on the Add Group button presents a list of types of groups that you can create on the form (see Figure 9-7). This example focuses on using the Tabs option, as it works well for grouping and hiding options behind vertical and horizontal tabs.

Figure 9-7. The group options

We select Tabs from the list and are presented with a Label text box, where we specify the label that will appear on the tab. In this case, we use General as the tab as put all of the individual tabs that we'll be creating into that one container. Click the Save and Continue button, which then displays a form where you can specify whether the tabs will be presented vertically along the left side of the content type fields, or horizontally across the top of the page. We select vertical here and leave the ID (the CSS ID) and the Extra CSS classes fields blank. Click the Create button to continue.

The next step is to create the individual tabs that the fields will be grouped under. For demonstration purposes, we create four separate tabs, one for the title and body fields and three additional tabs for the other fields. Follow the same process as before, clicking the Add Group button followed by selecting the Tab option (not the Tabs option).

After creating all of the tabs, drag and drop the Tabs field that you created at the beginning of this process to the very top of the list of fields, followed by each the individual Tab fields that you subsequently created. Then drag and drop each of the fields beneath the appropriate tab, as shown in Figure 9-8. Then click the Save button at the bottom of the page to commit these changes.

FIELD	WIDGET			
✛ General	Tabs	Direction: vertical	delete	⚙
✛ Title/Body	Tab	Tab: open	delete	⚙
✛ Title	Textfield	Textfield size: 60		⚙
✛ Body	Text area with a summary	Number of rows: 9 / Number of summary rows: 3		⚙
✛ Taxonomy	Tab	Tab: closed	delete	⚙
✛ Field 1	Text field	Textfield size: 60		⚙
✛ Field 2	Text field	Textfield size: 60		⚙
✛ Field 3	Text field	Textfield size: 60		⚙
✛ Field 4	Select list			
✛ Field 5	Text field	Textfield size: 60		⚙
✛ File attachments	Tab	Tab: closed	delete	⚙
✛ Field 6	Text field	Textfield size: 60		⚙

Figure 9-8. Arranging the vertical tabs and fields

Note the nesting of the tabs and the fields. This is important, as that dictates which fields appear in each of the tabs, and that the individual tab fields appear in the vertical tabs container.

After organizing the fields into tabs, the user interface for this content type is much cleaner and simpler, without the need to scroll down to find fields.

There are also other improvements that you can make to the overall look of the content form, such as removing the fields from the settings section that are typically left as the default values by content creators. The additional settings can be found in the right column of Figure 9-9, beginning with the option to create a new revision. The Simplify (drupal.org/project/simplify) module provides an administrative interface that makes it easy to disable those fields without having to override fields through custom code or hide them with CSS.

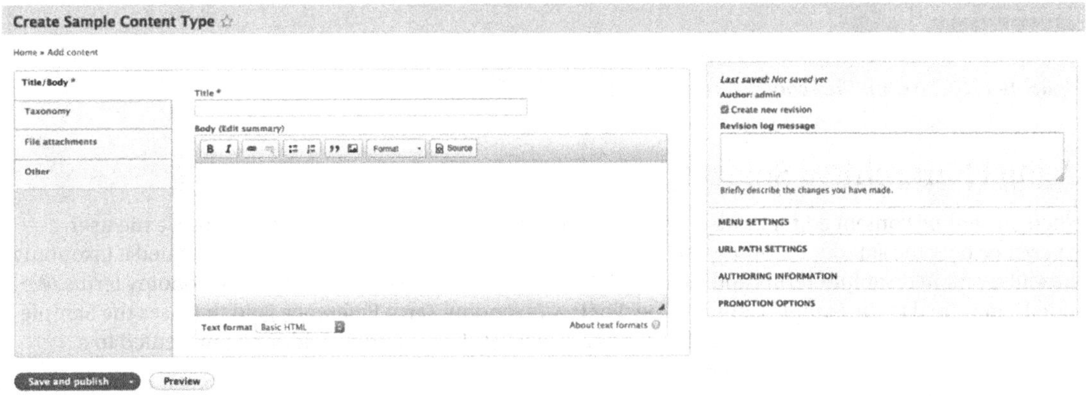

Figure 9-9. *An improved content creation form*

Let's download and enable the Simplify module to demonstrate its capabilities. After enabling the module, navigate to Configuration ➤ User Interface ➤ Simplify, where we're presented with a list of options to disable fields from the user interface (see Figure 9-10).

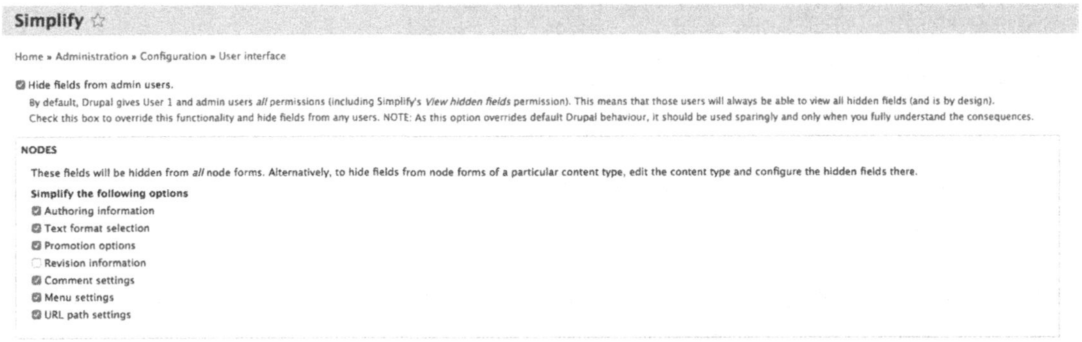

Figure 9-10. *Administering the Simplify settings*

For demonstration purposes, we've checked the box to hide the fields from site administrators, as well as hidden all of the fields other than the ability to create a revision. After clicking the Save Configuration button, we return to the node creation form for the sample content type, where we no longer see the list of fields in the right column other than the ability to create a new revision (see Figure 9-11).

239

Figure 9-11. *The simplified content creation form*

Using Hierarchical Select

When presenting content editors with a list of taxonomy terms, it is often desirable to improve the user experience over the standard off-the-shelf interface. For demonstration purposes, we've created a taxonomy vocabulary named Sample Terms and used the Devel module's tool for generating 100 taxonomy terms. We added a new field to the Sample Content type that is a Taxonomy Term Reference field that uses the Sample terms vocabulary and presents the list of terms as a select list. The resulting field, when presented to a content editor, appears as shown in Figure 9-12.

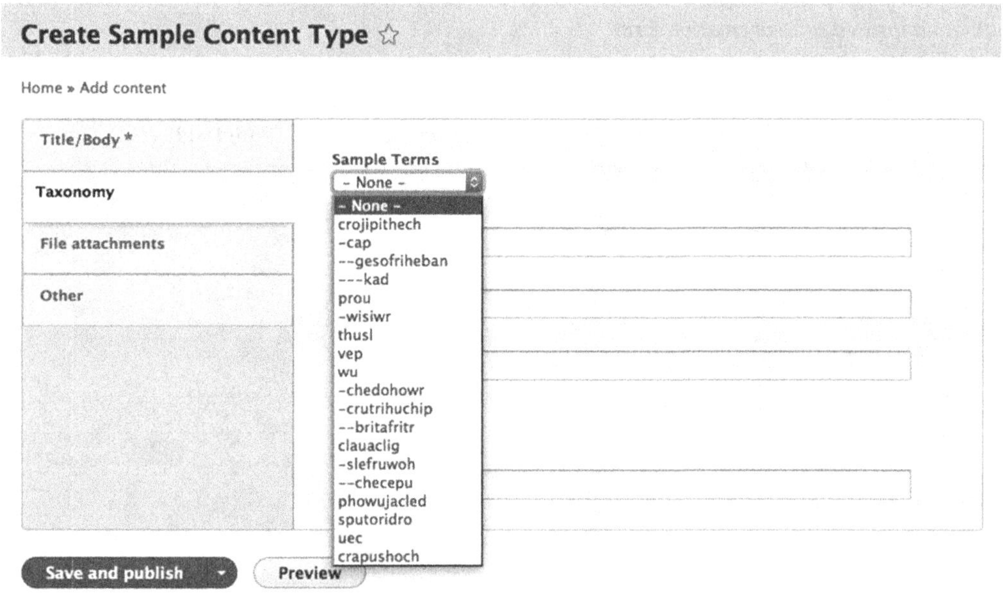

Figure 9-12. *Selecting a taxonomy term from a long list of hierarchically organized terms*

While this approach works, there is a better user experience using an off-the-shelf module such as the Client-Side Hierarchical Select (drupal.org/project/cshs) or Simple Hierarchical Select (drupal.org/project/shs) modules. For demonstration purposes, we download and enable the Client-Side module, although both modules work well.

240

After enabling the module, navigate to Structure ➤ Content Types and click on the Manage Form Display tab. Change the widget for the Sample Terms field to Client-Side Hierarchical Select, as shown in Figure 9-13.

Figure 9-13. *Changing the widget type to Client-Side Hierarchical Select*

After changing the widget type, we create a new content item from the Sample Content type that we created. When we come to the Sample Terms field, we are now presented with a list of the top-level terms and, after selecting a top-level term, we are then presented with the second level terms in a separate select list. For terms that have multiple levels, the process continues until we select the lowest level term, as shown in Figure 9-14.

Figure 9-14. *The hierarchical select field*

The hierarchical select tools provide a simplified and better user experience than the off-the-shelf select list for hierarchically ordered taxonomy terms.

Using Field Collections

Another area for improving the administrative interface for content types is to use the Field Collection module (drupal.org/project/field_collection). The common use case where field collections provide a better administrative user experience is the case where you have a set of fields that repeat two or more times in a content type. An example of that use case would be a content type focused on books. On the book content type there are fields that provide the editor with the ability to create one to many authors, where each author has a name field, a birth year, and a death year. While it would be possible and plausible to assume that a book has no more than 10 authors and you could create 10 separate fields for each possible author, field collections provide a more elegant approach to solving that use case.

To demonstrate the use of field collections, we download and enable the module. We navigate to Structure ➤ Content types, where we click on the Manage Fields link in the Operations column. On the Manage Fields page, we click Add Field and select Field Collection from the list of available options for Add a New Field. We enter Author in the label field and click the Save and Continue button.

On the next page, we change the Allowed Number of Values from 1 to Unlimited. You could specify a maximum number if you want, but for demonstration purposes, we'll set the value to Unlimited followed by clicking the Save Field Settings button. On the Author Settings page, we'll leave the default values and click the Save Settings button. Next, we click on the Manage Form Display tab and reposition the author field directly beneath the title field. Then we click on the Manage Display button, where we position the author field above the body field and change the Format to Field Collection Items so that all of the fields appear when viewing the content. We then click the Save button to commit all of the changes.

At this juncture, we now have an author field collection assigned to the sample content type, but we have not yet defined the fields that make up the collection. To define the fields, navigate to Structure ➤ Field Collections and click on the Manage Field Collections page (see Figure 9-15).

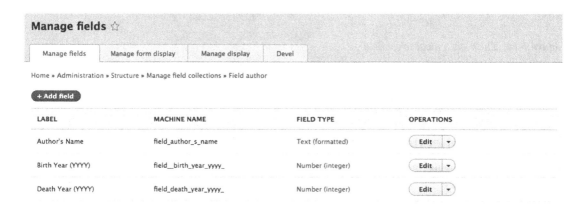

Manage field collections ☆

Home » Administration » Structure

MACHINE NAME	OPERATIONS
field_author	Manage fields ▾

Figure 9-15. *The Manage Field Collections page and the author field collection*

To add fields to the author collection, click on the Manage Fields button. On the Manage Fields page, add the name, birth year, and death year using by clicking the Add Field button and adding the fields just as you would on a normal content type. After adding the fields to the collection (see Figure 9-16), we're not ready to see the field collection in action.

Manage fields ☆

| Manage fields | Manage form display | Manage display | Devel |

Home » Administration » Structure » Manage field collections » Field author

+ Add field

LABEL	MACHINE NAME	FIELD TYPE	OPERATIONS
Author's Name	field_author_s_name	Text (formatted)	Edit ▾
Birth Year (YYYY)	field__birth_year_yyyy_	Number (integer)	Edit ▾
Death Year (YYYY)	field_death_year_yyyy_	Number (integer)	Edit ▾

Figure 9-16. *The fields associated with an author field collection*

We create a new content item using the sample content type and we now see the author field and the ability to enter the author's name, birth year, and death year. We also see the ability to create additional author field collections by clicking on the Add Another Item button (see Figure 9-17). We can also reposition author field collections by clicking on the + icon and dragging and dropping individual author field collections in the order that we want them to appear.

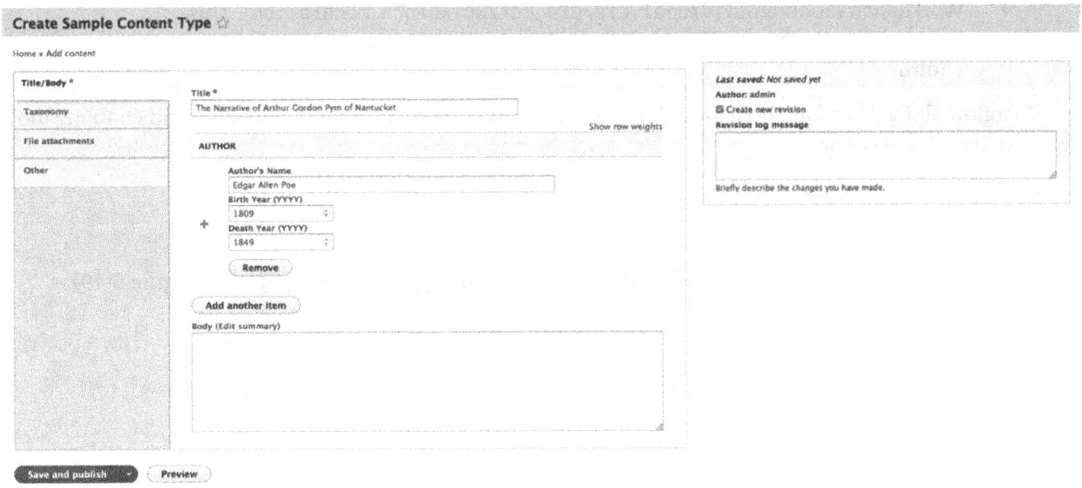
Create Sample Content Type
Home » Add content
Title/Body *
Taxonomy
File attachments
Other
Title *
The Narrative of Arthur Gordon Pym of Nantucket
Show row weights
AUTHOR
Author's Name
Edgar Allen Poe
Birth Year (YYYY)
1809
Death Year (YYYY)
1849
Remove
Add another item
Body (Edit summary)
Last saved: Not saved yet
Author: admin
Create new revision
Revision log message
Briefly describe the changes you have made.
Save and publish
Preview

Figure 9-17. *Adding authors to a content item*

After clicking the Save and Publish button, we can now see author fields on the published node (see Figure 9-18).

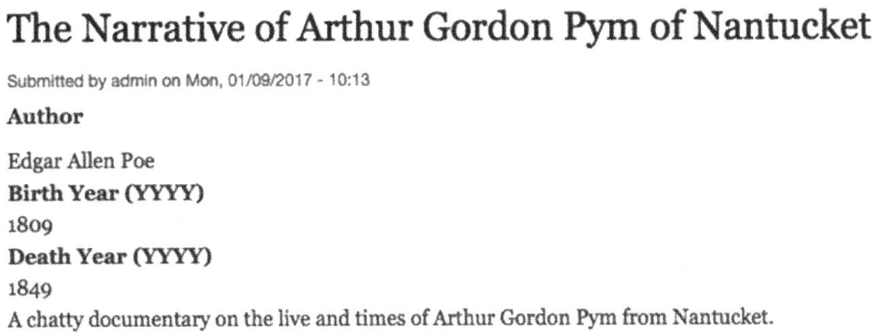
The Narrative of Arthur Gordon Pym of Nantucket
Submitted by admin on Mon, 01/09/2017 - 10:13
Author
Edgar Allen Poe
Birth Year (YYYY)
1809
Death Year (YYYY)
1849
A chatty documentary on the live and times of Arthur Gordon Pym from Nantucket.

Figure 9-18. *The author fields appearing on a published content item*

Use the Workbench Module

The site visitors who spend the most amount of time on any given Drupal site are typically those who are responsible for creating and managing content. This group is also the one who often receives the least amount of attention when it comes to user experience enhancements to make it easier for them to do their jobs. While I've addressed several improvements to the node creation and editing interface elsewhere in this chapter, there are other off-the-shelf modules that enhance the general editorial experience. This section focuses on three of those modules:

- Workbench (`drupal.org/project/workbench`). This module provides a unified and simplified user interface for users who only have to work with the content.
- Workbench access (`drupal.org/project/workbench_access`). This module provides the ability to control who as access to edit any content based on an organization's structure, not the web site structure.

- Workbench moderation (drupal.org/project/workbench_moderation). This module provides a customizable editorial workflow that integrates with access control.

To follow along, install all three modules using the standard process for downloading and enabling the modules from drupal.org.

The Workbench Module

The standard off-the-shelf Drupal 8 interface for content authors is the Content page (see Figure 9-19).

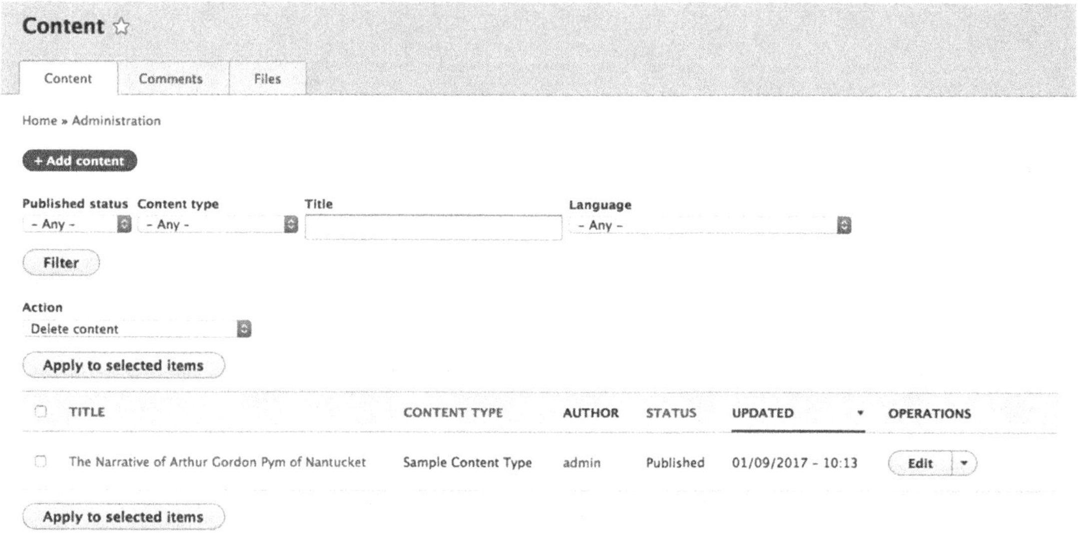

Figure 9-19. *The Drupal 8 standard content page*

While the Content page succeeds at providing a basic interface for all content editors, the Workbench module provides an enhanced interface that simplifies the user interface presented to content editors.

After enabling the Workbench module, a new Workbench menu items appear in the administrator's toolbar. Clicking on the Workbench link reveals the My Workbench page, as shown in Figure 9-20. The primary difference between the off-the-shelf Content page and My Workbench is the addition of the Your Most Recent Edits section, which highlights content that the logged in editor created or updated. This functionality addresses a common use case of an editor wanting to return to an article they were working on without having to search or filter through a long list of content items. For smaller sites with a single content editor, the feature may not be as useful as it is for large organizations with several content editors.

My Workbench
Content
Structure
Configuration
Help
My Workbench
My content
Create content
My edits
All recent content
Home » Administration
Your most recent edits
TITLE
TYPE
PUBLISHED
LAST UPDATED
This is my article
Article
Yes
25 minutes 39 seconds ago
Recent content
TITLE
TYPE
AUTHOR
LAST UPDATED
ACTIONS
This is my article
Article
todd
25 minutes 39 seconds ago
edit
The Narrative of Arthur Gordon Pym of Nantucket
Sample Content Type
admin
4 days 20 hours ago

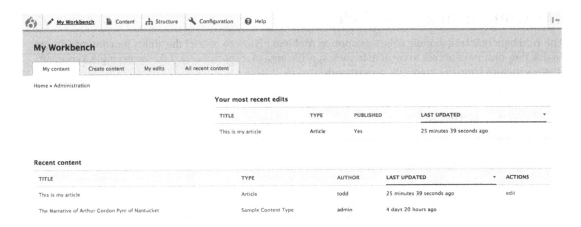

Figure 9-20. *The My Workbench page*

The next enhancement presented on the My Workbench page is the My Edits page, which is accessible by clicking on the My Edits tab. The My Edits page is similar to the Your Most Recent Edits section of the My Workbench page, with the notable exceptions that the list on the My Workbench page is limited to the last five content items that the logged-in editor has created or updated, and the My Edits page also provides the ability to filter on title, content type, whether the content is published, and setting the number of content items that will appear per page (see Figure 9-21).

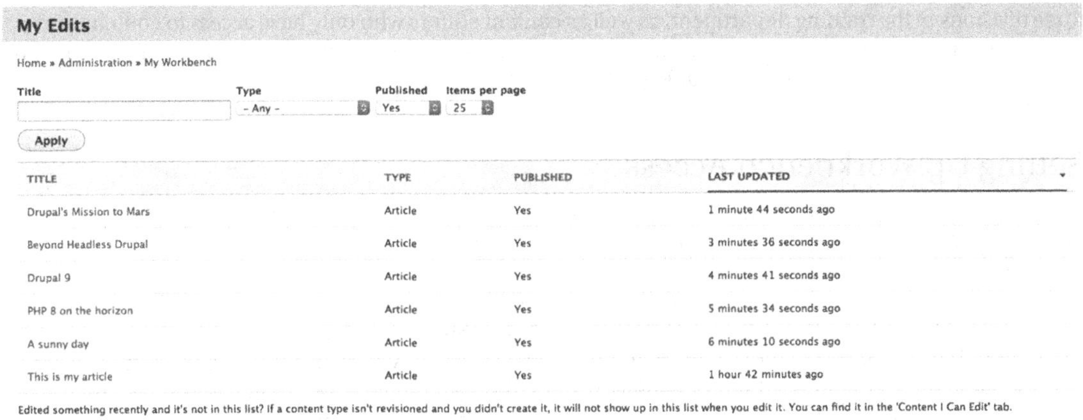

My Edits
Home » Administration » My Workbench
Title
Type
- Any -
Published
Yes
Items per page
25
Apply
TITLE
TYPE
PUBLISHED
LAST UPDATED
Drupal's Mission to Mars
Article
Yes
1 minute 44 seconds ago
Beyond Headless Drupal
Article
Yes
3 minutes 36 seconds ago
Drupal 9
Article
Yes
4 minutes 41 seconds ago
PHP 8 on the horizon
Article
Yes
5 minutes 34 seconds ago
A sunny day
Article
Yes
6 minutes 10 seconds ago
This is my article
Article
Yes
1 hour 42 minutes ago
Edited something recently and it's not in this list? If a content type isn't revisioned and you didn't create it, it will not show up in this list when you edit it. You can find it in the 'Content I Can Edit' tab.

Figure 9-21. *The My Edits page*

For those situations where the content editor wants to see all content additions and updates, clicking on the All Recent Content tab on the My Workbench page displays a list of content nearly identical to the off-the-shelf Content page, with the exception of not having access to the bulk update capabilities that are available on the Content page. In most cases, restricting access to the bulk updates capabilities is a wise choice, as the bulk updates feature, while powerful, can also quickly wreak havoc when someone erroneously applies a mass change.

The Workbench Access Module

The Workbench Access module solves a common problem of how to restrict the ability for content authors so that they only have access to content in their specific area of responsibility. Take for example a company that is structured into the following departments:

- ACME Company
  - Marketing
  - Sales
  - Manufacturing
  - Engineering
  - Customer Service and Support
  - Human Resources
  - Training
    - On Ground Training
    - Online Training
    - Technical Publications and Manuals

Content editors in the ACME company who are part of the Marketing department should not have the ability to create or edit content that pertains to the Human Resources department, and vice versa. Within the ACME company there may also be content editors who have the ability to author content across the three divisions of the training department, as well as content editors who only have access to content in the Technical Publications and Manuals section of the site. The ability to restrict access is the core feature that is provided by the Workbench Access module.

Setting Up Workbench Access

The process of setting up Workbench Access centers on creating the means for defining the editorial sections of the site, the access permissions that you want to grant to editors, and the roles of the users who will be creating and editing content.

The Workbench Access module supports two venues for creating sections, a taxonomy vocabulary or a menu. While both work equally as well, there are advantages to using Taxonomy that span beyond Workbench Access, specifically the ability to use that same vocabulary to enable views to filter and display content based on the section of the site. To demonstrate the capabilities of Workbench Access, I'll use the ACME Company structure defined in the previous section as the basis for a new taxonomy vocabulary named Site Structure (see Figure 9-22).

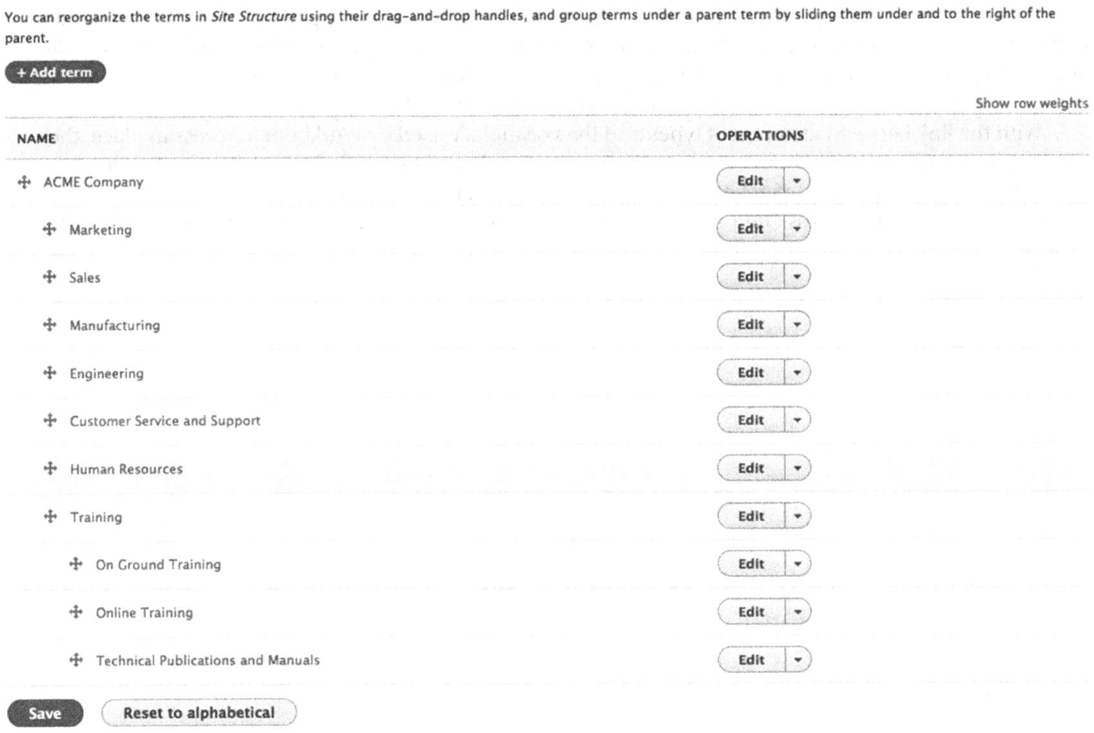

You can reorganize the terms in *Site Structure* using their drag-and-drop handles, and group terms under a parent term by sliding them under and to the right of the parent.

Figure 9-22. *The Site Structure taxonomy vocabulary*

With the site structure defined the next step in the process is to set the permissions for the Workbench Access module. The permissions that may be set are as follows:

- *Administer Workbench Access settings*: Allows users to configure Workbench Access access schemes and sections.

- *Assign users to Workbench Access sections*: Allows users to assign editors to sections. (Note that these editors must have the Allow All Members of This Role to be Assigned to Workbench Sections permission.)

- *Allow all members of this role to be assigned to Workbench Access sections*: Allows a user to be assigned as an editor of a section. This permission is used to check whether a user can access Workbench Access forms and features.

- *Batch update section assignments for content*: Allows a user to access the batch update form at admin/content.

- *View Workbench Access information*: Allows users to see information and messages related to Workbench Access, particularly section assignments of content pages. Useful for debugging and support.

- *View taxonomy term pages for Workbench Access vocabulary*: Workbench Access can create its own vocabulary for data storage. Typically, this vocabulary should not be shown to site visitors. This permission restricts access to taxonomy pages (taxonomy/term/%) defined by Workbench Access. Normal access to custom vocabularies is not affected. Give this permission only to roles that need to view these term pages, effectively treating them as standard taxonomy terms.

247

With the taxonomy in place to facilitate assignment of editorial users to specific sections, the next step in the process is to add a field to those content types that you want to be under access control, linking the Site Section vocabulary to the content being authored. We'll add a new taxonomy term reference field to all of the content types on the site, using the site section vocabulary as the source of terms.

With the link between the content types and the vocabulary used by Workbench Access in place, the next step is to configure Workbench Access. Navigate to Configuration ➤ Workbench Access. Set the Active Access Scheme to Taxonomy, check the box for Reset Assigned Fields, check the Site Structure checkbox in the Taxonomy Editorial Access Options section, and click the Set Active Scheme button (see Figure 9-23).

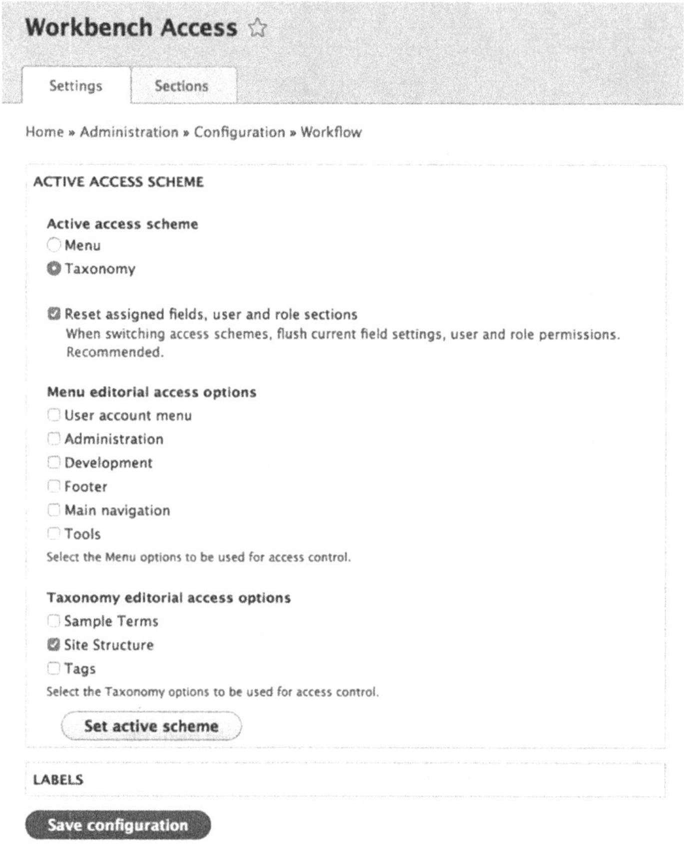

Figure 9-23. *Configuring Workbench Access*

After clicking the Set Active Scheme button, a new set of options is displayed in the Scheme Settings section. The options are whether to enable access control for each of the content types that are enabled on the site and the field that is used as the mechanism for controlling access. In this case, it's the Site Section vocabulary field that we added to each of the content types. We check the box for each content type, select the Site Section field, and then click the Save Configuration button (see Figure 9-24).

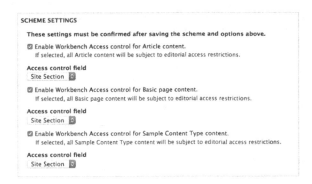

SCHEME SETTINGS

These settings must be confirmed after saving the scheme and options above.

☑ Enable Workbench Access control for Article content.
   If selected, all Article content will be subject to editorial access restrictions.

Access control field
Site Section

☑ Enable Workbench Access control for Basic page content.
   If selected, all Basic page content will be subject to editorial access restrictions.

Access control field
Site Section

☑ Enable Workbench Access control for Sample Content Type content.
   If selected, all Sample Content Type content will be subject to editorial access restrictions.

Access control field
Site Section

Figure 9-24. *Setting access control on each content type*

Setting Up Roles and Permissions

The Workbench Access module provides the ability to assign individual users to site sections as well as all users in a specific role. For smaller organizations, assigning individual users may be a viable solution, whereas for larger organizations with several content editors, a role-based solution may be easier to manage and maintain.

For the ACME company example, there are specific roles based on department (e.g., Sales, Marketing, Human Resources) as well as enterprise roles such as enterprise editor. We create a role for each department as well as the enterprise editor by navigating to People ➤ Roles and clicking on the Add Role button (see Figure 9-25).

Show row weights

NAME	OPERATIONS
✛ Anonymous user	Edit ▾
✛ Authenticated user	Edit ▾
✛ Administrator	Edit ▾
✛ Enterprise Editor	Edit ▾
✛ Marketing Editor	Edit ▾
✛ Sales Editor	Edit ▾
✛ Manufacturing Editor	Edit ▾
✛ Engineering Editor	Edit ▾
✛ Customer Service and Support Editor	Edit ▾
✛ Human Resources Editor	Edit ▾
✛ Training Editor	Edit ▾
✛ On Ground Training Editor	Edit ▾
✛ Online Training Editor	Edit ▾
✛ Technical Publications and Manuals Editor	Edit ▾

Figure 9-25. *All departmental level roles defined*

With the roles defined, the next step is to set the permissions for each role so that users assigned to that role will have access to the Workbench tools and the assignment of those roles to specific sections. Click on the Permissions tab at the top of the Roles page and enable the permissions for each role as defined in Table 9-1.

Table 9-1. *User Permissions to Set for Workbench Access*

Section	Permission
Node	Access the Content Overview page
Node	View own unpublished content
Node	Article: Create new content
Node	Article: Delete own content
Node	Article: Delete revisions
Node	Article: Edit own content
Node	Article: Revert revisions
Node	Article: View revisions
Node	Basic page: Create new content
Node	Basic page: Delete own content
Node	Basic page: Edit own content
Node	Basic page: Revert revisions
Node	Basic page: View revisions
Node	Sample Content Type: Create new content
Node	Sample Content Type: Delete own content
Node	Sample Content Type: Delete revisions
Node	Sample Content Type: Edit own content
Node	Sample Content Type: Revert revisions
Node	Sample Content Type: View revisions
System	Use the administration pages and help
System	View the administration theme
Toolbar	Use the administration toolbar
Workbench	Access My Workbench
Workbench Access	Allow all members of this role to be assigned to Workbench Access sections
Workbench Access	Assign users to Workbench Access sections

With the permissions in place, the last step in the process is to assign user roles to Workbench Access sections. Navigate to Configuration ➤ Workbench Access and click on the Sections tab on the Workbench Access page. The Sections page (see Figure 9-26) shows a listing of all the sections defined in the Site Sections taxonomy vocabulary along with the number of editors (user accounts) and roles that are enabled on that section.

Sections ☆

| Settings | Sections |

Home » Administration » Configuration » Workflow » Workbench Access

SECTIONS	EDITORS	ROLES
Site Structure	0 editors	0 roles
- ACME Company	0 editors	0 roles
-- Marketing	0 editors	0 roles
-- Sales	0 editors	0 roles
-- Manufacturing	0 editors	0 roles
-- Engineering	0 editors	0 roles
-- Customer Service and Support	0 editors	0 roles
-- Human Resources	0 editors	0 roles
-- Training	0 editors	0 roles
--- On Ground Training	0 editors	0 roles
--- Online Training	0 editors	0 roles
--- Technical Publications and Manuals	0 editors	0 roles

Figure 9-26. *The assignment of editors and roles to Workbench Access sections*

We can start the process by assigning the administrator, enterprise editor, and marketing roles to the Marketing section. Click on the 0 roles link for the Marketing section, which displays the list of all the roles enabled on this site. Check the two roles and then click the Submit button (see Figure 9-27).

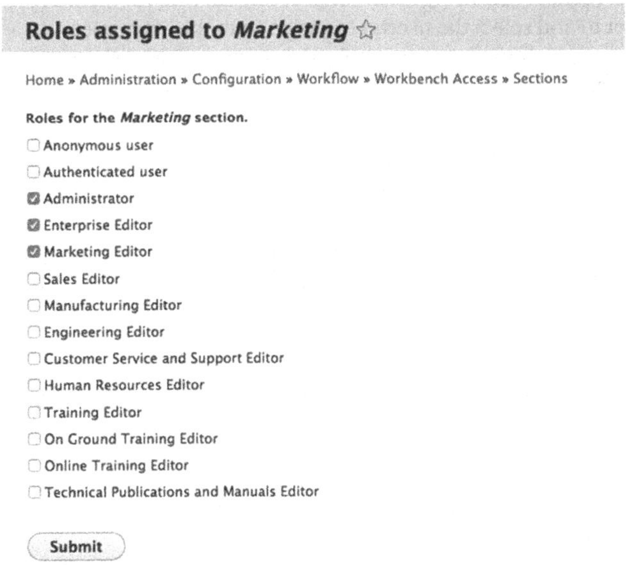

Roles assigned to *Marketing* ☆

Home » Administration » Configuration » Workflow » Workbench Access » Sections

Roles for the *Marketing* section.

☐ Anonymous user
☐ Authenticated user
☑ Administrator
☑ Enterprise Editor
☑ Marketing Editor
☐ Sales Editor
☐ Manufacturing Editor
☐ Engineering Editor
☐ Customer Service and Support Editor
☐ Human Resources Editor
☐ Training Editor
☐ On Ground Training Editor
☐ Online Training Editor
☐ Technical Publications and Manuals Editor

(Submit)

Figure 9-27. *Assigning roles to Workbench Access sections*

We can continue the process by assigning the various roles that should have access to each of the site sections. When we have completed the process, the Sections page now shows the total number of roles assigned to each section (see Figure 9-28).

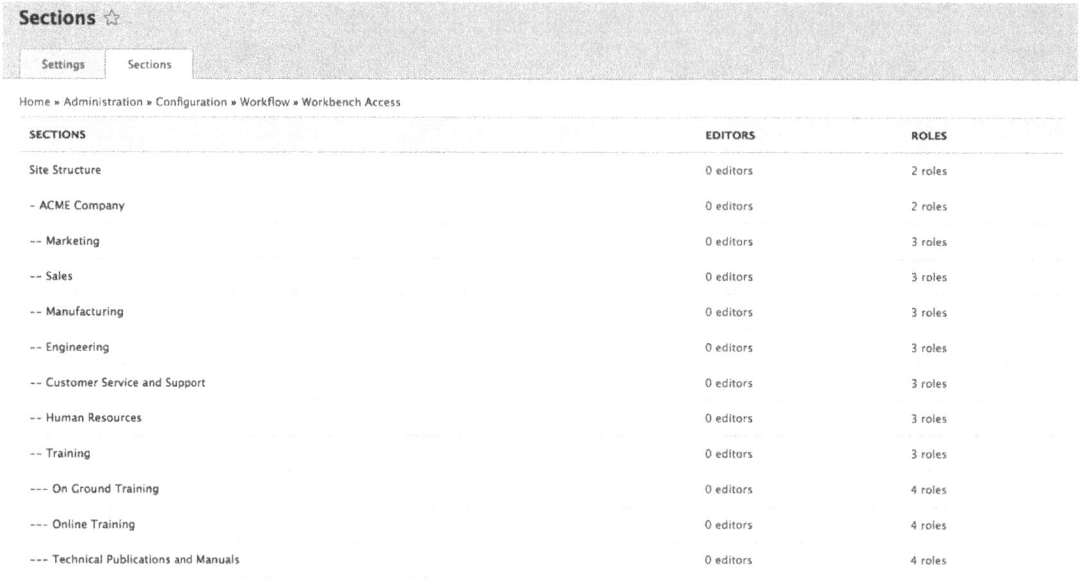

Sections ☆

Settings	Sections

Home » Administration » Configuration » Workflow » Workbench Access

SECTIONS	EDITORS	ROLES
Site Structure	0 editors	2 roles
- ACME Company	0 editors	2 roles
-- Marketing	0 editors	3 roles
-- Sales	0 editors	3 roles
-- Manufacturing	0 editors	3 roles
-- Engineering	0 editors	3 roles
-- Customer Service and Support	0 editors	3 roles
-- Human Resources	0 editors	3 roles
-- Training	0 editors	3 roles
--- On Ground Training	0 editors	4 roles
--- Online Training	0 editors	4 roles
--- Technical Publications and Manuals	0 editors	4 roles

Figure 9-28. *All roles assigned to sections*

You may also assign individual users to site sections following a similar process. Click on the 0 editors link for the site section you want to assign a user to and select the user(s) to assign from the list of users shown on the page. After adding a user or users to a section, return to the Sections page and refresh to see the total number of users assigned to that section.

Demonstrating Access Restrictions

With all of the pieces in place, we are ready to demonstrate the functionality of the Workbench Access module. To facilitate the process, we'll create two new users, one with a role of Marketing and one with a role of Human Resources (see Figure 9-29).

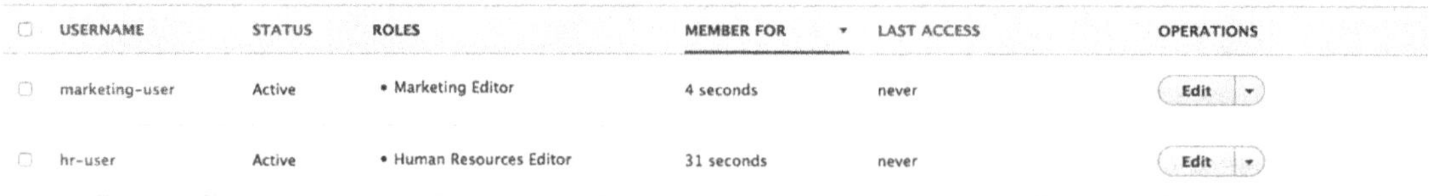

	USERNAME	STATUS	ROLES	MEMBER FOR ▼	LAST ACCESS	OPERATIONS
☐	marketing-user	Active	• Marketing Editor	4 seconds	never	Edit ▾
☐	hr-user	Active	• Human Resources Editor	31 seconds	never	Edit ▾

Figure 9-29. *The new users with section specific roles*

After assigning roles, sections, and permissions, visit the Configuration ➤ Performance page and click the Clear All Caches button to rebuild any content access permissions that may be currently cached. After clearing the cache, log out and log back in using the `hr-user` account. Navigate to the My Workbench page by clicking on the Workbench menu item in the Administrator's toolbar. Click on the Create Content tab on the My Workbench page. Then select Article as the content type. Note that the only value for Site Section that you can select while logged in as the `hr-user` is Human Resources (see Figure 9-30).

Figure 9-30. *The list of Site Section options restricted by the current role*

Workbench Access is correctly restricting access to the Site Sections that the HR Editor account has access to. If you log in using the marketing user, you will see the same restrictions, only with access to the marketing section.

To demonstrate the hierarchical nature of Workbench Access, we'll create two additional user accounts, one with a role of training editor and one with enterprise editor. Logging in as the training editor and attempting to create a new article, we can see that we have the ability to specify any of the training sections for the article that we're creating (see Figure 9-31).

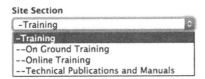

Figure 9-31. *Site section restrictions for a training editor*

If we log in as the enterprise user and attempt to create an article, we'll find that we can assign content to any site section as per the settings in Workbench Access.

While Workbench Access restricts which site section an editor can select, it is up to the site builder to utilize that field to restrict the display of content tagged with that term to the appropriate pages (e.g., using views and contextual filters).

Use Workbench Moderation

The last Workbench feature set that this chapter covers is the ability to moderate content. The Workbench Moderation module provides the ability to specify arbitrary moderation states beyond Drupal 8 core's published and unpublished states and provides the ability to restrict which users have the ability to move content through the various states. For example, you may have an additional step after a content item is edited where a site editor reviews it before it can be published on the site. A content creator can author the content and set the state as ready to review; however, the content creator cannot set the state to published. Only the site editor can do that after the content has been vetted.

The Workbench Moderation process focuses on node revisions instead of the node itself. This allows a node to remain published while updates are being made and pushed through the review process.

Configuring Workbench Moderation

After downloading and enabling the Workbench Moderation module (drupal.org/project/workbench_moderation), the next step is to define the moderation states that a node can travel through. Navigate to Configuration ➤ Workflow ➤ Workbench Moderation ➤ Moderation States to view the list of enabled states (see Figure 9-32).

Moderation states ☆

Home » Administration » Structure » Workbench moderation

+ Add Moderation state

MODERATION STATE	MACHINE NAME	OPERATIONS
Archived	archived	Edit ▼
Draft	draft	Edit ▼
Needs Review	needs_review	Edit ▼
Published	published	Edit ▼

Figure 9-32. *The off-the-shelf Workbench moderation states*

For demonstration purposes, we add a new state of Rejected, which the site editor can use to send a content item back to the content creator for updates. To add a state, you click on the Add Moderation state button (see Figure 9-33).

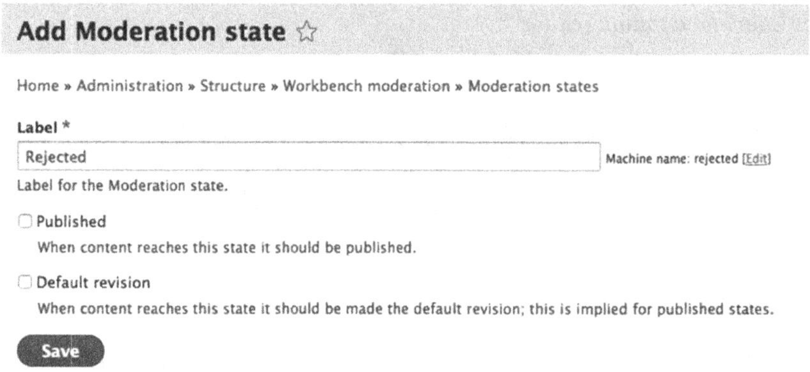

Add Moderation state ☆

Home » Administration » Structure » Workbench moderation » Moderation states

Label *

Rejected   Machine name: rejected [Edit]

Label for the Moderation state.

☐ Published
   When content reaches this state it should be published.

☐ Default revision
   When content reaches this state it should be made the default revision; this is implied for published states.

Save

Figure 9-33. *Adding a new workflow state*

After clicking save, you can now see the new Rejected state in the list of Moderation states.

The next step is to review and revise the moderation state transitions, meaning the flow of steps that a content item can transition through on its way to being published. The default off-the-shelf states are fine for my example site, with the one exception of needing to inject the Rejected state into the flow (see Figure 9-34).

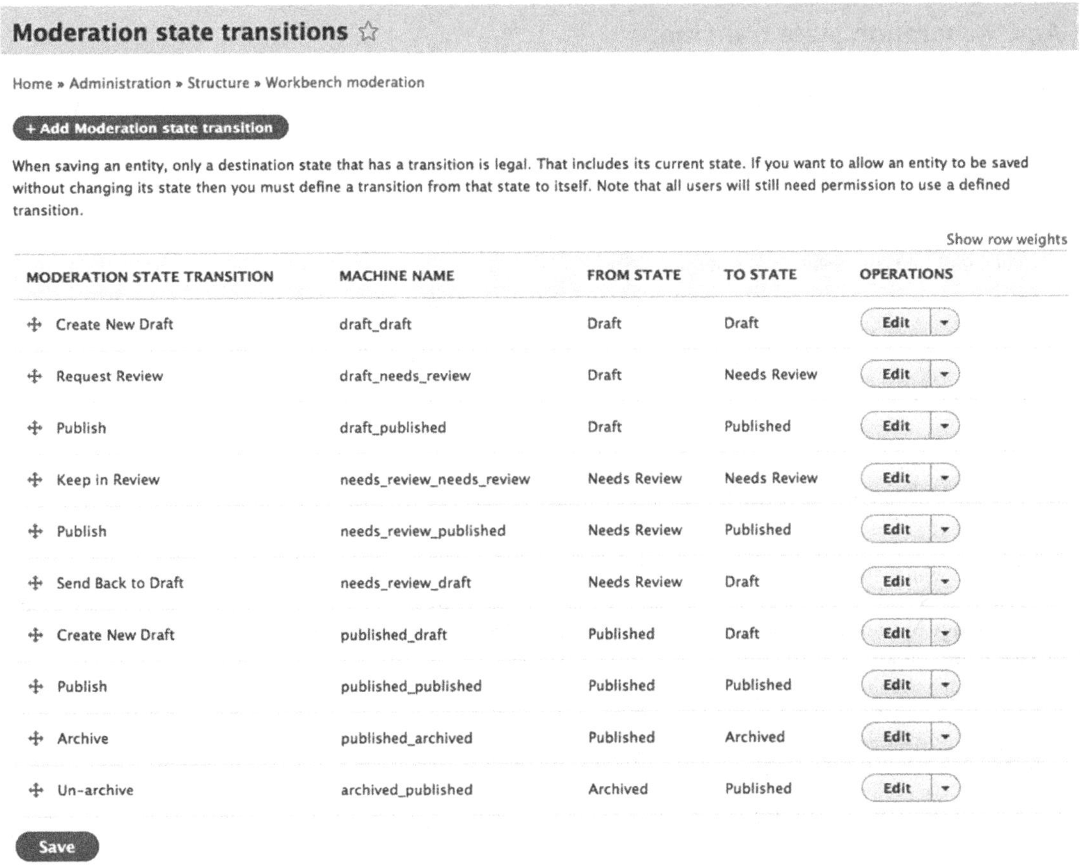

Moderation state transitions ☆

Home » Administration » Structure » Workbench moderation

+ Add Moderation state transition

When saving an entity, only a destination state that has a transition is legal. That includes its current state. If you want to allow an entity to be saved without changing its state then you must define a transition from that state to itself. Note that all users will still need permission to use a defined transition.

Show row weights

MODERATION STATE TRANSITION	MACHINE NAME	FROM STATE	TO STATE	OPERATIONS
✥ Create New Draft	draft_draft	Draft	Draft	Edit ▾
✥ Request Review	draft_needs_review	Draft	Needs Review	Edit ▾
✥ Publish	draft_published	Draft	Published	Edit ▾
✥ Keep in Review	needs_review_needs_review	Needs Review	Needs Review	Edit ▾
✥ Publish	needs_review_published	Needs Review	Published	Edit ▾
✥ Send Back to Draft	needs_review_draft	Needs Review	Draft	Edit ▾
✥ Create New Draft	published_draft	Published	Draft	Edit ▾
✥ Publish	published_published	Published	Published	Edit ▾
✥ Archive	published_archived	Published	Archived	Edit ▾
✥ Un-archive	archived_published	Archived	Published	Edit ▾

Save

Figure 9-34. The off-the-shelf moderation state transitions

To create the new transition, we click the Add Moderation State Transition button and enter Rejected in the Label field. We set the Transition from State to Needs Review, as that will be the current state when the site editor reviews the content, and the Transition To value will be set to Draft, as that will indicate to the content creator that there is work to do on the content item (see Figure 9-35).

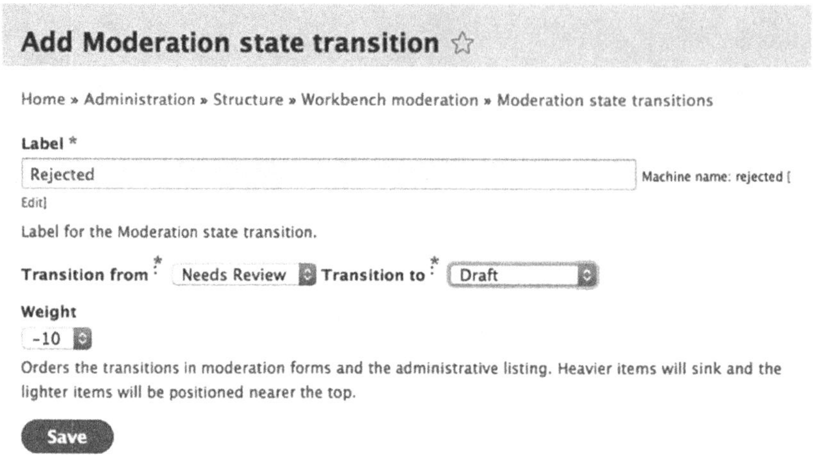

Add Moderation state transition ☆

Home » Administration » Structure » Workbench moderation » Moderation state transitions

Label *

Rejected   Machine name: rejected [
Edit]

Label for the Moderation state transition.

Transition from * Needs Review ◆ **Transition to** * Draft ◆

Weight

-10 ◆

Orders the transitions in moderation forms and the administrative listing. Heavier items will sink and the lighter items will be positioned nearer the top.

Save

Figure 9-35. *Defining the moderation state transitions.*

The next step is to enable moderation on each of the content types on your site. Navigate to Structure ➤ Content types and edit the Article Content type. A new tab appears on the Edit Article Content Type page named Manage Moderation. Click on that tab to see an option to enable moderation states for this content type (see Figure 9-36).

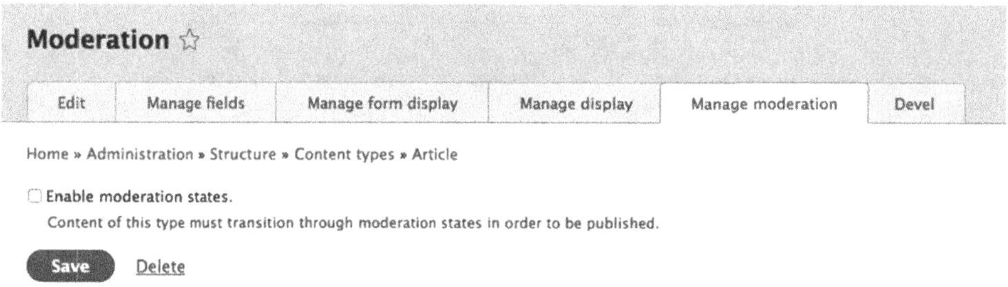

Moderation ☆

| Edit | Manage fields | Manage form display | Manage display | Manage moderation | Devel |

Home » Administration » Structure » Content types » Article

☐ Enable moderation states.

Content of this type must transition through moderation states in order to be published.

Save Delete

Figure 9-36. *Enabling moderation states on the Article Content type*

After checking the box, you'll be presented with the list of available moderation states, the state that is associated with the content being published, and the default state that is set when the node is initially created (see Figure 9-37). We'll leave all the values checked and the default state set to Draft. Click the Save button to enable moderation on the Article Content type.

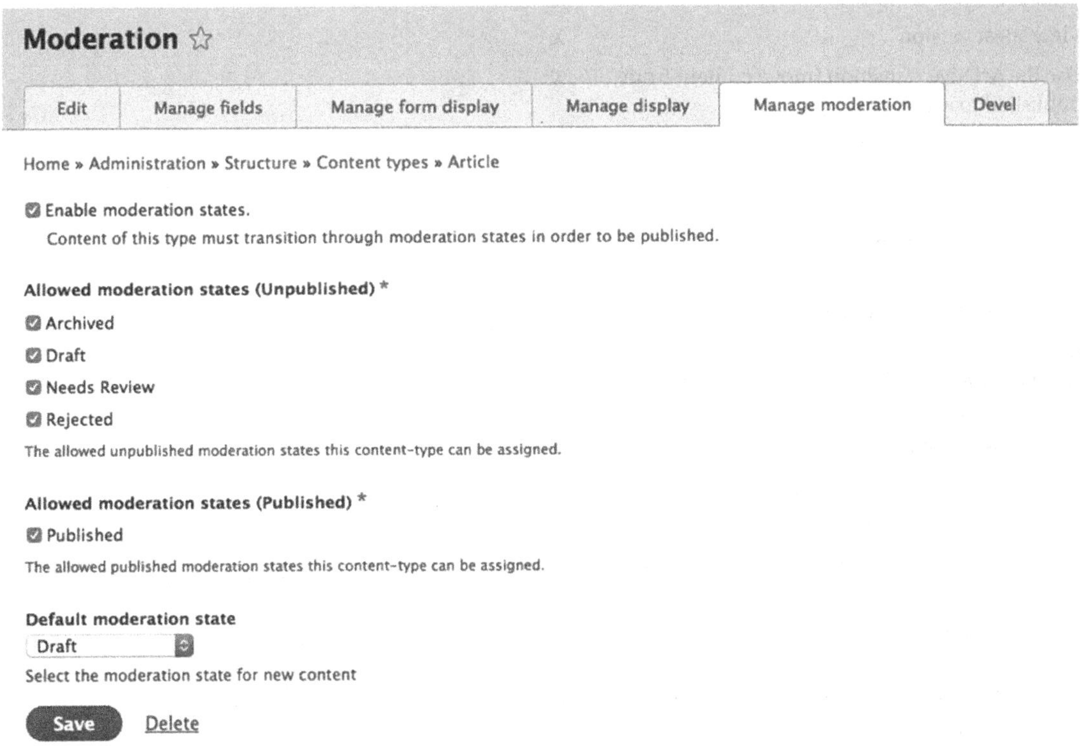

Moderation ☆

| Edit | Manage fields | Manage form display | Manage display | Manage moderation | Devel |

Home » Administration » Structure » Content types » Article

☑ Enable moderation states.
   Content of this type must transition through moderation states in order to be published.

Allowed moderation states (Unpublished) *

☑ Archived

☑ Draft

☑ Needs Review

☑ Rejected

The allowed unpublished moderation states this content-type can be assigned.

Allowed moderation states (Published) *

☑ Published

The allowed published moderation states this content-type can be assigned.

Default moderation state

| Draft ⬍ |

Select the moderation state for new content

Save   Delete

Figure 9-37. *Specifying the allowed moderation states*

Next we'll enable moderation on the other content types on the site before defining which user role has the ability to move content from one state to another.

Defining Workbench Moderation User Roles and Permissions

The final step in setting up workbench moderation is to define which user roles have the ability to move content through the various states. Navigate to People ➤ Permissions and, on the Permissions page, scroll to the Workbench moderation section. In that section, there are permissions for the following:

- Administering the configuration of the Workbench moderation module

- Viewing published and unpublished content

- Setting each moderation state that content can flow through

We'll use the existing user roles that we created earlier in this chapter, with the enterprise editor role being the only role that can reject and publish content. The details of the permissions and who can set them is listed in Table 9-2.

257

Table 9-2. *Setting the Workbench Moderation Permissions*

Permission	Enterprise Editor	All Other Editors
View any unpublished content	X	X
View moderation states	X	X
View latest version	X	X
Use the Archive transition (move content from published to archived)	X	
Use the Create New Draft transition (move content from Draft to Draft)	X	X
Use the Create New Draft transition (Move content from Draft to Published)	X	
Use the Keep in Review transition (Move content from Needs Review to Needs Review)	X	
Use the Publish transition (Move content from Needs Review to Published)	X	
Use the Publish transition (Move content from Published to Published)	X	
Use the Rejected transition (Move content from Needs review state to Draft)	X	
Use the Request Review transition (Move content from Draft to Needs review)	X	X
Use the Send Back to Draft transition (move content from Needs Review to Draft state)	X	X
Use the Send Back to Draft transition (Move content from Needs Review state to Draft state)	X	
Use the Un-archive transition (Move content from Archived state to Published state)	X	

To test the workflow, log out as the site administrator. Then log in as the marketing editor, who only has limited workflow permissions, specifically the ability to create a new draft of a content item and request review of that item once finished creating the content. We'll create a new article from the My Workbench page.

After entering the content, we're ready to save the article that we created and now only see two options available—we can save the article as a new draft or can save the article and request a review (see Figure 9-38). Let's save and request a review.

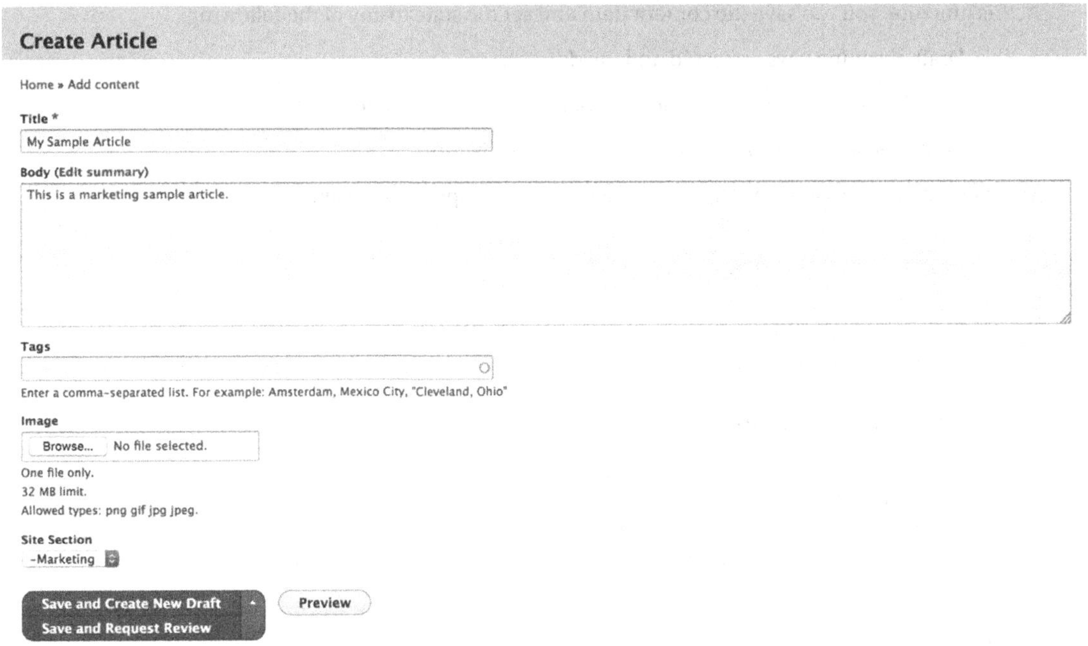

Figure 9-38. *Creating a new article with restricted publishing options*

After saving the article, the first thing that you'll notice is that the article has a pink background, which specifies that the article has not yet been published. (Note that the example is using the Bartik theme and other themes may use other colors or no color at all.)

Before reviewing the list of unpublished content that may need review, update the default workbench content view to include the moderation state field so that we can quickly see whether a node is in a state that needs editorial review. The view is Workbench: Recent Content and the field that we'll add is Content Revision: Moderation State, since it is revisions that are moderated and not the node itself.

Log out as the content editor and back into the site as a site administrator so you can update the view. After updating the view, navigate to the My Workbench page and click on the All Recent Content tab. Update the Published filter to "no" and click the Apply button, where you'll see the article that the marketing user created is in the Needs Review state (see Figure 9-39).

Figure 9-39. *The article that needs review is listed on the Recent Content page*

At this juncture, you can save the content item and set the state to any of the following:

- Draft, meaning it was rejected and needs work

- Keep in review so we can do more work on the article at a later time

- Published and viewable on the web site by site visitors

The content looks great, so we click the Save and Publish option (see Figure 9-40).

Figure 9-40. *Publishing the article after reviewing it*

While this example demonstrated the end-to-end use of the Workbench module and its various supporting modules, there is more that you can do with the capabilities presented by this suite of tools. Visit drupal.org and the various module homepages for details on other features and capabilities.

Summary

While the off-the-shelf Drupal administrative interface works well, there are opportunities for improving the experience for those who are responsible for the content that appears on your web site. Treat content editors well and enable them to do their jobs more effectively and your site will be better off in the end. As Drupal 8 matures there will likely be other modules that emerge to further improve the editorial and administrative backend of the CMS. Check drupal.org frequently for updates and new modules.

Providing a friendly user experience on the backend is great, but if your site doesn't perform well, nobody will be happy. The next chapter discusses the various areas to focus on when it comes to performance and scalability of your Drupal 8 web site.

CHAPTER 10

■ ■ ■

Scaling Drupal

You spend weeks and maybe months building a beautiful Drupal 8 web site and the day comes when you anxiously push the button to take your site live. You've done everything you can think of, including:

- Polishing the theme so that it is pixel-perfect across all devices

- Reviewing every piece of content on the site

- Setting user roles and permissions

- Running every piece of custom code through the coder module looking for issues

- Testing every page, every block, and every view

- Testing that the backups are running

You got kudos from the executive suite and your team is exhausted from the long days leading up to launch. You push code to the production server, point the DNS servers to your Drupal site, and launch. Thanks to the marketing department, there's an immediate groundswell of site traffic and you head home to finally get some sleep. By the time you pull in to your driveway, your phone begins to ring off the hook. Users are seeing blank pages and the site is unresponsive. The CEO calls you to remind you that every hour the site is down, the company loses tens of thousands of dollars. You go from being the organization's hero to being the one who everyone is blaming for the failed launch. You hate your job and wonder why you didn't go into construction instead of being the manager of the organization's web team. Suddenly your alarm clock goes off and you jump three feet off the bed as you realize that you were having the worst nightmare of your life. Fortunately it was a literal wake-up call. It's time to ensure that your site is set up to handle the anticipated traffic loads before the launch date. This true-to-life story is my own and fortunately I had the time to remedy the potential performance bottlenecks before the site launched. The goal of this chapter is to ensure that you don't experience the reality of my nightmare.

Understanding Potential Performance Bottlenecks

Before venturing out and implementing performance enhancements, let's go you through a typical scenario of an anonymous site visitor visiting your site's homepage. This section highlights the areas where you may want to apply resources to resolve potential performance issues.

For an off-the-shelf Drupal site that does not employ performance enhancement techniques, a site visitor navigating to your site's homepage travels through the following steps:

1. DNS servers route the visitor's request across the network to your hosting provider.

2. Drupal receives the request for your homepage and boots up.

3. Drupal connects to its database to pull together all of the elements on that page, including the blocks and content that is assembled via views.

© Todd Tomlinson 2017
T. Tomlinson, *Enterprise Drupal 8 Development*, DOI 10.1007/978-1-4842-0253-1_10

4. Drupal checks to ensure that all of the elements on the page can be viewed by an anonymous user (permissions).

5. PHP code turns the query results for all of the elements into an object, which is then passed to the theme engine.

6. The theme engine applies CSS and forms the HTML page.

7. The HTML page is returned to the user's browser.

While these steps represent a highly simplified version of what actually happens, they demonstrate that rendering a simple page actually takes several steps. If every step takes a few seconds, the overall time to deliver a page to a site visitor could add up to an unacceptably slow page load time.

If you look beyond the high-level steps, each user interaction with Drupal consumes PHP processes to execute the requests, such as making calls to the database to extract content. A PHP process may have to wait for milliseconds to seconds for a database query to complete, which ties up precious resources. There is a limit to the number of concurrent PHP processes that a server can run at any given point in time. When PHP processes are tied up, it means that Apache or Nginx must hold a request and wait for a process to become free. Eventually, when the queues for all of these services are too busy, requests will time out, resulting in blank pages being returned to users, as the requests are not fulfilled.

While you may be able to solve some of the performance bottlenecks by running your site on larger and larger servers, which results in rising costs, there is a better way. That is to employ performance optimization techniques that range from simple to complex. I start with the simplest solutions first, in hopes that you can solve your potential problem before you have to take more drastic measures.

Drupal Cache

One of the simplest approaches for significantly improving your site's performance is to utilize Drupal core's caching mechanisms. Caching is a means for storing the rendered version of a page, block, or view so that Drupal does not have to assemble those components every time a visitor requests a page. Take for example your homepage. Once the fully rendered page (HTML markup) has been stored in Drupal's cache tables, any subsequent visit to that page is served up from the cached version of that page instead of having to reassemble all of the content and apply the theme. This is a significantly faster process than going through the steps to recreate that page from scratch. A page that may take two or three seconds to fully assemble, theme, and return to the user may be rendered in milliseconds from the Drupal cache.

Enabling Drupal Cache

Drupal 8 core comes with two modules that empower caching on your site:

- *Internal Dynamic Page Cache*: This module caches pages for any user, anonymous or authenticated, handling dynamically generated pages correctly.

- *Internal Page Cache*: This module caches pages for anonymous users.

You will find both of these modules on the Extend page; both modules are enabled by default when installing Drupal 8. To utilize the power of these modules, you must set the page cache maximum age, which can be found by navigating to Configuration ➤ Performance and selecting a value from the drop-down. Select the value based on the volatility of your content. If the content on your site is constantly changing throughout the day then set the number low—for example, 15 minutes. A setting of 15 minutes instructs Drupal to set the cached version of a given page to expire in 15 minutes, after which it will be rebuilt the next time a visitor accesses that page. For sites that are relatively static, a value of 6 hours, 9 hours, 12 hours, or even 1 day may be more appropriate. For demonstration purposes, I select 6 hours and save the value by clicking the Save Configuration button.

A quick test of my very simple development site on my Mac Book Pro running MAMP shows that the homepage load time without caching is 88ms. With caching, the load time is 71ms (see Figure 10-1). Some of the time needed to load is based on the network itself and not on Drupal. When you look at the slice of time to load that is Drupal-specific (processing), the load time is actually 25% less than without caching. This site is so simple that it really doesn't represent the potential that may be achieved with simple caching for sites that have large pages and a significant amount of content is assembled before loading the page.

Page fully loaded after 88 ms. | **Page fully loaded after 71 ms.**

ⓘ	Offset	Duration	ⓘ	Offset	Duration
Redirect	0 ms	0 ms	Redirect	0 ms	0 ms
App cache	2 ms	0 ms	App cache	1 ms	0 ms
DNS lookup	2 ms	0 ms	DNS lookup	1 ms	0 ms
TCP connection	2 ms	0 ms	TCP connection	1 ms	0 ms
TCP request	3 ms	15 ms	TCP request	1 ms	17 ms
TCP response	18 ms	2 ms	TCP response	18 ms	0 ms
Processing	19 ms	69 ms	Processing	19 ms	52 ms
onload event	88 ms	2 ms	onload event	71 ms	1 ms

Figure 10-1. Page load times before (left) and after (right) caching

Caching Views

Another performance boost is to cache the output of views. This additional layer of caching speeds up rendering the output of views by caching the output and rendering the cached version of the output on subsequent page views where that view is displayed. For example, the Content page is built using views and is often a slow-loading page for sites that have a significant number of content items. On my demo Drupal 8 site with 1508 content items and without views caching, the page load time averaged 1947ms. After enabling caching on the Content view, the page load time decreased to 1035ms. Removing the network component of the page load time, the decrease in load time was nearly 53% (see Figure 10-2), a significant improvement over the non-cached version of the view. The cost of that boost in speed was a few moments to enable caching on the view.

Page fully loaded after 1947 ms. | **Page fully loaded after 1035 ms.**

ⓘ	Offset	Duration	ⓘ	Offset	Duration
Redirect	0 ms	0 ms	Redirect	0 ms	0 ms
App cache	2 ms	0 ms	App cache	1 ms	0 ms
DNS lookup	2 ms	0 ms	DNS lookup	1 ms	0 ms
TCP connection	2 ms	0 ms	TCP connection	1 ms	0 ms
TCP request	4 ms	1566 ms	TCP request	1 ms	706 ms
TCP response	1570 ms	23 ms	TCP response	707 ms	21 ms
Processing	1571 ms	376 ms	Processing	707 ms	328 ms
onload event	1947 ms	1 ms	onload event	1035 ms	2 ms

Figure 10-2. View load times before (left) and after (right) views caching

To enable views caching, navigate to Structure ➤ Views and edit the view that you would like to cache. In the Advanced column, look for Caching in the Other section. There are two options for setting the period in which a view is cached:

- *Tag based*: Tag-based has a significant benefit over time-based. Consider if you had a view that listed 10 items per page and was sorted descending by last update date and time. The view was cached and someone edits the eleventh item. In time-based cached views, the view will not be invalidated until the time period expires and that eleventh item will appear on the second page of the cached view until the time period expires. In a tag-based cache, editing and saving the eleventh item invalidates the cache and the view is rebuilt, with the eleventh item now listed as the first item.

- *Time based*: Selecting time-based works well for views of content that are relatively static, because updates to content will not invalidate the view until the time period has expired.

Select the solution that works best for your view. I suggest caching all views to take advantage of the boost in performance.

Caching Blocks

For those who are familiar with previous versions of Drupal, caching blocks was dependent on setting a configuration value that specified whether a block is cached or not. In Drupal 8 the approach changed. Blocks are automatically cached through the render_array() process.

If you are building custom blocks through code in Drupal 8, you can enable caching when building the renderable array for the block, as shown in the following code:

```
class MyCustomBlock extends BlockBase {
  public function build() {
    return array(
      '#markup' => $markup,
      '#cache' => array(
          'contexts' => array(
            'url.path',
          ),
      ),
    );
  }
}
```

In this case, caching is based on the URL in which the block is being rendered. For detailed information about caching and the Drupal 8 cache API, visit http://drupal.org/docs/8/api/cache-api/cache-api.

External Caching Mechanisms: Varnish Cache

Drupal 8's internal caching mechanisms, as demonstrated in the previous sections, provide a significant boost to the performance of your Drupal 8 site, but often Drupal 8's internal caching isn't enough to support the anticipated traffic to your site and you need to look for other alternatives, such as Varnish Cache.

Varnish Cache is a web application accelerator, which is also known as a caching HTTP reverse proxy server. It is installed on any server that supports HTTP and is configured to cache the content that passes through it. It is often installed on a server other than the application server where your Drupal site resides, and by its very nature, it sits between the Internet and your Drupal 8 application server (see Figure 10-3).

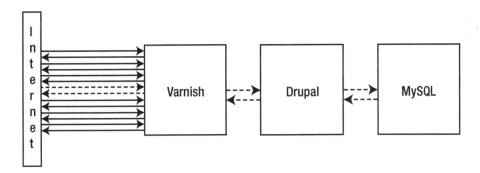

Figure 10-3. *Using Varnish Cache*

Varnish works by caching in memory the results of every request sent to Drupal. For example, suppose an anonymous site visitor wants to see your site's homepage and visits the URL of your site's homepage. When the homepage is sent back to the requesting site visitor, it is cached in Varnish's in-memory cache tables. When a subsequent request for the homepage is made by that visitor or another visitor, Varnish recognizes that the page exists in its cache table and that version of the homepage is returned to the site visitor. In that scenario, Drupal never sees the request, as shown in Figure 10-3 by the solid lines between the Internet and Varnish. The solid lines represent inbound requests for Drupal pages that are immediately served out of Varnish's cache table.

The dotted line in Figure 10-3 represents one of two scenarios, either the visitor has requested a page that does not exist in the Varnish cache table and must be generated by Drupal, or the visitor is an authenticated user. Varnish by default sends all authenticated traffic on to Drupal. How does Varnish know it's an authenticated user? There is information in the HTTP header that specifies that the user is authenticated.

Performance improvements by using a Varnish Cache server in front of your Drupal server are on the order of 300 to 1000 times faster than serving up that same page from Drupal, even with Drupal cache enabled. For more information about Varnish, visit `varnish-cache.org`.

Using a Content Delivery Network (CDN)

While Drupal's internal caching mechanisms and Varnish will significantly improve page load times, there's yet another tool for further boosting page load times, using a CDN.

A CDN is a globally distributed network of proxy servers that are deployed in multiple data centers. The goal of the CDN is to serve content to end users with high availability and high performance from servers that are closest to a user. Without a CDN in place, site visitors from around the world must wait for pages and assets (e.g., images, JavaScript, CSS, and files) to be transported from the server where your web site resides to their browser. With a CDN in place, the content and assets are delivered from a proxy server that is geographically nearest to them.

Take for example a web site that is hosted in Dallas Texas. A site visitor from Amsterdam must wait for the content and assets to be delivered from Texas because the site doesn't employ a CDN. In the case of that same site using a CDN, the content and assets will be delivered from a proxy server that likely resides in Amsterdam, thereby significantly decreasing network latency (see Figure 10-4).

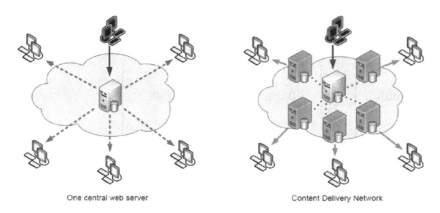

One central web server   Content Delivery Network

Figure 10-4. *With and without a CDN*

How CDNs Work

A content delivery network is a third-party provider service that enables your site to leverage the distribution of content and assets around the world. CDNs services are provided by a number of organizations, including:

- Cloudflare (`cloudflare.com`)

- Fastly (`fastly.com`)

- Amazon's CloudFront (`aws.amazon.com/cloudfront`)

- Akamai Edge (`akamai.com`)

- MaxCDN (`maxcdn.com`)

Each company provides similar services—the ability to serve your content and assets from their distributed network of proxy servers. A CDN's proxy servers route requests from site visitors through their network, caching pages and assets as site visitors browse your web site. If a page is cached in their network, the content and assets will be served up to that site visitor from the closest proxy server, which is likely located significantly closer to their physical location than where your web site is hosted.

Although there is a cost for using a CDN, the ability to off-load traffic from your server to the CDN providers network of proxy servers often means lower hosting costs. That's because the demands on your local server are lower.

Integrating a CDN into your Drupal 8 site differs by provider. Visit the provider's web sites for details about how to integrate their services into your site.

Considering Nginx Over Apache

For decades Apache has been the standard web server used by organizations around the world to serve up content to the web. While Apache is still the top web server for Drupal, many organizations are employing Nginx as an alternative to Apache, or in conjunction with Apache, to address the shortcomings of Apache when it comes to effectively serving thousands of concurrent requests.

The issue that many have with Apache is that it often reaches a limit as to the number of concurrent connections it can effectively manage due to process startup, memory consumption, and CPU constraints. As requests come into Apache, it must start up a new process, allocate memory, and access the CPU to address each request. As more requests come in, more processes are created, and each process is allocated memory. Processes are kept alive to minimize the startup and shutdown costs, assuming that subsequent requests may come in from that same browser. As the number of requests grow, processes and memory usage grow.

When you consider that each browser typically creates six or more TCP connections to a web server, 1,000 concurrent visitors equates to 6,000 active connections and each of those connections results in a new process and memory consumption. As traffic increases, Apache begins to thrash as memory is swapped to and from disk to handle the volume of connections. This issue is well documented and is often called the *C10K problem* (en.wikipedia.org/wiki/C10k_problem). Nginx, on the other hand, was architected more recently and under the assumption that it must effectively handle large numbers of connections without being affected by the C10K problem. Nginx, unlike Apache, does not create new processes to handle incoming requests. It runs with a set number of processes, typically one per CPU core, and each of its few processes uses a single thread to handle thousands of requests at a time.

Although you could replace Apache with Nginx, there are benefits to having Apache in the architecture, specifically serving up dynamic content. Nginx, on the other hand, does an excellent job of serving up static content, delivering pages at lightning speed. When you combine the two—using Nginx as the proxy server that delivers cached content and Apache as the delivery mechanism for dynamic content, the end result is faster all around page load speeds.

For more information about Nginx, visit nginx.com. For more information about Apache, visit httpd.apache.org.

Using Memcache or Redis

All of Drupal's internal caching mechanisms rely on database tables as the storage mechanism for cached elements. A relatively simple way of significantly speeding up the loading of cached elements is to employ a memory-based caching mechanism such as Memcache or Redis. Instead of having to retrieve cached elements from the database, Memcache and Redis serve up those elements from memory, significantly faster than loading them from the database. Due to the wide range of operating systems and hosted environments, visit memcached.org or redis.io for details on how to download and install Memcache or Redis on your server. If you are running on a hosted platform such as Pantheon, Redis is already installed and available for you to use. If you are running your site on Acquia, Memcache is available to all paid subscriptions.

Optimizing MySQL

The last area that I address in this chapter is optimizing MySQL. As a consultant one of the most frequent requests that I receive is helping an organization resolve their slow page loads. The first thing I look at is whether they have correctly enabled caching. Often just fixing a caching problem solves the page load time issue, but when it doesn't, the next step I take is to look at page complexity. If a page is overly complex with dozens of database queries, there is little you can do to radically improve page load times, short of simplifying the page and reducing the number of queries. When I run across situations where complex pages are loading slowly and the organization says that they need that level of complexity, my next question is whether they are willing to sacrifice site visitors for page complexity, as slow load times often equate to visitors leaving and never coming back.

If pages are not complex, have few assets such as images, and CSS and JavaScript are compressed, yet still load slowly, I often then turn to tools such as New Relic to further narrow down the source of slow load times. If I find that the majority of the page load time is MySQL related, the next activity is to look at how much data is being loaded on the page. For example, if a view is unrestricted in the number of records that it will return and often returns hundreds of rows, my first focus is to look for ways to limit the number of records returned. I do this by providing some form of exposed filtering on the view and limiting the number of records returned. If I'm still faced with slow page load times, I'll then look at tools such the slow query log to see which database queries are taking excessive time to complete. If I find queries in the log I'll then use the MySQL EXPLAIN statement to identify opportunities for adding indexes to speed the performance of those queries. On a recent project where queries were running extremely slow, using the information from the slow query log and running EXPLAIN on those queries identified potential additional indexes that, when added, completely eliminated the performance problems. An hour examining the log, running EXPLAIN, and adding indexes reduced page load times by over 80%—time well spent.

If caching, simplification, and adding indexes fail to address your performance issues, the next step is to examine the MySQL configuration files to check for a misconfigured value. The following are common settings that will significantly impact MySQL performance:

- innodb_buffer_pool_size: This is the first setting to check. This is the buffer pool where data and indexes are cached. Having it as large as possible will ensure that memory is used for queries instead of disk. Typical values are 5-6GB (8GB of RAM), 20-25GB (32GB of RAM), and 100-120GB (128GB of RAM).

- inndb_log_file_size: This is the size of the redo logs. The redo logs are used to ensure that writes are fast and durable and also support crash recovery. Start with innodb_log_file_size set to 4G for MySQL 5.6 and above. For older versions, use 512M.

- max_connections: If you see the "too many connections" error in your log, max_connections is typically set too low. The default value is 151 connections, but use caution when increasing this number as values above 1000 will typically cause your server to become unresponsive. Start with small incremental changes and test.

- innodb_flush_log_at_trx_commit: This is one setting that you may want to consider changing only as a last result. By default, the value is set to 1, meaning that InnoDB is fully ACID compliant. It's the best value when you are concerned with data safety; however, it can have a significant overhead on systems with slow disks due to the additional actions required to flush each change to the redo logs. Setting it to 2 is less reliable because committed transactions will be flushed to the redo logs only once per second, which means that in the case of a crash, you may lose a transaction that was committed to the redo log in the last second.

- innodb_log_buffer_size: This setting controls the size of the buffer for transactions that have not yet been committed. The default value is 1MB, which is typically sufficient for transactions without large blob/text fields. Larger fields will fill the buffer quickly and trigger extra I/O. Examine the innodb_log_waits status and, if it's not zero, then increase innodb_log_buffer_size.

- query_cache_size: This setting is a well-known bottleneck. The best solution is to disable it by setting the value to 0.

A great free tool that will help you identify the best configuration options for your MySQL database can be found at tools.percona.com.

If, after trying all these fixes, you are still running into performance problems with MySQL, it may warrant the creation of a MySQL cluster. This is where a master MySQL server replicates your Drupal database to multiple slave servers, thereby distributing the workload.

Scaling Hardware

When you have exhausted all of the methods described previously, it is likely that you'll need to replace or replicate your hardware. Attempting to run a large Drupal 8 web site on antiquated hardware or servers that lack adequate resources is likely to result in a poorly performing Drupal 8 web site. When replacing hardware, look for details on current specifications on drupal.org. When scaling Drupal 8, there are multiple options that vary based on the types of performance bottlenecks you are experiencing. Figure 10-5 depicts the various layers in the hardware architecture and the options for scaling servers.

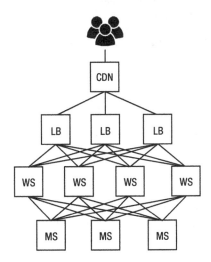

Figure 10-5. *Scaling hardware*

The first layer between the end user and your Drupal site is the CDN. As described earlier in this chapter, a CDN may give your site an immediate boost without having to add or upgrade hardware. While there is a cost associated with most CDNs, it's usually significantly less than adding hardware to your infrastructure.

The next layer in the hardware architecture to consider scaling is the load balancers (LB). Using Nginx as the reverse proxy and Varnish as the caching mechanism on your load balancer often minimizes the traffic that has to flow deeper into your architecture. This is because the load balancers are serving up cached versions of pages and the CDN is serving up cached versions of assets such as images, CSS, and JavaScript.

The workhorse layer of the architecture is the web server, which is typically Apache in the case of Drupal 8. You may spread the load across multiple web servers when you find that the CDN and load balancers aren't shielding the web server. This is typically a case when your site visitors are authenticated (versus anonymous) or the page content is highly dynamic, as opposed to static content that can be cached.

The final layer in the architecture is MySQL and the servers that support your Drupal 8 MySQL database. If you are running MySQL you may consider running one of the higher performance MySQL options, such as Percona or MariaDB, before taking the step of clustering your MySQL databases. If you have exhausted your options and the database is a bottleneck then consider implementing a MySQL cluster with a master/slave architecture that provides the ability to distribute the query loads across multiple servers.

The options are nearly limitless as to how to arrange and scale hardware. Carefully examine and evaluate the bottlenecks before applying additional hardware. Often a CDN and an effective caching strategy can mitigate the need for additional hardware.

Hosting Your Drupal 8 Site

Historically, many enterprise class web sites were hosted internally on corporate hardware in corporate data centers. While that still exists, the trend is to leverage the capabilities and expertise of organizations such as Pantheon or Acquia to host large enterprise sites. The capabilities of providers such as Pantheon and Acquia remove the costs associated with acquiring, installing, configuring, and maintaining a complex server environment to support a large-scale Drupal 8 implementation. Their cost is often less than owning your own hardware, paying the licensing and maintenance costs on that hardware and software, and the salaries associated with maintaining an in-house staff that handles all of the tasks associated with effectively managing a large infrastructure. Hosting in the cloud also makes sense for sites that experience periodic spikes in traffic. Instead of having to buy hardware to support your peak traffic volumes, you can lean on the services of Pantheon or Acquia to provide on-demand capacity when those peaks occur without paying for it 24 hours a day, 365 days a year.

Summary

Performance and scalability should be at the forefront of your Drupal team's every thought and action. Teams often miss simple configuration changes that would significantly boost the performance of their Drupal 8 sites or severely impact the speed of their sites. Statistics show that 40% of site visitors fail to return to sites with page load times of greater than three seconds, so performance should be at the center of all that your Drupal team does. Fortunately, following the few relatively simple actions outlined in this chapter, you can mitigate the risk of a slow site.

The next chapter dives into the world of DevOps, focusing on the tools and processes that will make it simpler and quicker to manage and maintain your Drupal 8 web site.

■ ■ ■

## CHAPTER 11

Drupal 8 DevOps

DevOps is a term for common practices that have catalyzed into a movement that is rapidly spreading throughout the development community, and it not relegated just to Drupal development. DevOps represents the marriage of development and operations into a set of cultural philosophies, common practices, and tools that enable an organization to deliver applications and services at a velocity that most organizations have traditionally failed to achieve. Historically the time from concept to it being realized in software that is running in production was weeks, months, and sometimes years. While it may have been suitable in the past to deliver new solutions on a quarterly basis, in today's world, you must deliver new capabilities in near real time or sit by and watch your competitors race by you. Today you may receive a new requirement on Monday morning with the expectation that the functionality will be deployed by end-of-day on Tuesday, and yes, Tuesday of that same week. The old culture, processes, tools, and siloed organizations will surely fail to deliver the solutions in timeframes that were unheard of in the past, but that are commonplace in today's market.

Traditional Versus DevOps

In a traditional development and operations approach, the development team is responsible for building and testing the solutions that the organization then hands to the operations team to deploy to the production environment. In most organizations the development team "washes their hands" of the solution at the handoff between the development and operations teams. Operations is then responsible for deploying the code to the production environment and monitoring that solution for performance and reliability. The handoff of the "golden" ZIP file is the only semi-automated piece of the process, as it's copied into a directory where operations can then pick it up and copy and extract the archive on the production system. In Figure 11-1, the development team handles the build and test processes, and the operations team handles the deployment and monitoring processes, with very little if any collaboration happening during the planning process.

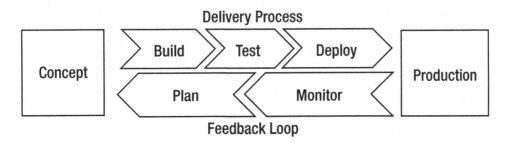

Figure 11-1. *The typical delivery and operations process flow*

In a DevOps model, development and operations are no longer siloed in their own organizations; they are often merged into a single team where engineers work across the entire process from concept to production, building skills across the various disciplines of development, testing, and operations. Often, quality assurance and security team members are rolled into the single organization and become an integral part of the team, applying their domain expertise to every step of the process, from concept to deployment.

In conjunction with the new organizational structure, DevOps brings with it a suite of tools that automates the processes that have traditionally required human intervention and were therefore slow, enabling the process to move from weekly, monthly, quarterly, or yearly to deployments that occur several times a day. This concept wasn't possible in the past, without this revised way of organizing development and operations teams and employing tools to automate the process.

The Benefits of Embracing DevOps

One of the most often quoted benefits of DevOps is speed. With the tools, processes, and team in place, organizations are now able to move from concept to production at a velocity that was unimaginable in the past. Organizations can now innovate on a daily basis, adapt to changing markets faster, and are far more effective and efficient at driving business results. The DevOps model enables your development and operations teams to achieve results that were impossible in the past.

With speed comes rapid delivery. Employing DevOps provides the ability to increase the frequency and pace of releases to production. The faster you can release new features and bug fixes, the faster you can respond to your customers' needs and competitive challenges. Continuous integration and continuous delivery, which I cover in detail later in this chapter, are DevOps practices that remove the human intervention in the software release process, automating every step from build to deploy.

DevOps also improves reliability. By employing rigorous automated testing, your organization can quickly deploy changes to your applications and infrastructure with a high degree of confidence that the changes will maintain a positive experience for your end users.

A cornerstone of DevOps is improved collaboration between the various roles that are responsible for the tasks associated with development through deployment and operations. The DevOps cultural model focuses on ownership and accountability throughout the process, requiring a higher level of collaboration and sharing of responsibility across the development and deployment workflow. This increased level of integration and collaboration saves time and reduces and often eliminates handoffs, speeding the delivery of new solutions to your production environments.

DevOps may improve security by automating the process and putting the checks and balances in the automated testing processes to ensure that the systems you deploy to your end users comply with your organization's compliance policies and controls.

Adopting DevOps

While the previous sections make DevOps sound like the best thing since sliced bread, there is work involved in implementing it into your organization.

The first step is changing the culture and mindset of those in the organization who are responsible for development and delivery. It typically requires merging what have been two separate teams that were effectively siloed into a single organization, requiring a higher level of collaboration between team members who traditionally may not have worked very well together. With the merging of the team comes a new set of roles and responsibilities. Developers who may not have had anything to do with quality assurance or deployments will find themselves required to build automated test scripts for their code and to ensure that their code successfully passes those tests and is deployed in production. Operations team members who have not been responsible for development or quality assurance may find themselves responsible for developing DevOps tools and scripts and testing and deploying those tools and capabilities using the same processes that the developers do for business applications. It may be an uncomfortable situation for many on the team, now having the accountability and responsibility for the end-to-end processes of building and deploying their solutions. Overcoming those challenges is by no means easy, nor is it impossible. There are excellent resources through organizations such as the Agile community who have focused on this aspect for years.

The next step is to reduce the scope and velocity of changes that are deployed into the production environment by deploying frequent, often daily or even hourly, small updates. Releasing small incremental changes lowers the risk of deployments by making it easier to identify and remediate bugs. Drupal's modular architectural makes it easy to deploy incremental changes by releasing changes to individual elements such as .yml configuration files and modules.

DevOps Best Practices

Reorganizing the team, adopting microservices architecture, and performing smaller more frequent incremental deployments are supported by well-known best practices. While the optimal approach is to adopt all of these in your organization, doing so all at once is often overwhelming. Beyond merging the development and operations groups into a single entity, you may consider implementing the following best practices in the order outlined here:

- *Continuous integration.* This best practice focuses on the tools that developers use to manage their code. A central repository, such as GitHub, becomes the single source of truth for all code in the organization. Developers regularly merge their code updates into this central repository where automated processes build and test the updates. The objectives of continuous integration are to find and address bugs quicker, improve software quality, and reduce the time it takes to validate and release new software updates.

- *Continuous delivery* is the next best practice to implement. This DevOps solution takes the output of continuous integration and prepares and deploys the fully tested updates to the production environment.

- *Microservices* is the best practice that focuses on dividing a larger application into smaller services that are focused on a small subset of the overall functionality of the solution being managed and deployed. Drupal 8 already falls into the microservices architecture model by its very nature of being built through modules, both core and contributed, as well as elements such as content types, themes, and configuration files.

- *Infrastructure as code* is a practice in which infrastructure is provisioned and managed using code and software development techniques such as version control and continuous integration. For organizations that host their Drupal 8 sites in the cloud on services provided by companies such as Pantheon and Acquia, this process is handled by the cloud services provider. For organizations that host Drupal 8 on their own infrastructure, this approach may be difficult to adopt broadly across all of the infrastructure in the organization.

Since most IT organizations support more than just Drupal, the footprint of Drupal in their portfolio is often too small to justify an overhaul of the entire IT organization's structure, processes, and tools. While organizations will gain significant benefits from adopting a DevOps culture and approach, it may be too big to bite off all at once.

While DevOps may be too big of an undertaking at the enterprise level, you may want to consider adopting a portion of it as a starting point by implementing continuous integration and continuous deployments for your Drupal 8 web sites.

Drupal 8 Continuous Integration and Deployment

The concept of continuous integration (CI) and continuous deployment (CD) is nothing new; it's been around since the 90's when Grady Booch, the father of object orientation, described the need for developers to integrate their code into a single repository on a frequent basis. This was to avoid the issues of integrating everyone's code, only to find out that two or three or more people worked on the same code. How do you effectively interweave the changes from each developer without destroying the code that was so diligently worked on? While Booch didn't envision nor advocate merging code several times a day, the extreme programming (XP) community came along and said that integrations need to happen frequently to avert the issues with several developers working together on a common solution.

Drupal is not unlike other software solutions; developers create custom modules and often on larger teams more than one person works on a common set of functionality. Add to that Drupal 8's configuration management in code and you can quickly run into scenarios where collisions happen when long periods of time between merges occur. While the advent of source code control systems such as Git resolve many of the issues, there are further steps that you can take as an organization that make the merging and testing of code more robust, including the ability to automate testing and immediately identify code issues.

More recently the concepts of CI and CD have evolved to include the creation of virtual environments that are spun up when a developer checks in code, where production quality content is sourced from the production server to enable realistic testing of software changes against production data. If the tests run successfully, the environments are "torn down" and the code is staged for pushing to production where the CD elements of the DevOps solution push the code and configuration changes to the live production environment. If there are errors, that environment may be configured to live beyond the execution of the test so that your developers and quality assurance team can dive into the root cause of the test failure.

The CI/CD Process Flow

The typical process flow for CI/CD is as follows:

- A developer commits code to a repository, typically using Git

- The developer pushes the committed code up to the central repository (e.g., GitHub)

- The update to the repository triggers a job on your CI server (e.g., Jenkins)

- The job kicks off code deployment automatically, copying the code from the repository to your server

- It runs Drush commands to update the database

- It runs some tests on the site build

- It reports the status to you, e.g., pass/fail

- If the tests pass, the code and configuration are pushed to the live production environment

While you may have variations (e.g., spinning up a new virtual environment and copying the production database to the new virtual environment), the basic flow is the same.

CI/CD Tools

The starting point for CI/CD is to have a centralized repository where your developers check in and check out their code. Without that central repository, it will be difficult to enable an effective CI process flow. GitHub and BitBucket are two popular services. If you host your site on Pantheon or Acquia, you may use their repositories as well.

The next component of CI/CD is to find and install a CI server. There are several open source and commercially available products in the market. Examples of commonly used CI servers in Drupal environments include the following:

- Jenkins (`jenkins.com`)

- CircleCI (`circleci.com`)

- TravisCI (`travisci.org` for the community version or `travisci.com` for the commercial version)

While there are other solutions in the market, these are the ones that are most frequently referenced. Each of these solutions provides similar functionality and relatively simple setup and configuration processes. For example, the process for setting up CircleCI consists of logging in to CircleCI with your GitHub or BitBucket credentials, posting your SSH keys that are known to your code repository, and filling out a few configuration values.

Once you have your CI/CD server set up, the next step is to configure the workflow. Each tool differs in their approach for configuring the workflow. I suggest visiting the site for each of these CI/CD vendors and reading through the installation and configuration documentation.

Automated Testing

Continuous integration and deployment really doesn't work well without automated testing. While you could automatically merge and deploy your untested code to production, it's surely not a best practice and will likely result in the destruction of any confidence in your team's ability to manage and maintain a production Drupal 8 site. Fortunately there are tools that make testing, and specifically automated testing, relatively straightforward and easy.

The Drupal community has adopted automated testing as a means to verify and validate all of the elements of Drupal core. The approach consists of both unit tests, which test and validate the functionality of classes at the lowest level of code, and functional tests that validate that Drupal core does what it's supposed to do from a functional perspective. Every time new code is committed to the code repository, it is automatically tested to ensure that it doesn't break any existing functionality.

As developers we need to adopt the same approach as we build Drupal sites using Drupal core and extend the functionality of our sites through the addition of contributed and custom modules. As new code is added, the code should be tested through unit tests, and before merging that new code into the master branch of the code repository, a complete regression test of the functionality should be performed. Every build should be thoroughly tested before deploying that code to the production environment. In a Drupal 8 environment, there are tools and techniques for writing unit and functional tests, such as PHPUnit and Simpletest.

Writing PHPUnit Tests for Classes

The fundamental building block of Drupal 8 modules are PHP classes. The PHPUnit test framework is the tool that the Drupal community uses for testing classes in Drupal 8 core. Writing tests in the PHPUnit testing framework allows a developer or quality assurance tester to evaluate whether the class itself performs the required functionality, and it does so in a manner that generates the correct results.

Writing a PHPUnit test is relatively straightforward:

- Begin by defining a class that extends `\Drupal\Tests\UnitTestCase`.

- The name of the class should end with the word `Test`.

- Specify the namespace as a subspace/subdirectory of `\Drupal\<modulename>\Tests`, where `<modulename>` is your test module's machine name.

- Store the test class file in the `<modulename>/tests/src/Unit` directory, using a PSR-4 naming standard.

- Incorporate a `phpDoc` comment block at the top of the class that describes the test.

- Create test cases in your class by creating methods that start with the word `test`. Each method should be limited in scope to a test that examines a specific functional or technical requirement.

You can find several examples of PHPUnit tests in your site's `/core/tests/Drupal/Tests/Component` directory. A great place to learn the pattern of creating unit tests is to examine existing tests.

For additional details, see:

- `drupal.org/phpunit` for details on how to use PHPUnit tests with Drupal

- `phpunit.de` for information how to use the PHPUnit testing framework

Writing Functional Tests

Functional tests examine the results of doing something on your Drupal site, such as clicking on a link, adding a content item, updating a user account, or filling out a form. The framework that has been used by the Drupal community for years is Simpletest. Using Simpletest consists of creating actions and defining assertions, where actions are what the test is supposed to do and the assertions evaluate the results of the action by comparing the output of the action against a predefined expected result. Examples of Simpletests in Drupal core can be found in the `/core/tests/Drupal/FunctionalTests/` directory.

To write a Simpletest:

- For tests that assume interaction through a web browser, create a class that extends `\Drupal\simpletest\WebTestBase`. This base class includes an internal web browser that includes test assertion methods that you can use to simulate interaction with your site through a browser.

- For test that do not test interaction through a web browser, create a class that extends `\Drupal\KernelTests\KernelTestBase`.

- Use a namespace that is a subspace/subdirectory of `\Drupal\<modulename>\Tests`, where `<modulename>` is your test module's machine name.

- Create the test class file and save it to the `<modulename>/src/Tests` directory, following the PSR-4 naming standards.

- Create a `phpDoc` comment block at the top of your class that contains a description of the tests that are covered in this class.

- In most cases, you will create a separate test module to define your functional tests, as opposed to writing tests in your modules. Store standalone modules under the `<modulename>/tests/modules` directory.

- Create test cases in your class by creating methods that start with the word `test`. Each method should be limited in scope to a test that examines a specific functional or technical requirement.

For additional details, visit `drupal.org/simpletest`.

Write Functional JavaScript Tests (PHPUnit)

A Drupal 8 solution often extends beyond just PHP code and includes JavaScript as a portion of the overall solution. JavaScript code, just like PHP code, needs to be thoroughly tested to ensure it generates the expected results. To write a test for JavaScript:

- Begin with `Extend \Drupal\FunctionalJavaScriptTests\JavascriptTestBase` to build upon the baseline testing framework.

- Save the test file into the `<modulename>/tests/src/FunctionalJavascript/` directory and use the `\Drupal\Tests\<modulename>\FunctionalJavaScript` namespace according to the PSR-4 naming standards.

- At the top of the file, incorporate an `@group` annotation using `<modulename>` as the group name.

- Install and configure PhantomJS on your computer; see `phantomjs.org/download.html`.

- To execute JavaScript tests, see the `core/tests/README.md` file.

For more details on testing JavaScript through PHPUnit, see:

- `drupal.org/docs/8/phpunit/phpunit-javascript-testing-tutorial` for details on how to write PHPUnit JavaScript tests

- `drupal.org/phpunit` for details on how to effectively write PHPUnit tests for your Drupal site

Executing Tests

To run a test, begin by enabling the Drupal 8 core testing module. After enabling the module tests can be executed from the Testing modules administrative interface or via Drush by using the `core/scripts/run-tests.sh` script.

You may also execute PHPUnit tests from the command line. Visit `drupal.org/node/2116263` for details.

You may also run tests from within the CI/CD solution that you choose. Each has its own means for executing automated tests. Visit the documentation for the solution you selected to find the details on how to run tests and utilize the output of those tests to stop the deployment process when tests fail.

Other Testing Tools

While Simpletest and PHPUnit tests are the tools utilized by the Drupal community to test Drupal itself, there are alternatives that you may want to consider such as Behat (`behat.org`). While PHPUnit and Simpletest scripts are very "coder-centric," Behat takes a slightly different approach by providing a nearly English scripting language for authoring tests. Take, for example, a scenario where you need to test a Drupal Commerce web site in which customers put items into their shopping cart. A description of the test in Behat would look something like this:

```
Feature:  Shopping Cart
  In order to purchase items
  As a customer
  I need to be able to add items to my shopping cart
```

This description of the feature that the script is testing provides a relatively easy-to-follow explanation of what is to be tested. As a customer we want to put products into a basket. But there is more to the test. While speaking with a business stakeholder, we come to find out that we need to collect a 9% sales tax and that there are rules on the cost of delivering the goods to the customers. Expanding the description of the test, we now have:

```
Feature:  Shopping Cart
  In order to purchase items
  As a customer
  I need to be able to add items to my shopping cart

Rules:
  -  Sales Tax is 5%
  -  Delivery for shopping cart under $20 is $5
  -  Deliver for shopping cart over $20 is $3
```

The description is great; it talks about the general capabilities of adding products to a basket as a customer, and the expected outcomes of sales tax and delivery costs. What it doesn't speak to is the various scenarios that might occur and the specific expected outcomes for each of those scenarios. Expanding the Behat script to address those scenarios is relatively straightforward, as shown here:

```
Feature:  Shopping Cart
  In order to purchase items
  As a customer
  I need to be able to add items to my shopping cart

Rules:
  -  Sales Tax is 5%
  -  Delivery for shopping cart under $20 is $5
  -  Deliver for shopping cart over $20 is $3

Scenario:
   Buying a single item under $10
   Given there is a "Drupal Book", which costs $5
   When I add the "Drupal Book" to the shopping cart
   Then I should have 1 item in the shopping cart
   And the overall shopping cart price should be $10.25

Scenario: Buying a single item over $20
   Given there is a "JavaScript Book", which costs $25
   When I add the "JavaScript Book" to the shopping cart
   Then I should have 1 item in the shopping cart
   And the overall shopping cart price should be $29.25

Scenario: Buying two products over $20
   Given there is a "Drupal Book", which costs $5
   And there is a "JavaScript Book", which costs $25
   When I add the "Drupal Book" to the shopping cart
   And I add the "JavaScript Book" to the shopping cart
   Then I should have 2 items in the shopping cart
   And the overall shopping cart price should be $34.50
```

The scenarios in the test describe context, event, and outcome for each of the scenarios to be tested, in the following general framework:

```
Scenario:  Some description of a specific scenario to be tested
  Given a contextual condition
  When some event occurs
  Then the expected results are
```

You can expand on the scenarios to include additional keywords such as And and But:

```
Scenario:  A description of what is  to be tested
  Given a contextual condition    And more contextual conditions
  When some event occurs
  And a second event occurs
  Then the expected results
  And another expected result
  But another expected result
```

Unlike PHPUnit and Simpletest scripts, which require some level of coding expertise, Behat makes it relatively easy for those who write functional specifications to also write Behat test scripts.

PHPUnit, Simpletest, and Behat provide a majority of the testing capabilities required to successfully test your site; however, there are other tools that integrate well into the CI/CD workflow that you may want to consider, such as Selenium, which is a tool that provides browser testing, allowing a test script to simulate a site visitor clicking around your site and entering values into fields.

Summary

DevOps is often one of the last elements to implement in a Drupal team and is often overlooked due to the demands of constantly delivering new functionality to the web for the organizations that we work for. The interesting point is that if we stopped long enough to implement DevOps in our organizations, we could deliver more functionality faster and easier than doing it the traditional ways that Drupal development teams have done for over a decade.

DevOps takes the pressure off of the development team and provides the ability to once again enjoy our weekends as we're not getting up at the crack of dawn on a Sunday morning to deploy code when the site traffic is at its lowest point of the week. It also eliminates those "oops I forgot to do…" scenarios that we often face when we walk in the doors of our office on Monday morning. It's well worth the time and effort to adopt the DevOps mindset of small incremental changes and to use the tools to test and deploy code that works the way it's supposed to work the first time.

## CHAPTER 12

Migrating to Drupal 8

Migrating from one version of a software package to another is often a Herculean task fraught with problems, missed deadlines, and blown budgets. Drupal can fit into that category depending on the custom modules that you developed and the complexity of your site. Fortunately there are tools to help ease the burden of migrating a Drupal 6 or 7 site to Drupal 8, which is the focus of this chapter.

The Migrate Modules in Drupal 8 Core

Drupal 8 core ships with three modules that support the process of migrating a Drupal 6 or 7 site to Drupal 8. The Migrate, Migrate Drupal, and Migrate Drupal UI modules perform the functions of moving content, taxonomy, users, and configuration from a Drupal 6 or 7 site into Drupal 8, and they do so with relative ease. To demonstrate the process in this chapter, we migrate a standard off-the-shelf Drupal 7 site to Drupal 8.

To begin, we create a Drupal 7 site and populate the site with users, taxonomy, and content using the Devel module's generate features (drupal.org/project/devel). The resulting site with content appears in Figure 12-1.

© Todd Tomlinson 2017

T. Tomlinson, *Enterprise Drupal 8 Development*, DOI 10.1007/978-1-4842-0253-1_12

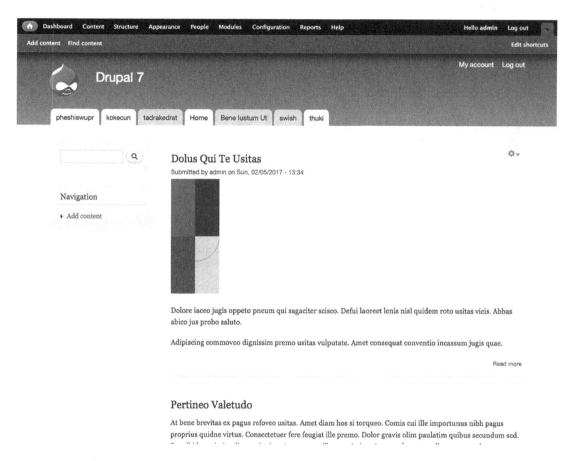

Figure 12-1. *The Drupal 7 site to be migrated*

Next, we install Drupal 8 as the target site for where the Drupal 7 site will be migrated. Visit the Extend page and enable the three Drupal 8 migrate modules (see Figure 12-2).

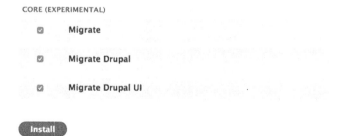

Figure 12-2. *The Migrate modules*

After enabling the modules, we back up the Drupal 7 and Drupal 8 sites, including the database, files, and codebase, to ensure that we can restore both sites in the event of a failure. After backups are completed, we navigate to upgrade on the Drupal 8 site to begin the process. On the Upgrade page, you will find a list of instructions and recommendations (see Figure 12-3).

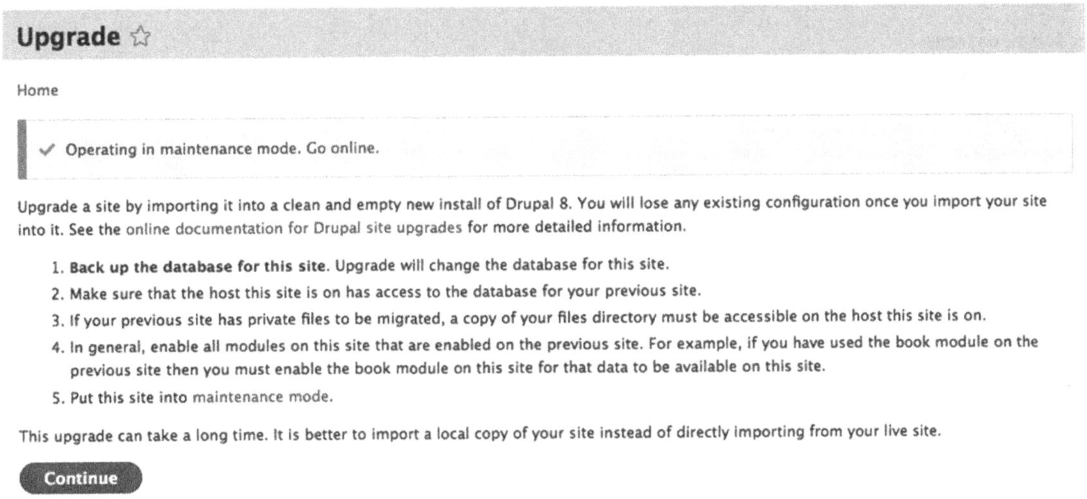

Upgrade ☆

Home

✓ Operating in maintenance mode. Go online.

Upgrade a site by importing it into a clean and empty new install of Drupal 8. You will lose any existing configuration once you import your site into it. See the online documentation for Drupal site upgrades for more detailed information.

1. **Back up the database for this site.** Upgrade will change the database for this site.
2. Make sure that the host this site is on has access to the database for your previous site.
3. If your previous site has private files to be migrated, a copy of your files directory must be accessible on the host this site is on.
4. In general, enable all modules on this site that are enabled on the previous site. For example, if you have used the book module on the previous site then you must enable the book module on this site for that data to be available on this site.
5. Put this site into maintenance mode.

This upgrade can take a long time. It is better to import a local copy of your site instead of directly importing from your live site.

Continue

Figure 12-3. The Upgrade instructions

Following the instructions, do the following:

- Back up the database. Make sure that the host of the Drupal 7 site is accessible and that you have the database credentials and the ability to access that database from the Drupal 8 instance.

- Manually move any private files to the Drupal 8 site. You must ensure that all enabled modules on the Drupal 7 site are also present on the Drupal 8 site as the Drupal 8 equivalent of those modules. In the case of these example sites, the only contributed module is the Devel module. If you have modules that do not have a Drupal 8 equivalent, you can replace those modules with other modules that are available for Drupal 8, or following the steps outlined later in this chapter, migrate the module manually.

- Put the Drupal 8 site into maintenance mode.

Click the Continue button to move to the next step in the process. On the Drupal Upgrade page, we specify the type of database, the database host, database name, database user name, database password, and files directory on the Drupal 7 site (see Figure 12-4).

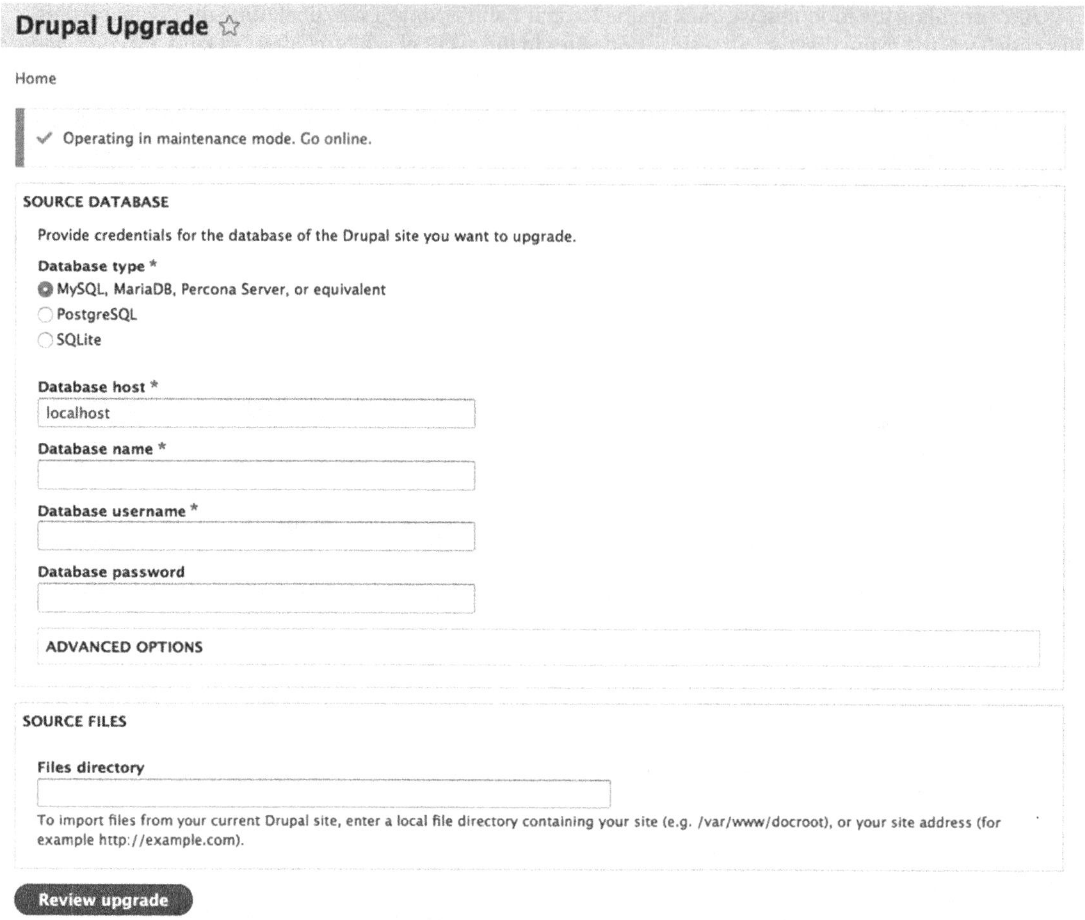

Drupal Upgrade ☆

Home

✓ Operating in maintenance mode. Go online.

SOURCE DATABASE

Provide credentials for the database of the Drupal site you want to upgrade.

Database type *
- ⦿ MySQL, MariaDB, Percona Server, or equivalent
- ◯ PostgreSQL
- ◯ SQLite

Database host *

> localhost

Database name *

Database username *

Database password

ADVANCED OPTIONS

SOURCE FILES

Files directory

To import files from your current Drupal site, enter a local file directory containing your site (e.g. /var/www/docroot), or your site address (for example http://example.com).

Review upgrade

Figure 12-4. *Specifying the source database credentials and files directory*

After entering the values, we click the Review Upgrade button to examine the list of modules on the Drupal 7 site that are missing their counterpart on the Drupal 8 site, as well as the list of modules that match between the two sites (see Figure 12-5).

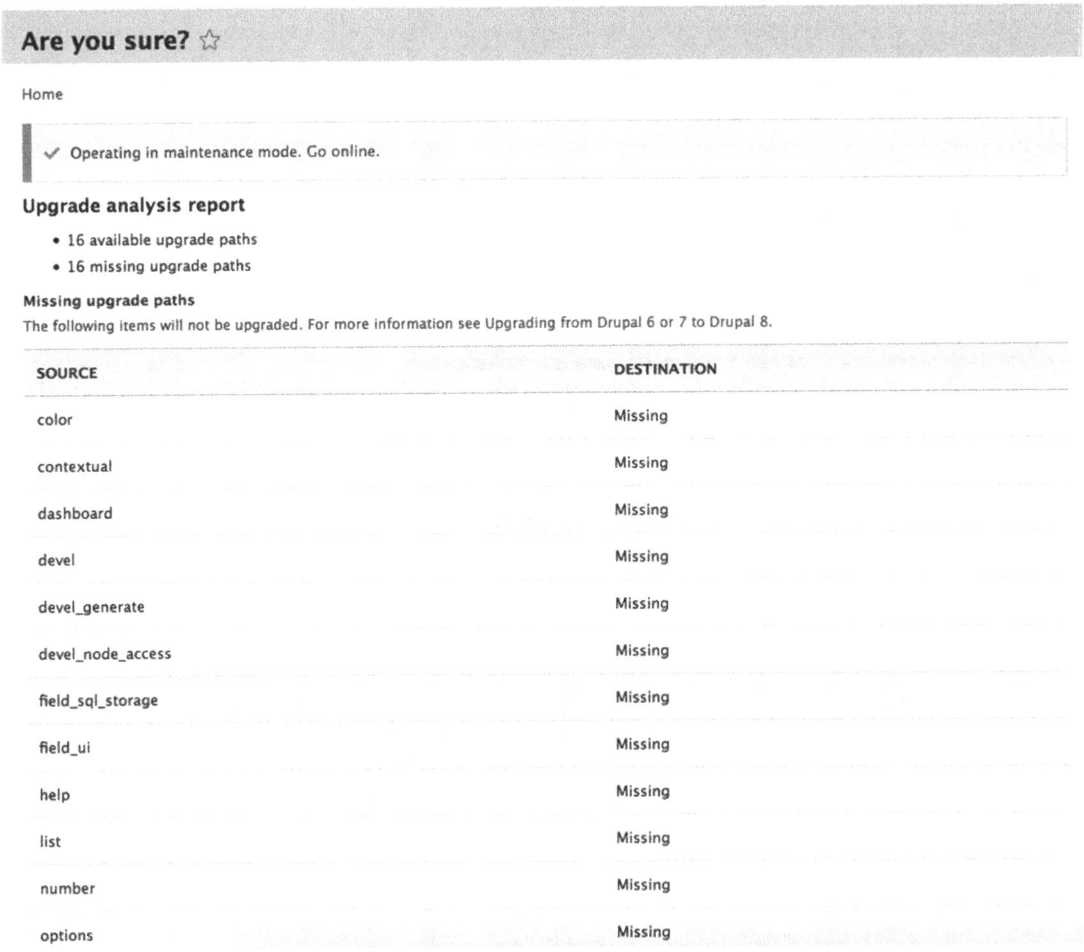

Are you sure? ☆

Home

✓ Operating in maintenance mode. Go online.

Upgrade analysis report

- 16 available upgrade paths
- 16 missing upgrade paths

Missing upgrade paths
The following items will not be upgraded. For more information see Upgrading from Drupal 6 or 7 to Drupal 8.

SOURCE	DESTINATION
color	Missing
contextual	Missing
dashboard	Missing
devel	Missing
devel_generate	Missing
devel_node_access	Missing
field_sql_storage	Missing
field_ui	Missing
help	Missing
list	Missing
number	Missing
options	Missing

Figure 12-5. The available and missing upgrade paths

After reviewing the list of missing upgrade paths, we decide to continue with the upgrade. If there were modules that were missing upgrade paths that are critical to the functionality or appearance of your site, you could:

- Abandon the upgrade and look for the Drupal 8 equivalent modules before proceeding. After downloading and installing those modules, you could then visit the upgrade page and attempt the upgrade again.

- Continue with the upgrade with the understanding that some site functionality and the appearance of the site may differ on Drupal 8. You then have to look for alternative solutions to address the missing functionality and make the appropriate adjustments.

For demonstration purposes, we continue with the upgrade, understanding that the items listed in the missing upgrade paths will not be migrated to this Drupal 8 site. WE click the Perform Upgrade button at the bottom of the page to continue the upgrade process. As the upgrade progresses, the module reports the status of the process, as shown in Figure 12-6.

Figure 12-6. *The migration from Drupal 7 is in process*

When the upgrade is complete, a summary of the migration activities is displayed on your homepage, as shown in Figure 12-7.

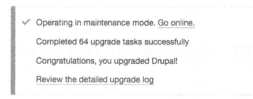

Figure 12-7. *The upgrade summary*

Clicking on the Review the Detailed Upgrade Log link displays a list of messages that detail the actions taken during the upgrade process (see Figure 12-8).

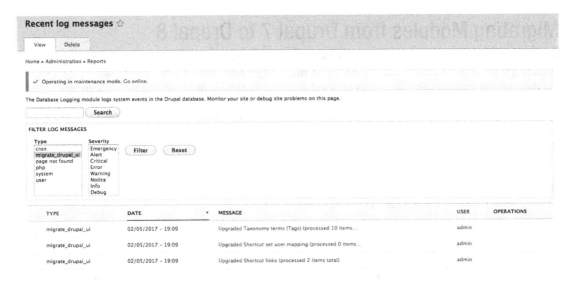

Figure 12-8. *The upgrade log*

After upgrading, you need to comb through the site to find all of the areas that were not successfully migrated and manually migrate the remaining elements. In the case of this sample site, all of the nodes, taxonomy terms, menu items, and users were successfully migrated.

Migrating Themes

Migrating a Drupal 6 or 7 theme to Drupal 8 is relatively straightforward, with the primary changes being the following:

- The Drupal 6 or 7 theme's `.info` file will need to be converted to a Drupal 8 `.info.yml` file.

- Certain core CSS classes have changed, including:

  - `element-hidden` has become `hidden`

  - `element-invisible` has become `visually-hidden`

  - `element-focusable` has become `visually-hidden focusable`

  - The addition of `invisible`, which was not available in Drupal 6 or 7

- All `.tpl.php` template files are now `.html.twig` files. All PHP code that was contained in Drupal 6 and 7 `.tpl.php` files are replaced with Twig. For details, see Chapter 5.

- The `template.php file` is now contained in the `.theme` file.

There are limited and somewhat cryptic instructions on `drupal.org` for migrating themes from Drupal 7 to Drupal 8. Visit `drupal.org/docs/8/theming/upgrading-7x-themes-to-8x` for up-to-date details on migrating your theme.

Migrating Modules from Drupal 7 to Drupal 8

Migrating content, users, and taxonomy from Drupal 6 or 7 to Drupal 8 was relatively easy as compared to migrating themes and modules. For the most part, migrating themes is next in the list of "easy-to-do" tasks, but that easy list ends quickly when we get to modules. Migrating modules from Drupal 7 to Drupal 8 often requires significant surgery, as the underlying core functionality has changed from straight PHP and PDO to Symfony, with all of its structure and syntax. Fortunately there's a tool that takes some of the pain out of the process, called the Drupal Module Upgrader.

To install the Drupal Module Upgrader, navigate to your Drupal 8 site's root directory and run the following commands in order:

```
drush dl drupalmoduleupgrader
cd modules/drupalmoduleupgrader
composer install
drush en drupalmoduleupgrader -y
```

You are now ready to attempt to upgrade a Drupal 7 module to Drupal 8. The `drupalmodulegrader` (DMU) is a command-line script that scans the source of a Drupal 7 module, flags any code that requires updating to Drupal 8, points to any relevant API change notices, and, when possible, attempts to convert the Drupal 7 code automatically to the Drupal 8 version. The goal of the module is to address the most widely used Drupal hooks and ensure there's coverage for them.

To demonstrate the DMU tool, we use a simple Drupal 7 module, the Pirate module. This simple module filters text on your site on the International Talk Like a Pirate Day (September 19th) and converts appropriate English phrases and words into pirate speak. You can download the Drupal 7 version of Pirate (`drupal.org/project/pirate`) to the `modules` directory on your Drupal 8 site.

After downloading the module, we generate a report by navigating to the Drupal 8 site's root directory and executing the following command:

```
drush dmu-analyze pirate
```

The output generated by `dmu-analyze` is stored in the module's root directory with a name of `upgrade-info.html`. You can use your browser to view the file by visiting `mysite.com/modules/pirate/upgrade-info.html`, where you'll see a list of required changes, as shown in Figure 12-9.

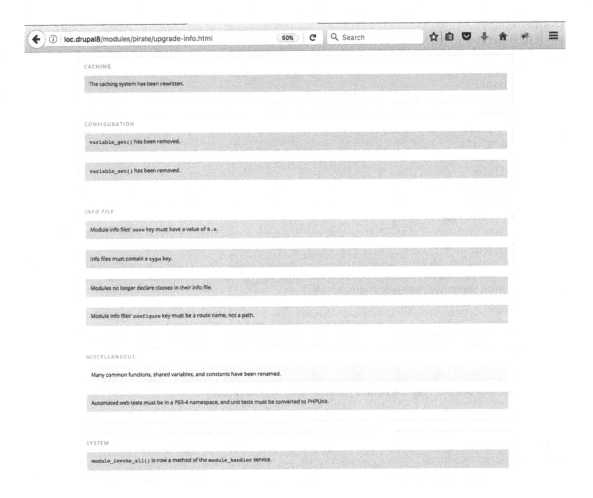

Figure 12-9. *The list of required changes for the Pirate module*

We can now try to automatically upgrade the module by executing the following command from the root directory of the Drupal 8 site:

```
drush dmu-upgrade pirate
```

If the DMU upgrader runs into problems during the upgrade, it will report those problems during the upgrade process. In the case of the Pirate module, no errors were generated. If you navigate to /modules/ pirate, you will now see that the module has been converted to Drupal 8.

```
├── INSTALL.txt
├── LICENSE.txt
├── README.txt
├── config
│   ├── install
│   │   └── pirate.settings.yml
│   └── schema
│       └── pirate.schema.yml
├── pirate.api.php
├── pirate.drush.inc
├── pirate.info
├── pirate.info.yml
├── pirate.module
└── upgrade-info.html

3 directories, 11 files
```

Navigating to the Extend page, you can now see the Drupal 8 version of the Pirate module, ready to install and use on September 19th (see Figure 12-10).

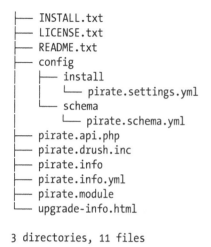

Figure 12-10. *The Drupal 8 version of the Pirate module ready to enable*

Not all modules will convert as cleanly as the Pirate module. For detailed steps on how to manually convert a Drupal 7 module to Drupal 8, visit `drupal.org/docs/8/converting-drupal-7-modules-to-drupal-8`.

Contributed Modules

Although the Pirate module is relatively easy to migrate to Drupal 8, not all Drupal 7 modules have been migrated to Drupal 8 and you may be in a position in which there's no clear path for a Drupal 7 contributed module to be ported to Drupal 8. In that case, your options are as follows:

- Undertake the migration of the module from Drupal 7 to Drupal 8. Reach out to the module's maintainer on `drupal.org` and ask if they would be willing to let you migrate the module for them. In most cases, the module maintainer will jump at the opportunity to have someone take on the migration effort. There may be cases where the migration is already underway and you can participate in that process, again by asking the module maintainer if you can assist.

- Look for alternative modules. There may be other similar contributed modules that provide similar functionality and have been ported to Drupal 8 or were created for the first time on Drupal 8.

- Look for alternative solutions. Often a combination of a custom content type and a view or two can solve a common problem that a contributed module solved in the past.

- Develop your own custom Drupal 8 module using the scaffolding approach described in Chapter 7 to jumpstart the development of your module.

- Reach out to the community on the various forums and IRC channels. It's likely that you're not the first one on the planet to run into the situation where a popular contributed module has not been ported to Drupal 8. It's likely you'll find others in the same situation who are willing to help or who have alternative solutions that have worked for them.

Summary

Migrating to Drupal 8 has become significantly easier than migrating between major Drupal releases in the past. The community has focused on making the upgrade path as painless as possible to ensure the adoption of Drupal 8 as the platform for the future. Not everything will be easy and, in those situations, the best approach is to reach out to the Drupal community for help. The adoption of Drupal 8 is critical to the long-term success of the Drupal community and there are thousands of developers around the world whose careers depend on the success of the platform. You will likely find a group of people who are ready and willing to lend a hand.

Contributing to the Drupal Community

There are several ways to contribute to the Drupal community; you don't have to be a developer to have a significant role. The following are areas that you might consider helping the Drupal community.

User Support

Even the most gifted Drupal developers begin at ground zero, and if you are a Drupal developer today there is a good chance that someone helped you along the way. No matter what your skill level is you can give back by sharing what you know with other users. To help others, you might consider participating:

- In the support forums (`drupal.org/forum/18`). This is the place where people from around the world post their questions and search for answers

- On the Drupal Answers part of Stack Exchange (`drupal.stackexchange.com`). While not officially part of the Drupal community, it is a channel that people use to look for answers to common and not-so-common Drupal issues.

- In local Drupal user groups. Visit `groups.drupal.org` for a list of groups near you.

- On the support mailing list. Register at `lists.drupal.org/listinfo/support` to begin receiving e-mails with requests for support.

- In the active support requests in the bug tracker (`drupal.org/project/issues?text=&projects=&status=Open&priorities=All&categories=4`).

- Via real-time chat in IRC, specifically the #drupal-support channel on `ir.freenode.net`.

Documentation

Whether you're interested in providing fine-grained API documentation, writing step-by-step tutorials for the handbook, or producing multimedia screencasts to show people how Drupal works, you can help improve Drupal's documentation and provide a valuable resource to the community. You might consider participating on one of the following:

- The community documentation pages on `drupal.org` (`drupal.org/documentation`)

- The Programming API reference documentation on `api.drupal.org`

© Todd Tomlinson 2017
T. Tomlinson, *Enterprise Drupal 8 Development*, DOI 10.1007/978-1-4842-0253-1

- Community initiative pages on `drupal.org` (`drupal.org/community-initiatives`)

- The help pages within the core Drupal software

- Documentation that is embedded in and distributed with contributed modules and themes

- Externally hosted documentation through blog postings or other third-party sites

Translations

Drupal supports many languages from around the world. If you know another language you can contribute by helping to maintain Drupal core or contribute to module translations. You can contribute by:

- Contributing to the translations that are managed on `localize.drupal.org`.

- Adding a new language that is not currently supported by Drupal. Follow the procedures at the bottom of the `localize.drupal.org` page for details on how to contribute new languages.

Testing

If you have a keen eye for detail or even just a knack for breaking things, you can help Drupal with testing. Good testing directly contributes to the stability of the platform and is an excellent way for people of all backgrounds to make a valuable contribution to the project. You can get involved in testing by:

- Reviewing and testing patches (`drupal.org/patch/review`)

- Providing usability feedback (`drupal.org/node/1237450`)

- Writing unit tests (`drupal.org/docs/8/testing`)

Design and Usability

Are you helping someone who has never used Drupal before? Or are you new to Drupal yourself? Do you have specialized knowledge in web accessibility and other standards? Contribute feedback to Drupal's usability group (`groups.drupal.org/usability`) or to the Drupal 8 User Experience team (`drupal.org/community-initiatives/drupal-core/usability`).

Donations

Want to contribute but don't have the time? Want to say "thank you" to the folks who put work into making Drupal what it is? Want to ensure that Drupal's infrastructure stays healthy and strong? Why not consider a monetary donation? You may contribute financially by visiting `association.drupal.org/donate`.

Development

Drupal thrives on developer contributions in the form of both contributed modules and patches to core. Helping out in development helps the project move forward and stay competitive, and it is the best way to ensure that Drupal can do what you need it to do on your next project.

Ways to Contribute Code: Drupal Core, Contributed Projects, and Patches

The Drupal code ecosystem encompasses the core of Drupal (the files that you get when you download Drupal from the Drupal project page (drupal.org/project), and "contrib" projects, which encompass all contributed code (modules, themes, installation profiles, etc.). You can read more about this distinction between the core and the contributed projects at this page (drupal.org/node/22286). You can also improve Drupal core and the contributed projects by submitting patches.

You can find more information about helping Drupal core by visiting (drupal.org/node/717162).

Improving Existing Projects and Core with Patches

If you want to make improvements (bug fixes, new features, and so on) to existing projects, such as Drupal core (drupal.org/project/drupal) or to one of our contributed modules (drupal.org/project/project_modules) or themes (drupal.org/project/project_themes), this section is for you.

Contributions to existing projects come in the form of patches (drupal.org/patch), which allow you to share modifications you made to a project with the maintainer and other users in the project's issue queue (drupal.org/node/317). To learn more, read:

- What is a patch? (drupal.org/node/367392)
- Creating patches (drupal.org/node/707484)
- The advanced patch contributors guide (drupal.org/node/1054616)
- Applying patches (drupal.org/patch/apply)
- Applying patches using Git (drupal.org/node/1054616#applying-patches)

Contributing New Projects

If you developed a new module or theme, you can also create your own project to contribute your code to drupal.org.

There are two types of projects that you can create:

- **Full projects**, the standard downloadable modules and themes like Views and Zen. To read more about contributing a new module or theme, visit drupal.org/node/1015224.

- **Sandbox projects**, which are for experimental code, or code from new contributors who've not been through a vetting process yet. To read about sandbox projects, visit drupal.org/node/1011196.

In order to contribute new code, you must obtain Git access on drupal.org (drupal.org/node/1047190) and, in order to promote sandbox projects to full projects, they must go through a one-time approval process (drupal.org/node/1011698).

All project pages on drupal.org have a Version Control tab, which contains information on how to create and maintain your project with Git.

Collaboration Rather than Competition

The Drupal community holds a strong collaboration rather than competition ethos, which values joining forces on improving one awesome project rather than building several substandard ones that overwhelm end users with choices. While not outright forbidden, duplicate projects are generally discouraged without good reason (such as a fundamentally different architectural approach). Remember to search existing modules and themes first before embarking on your quest or taking over an abandoned project (`drupal.org/node/251466`). You could save yourself some time and earn community Karma by helping others.

Additional Resources

As you begin (and continue) your journey of learning Drupal, there will likely be times when you'll need to find a Drupal module, a Drupal theme, additional details about specific Drupal technologies (such as theming), and operating system–level commands (for tasks such as backing up the site from the command line). This appendix points you to recommended web sites where you can find additional resources to help you along your journey.

Drupal Modules

The primary site for finding modules is the `drupal.org` web site (`www.drupal.org/project/project_module`). Every Drupal-contributed module has its own "homepage" that describes the module, provides links for downloading the various versions of the module, and, in most cases, links to additional documentation and examples.

Drupal Themes

The primary source of Drupal themes is the `drupal.org` web site (`www.drupal.org/project/project_theme`). You can browse through dozens of themes, see screenshots of each, and download the themes you like from `drupal.org`.

Drupal Documentation

The Drupal community has assembled a number of online guides (`www.drupal.org/docs/8`) that are chock-full of information about Drupal 8. You will find the following guides under the designated categories:

- Understanding Drupal—This guide gives you the big picture overview of Drupal concepts, helping you understand the foundation of Drupal.

- System requirements—This guide covers detailed system requirements for a Drupal 8 installation.

- Extending Drupal 8—Learn how to extend your Drupal 8 site's functionality with contributed modules or alter its appearance with contributed themes.

- Configuration Management—This guide explains how to import and export your site's configuration and manage it with version control.

© Todd Tomlinson 2017

T. Tomlinson, *Enterprise Drupal 8 Development*, DOI 10.1007/978-1-4842-0253-1

- Migrating to Drupal—This guide explains the processes and tools for migrating to Drupal 8.

- Contributed Modules—This is the documentation for contributed modules in Drupal 8.

- Clean URLs in Drupal 8—Enabled by default, this document describes how clean URLs improve search engine indexing and how they provide a cleaner, user-friendly URL structure.

- Drupal 8 APIs—This guide describes Drupal 8's APIs, which make it easier to alter and extend Drupal. It helps developers with common tasks associated with developing on Drupal.

- Mobile Guide—This guide shares the details of developing mobile-friendly Drupal 8 sites.

- PHPUnit in Drupal 8—This guide explains in detail how to write and execute tests in Drupal's implementation of PHPUnit.

- Theming in Drupal 8—This is the guide for creating themes for Drupal 8.

- Upgrade to Drupal 8—This explains the process for upgrading your Drupal 6 or 7 site to Drupal 8.

- Core Modules and Themes—This guide describes the modules and themes included in Drupal 8's core.

- Testing—This guide provides an overview of the testing framework in Drupal 8.

- Understanding Drupal Version Numbers—This guide provides a detailed description of Drupal's versioning numbering scheme for Drupal core, and for contributed modules and themes.

- Installing Drupal 8—This guide covers preparing, running, and installing Drupal 8 and the steps that should be performed after the installation script has completed.

- Cron Automated Tasks—This guide describes how to configure Cron and the automated tasks it performs on your Drupal 8 site.

- Administering Drupal 8—This guide provides the details of how to monitor and administer a Drupal 8 site.

- Multisite Drupal—This guide provides an overview of using multisite to create and configure multiple Drupal 8 sites from a single codebase.

- Accessibility—This guide outlines the accessibility capabilities and features in Drupal 8.

- Creating Custom Modules—This guide details the steps required to create a custom module in Drupal 8.

- Managing Site Performance and Scalability—This guide describes the processes and tools for monitoring your Drupal 8 site's performance.

- Multilingual Guide—This document details the steps for enabling multilingual capabilities in a Drupal 8 site, and for creating and managing multilingual content.

- Security in Drupal 8—This document details how to secure your Drupal 8 site.

- Updating a Drupal 8 Site—This document outlines how to upgrade your Drupal 8 site from one version to the next (e.g., 8.0.1 to 8.0.2).

- Converting Drupal 7 Modules to Drupal 8—This guide walks you through the steps of migrating a Drupal 7 module to Drupal 8 and the tools that are available to assist you in that process.

- Creating Distributions—This guide outlines the steps for creating a Drupal 8 profile and distribution.

Where to Go When You Have Problems

One of the best sources for Drupal help is the Community Forum on the `drupal.org` web site (`www.drupal.org/forum`). There are hundreds of thousands of postings on just about every conceivable topic. If you run into an issue, you're likely to find that the solution to your problem is already documented in the forum. If you can't find a solution, you can post a question to the forum and you'll often receive a solution to your problem within hours of posting the issue. Another great resource is Drupal Answers at Stack Exchange (`http://drupal.stackexchange.com`). When I'm looking for an example, Stack Exchange is my second stop along the journey of finding a solution.

Where to Host Your Drupal Site

If you are looking for a place to host your web site, an excellent resource is the `drupal.org` site (`www.drupal.org/hosting`). The Hosting page lists a number of companies that are known to support Drupal.

Where to Go to Learn HTML and CSS

A great resource to help you learn HTML and CSS is the W3Schools web site (`www.w3schools.com`). You'll find easy-to-understand tutorials and excellent examples. Other alternatives exist, such as the Code School (`www.codeschool.com`), which has several free tutorials on HTML and CSS.

Video Tutorials

There are thousands of YouTube (`www.youtube.com`) videos that cover a wide variety of Drupal topics. It is a great source for learning various aspects of Drupal. Enter "Drupal" in YouTube's search box and you'll see a very long list of Drupal-related videos. There are also excellent paid training sites, such as `Drupalize.Me` (`https://drupalize.me`) and `BuildAModule` (`http://buildamodule.com`).

Drupal Podcasts

Another great source for learning Drupal is podcasts. There are a number podcasts that cover Drupal on iTunes.

Creating a Drupal 8 Profile

When developing Drupal 8 sites in your organization you may find that there are several common characteristics of sites that you're having to configure over and over again every time you spin up a new Drupal 8 site. You can eliminate the need to repeat those processes by creating a Drupal 8 installation profile, and in some cases you may find yourself creating several installation profiles for specific use cases—such as a simple marketing site, an online community site, a promotional site, and a commerce site. The number of profiles is limited only by the number of site types that your organization will create and maintain.

Installation profiles in Drupal 8 have all the functionality of modules, including access to hooks and plugins and, critically, the ability to provide configuration for your site in the form of .yml files.

Picking a Machine Name

First, you need a machine name for your profile. This is a name consisting only of lowercase letters and underscores. From here on, all references to *profilename* imply the profile machine name.

For example, if your profile is for *Acme starter kit,* valid profile machine names would include:

- acme_starter_kit
- acme_starter
- acme_starter_profile
- acme_kit

The following names would be invalid:

- acme-starter-kit
- acme-kit

This is because profiles are just like modules, and they hence can implement hooks. But acme-kit_ form_alter would not constitute a valid PHP function name.

© Todd Tomlinson 2017
T. Tomlinson, *Enterprise Drupal 8 Development*, DOI 10.1007/978-1-4842-0253-1

Creating the File Structure

Your installation profile will reside in its own *profilename* directory in the /profiles directory of a Drupal 8 site.

All installation profiles must have a profilename.info.yml file, which I describe in the next section. They may also have the following:

- profilename.profile
- profilename.install file
- config folder
- translations folder

Each of which I describe in the following sections. When packaged, your installation profile will also have modules, src, and themes directories as needed.

The .info.yml File

The profilename.info.yml file should look similar to this:

```
name: Profile Name
type: profile
description: 'Description of your profile.'
core: 8.x

# Optional: Declare your installation profile as a distribution.
# This will make the installer auto-select this installation profile.
# The distribution_name property is used in the installer and other
# places as a label for the software being installed.

distribution:
  name: Distribution Name

# Required modules dependencies:
  - node
  - history
  - block
  - block_content
  - breakpoint
  - color
  - config
  - comment
  - contextual
  - contact
  - quickedit
  - help
  - image
  - options
  - path
  - taxonomy
  - dblog
```

```
    - search
    - shortcut
    - toolbar
    - field_ui
    - file
    - rdf
    - views
    - views_ui
    - editor
    - ckeditor
```

The .install File

The `.install` file should look similar to this:

```php
<?php
/**
 * @file
 * Install, update and uninstall functions for the profilename install profile.
 */

/**
 * Implements hook_install().
 *
 * Perform actions to set up the site for this profile.
 *
 * @see system_install()
 */

function profilename_install() {
  // First, do everything in standard profile.
  include_once DRUPAL_ROOT . '/core/profiles/standard/standard.install';
  standard_install();

  // Can add code in here to make nodes, terms, etc.
}
```

The .profile File

The `profilename.profile` file has access to almost everything a normal Drupal `modulename.module` file does because Drupal is fully bootstrapped before almost anything in the profile runs.

```php
<?php
/**
 * @file
 * Enables modules and site configuration for a standard site installation.
 */

// Add any custom code here like hook implementations.
```

Configuration Files

Drupal 8 installation profiles can contain configuration files. You can start by taking the configuration directory (the `config` folder) of an installed, configured site and copying it into the `config/install` folder in your profile.

Once that's in place, there are some other required tasks:

- Copy all of the modules and themes listed in `core.extension.yml` into your profile's `.info` file (using the new info file's format).

- Delete `core.extension.yml`.

- Remove all of the UUIDs from your config files so that they don't conflict with those of new sites. This can be done quite easily on the command line like so, all on one line:

```
find /path/to/PROFILE_NAME/config/install/ -type f -exec sed -i
'' -e '/^uuid: /d' {} \;
```

If you just want to grab an existing site's configuration and you don't need to end up with a formal installation profile (for sharing on `drupal.org`, for example), you can use the Configuration installer (`drupal.org/project/config_installer`) installation profile to install a new site from the configuration of another site.

Default Content

You can also include default content by making default content (`drupal.org/project/default_content`) a dependency of your installation profile and using it to import JSON-formatted content.

The configuration that needs content to work is possible by putting content (and configuration as needed) in modules you make (which your profile can depend on), which themselves depend on `default_content`.

Index

A

Administrative interface
  admin themes, 233
  content type (*see* Content types)
  drop-down menus, 236
  Seven theme, 234–235
  Workbench (*see* Workbench module)
Apache Solr, 149, 208
API documentation, 293
Automated testing
  functional tests, 276
  JavaScript, 277
  PHPUnit, 275–276

B

Blocks creation, 57–62
Breakpoint module, 131–132
Business system analyst (BSA), 19

C

C10K problem, 31
Caching
  blocks, 264
  Internal Dynamic, 262
  Internal Page, 262
  Varnish, 264
  views, 263–264
Cascading stylesheets (CSS), 299
  libraries.yml file, 128–129
  stylesheets, 127
Content delivery network (CDN), 265–266
Content management system (CMS)
  contributed module, 3
  creating content
    Add content link, 5
    basic page, 6
    content-authoring screens, 4
    content type, 5
    front page, 6–7

  definition, 1
  Drupal, 2
    core, 2
    themes, 4
  features, 1
Content staging
  configuration
    multiversion, 140–142
    RELAXed web services modules, 145–148
    workspaces module, 142–145
  deploy module, 138
  multiversion module, 139
  RELAXed Web Services module, 139
  replication module, 139
  trash module, 140
  use cases, 137–138
  workspace module, 139
Content translation
  article page, 171
  languages status, 170
  option, 170
Content types, 10
  administration form, 178
  analysis spreadsheet, 174
  Article Type taxonomy, 174
  baseFieldDefinitions function, 183
  buildHeader and buildRow functions, 185, 186
  Create Article page, 176
  custom entity, 179
  Customer addition, 188
  customer entity module, 186
  Customer list page, 187
  Drupal Console, 180–183
  field collections, 241–243
  field group
    configuration, 175
    options, 175
    rearrangement, 176
  fields, 236–237
  form creation, 239–240
  group options, 237–238

© Todd Tomlinson 2017
T. Tomlinson, *Enterprise Drupal 8 Development*, DOI 10.1007/978-1-4842-0253-1

Content types (*cont.*)
    hierarchical selection, 240–241
    Node Edit form, 177–178
    Simplify module, 239
    Structure page, 187
    Where Used taxonomy, 174
Continuous deployment (CD). *See* Continuous
        integration (CI)
Continuous integration (CI)
    process, 274
    tools, 275
Contributed modules, 13
Custom content types, 11, 13
Custom forms
    elements addition, 67–70
    file creation, 62, 64
    form submission, 66
    menu item, 66
    routing file, 64
    subdirectory creation, 62
    submitForm function, 71
    validation, 65
Custom RESTful APIs, 229–232

▒ D

Database servers
    MariaDB and Percona, 32
    MySQL clustering, 32
Davinci theme, 135–136
Davinci Theme Directory, 91
Design and usability, 294
Design elements, 13
DevOps
    automated test (*see* Automated testing)
    benefits, 272
    CI (*see* Continuous integration (CI))
    executing tests, 277
    microservices architecture, 273
    vs. traditional development, 271
Distribution architectural approach, 34
Documentation, 297–298
Donations, 294
Drop-down menu items, 11
Drupal
    Console, 179–183
    core, 2, 295
    methodology, building sites, 9–10, 12–14
    themes, 4
Drupal 8, creation
    configuration, 304
    default content, 304
    file structure, 302
    info.yml file, 302
    installation, 303
    machine name, 301

Drupalmodulegrader (DMU), 288
Drupal team building
    business system analyst
        metrics and measurements, 19
        qualifications, 19
        roles and responsibilities, 19
    developer, roles and
        responsibilities, 21–22
    development lead
        metrics and measurements, 21
        minimum qualifications, 20–21
        roles and responsibilities, 20
    project manager
        metrics and measurements, 17
        planning and forecasting, 15
        project execution, 16
        qualifications, 16
        reporting, 16
    quality assurance specialist, 26
    senior architect
        metrics and measurements, 18
        qualifications, 18
        roles and responsibilities, 17–18
    site administrator, 27–28
    site builder, 22, 25
    themer, 25
    user experience (UX) designer, 23
    visual designer, 24

▒ E, F, G

Elevator pitch, 10
Enterprise Drupal architecture
    component defining, 30
    contributed modules, 35
    custom modules, 36
    database servers, 32
    distribution, 34
    entities
        content, 37
        taxonomy, 38
        users, 38
    installation profiles, 34
    multisite, 33
    network and web server, 31
    pages, 41
    requirements, 29–30
    rules, 41–42
    single-site, 33
    taxonomy, 38–40
    themes, 42
    user interface, 43–44
    user roles and
        permissions, 42
    views, 40
    web services, 43

Entities
    content, 37
    customer content type, 76–77, 79–80
    customer node edit form, 81
    deletion, 87
    field area elements, 78
    files creation, 84
    finding existing entities, 72, 74
        form creation, 71–73
        Node ID, 75
        node not found modal, 76
        routing file, 74
        search form, 75
    menu links, 86
    nodes creation, 82–84
    nodes with images, 84–85
    taxonomy, 38
    taxonomy terms, 85–86
    update, 86–87
    users, 38

H

Hosting platforms, 12
Hosting provider, 12
HTML, 299

I

Integration options, 232
Interface translation, 168

J, K

JavaScript, 129–131

L

Leveraging taxonomy
    Add View page, 192
    articles creation, 191–192
    Banner image field, 191
    Block Layout page, 192
    block visibility, 189
    fields
        creation, 189
        details, 190
        types, 190
    multipurpose pages, 194–195
    product content type
        default page, 198
        field order, 197
        and fields, 197
    product line terms, 196
    product page

        Add Block form, 204
        creation, 201
        layout options, 202–203
        product line, 206
        updated, 206–207
        URL argument, 201
        views list, 204
    product views, 198–200
Location of content, enterprise setting, 207–208
Lucene, 149–150

M

MariaDB, 32
Memcache/Redis, 267
Migrate modules
    contributed module, 290–291
    database credentials and files directory, 284
    Drupal 7, 281–282
    Drupal 7 to Drupal 8, 288–290
    missing upgrade paths, 285–286
    themes, 287–288
    upgrade instructions, 283
    upgrade log, 287
    upgrade process, 287
Minimal viable product (MVP), 14
Model-View-Controller (MVC), 50
Modules, 297
Modules creation
    adding function, 55
    controller, 51–52, 55
    directory, 48
    extend page, 52
    info file, 48–49
    menu item, 52–54
    module file, 49
    predefined modules, 46
    routing file, 50, 56–57
    Symfony, 47
    text display, 47
Multilingual capabilities
    base languages, 165
    configuration options, 165
    content translation, 167
    entities, 168
    interface translation, 168
    language activation configuration, 166
    list of, 164
    modules list, 164
    switcher block of language, 167
    translating content, 170
Multisite architectural approach, 33
MySQL, 267–268
    clustering, 32
    full text search, 148

N

Navigational structure, 11
Network and web server architecture, 31
Nginx, 266–267

O

Off-the-shelf *vs.* custom development, 209–210
OpenSolr, 150–151

P, Q

Page content type, 11
Page templates, 41
PHPUnit, 277–279
Podcasts, 299

R

Really Simple Syndication (RSS), 10
RESTful web services
    advantages, 214
    content retrieval, 215–216
    deletion, 221
    in Drupal 8 core, 214–215
    nodes creation, 216–220
    output formats, 227–228
    update, 220–221
    updates, 221
    view
        articles list, 223–225
        contextual filter, 226
        limited search, 227
RSS feed-based view, 228–229

S

Scaling Drupal
    caching mechanisms (*see* Caching)
    CDN, 265–266
    hardware, 269
    Memcache/Redis, 267
    MySQL, 267–268
    Nginx, 266–267
    potential performance, 261
Scaling hardware, 269
Search
    adding fields, 158–159
    Add Search Index form, 154
    Apache Solr, 149
    indexed items, OpenSolr, 155–156
    Index Status page, 155
    Lucene, 149–150
    OpenSolr, 150–152
    Search API, 150, 152

Search API Solr, 150
    Solr index, 157
Simpletest, 277–279
Single-site architectural approach, 33
Solr
    adding fields, 158, 160
    content rendering, 161
    Content Type block, 162
    Facets page, 161–163
    federated search, 163
    indexed field, 160
    indexed information, 209
    Search API module, 208
    Search Solr API module, 208
    Solr index, 157

T

Taxonomy, 38–40
Taxonomy structure, 11
Testing, 294
Themes, 297
    CSS
        libraries, .info.yml file, 128–129
        libraries.yml file, 128
        libraries.yml file, creation, 128
        stylesheets creation, 127, 128
    files creation
        Davinci theme directory, 91–92
        looping, 101
        regions, 93–95
        Twig (*see* Twig)
    JavaScript, 129–131
    role, 89
    settings, 133–134
    structure, 90
    subthemes, 134–136
Translating content. *See* Content translation
Twig
    attribute array, 116
    conditional, 98–100
    displaying and hiding content fields, 115
    Drupal 8 templates, 107–108
    filters, 101–103
    looping, 101
    math functions, 104
    syntax, 96
    template files, 104–107
    template modifications
        field.html.twig, 118–120
        node.html.twig, 114–117
        page.html.twig, 108–111, 113–114
    templating engine, 89
    tests, 103
    variables, 96–97

forums.html.twig, 126
forum_theme function, 122–126
hook_theme, 121

■ U

User interface, 43–44
User roles and permissions, 42
User support, 293

■ V

Varnish cache, 264
Views, 40
Visitor types, 10–11
Visual design, 12

■ W, X, Y, Z

Web services, 43
Workbench moderation process
    configuration, 254–257
    user roles and permissions, 257–259
Workbench module
    Access module, 246
    access restrictions, 252–253
    content, 244
    Moderation process (*see* Workbench
        moderation process)
    My Edits, 245
    My Workbench, 245
    permissions, 249–252
    setti ng up, 246–249

Get the eBook for only $5!

Why limit yourself?

With most of our titles available in both PDF and ePUB format, you can access your content wherever and however you wish—on your PC, phone, tablet, or reader.

Since you've purchased this print book, we are happy to offer you the eBook for just $5.

To learn more, go to http://www.apress.com/companion or contact support@apress.com.

Apress®

Printed in the United States
By Bookmasters